perspectives

Educating Exceptional Learners

Academic Editor
David Podell
College of Staten Island
City University of New York

coursewise
publishing
inc.

Boulder • Bellevue • Dubuque • Madison

Our mission at **coursewise** is to help students make connections—linking theory to practice and the classroom to the outside world. Learners are motivated to synthesize ideas when course materials are placed in a context they recognize. By providing gateways to contemporary and enduring issues, **coursewise** publications will expand students' awareness of and context for the course subject.

For more information on **coursewise** visit us at our web site: http://www.coursewise.com

coursewise publishing editorial staff

Thomas Doran, ceo/publisher: Journalism/Marketing/Speech
Edgar Laube, publisher: Geography/Political Science/Psychology/Sociology
Linda Meehan Avenarius, publisher: **courselinks**
Sue Pulvermacher-Alt, publisher: Education/Health/Gender Studies
Victoria Putman, publisher: Anthropology/Philosophy/Religion
Tom Romaniak, publisher: Business/Criminal Justice/Economics

Cover photo: Copyright © 1997 T. Teshigawara/Panoramic Images, Chicago, IL. All Rights Reserved.

Interior design and cover design by Jeff Storm

Printed in the United States of America by **coursewise publishing,** Inc.
1379 Lodge Lane, Boulder, CO 80303

10 9 8 7 6 5 4 3 2

from the
Publisher

coursewise publishing

Sue Pulvermacher-Alt

"Handle with Care"

A few years ago my brother feigned a handicap. He pretended to be blind so he could sneak his dog Zack into a hospital. Zack had been acting depressed since my brother's hired farmhand, Jim, had been hospitalized. My brother cared about his dog and his friend, and he thought the visit would do both Zack and Jim some good. He violated more health codes and hospital policies than I care to mention. In the end he was right—both Zack and Jim felt better after what my family came to call "the visit."

The intriguing thing is what happened along the way. Hospital personnel and hospital visitors cared and, in fact, bent over backward to help my brother as he and Zack meandered through the hospital en route to and from Jim's room. No one questioned him or even seemed to notice the unusual sight of a supposed guide dog on a chain (rather than a harness) or my brother tapping a white metal fence pole (rather than a cane). My brother experienced caring kindness and an absence of judgment that day. (Of course, had someone seen them in the parking ramp [as my brother slid into the driver's seat], it could have been a very different story. . . .)

What does this story have to do with *Perspectives: Educating Exceptional Learners?* I mention it as a prelude to your own reflection. Was my brother right or wrong in his pretending to have a disability? Was he right or wrong to violate hospital policy for the betterment of individuals? Was his very positive experience common among people with disabilities? The same answer applies to all three questions—maybe; maybe not.

I don't know you, but I bet you care about learners with exceptionalities. The field of special education is filled with caring people. A caring attitude is critical. Unfortunately, it isn't enough. The issues surrounding special education and learners with exceptionalities are complex. The range of both exceptionalities and the responses to people with exceptionalities is wide. Debates continue over such issues as funding, placement, identification, and instructional methods.

You need to examine many sides of these complex issues and come to your own conclusions and decisions. If you care, you need to put forth the energy to understand.

In this volume, we've tried to pull together articles that help you sort out the important issues and become an informed educator. The first section has articles that raise unsettling issues about how society values (or devalues) individuals with disabilities. The second section consists of articles that present different sides of the current debate about special education. The next three sections address difficult challenges facing educators who work with students with disabilities. And the two final sections focus on recent and important trends in the field.

In addition to the articles in this volume, you'll find web sites that we hope will expand your understanding of the issues. The R.E.A.L. sites listed throughout this *Perspectives* volume and at the **courselinks**™ site were chosen because they are particularly useful. You, however, still need to be the critical consumer of the information. Read the annotations and decide if the site is worth visiting. Do the activities so you can get to know the site better. Search our **courselinks**™ site by key topic and find the information you need to be a more informed special educator.

As publisher for this volume, I had the good fortune to work with David Podell as the Academic Editor. I've known David for several years, and we've worked together on other projects. I enjoy and appreciate his calm, professional manner. David cares—about his colleagues, about his students, about the families he counsels, and about his own family. From the effort he put into this volume, you can believe he cares about you, too. He wants to give you a tool to make your college coursework more meaningful.

David and I were helped by a hard-working, top-notch Editorial Board. At **coursewise** we're working hard to publish Relevant, Exciting, Approved, and Linked (what we call R.E.A.L.) learning tools. Articles and web sites are selected with these criteria in mind. Members of the Editorial Board offer critical feedback and pose interesting challenges. They know their content and are a web-savvy bunch. The result is a R.E.A.L. learning tool. My thanks to David and the entire Editorial Board.

Show me you care. Tell me what you think about my brother and his questionable judgment, about the articles in this volume, about the issues we chose to cover, or about the R.E.A.L. sites we selected. I welcome your feedback. And you can bet I'll be back in touch because I care what you think.

from the
Academic Editor

David Podell

David Podell

College of Staten Island

David M. Podell is associate professor and chairperson of the Department of Education at The College of Staten Island, City University of New York. He earned his master's degree from Harvard University and his Ph.D. from New York University. His research concerns teacher efficacy, special education placement and referral, and instructional applications of technology. He is the co-author of *Educational Psychology: Windows on Teaching*.

When an opportunity arose to edit a book of articles on educating exceptional learners, I could not resist. Because many excellent articles on important topics are published in a variety of sources, instructors and students can miss them. To assemble these articles in one book (and with highlighted Internet sites) allows me to feature topics and articles that I think are of particular value. I hope that these articles will enhance discussion in the college classroom and promote a deeper understanding of many current issues.

The articles were selected for their contributions to pertinent topics and for their currency. In the first section, "Exceptionality: In the Eye of the Beholder?", I included articles that I hoped would raise unsettling issues about how society values (or devalues) individuals with disabilities. I also wanted readers to hear how some persons with disabilities and their family members express *in their own words* their interactions with society.

Often, in college classes concerning the education of students with disabilities, the professor is "preaching to the converted." We possess a number of assumptions about special education, one of which, for many, is that special education is desirable and justifiable. Those assumptions are by no means universal. In the second section, "The Special Education Controversy," I included articles that present different sides to the current debate about special education. The authors of these articles address questions regarding special education's cost, effectiveness, and desirability.

The next three sections concern difficult challenges facing educators who work with students with disabilities. The first challenge is preparing students for their future, either in the work force or in higher education. The articles in section 3, "The Transition to Adulthood: Challenges for the Exceptional Individual," present techniques for helping students prepare for their adulthood. The second challenge is the interplay between "Exceptionality and Cultural Diversity," the topic of section 4. Here, the authors address a variety of complex problems, including inappropriate placement of students from minority backgrounds both in special education and in regular education, and teaching language-minority students with special needs. The third challenge is the emergence of "Attention Deficit Disorder: The Newest Disability," the topic of section 5. The articles in this section describe the needs of students with attention deficits from the perspectives of both a parent and a teacher.

The two final sections examine recent and important trends in the field. In section 6, "Innovations in Assessment and Instruction," articles address new assessment practices and the impact of technology on instruction for exceptional learners. Section 7, "Inclusion: The Issue of the 21st Century," includes articles presenting different positions on the most highly debated issue of the present day: the inclusion of *all* students, regardless of their disability, in age-appropriate classes. The authors are all concerned about the quality of education for students with disabilities; however, they differ dramatically in their positions on how quality is to be achieved.

I hope that the articles in *Perspectives: Educating Exceptional Learners* provoke much discussion and debate, and help readers gain insight on positions that differ from their own. I thank the various authors and publishers for their permission to reprint their articles in this book. In addition, I am grateful to the members of the Editorial Board, whose suggestions and guidance contributed to the organization of this book and article selection. Finally, many thanks to the staff of **coursewise** and, in particular, Sue Pulvermacher Alt, for the friendly help I received throughout the preparation of *Perspectives: Educating Exceptional Learners*.

Editorial Board

WiseGuide Introduction

Critical Thinking and Bumper Stickers

Question Authority

The bumper sticker said: Question Authority. This is a simple directive that goes straight to the heart of critical thinking. The issue is not whether the authority is right or wrong; it's the questioning process that's important. Questioning helps you develop awareness and a clearer sense of what you think. That's critical thinking.

Critical thinking is a new label for an old approach to learning—that of challenging all ideas, hypotheses, and assumptions. In the physical and life sciences, systematic questioning and testing methods (known as the scientific method) help verify information, and objectivity is the benchmark on which all knowledge is pursued. In the social sciences, however, where the goal is to study people and their behavior, things get fuzzy. It's one thing for the chemistry experiment to work out as predicted, or for the petri dish to yield a certain result. It's quite another matter, however, in the social sciences, where the subject is ourselves. Objectivity is harder to achieve.

Although you'll hear critical thinking defined in many different ways, it really boils down to analyzing the ideas and messages that you receive. What are you being asked to think or believe? Does it make sense, objectively? Using the same facts and considerations, could you reasonably come up with a different conclusion? And, why does this matter in the first place? As the bumper sticker urged, question authority. Authority can be a textbook, a politician, a boss, a big sister, or an ad on television. Whatever the message, learning to question it appropriately is a habit that will serve you well for a lifetime. And in the meantime, thinking critically will certainly help you be course wise.

Getting Connected

This reader is a tool for connected learning. This means that the readings and other learning aids explained here will help you to link classroom theory to real-world issues. They will help you to think critically and to make long-lasting learning connections. Feedback from both instructors and students has helped us to develop some suggestions on how you can wisely use this connected learning tool.

WiseGuide Pedagogy

A wise reader is better able to be a critical reader. Therefore, we want to help you get wise about the articles in this reader. Each section of *Perspectives* has three tools to help you: the WiseGuide Intro, the WiseGuide Wrap-Up, and the Putting It in *Perspectives* review form.

WiseGuide Intro

In the WiseGuide Intro, the Academic Editor introduces the section, gives you an overview of the topics covered, and explains why particular articles were selected and what's important about them.

Also in the WiseGuide Intro, you'll find several key points or learning objectives that highlight the most important things to remember from this section. These will help you to focus your study of section topics.

At the end of the Wiseguide Intro, you'll find questions designed to stimulate critical thinking. Wise students will keep these questions in mind as they read an article (we repeat the questions at the start of the articles as a reminder). When you finish each article, check your understanding. Can you answer the questions? If not, go back and reread the article. The Academic Editor has written sample responses for many of the questions, and you'll find these online at the **courselinks**™ site for this course. More about **courselinks**™ in a minute. . . .

WiseGuide Wrap-Up

Be course wise and develop a thorough understanding of the topics covered in this course. The WiseGuide Wrap-Up at the end of each section will help you do just that with concluding comments or summary points that repeat what's most important to understand from the section you just read.

In addition, we try to get you wired up by providing a list of select Internet resources—what we call R.E.A.L. web sites because they're Relevant, Exciting, Approved, and Linked. The information at these web sites will enhance your understanding of a topic. (Remember to use your Passport and start at http://www.courselinks.com so that if any of these sites have changed, you'll have the latest link.)

Putting It in *Perspectives* Review Form

At the end of the book is the Putting It in *Perspectives* review form. Your instructor may ask you to complete this form as an assignment or for extra credit. If nothing else, consider doing it on your own to help you critically think about the reading.

Prompts at the end of each article encourage you to complete this review form. Feel free to copy the form and use it as needed.

The courselinks™ Site

The **courselinks**™ Passport is your ticket to a wonderful world of integrated web resources designed to help you with your course work. These resources are found at the **courselinks**™ site for your course area. This is where the readings in this book and the key topics of your course are linked to an exciting array of online learning tools. Here you will find carefully selected readings, web links, quizzes, worksheets, and more, tailored to your course and approved as connected learning tools. The ever-changing, always interesting **courselinks**™ site features a number of carefully integrated resources designed to help you be course wise. These include:

- **R.E.A.L. Sites** At the core of a **courselinks**™ site is the list of R.E.A.L. sites. This is a select group of web sites for studying, not surfing. Like the readings in this book, these sites have been selected, reviewed, and approved by the Academic Editor and the Editorial Board. The R.E.A.L. sites are arranged by topic and are annotated with short descriptions and key words to make them easier for you to use for reference or research. With R.E.A.L. sites, you're studying approved resources within seconds—and not wasting precious time surfing unproven sites.

- **Editor's Choice** Here you'll find updates on news related to your course, with links to the actual online sources. This is also where we'll tell you about changes to the site and about online events.

- **Course Overview** This is a general description of the typical course in this area of study. While your instructor will provide specific course objectives, this overview helps you place the course in a generic context and offers you an additional reference point.

- **www.orksheet** Focus your trip to a R.E.A.L. site with the www.orksheet. Each of the 10 to 15 questions will prompt you to take in the best that site has to offer. Use this tool for self-study, or if required, email it to your instructor.

- **Course Quiz** The questions on this self-scoring quiz are related to articles in the reader, information at R.E.A.L. sites, and other course topics, and will help you pinpoint areas you need to study. Only you will know your score—it's an easy, risk-free way to keep pace!

- **Topic Key** The Topic Key is a listing of the main topics in your course, and it correlates with the Topic Key that appears in this reader. This handy reference tool also links directly to those R.E.A.L. sites that are especially appropriate to each topic, bringing you integrated online resources within seconds!

- **Web Savvy Student Site** If you're new to the Internet or want to brush up, stop by the Web Savvy Student site. This unique supplement is a complete **courselinks**™ site unto itself. Here, you'll find basic information on using the Internet, creating a web page, communicating on the web, and more. Quizzes and Web Savvy Worksheets test your web knowledge, and the R.E.A.L. sites listed here will further enhance your understanding of the web.

- **Student Lounge** Drop by the Student Lounge to chat with other students taking the same course or to learn more about careers in your major. You'll find links to resources for scholarships, financial aid, internships, professional associations, and jobs. Take a look around the Student Lounge and give us your feedback. We're open to remodeling the Lounge per your suggestions.

Building Better Perspectives!

Please tell us what you think of this *Perspectives* volume so we can improve the next one. Here's how you can help:

1. Visit our **coursewise** site at: http://www.coursewise.com

2. Click on *Perspectives*. Then select the Building Better *Perspectives* Form for your book.

3. Forms and instructions for submission are available online.

Tell us what you think—did the readings and online materials help you make some learning connections? Were some materials more helpful than others? Thanks in advance for helping us build better *Perspectives*.

Student Internships

If you enjoy evaluating these articles or would like to help us evaluate the **courselinks**™ site for this course, check out the **coursewise** Student Internship Program. For more information, visit:

http://www.coursewise.com/intern.html

Contents

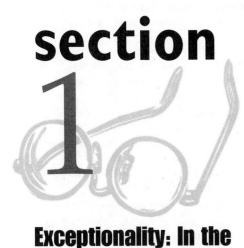
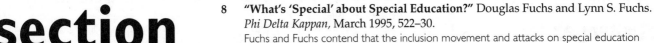

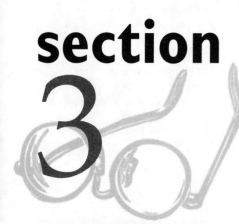

section

3

The Transition to Adulthood: Challenges for the Exceptional Individual

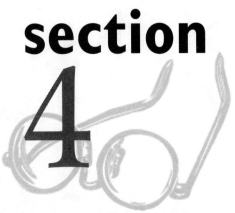

section 4

Exceptionality and Cultural Diversity

section 5

Attention Deficit Disorder: The Newest Disability

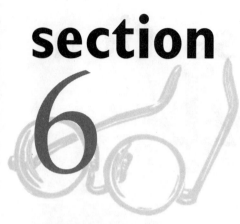

section 6

Innovations in Assessment and Instruction

section 7

Inclusion: The Issue of the 21st Century

Topic Key

This Topic Key is an important tool for learning. It will help you integrate this reader into your course studies. Listed below, in alphabetical order, are important topics covered in this volume. Below each topic you'll find the article or articles and R.E.A.L. web site addresses relating to that topic. Note that the Topic Key might not include every topic your instructor chooses to emphasize. If you don't find the topic you're looking for in the Topic Key, check the index or the OnLine Topic Key at the **courselinks**™ site.

Accommodations
www.cc.ndsu.nodak.edu/at/

Advocacy
www.downsyndrome.com
www.eskimo.com/~jlubin/disabled.html

African American Students
R18 The Overrepresentation of African American Children in Special Education: The Resegregation of Educational Programming?

Assistive Devices
www.eskimo.com/~jlubin/disabled.html

Attention Deficit Hyperactivity Disorder
R21 Teaching Tommy: A Second-Grader with Attention Deficit Hyperactivity Disorder
R22 Attention Deficit Hyperactivity Disorder: A Parent's Perspective
www.chadd.org/

Attitudes
R1 Living with 'The Look'
laran.waisman.wisc.edu/fr/www/general/disability-awareness.html

Authentic Assessment
R23 Authentic Assessment Strategies: Alternatives to Norm-Referenced Testing

Autism
R1 Living with 'The Look'

Behavioral Disorders
R29 Inclusion of All Students with Emotional or Behavioral Disorders? Let's Think Again

Culture
R7 Culture *as* Disability

Curriculum
darkwing.uoregon.edu/~ncite/index.html

Disability Rights
R5 Not Dead Yet

Emotional Disorders
R29 Inclusion of All Students with Emotional or Behavioral Disorders? Let's Think Again

Employment
R3 A Good Investment
www2.interaccess.com/netown/
www.ici.coled.umn.edu/schooltowork/

Families
R1 Living with 'The Look'
R2 Life as We Know It
www.downsyndrome.com
rdz.stjohns.edu/library/support/our-kids
schoolnet2.carleton.ca/sne/
www2.interaccess.com/netown/
www.irsc.org/

Genetics
R2 Life as We Know It

Government
www.ed.gov/offices/OSERS/
www.ed.gov/offices/OSERS/OSEP/index.html
www.ed.gov/pubs/OSEP96AnlRpt/

Inclusion
R26 Full Inclusion as Disclosing Tablet: Revealing the Flaws in Our Present System
R27 The Challenge of Inclusion
R28 The Real Challenge of Inclusion: Confessions of a 'Rabid Inclusionist'
R29 Inclusion of All Students with Emotional or Behavioral Disorders? Let's Think Again
R30 Small Victories in an Inclusive Classroom

www.weac.org/resource/june96/speced.htm
www.uni.edu/coe/inclusion/index.html
www.asri.edu/cfsp/brochure/abtcons.htm

Individuals with Disabilities Education Act (IDEA)
www.ed.gov/offices/OSERS/
www.ed.gov/pubs/OSEP96AnlRpt/
www.dssc.org/frc/index.htm

Internet Resources
schoolnet2.carleton.ca/sne/
www.hood.edu/seri/serhome.htm
www.irsc.org/
unr.edu/homepage/maddux/

Language-Minority Students
R19 The Language-Minority Student and Special Education: Issues, Trends, and Paradoxes
R20 Conversations with a Latina Teacher about Education for Language-Minority Students with Special Needs

Law
www.ed.gov/offices/OSERS/
www.ed.gov.pubs/OSEP96AnlRpt/
www.chadd.org/
www.weac.org/resource/june96/speced.htm
www.uni.edu/coe/inclusion/index.html
www.hood.edu/seri/serhome.htm

Medical Information
www.eskimo.com/~jlubin/disabled.html

Microcomputers
home.earthlink.net/~thecatalyst/

Minorities
R18 The Overrepresentation of African American Children in Special Education: The Resegregation of Educational Programming?
R19 The Language-Minority Student and Special Education: Issues, Trends, and Paradoxes

section

1

Learning Objectives

After studying this section, the reader will:

- Understand how exceptionality is a culturally determined phenomenon.

- Know some of the responses of persons with disabilities and their families to how society views the individual who is disabled.

- Be able to identify reasons why people with disabilities wish to be advocates for themselves.

- Understand how disability rights advocates are responding to the assisted suicide movement.

- Grasp the implications of the policy of failing to sustain life in infants born with disabilities.

- Know three different ways of looking at disabilities: the deprivation approach, the difference approach, and the culture-as-disability approach.

Exceptionality: In the Eye of the Beholder?

What is exceptionality? Society has traditionally classified people as having "learning disabilities," "mental retardation," "autism," "physical disabilities," "giftedness," and so on. But *where* do these exceptionalities lie? Are they *within* the individual? Or, do they exist in society's judgment of an individual? Put differently, are exceptionalities in the eyes of the beholder?

Increasingly, educators are contending that, while individuals possess different characteristics, cultures define when those differences are viewed as exceptionalities. When society was agricultural, many individuals who we might now classify as having mild mental retardation might not have been viewed as disabled. If they were able to meet the demands of their culture, there was no need to label them. Did anyone have dyslexia before the need to be able to read became commonplace in society? In fifty years, will we describe individuals as having a *computer disability* if they are inept at using a computer? Will we describe people who cannot operate a mouse as having *dysmousia*?

This first section explores exceptionality and disability in a cultural context. How does society treat individuals who are different and, more importantly, *why* are people with exceptional characteristics treated differently?

The first two articles are by fathers of children with disabilities. In "Living With 'The Look'", Robert Hughes examines the reaction of people who see his son, who has autism, on the street; he further examines his own response to their reaction. In "Life As We Know It," Michael Bérubé considers how the birth of his son, who has Down syndrome, has influenced his understanding of the interplay between genetics and social practices.

The next two articles are concerned with persons with disabilities as advocates for themselves. Jerome Lee, in "A Good Investment," asks society to consider the value of preparing individuals with disabilities for jobs and providing them with job opportunities. Michael Kennedy, in "Thoughts About Self-Advocacy," explains the need for people with disabilities to be their own advocates, recognizing both their rights and responsibilities as citizens.

The following two articles, both by Nat Hentoff of *The Village Voice*, explore issues relating to how society values the lives of people with disabilities. In "Not Dead Yet," he examines how disabilities rights activists are protesting the assisted suicide movement. In "Getting Rid of Damaged Infants," he challenges the practice of medical personnel to encourage parents to allow their children who are born with severe disabilities to die through lack of feeding.

Finally, in "Culture *As* Disability," Ray McDermott and Hervé Varenne explore how cultures create disabilities. Taking an anthropological view, they look specifically at learning disabilities and illiteracy, examining how cultures address individuals who present "problems" in a culture reaching its goals.

? ? ? Questions ?

R1. How would you characterize Hughes' response of the people on the street to his son? What do you think is the cause of "The Look" described by Hughes and what response do you think Hughes would prefer?

R2. How does Bérubé view "political correctness"? From Bérubé's perspective, is disability a physical reality or a social construction?

R3. How does Lee try to persuade the reader that disability status is unique among minority groups? Based on Lee's article, what are the primary obstacles to obtaining employment for people with disabilities?

R4. How does Kennedy respond to the issue that some persons with disabilities may be too low functioning to participate meaningfully in self-advocacy? According to Kennedy, how is self-advocacy accomplished?

R5. What do you think Diane Coleman means when she says, "The disability community is the canary in the coal mine?" Why do you think the disability rights advocates see a need to mount their protest against assisted suicide and euthanasia so strongly?

R6. What is the central argument presented by Congressman Henry Hyde, and endorsed by Hentoff, for preventing parents and medical personnel from allowing an infant with disabilities to die? Why do you think Hentoff presents the case of the Bloomington Baby?

R7. Why do McDermott and Varenne introduce the H. G. Wells character "Nunez" and his experience in the Country of the Blind? What do the authors mean when they say "culture *as* disability"?

How would you characterize Hughes' response of the people on the street to his son? What do you think is the cause of "The Look" described by Hughes and what response do you think Hughes would prefer?

Living with 'The Look'

How passersby see my autistic son's antics is making me change the way I see myself

Robert Hughes

Hughes teaches English at Truman College in Chicago.

I am walking down a busy Chicago street with Walker, my autistic 11-year-old son, and people are staring at him. He's a boy blessed with terrific good looks—tall and straight, with big dark eyes, glossy hair and a movie star's smile—but this isn't what's turning heads.

Walker isn't actually walking down the street; he's running and somehow skipping at the same time. And he isn't talking to me; he's loudly singing "Jingle Bell Rock," though this is the middle of July. And he isn't, like me, trying unsuccessfully to look everywhere but into people's eyes; he's looking and smiling directly at everyone he passes with his fingers in his ears, his elbows flared out on either side. And, further baffling the bourgeoisie, he occasionally stops, shouts, spits twice and pulls up his shirt.

Although I'm secretly proud of every bit of this sidewalk rou-

tine of his, I'm all too aware of the faces of the people we pass. Some smile, even laugh appreciatively, at his obvious joy. Some nod to me sadly and knowingly: "Ah, I know how hard your life must be," they seem to say. Some flinch in exaggerated horror as though from some ghastly space alien from Warner Brothers. Others are cool, spot him far off and pretend not to see him when they pass. Still others are so used to such surpassing weirdness in the city that our little show comes nowhere near their threshold of surprise.

One reaction, however, is more puzzling to me than all the others. I have come to think of it as "The Look." The passerby's face becomes still and thoughtful. The eyes become narrow, like those of the cunning psychiatrist in an old movie when he asks a patient what the inkblots look like. A hand goes up to the lips and, shifting into field anthropologist mode, the eyewitness stops and stares and nods silently as though making a mental note to write this one down in the jour-

nal. It's a locked-on-target look. A piano falling onto the pavement nearby wouldn't jar the stunning logical processes at work.

Having been upset by The Look about a thousand times, and being something of an amateur field anthropologist myself, I have often asked this question: "Why do these people act this way?" The best answers that I have been able to come up with are these:

a. They are heartless and rude and should be tortured in some hideous way for upsetting a really nice father.

b. They are ignorant and think that humans come in solidly "normal" and "abnormal" forms and have no doubt about what kind they themselves are.

c. They saw the movie "Rain Man" and are now experts on autism.

d. They are fearful and are trying to achieve distance from a scary sight by trying to regard it as a rare scientific phenomenon.

e. They are curious, as the father would be, too, in their

situation, at seeing a normal-looking boy acting strangely.

f. They aren't even aware that they have an expression on their faces and actually feel sympathetic toward the boy.

g. They really are psychiatrists, and their work is a big help to humanity.

Which answer I choose is largely dependent on my mood. If I'm feeling defensive and hypersensitive (most of the time), I gravitate toward letters *a*, *b* and *c*. If I'm feeling wise and magnanimous (not very often), I go for letters *d*, *e* and *f*. And if I'm feeling lighthearted (once or twice a year), I amuse myself with some variation of *g*.

But I know that I can conjecture forever and never really be sure what The Look means.

One thing I am sure of is the look on Walker's face. Unable to talk normally, he deploys a heavy arsenal of expression and movement to communicate. The beaming smile, the direct gaze, the skip-running and shout-singing, even the vigorous spitting—all of it—tells me Walker is working his audience hard. "Here I am! Look at me! I'm having fun! Aren't you impressed?" The message goes out, and some people, remarkably, seem to pick it up. Most, understandably, do not.

But what about my face, my look? Inside the house I do a fair job of attempting to see the world as Walker sees it and understanding him as far as possible on his own terms. Thus a game of catch is, for us, not a Ward and the Beaver experience in the backyard. Performed Walker style, catch is an "extreme sport," with rules that are reinvented by him daily. Currently the game must be played in the house while Walker jumps wildly on his exercise trampoline, and there must be loud music playing, and he must catch the ball and throw it back while airborne. At unpredictable moments, Walker must leap off the trampoline and dash in and out of the room. The one unvarying rule is this: Dad must never stop paying attention. The result is that I long ceased aching for the "normal" game of catch and learned to love the in-house version we share.

At home, I stretch my notions of the "appropriate" to accommodate Walker's ideas on: a bedroom (the dining room, lights on); breakfast, lunch and dinner (cooked spaghetti, no sauce); and entertainment (every morning, the video of "The Wind in the Willows").

When I step outside the house, however, a different, less noble point of view grips me, and I start to speculate needlessly on how outsiders see my son. Lost in a fog of anger or avoidance or criticism, I must present an uninviting picture for him and the world to look at. Why shouldn't passersby stare at the friendly son when the father's face is cloudy with conflict and questioning?

So I'm working on my look. I'm shooting for, at minimum, a near-frequent smile. I want to face the sidewalk parade as Walker does, with joy and hope and, most important of all, with a saving sense of fun.

 Article Review Form at end of book.

How does Bérubé view "political correctness"? From Bérubé's perspective, is disability a physical reality or a social construction?

Life as We Know It

A father, a son, and genetic destiny

Michael Bérubé

Michael Bérubé is the author of Marginal Forces/Cultural Centers *(Cornell University Press) and* Public Access: Literary Theory and American Cultural Politics *(Verso). He is an associate professor of English at the University of Illinois at Urbana-Champaign.*

In my line of work I don't think very often about carbon or potassium, much less about polypeptides or transfer RNA. I teach American and African-American literature; Janet Lyon, my legal spouse and general partner, teaches modern British literature and women's studies. Nothing about our jobs requires us to be aware of the biochemical processes that made us—and, more recently, our children—into conscious beings. But in 1985–86, when Janet was pregnant with our first child, Nicholas, I would lie awake for hours, wondering how the baseball-size clump of cells in her uterus was really going to form something living, let alone something capable of thought. I knew that the physical processes that form dogs and drosophilas are more or less as intricate, on the molecular level, as those that form humans; but puppies and fruit flies don't go around asking how they got here or how (another version of the same question) DNA base-pair sequences code for various amino acids. And though humans have been amazed and puzzled by human gestation for quite a while now, it wasn't until a few nanoseconds ago (in geological time) that their wonder began to focus on the chemical minutiae that somehow differentiate living matter from "mere" matter. The fact that self-replicating molecules had eventually come up with a life-form that could actually pick apart the workings of self-replicating molecules . . . well, let's just say I found this line of thought something of a distraction. At the time, I thought that I would never again devote so much attention to such ideas. I figured the miracle of human birth, like that of humans landing on the moon, would be more routine than miracle the second time around. It wasn't.

James appeared tangled in his umbilical cord. "He looks Downsy around the eyes," I heard. Downsy?

Five years later, in September 1991, Janet was pregnant again, another fall semester was beginning, and I was up late writing. At 2:00 A.M., Janet asked when I was coming to bed. At 4:00 A.M., she asked again. "Soon," I said. "Well, you should probably stop working now," she replied, "because I think I'm going into labor." At which point she presented me with an early birthday present, a watch with a second hand.

That was the first unexpected thing: James wasn't due for another two weeks. Then came more unexpected things in rapid succession.

Eight hours later, in the middle of labor, Janet spotted a dangerous arrhythmia on her heart monitor. The only other person in the room was an obstetrics staff nurse; Janet turned to her and barked, "That's V-tach. We need a cardiologist in here. Get a bolus of lidocaine ready, and get the crash cart." (Being an ex-cardiac-intensive-care nurse comes in handy sometimes.) Pounding on her chest and forcing herself to cough, she broke out of what was possibly a lethal heart rhythm. Labor stalled; Janet and I stared at each other for an hour. Suddenly, at a strange moment when she and I were the only people in the room, James's head presented. I hollered down the hall for help. James appeared within minutes, an unmoving baby of a deep, rich, purple hue, tangled in his umbilical cord. "He looks Downsy around the eyes," I heard. Downsy? He looks stillborn, I thought. They unwrapped the cord, cut it, gave him oxygen. Quickly, incredibly, he revived. No cry, but who cared? They gave him an Apgar score of 7, on a scale of 1 to 10. I remember feeling an immense relief. My wife was alive, my second child was alive. At the end of a teeth-grating hour during which I'd wondered if either of them would see the end of the day, Down syndrome somehow seemed like a reprieve.

Over the next half hour, as the nurses worked on James, and Janet and I tried to collect our thoughts, I realized I didn't know very much about Down's, other than that it meant James had an extra chromosome and would be mentally retarded. I knew I'd have some homework to do.

But what kind of homework were we talking about? Would we ever have normal lives again? We'd struggled for eight years on salaries that left us able to peer at the poverty line only if one of us stood on the other's shoulders. A mere three weeks earlier, the university had hired Janet, thus making us one of the extremely rare dual-career academic couples working in the same department; we knew how lucky we were, and we thought we were finally going to be "comfortable." But now were we going to spend the rest of our days caring for a se-verely disabled child? Would we have even an hour to ourselves? Christ, we'd only just finished paying off the bills for *Nick's* birth two months earlier, and now were we facing the kind of catastrophic medical debt that fills the op-ed pages? These were selfish thoughts, and the understanding that such thoughts are "natural" didn't make them any less bitter or insistent.

We went over the past few months. The pregnancy had been occasionally odd but not exactly scary. We'd decided against getting an amniocentesis, on the grounds that a sonogram would pick up nearly any serious problems with the fetus *except* Down syndrome, and the chances of having a child with Down syndrome at Janet's age, thirty-six, were roughly equal to the chances of an amniocentesis-induced miscarriage (1 in 225 and 1 in 200, respectively). Later, there were some hitches: reduced fetal movements, disproportionate fetal measurements on sonograms, low weight gain, and so on. Our worries were vague but persistent.

Back in the present, over on his table in the birthing room, James wasn't doing very well. He still wasn't moving, he had no sucking reflex, and he was getting bluer. It turned out that the fetal opening in his heart hadn't closed fully. You and I had the same arrangement until around the time of birth, when our heart's ventricles sealed themselves off in order to get us ready to start conducting oxygen from our lungs into our bloodstream. But James still had a hole where no hole should be, and wasn't oxygenating properly.

There was more. Along with his patent ductus arteriosus and his trisomy 21, there was laryngo-malacia (floppy larynx), jaundice, polycythenia (an abnormal increase in red blood cells), torticollis, vertebral anomaly, scoliosis, hypotonia (low muscle tone), and (not least of these) feeding problems. That's a lot of text to wade through to get to your kid.

Basically, James was in danger. If he made it through the night he would still be a candidate, in the morning, for open-heart surgery *and* a tracheostomy. Because of the laryngomalacia, which isn't related to Down's, he couldn't coordinate sucking, swallowing, and breathing, and his air supply would close off if he slept on the wrong side. The vertebral problems, we learned, occur in roughly one of six kids with Down's; his first three vertebrae were malformed, his spinal cord vulnerable. And his neck muscles were abnormally tight (that's the torticollis), leaving him with a 20-degree head tilt to the left. He was being fed intravenously and had tubes not only in his arm but in his stomach as well, run neatly through his umbilical artery, still viable from the delivery. Our first Polaroid of him shows a little fleshy thing under a clear plastic basin, lost in machinery and wires. I remember thinking, it's all right that they do all this to him now because he'll never remember it. But it can't be a pleasant introduction to the world.

Within days things got better, and one anxiety after another peeled away: Jamie's duct closed, and as I entered the intensive-care unit one morning I found that the staff had erased from his chart the phone number of the emergency helicopter service that would have flown him to Peoria for heart

We sneaked a peek at a nurse's notes: "Parents intellectualizing." That seemed accurate enough."

surgery. His blood-oxygen levels reached the high 90s and stayed there, even as he was weaned from 100 percent oxygen to a level just above the atmospheric norm. A tracheoscopy (that is, a viewing of his throat with an eyepiece at the end of a tube) confirmed that he didn't need a tracheostomy. He still wasn't feeding, but he was opening an eye now and then and looking out at his brother and his parents.

I got hold of everything I could on genetics, reproduction, and "abnormal" human development, dusting off college textbooks I hadn't touched since before Nick was born. At one point a staff nurse was sent in to check on *our* mental health; she found us babbling about meiosis and monoploids, wondering anew that Jamie had "gotten" Down syndrome the second he became a zygote. When the nurse inadvertently left behind her notes, Janet sneaked a peek. "Parents seem to be intellectualizing," we read. "Well," Janet shrugged, "that seems accurate enough."

Looking over the fossil record, I really don't see any compelling logic behind humans' existence on the planet. I'm told that intelligence has obvious survival value, since organisms with a talent for information processing "naturally" beat out their competitors for food, water, and condos, but human history doesn't convince me that *our* brand of intelligence is just what the world was waiting for. Thus I've never believed we were supposed to survive the Ice Age, or that some cosmic design mandated that cataclysmic collision in the late Cretaceous period that gave us an iridium layer in our soil and may have ended the dinosaurs' reign. Bacteria and horseshoe crabs un-

modified for aeons are still with us, but what has become of *Eusthenopteron,* introduced to me by then-five-year-old Nicholas as the fish that could walk on land? If you were fighting for survival 350 million years ago, you'd think you'd have had a leg up on the competition if you developed small bones in your fins, enabling you to shimmy onto shore. But you'd be wrong: these days, *Eusthenopteron* is nothing more than a card in Nick's "prehistoric animals" collection, alongside the Ankylosaur, the mastodon, and the jessehelms. I figure we were here thanks to dumb luck, and though we have managed to understand our own biochemical origins and take neat close-up pictures from the far side of Saturn, we also spend much of our time exterminating ourselves and most other species we meet. And nothing in Nick's cards says we too won't wind up in nature's deck of "prehistoric" animals.

Still, it wasn't until I got to college and started thinking about sex and drugs in rather immediate ways that I began to realize that the workings of chance on the molecular level are even more terrifying than on the evolutionary plane. Of course, the molecular and the evolutionary have everything to do with each other; it's just that the minutiae of mitosis are more awe-inspiring to me, *because* more quotidian, than the thought of random rocks slamming into my home planet every couple of hundred million years. For those who don't feel like cracking open old textbooks, Richard Powers's novel *The Gold Bug Variations* offers some idea of what's involved in cell division: "seven feet of aperiodic crystal

unzips, finds complements of each of its billion constituents, integrates them perfectly without tearing or entangling, then winds up again into a fraction of a millimeter, all in two minutes." And this is just the ordinary stuff your cells are doing every moment. Sex, as always, is a little more complicated.

So let's talk about sex. Of the 15 percent of pregnancies that end in miscarriage, more than half are the result of chromosomal abnormalities, and half of these are caused by trisomy—three chromosomes where two should be. Of the myriad possible genetic mistransmissions in human reproduction, excluding anomalies in the sex chromosomes, it appears that only three kinds of trisomies make it to term: people with three thirteenth chromosomes (Patau's syndrome), three eighteenth chromosomes (Edwards' syndrome), and three twenty-first chromosomes (Down syndrome). About one in four or five zygotes with Down's winds up getting born, and since Down's accounts for one of every 600 to 800 live births, it would appear that trisomy 21 happens quite often, maybe on the order of once in every 150 to 250 fertilizations. Kids with Edwards' or Patau's syndrome are born severely deformed and profoundly retarded; they normally don't live more than a few months. That's what I would expect of genetic anomaly, whatever the size of the autosome: though the twenty-first chromosome is the smallest we have, James still has extra genetic material in every single cell. You'd think the effects of such a basic transcription error would make themselves felt pretty clearly.

The workings of chance on the molecular level are even more terrifying than on the evolutionary plane.

But what's odd about Down's is how extraordinarily subtle it can be. Mental retardation is one well-known effect, and it can sometimes be severe, but anyone who's watched Chris Burke on TV's *Life Goes On*" or "Mike" in McDonald's commercials knows that the extent of such retardation can be next to negligible. The *real* story of Down's lies not in intelligence tests but in developmental delays across the board, and for the first two years of James's life the most important of these were physical rather than mental (though thanks to James I've come to see how interdependent the mental and physical really are). His muscles are weaker than those of most children his age, his nasal passages imperceptibly narrower. His tongue is slightly thicker; one ear is crinkly. His fingers would be shorter and stubbier but for the fact that his mother's are long, thin, and elegant. His face is a few degrees flatter through the middle, his nose delicate.

Down's doesn't cut all children to one mold; the relations between James's genotype and phenotype are lacy and intricate. It's sort of like what happens in Ray Bradbury's short story "A Sound of Thunder," in which a time traveler accidentally steps on a butterfly while hunting dinosaurs 65 million years ago and returns home to find that he's changed the conventions of English spelling and the outcome of the previous day's election. As he hit the age of two, James was very pleased to find himself capable of walking; by three, he had learned to say the names of colors, to count to ten, and to claim that he would *really* be turning four. Of all our genetic nondisjunctions (with the possible exception of hermaphroditism), only Down

syndrome produces so nuanced, so finely articulated a variation on "normal" reproduction. James is less mobile and more susceptible to colds than his peers, but—as his grandparents have often attested—you could play with him for hours and never see anything "wrong."

And then there's a variant form of Down's, called mosaicism, which results from the failure of the chromosome to divide not *before* fertilization but immediately *after,* during the early stages of cell division. Only one in a hundred people with Down's are mosaics, but it's possible for such folks to have some normal cells and some with trisomy 21; there's something about the twenty-first, then, that produces anomalies during either meiosis *or* mitosis. Now, that's truly weird. There's also translocation, in which the twenty-first chromosome splits off and joins the fourteenth or fifteenth, producing people who can be called "carriers"; they can give birth to more translocation carriers, normal children, or translocation kids with Down's. And although everyone knows that the incidence of Down's increases with maternal age, almost no one knows that three quarters of all such children are born to mothers under thirty-five, or that fathers are genetically "responsible" for about one fifth of them.

Parents seem to be intellectualizing. And why not?

There has never been a better time than now to be born with Down syndrome—and that's really saying something, since it has recently been reported in chimpanzees and gorillas. Because our branch of the evolutionary tree split off from the apes' around 15

to 20 million years ago, these reports would seem to suggest that we've produced offspring with Down syndrome with great regularity at every point in our history as hominids—even though it's a genetic anomaly that's not transmitted hereditarily (except in extremely rare instances) and has no obvious survival value. The statistical incidence of Down's in the current human population is no less staggering: there may be 10 million people with Down's worldwide, or just about one on every other street corner.

At no time in our history did hominids not give birth to offspring with Down's syndrome.

But although *Homo sapiens* (as well as our immediate ancestors) has always experienced some difficulty dividing its chromosomes, it wasn't until 1866 that British physician J. Langdon Down diagnosed it as "mongolism" (because it produced children with almond-shaped eyes reminiscent, to at least one nineteenth-century British mind, of central Asian faces). At the time, the average life expectancy of children with Down's was under ten. And for a hundred years thereafter—during which the discovery of antibiotics lengthened the life span of Down's kids to around twenty—Down syndrome was formally known as "mongoloid idiocy."

The 1980 edition of my college genetics textbook, *The Science of Genetics: An Introduction to Heredity,* opens its segment on Down's with the words, "An important and tragic instance of trisomy in humans involves Down's syndrome, or mongoloid idiocy." It includes a picture of a "mongoloid idiot" along with a karyotype of his chromosomes and the information that most people with Down's have IQs in the low 40s.

The presentation is objective, dispassionate, and strictly "factual," as it should be. But reading it again in 1991, I began to wonder: is there a connection between the official textual representation of Down syndrome and the social policies by which people with Down's are understood and misunderstood?

You bet your life there is. Anyone who has paid attention to the "political correctness" wars on American campuses knows how stupid the academic left can be: we're always talking about language instead of reality, whining about "lookism" and "differently abled persons" instead of changing the world the way the real he-man left *used* to do. But you know, there really is a difference between calling someone "a mongoloid idiot" and calling him or her "a person with Down syndrome." There's even a difference between calling people "retarded" and calling them "delayed." Though these words may appear to mean the same damn thing when you look them up in Webster's, I remember full well from my days as an American male adolescent that I never taunted my peers by calling them "delayed." Even from those of us who were shocked at the frequency with which "homo" and "nigger" were thrown around in our fancy Catholic high school, "retard" aroused no comment, no protest. In other words, a retarded person is just a retard. But *delayed* persons will get where they're going eventually, if you'll only have some patience.

One night I said something like this to one of the leaders of what I usually think of as the other side in the academic culture wars. Being a humane fellow, he replied that although epithets like "mongoloid idiot" were undoubtedly used in a more benighted time, there have always been persons of goodwill who resisted such phraseology. A nice thought, but it just ain't so. Right through the 1970s, "mongoloid idiot" wasn't an epithet; it was a *diagnosis*. It wasn't uttered by callow, ignorant persons fearful of "difference" and central Asian eyes; it was pronounced by the best-trained medical practitioners in the world, who told families of kids with Down's that their children would never be able to dress themselves, recognize their parents, or live "meaningful" lives. Best to have the child institutionalized and tell one's friends that the baby died at birth. Only the most stubborn, intransigent, or inspired parents resisted such advice from their trusted experts. Who could reasonably expect otherwise?

It's impossible to say how deeply we're indebted to those parents, children, teachers, and medical personnel who insisted on treating people with Down's as if they *could* learn, as if they *could* lead "meaningful" lives. In bygone eras, parents who didn't take their children home didn't really have the "option" of doing so; you can't talk about "options" (in any substantial sense of the word) in an ideological current so strong. But in the early 1970s, some parents did bring their children home, worked with them, held them, provided them physical therapy and "special learning" environments. These parents are saints and sages. They have, in the broadest sense of the phrase, uplifted the race. In the 15-million-year history of Down syndrome, they've allowed us to believe that we're finally getting somewhere.

Of course, the phrase "mongoloid idiocy" did not cause Down syndrome any more than the word "homo" magically induces same-sex desire. But words and phrases are the devices by which we beings signify what homosexuality, or Down syndrome, or anything else, will mean. There surely were, and are, the most intimate possible relations between the language in which we spoke of Down's and the social practices by which we understood it—or refused to understand it. You don't have to be a poststructuralist or a postmodernist or a post-*anything* to get this; all you have to do is meet a parent of a child with Down syndrome. Not long ago, we lived next door to people whose youngest child had Down's. After James was born, they told us of going to the library to find out more about their baby's prospects and wading through page after page of outdated information, ignorant generalizations, and pictures of people in mental institutions, face down in their feeding trays. These parents demanded the library get some better material and throw out the garbage they had on their shelves. Was this a "politically correct" thing for them to do? Damn straight it was. That garbage has had its effects *for generations*. It may only look like words, but perhaps the fragile little neonates whose lives were thwarted and impeded by the policies and conditions of institutionalization can testify in some celestial court to the power of mere language, to the intimate links between words and social policies.

Some of my friends tell me this sounds too much like "strict social constructionism"—that is,

Right through the seventies, "mongoloid idiot" wasn't an epithet, it was a diagnosis.

too much like the proposition that culture is everything and biology is only what we decide to make (of) it. But although James is pretty solid proof that human biology "exists" independently of our understanding of it, every morning when he gets up, smiling and babbling to his family, I can see for myself how much of his life depends on our social practices. On one of those mornings I turned to my mother-in-law and said, "He's always so full of mischief, he's always so glad to see us—the only thought I can't face is the idea of this little guy waking up each day in a state mental hospital." To which my mother-in-law replied, "Well, Michael, if he were waking up every day in a state mental hospital, he wouldn't *be* this little guy."

There are days I catch myself believing that people with Down's are here for a specific purpose.

As it happens, my mother-in-law doesn't subscribe to any strict social constructionist newsletters; she was just passing along what she took to be good common sense. But every so often I wonder how common that sense really is. Every ten minutes we hear that the genetic basis of something has been "discovered," and we rush madly to the newsweeklies: Disease is genetic! Homosexuality is genetic! Infidelity, addiction, obsession with mystery novels—all genetic! Such discourses, it would seem, bring out the hidden determinist in more of us than will admit it. Sure, there's a baseline sense in which our genes "determine" who we are: we can't play the tune unless the score is written down somewhere in the genome. But one does not need or require a biochemical explanation for literary taste, or voguing, or faithless lovers. In these as in all things

human, including Down's, the genome is but a template for a vaster and more significant range of social and historical variation. Figuring out even the most rudimentary of relations between the genome and the immune system (something of great relevance to us wheezing asthmatics) involves so many trillions of variables that a decent answer will win you an all-expenses-paid trip to Stockholm.

I'm not saying we can eradicate Down's—or its myriad effects—simply by talking about it more nicely. I'm only saying that James's intelligence is doing better than it would in an institution, and people who try to deny this don't strike me as being among the geniuses of the species. And every time I hear some self-styled "realist" tell me that my logic licenses the kind of maniacal social engineering that produced Auschwitz, I do a reality check: the people who brought us Auschwitz weren't "social constructionists." They were eugenicists. They thought they knew the "immutable laws" of genetics and the "fixed purpose" of evolution, and they were less interested in "improving" folks like Jamie than in exterminating them. I'll take my chances with the people who believe in chance.

And yet there's something very seductive about the notion that Down syndrome wouldn't have been so prevalent in humans for so long without good reason. Indeed, there are days when, despite everything I know and profess, I catch myself believing that people with Down syndrome are here for a specific purpose—perhaps to teach us patience, or

humility, or compassion, or mere joy. A great deal can go wrong with us in utero, but under the heading of what goes wrong, Down syndrome is among the most basic, the most fundamental, the most common, *and* the most innocuous, leavening the species with children who are somewhat slower, and usually somewhat gentler, than the rest of the human brood. It speaks to us strongly of design, if design may govern in a thing so small.

After seventeen days in the ICU, James was scheduled for release. We would be equipped with the materials necessary for his care, including oxygen tanks and an apnea monitor that would beep if his heart slowed, became extremely irregular, or stopped. To compensate for his inability to take food orally, James would have a gastrostomy tube surgically introduced through his abdominal wall into his stomach. Janet and I balked. James had recently made progress in his bottle feeding; why do preemptive surgery? We nixed the gastrostomy tube, saying we'd prefer to augment his bottle feedings with a nasal tube and we'd do it ourselves. James stayed three more days in the ICU, and came home to a house full of flowers and homemade dinners from our colleagues.

For the most part, I've repressed the details of that autumn. But every once in a while, rummaging through the medicine closet for Ace bandages or heating pads, I come across the Hypafix adhesive tape with which we attached James's feeding tube to the bridge of his nose, or the strap we wrapped around his tiny chest for his apnea monitor. It's like discovering evidence of another life, dim but indelible, and you realize that once upon a time you could cope with practically anything. Running a small tube through your baby's nose to his stomach is the worst kind of counterintuitive practice. You have to do it carefully, measuring your length of tubing accurately and listening with a stethoscope to make sure you haven't entered the lung. Whenever James pulled out his tubes, we had to do the whole thing over again, in the other nostril this time, lubricating and marking and holding the tube while fumbling with the world's stickiest tape. It's a four-handed job, and I don't blame the staff doctors for assuming we wouldn't undertake such an enterprise alone.

But slowly we got James to bottle feed. After all, for our purposes, Jamie's nasal tube, like unto a thermonuclear weapon, was there precisely so that we *wouldn't* use it. Each week a visiting nurse would set a minimum daily amount for Jamie's milk intake, and whatever he didn't get by bottle would have to go in by tube. So you can see the incentive at work here. Within a month we began to see glimpses of what James would look like sans tube. Then we stopped giving him oxygen during the night, and gradually his tiny nostrils found themselves a lot less encumbered. He still didn't have a voice, but he was clearly interested in his new home and very trusting of his parents and brother.

In the midst of that winter James began physical therapy and massages. We stretched his neck every night, and whenever we could afford it we took him to a local masseuse who played ambient music, relaxed us all, and worked on James for an hour. His

I don't blame the staff doctors for assuming we wouldn't want to undertake such an enterprise alone.

physical therapist showed us how everything about James was connected to everything else: His neck, if left uncorrected, would reshape the bones of his face. The straighter his neck, the sooner he'd sit up, the sooner he'd walk. If he could handle simple solid foods with equal facility in both sides of his mouth, he could center himself more easily; and the sooner he could move around by himself, the more he'd be able to explore and learn. In other words, his eating would affect his ability to walk, and his thighs and torso would impinge upon his ability to talk. I suppose that's what it means to be an organism.

Not only did we realize the profound interdependence of human hearts and minds; we also discovered (and had to reconfigure) our relations to a vast array of social practices and institutions. "Developmental" turns out to be a buzzword for a sprawling nexus of agencies, state organizations, and human disabilities. Likewise, "special needs" isn't a euphemism, it's a very specific marker. We're learning about the differences between "mainstreaming" and "inclusion," and we'll be figuring out the Americans with Disabilities Act for the rest of our lives. Above all else, we know that James is extremely lucky to be so well provided for; when every employer is as flexible as ours, when parental leave is the law of the land, when private insurers can't drop families from the rolls because of "high risk" children, when every child can be fed, clothed, and cared for—*then* we can start talk-

Nothing will delight James so much as the realization that you have understood him.

ing about what kind of a choice "life" might be.

Because, after all he's been through, James is thriving. He's thrilled to be here and takes a visible, palpable delight in seeing his reflection in the oven door as he toddles across the kitchen, or hearing his parents address him in the voices of the *Sesame Street* regulars, or winging a Nerf ball to his brother on the couch. He knows perfectly well when he's doing something we've never seen before, like riding his toddler bicycle down the hall into the laundry room or calling out "Georgia" and "Hawaii" as he flips through Nick's book of the fifty states. He's been a bibliophile from the moment he learned to turn pages. His current favorite is Maurice Sendak's classic *Where the Wild Things Are,* surely a Great Book by any standard; he began by identifying with Max and then, in one of those "oscillations" described by reader-response criticism and feminist film theory, switched over to identifying with the wild things themselves— roaring his terrible roar and showing his terrible claws.

He has his maternal aunts' large deep eyes, and a beautiful smile that somehow involves his whole body. He's not only an independent cuss, but he also has an attention span of about twenty minutes— eighteen minutes longer than the average American political pundit. He's blessed with a preternaturally patient, sensitive brother Nick, who, upon hearing one of his classmates' parents gasp "Oh my God" at the news that Jamie had Down's, turned to her and said with a fine mixture of reassurance and annoyance, "He's perfectly all *right*." Like Nick, James has a keen sense of humor; the two of them can be set agiggle by pratfalls, radical incongruities, and mere sidelong looks. He's just now old enough to be curious about what he was like as a baby: as he puts it, all he could do was go "waaah" (holding his fists to his eyes). Barring all the contingencies that can never be barred, James can expect a life span of anywhere from thirty-five to fifty-five years. For tomorrow, he can expect to see his friends at day care, to put all his shapes in his shapes box, and to sing along with Raffi as he shakes his sillies out and wiggles his waggles away.

Before James was born, I frankly didn't think very highly of appeals to our "common humanity." I thought such appeals were well intentioned but basically inconsequential. Clearly, Muslim and Christian do not bond over their common ancestor in *Australopithecus*. Rwandan Hutu and Rwandan Tutsi do not toast to the distinctive size of their cerebral cortices. The rape of Bosnia, and Bosnian women, does not stop once Serbian soldiers realize that they too will pass from the earth.

And yet we possess one crucial characteristic: the desire to communicate, to understand, to put ourselves in some mutual, reciprocal form of contact with one another. This desire hasn't proven any better at disarming warheads than any of the weaker commonalities enumerated above, but it stands a better chance nonetheless. For among the most amazing and hopeful things about us is that we show up, from our day of birth, programmed to receive and transmit even in the most difficult circumstances; the ability to imagine mutual communicative relations is embedded in our material bodies, woven through our double-stranded fibers. Granted, it's only one variable among trillions, and it's not even "fundamentally" human— for all we know, dolphins are much better at communication than we are. And the sociohistorical variables of human communication will always be more significant and numerous than any genetic determinism can admit. All the same, it's in our software somewhere, and, better still, it's a program that teaches itself how to operate each time we use it.

Whether you want to consider reciprocal communication a constant or a variable, though, the point remains that it's a human attribute requiring other people if it's going to work. Among the talents we have, it's one we could stand to develop more fully. It's only natural: among our deepest, strongest impulses is the impulse to mutual cuing. Nothing will delight James so much as the realization that you have understood him—except the realization that he has understood *you*, and recursively understood his own understanding and yours. Perhaps I could have realized our human stake in mutual realization without James's aid; any number of other humans would have been willing to help me out. But now that I get it, I get it for good. Communication is itself self-replicating. Sign unto others as you'd have them sign unto you. Pass it on.

 Article Review Form at end of book.

How does Lee try to persuade the reader that disability status is unique among minority groups? Based on Lee's article, what are the primary obstacles to obtaining employment for people with disabilities?

A Good Investment

People with disabilities do a better job because we have something to prove. Don't write us off.

Jerome Lee

Lee, 42, lives in Brooklyn, N.Y.

I had worked in construction for more than 22 years. As a site manager, I was used to being out in the open, organizing workers and materials and getting things done. I loved my work, was good at it and didn't really know any other occupation. But in 1992, in one instant, my whole life changed.

I was standing on the 135th Street Bridge in Manhattan, enjoying the view of the Harlem River, when I was shot in the spine in broad daylight by a young man on a bicycle. The police called it an attempted robbery. If two people passing by hadn't rescued me, I would have died. The bullet left me paralyzed. I am now paraplegic and use a wheelchair.

I spent three weeks at Harlem Hospital. Fearing I would lose all movement in my neck in addition to my lower spine, the doctors decided not to remove the bullet, which is still lodged in my spine. I then was sent to Mount Sinai Hospital for three months of rehabilitation.

I met many new people while in rehab and heard a variety of stories. One of the things that surprised me most was that, like me, nearly all of the minority patients were there not because of car accidents, or because they had fallen off ladders at work, or because they'd suffered sports injuries but because they had been shot. The discovery disturbed me very much.

This was a hard time in my life, but much to my amazement, I did not despair. I felt that my injury would be a temporary thing. I believed that I would walk again, that God would heal me, that I'd return to the world I'd known. It never occurred to me that I would not be able to resume my work in construction.

My doctors told me that if a person was bitter before an injury, he'd likely be more bitter afterward. But if he'd had a positive attitude, he'd bring that to the new situation as well. I had always worked and been financially independent. I had always believed in building a future. In spite of my difficulties, that part of me did not change. And my faith helped me to help others. While undergoing rehab, I found myself being called upon by doctors and nurses to assist with their other patients. "Just talk to him," they'd say. "Help us motivate this kid to get better." And sometimes I was able to do that.

Eventually I began to accept what I had been told by so many people—that I would never be able to work in construction again. I was referred to the International Center for the Disabled in New York City for rehabilitation and vocational services to help me make a career change. ICD was the first outpatient rehab center in the United States. It's a wonderful place with a staff that really understands what you are going through, a staff that doesn't give up. Because I love working with young people and seem to be good at motivating others, I trained as a human services assistant and received certification in that program.

But I hated to throw away all my years of experience and all that I knew and loved about construction work. I had many discussions about this with the director of ICD's Business Opportunities Development Department. Together we came up with a way to combine my years of experience in construction and love of that work with my training in human services and interest in young people. I now manage ICD's painting crew, which is made up entirely of people with disabilities. These men and women come from all kinds of backgrounds and have many kinds of disabilities, including head injuries, visual limitations, kidney failure, developmental problems, learning disabilities and seizure disorders. Several are partly paralyzed.

I bid on jobs, organize the workload, order supplies, assemble the work teams, supervise the jobs—and do a lot of the plastering and painting myself. My crews have renovated, refurbished and painted government offices, medical suites, apartments and the offices at ICD. We do a better job than anyone else because we're out to prove something.

I teach my crew members a trade they can really use. By sharing my confidence, they gain confidence, too. We sometimes surprise people who don't expect to see individuals with disabilities doing this kind of work. To me, we are proof that no one should be denied the chance to work because he or she has a disability.

There are more than 49 million Americans with disabilities, more than one person in every five. In fact, we are the country's largest minority—and the only one that any person can join at any time. Disability doesn't discriminate. As I have learned, no one is guaranteed safety from accident, illness or violence. I had never thought about becoming disabled before I was shot. Most people don't. I had never thought I'd have to change my life.

Despite passage of the Americans With Disabilities Act in 1990, 70 percent of people with disabilities between the ages of 18 and 65 are still unemployed. Each year the federal government spends 40 times more money to support people with disabilities not working than it spends to help us prepare for and find jobs. The cost to society is tremendous—in both human and economic terms.

Many people assume that we don't want to work. But I do want to work. Most of the people I know want to work. A large number of us were employed before we became disabled and want to return to a regular, productive life.

But we need help to do it. We need long-term rehabilitation and medical coverage we can count on. We need to be free from the threat of losing our health and social-security benefits if we become employed. And most important, we need job-training programs that work—and real job opportunities.

I believe that government and business should not write off people with disabilities but should invest in us. In this time of cutbacks in government spending, a changing policy toward government "handouts" and downsizing in business, everyone has to do more than "talk the talk" so that we can "walk the walk." Give us the job-training programs we need—and hire us. It's a good investment for the whole country.

 Article Review Form at end of book.

How does Kennedy respond to the issue that some persons with disabilities may be too low functioning to participate meaningfully in self-advocacy? According to Kennedy, how is self-advocacy accomplished?

Thoughts about Self-Advocacy

Michael Kennedy, with Bonnie Shoultz

I give quite a few talks around the country on self-advocacy. Most of those talks are to service providers and parents, although there are some people with disabilities in some of the audiences. One thing that amazes me still is that although self-advocacy has been around for a long time now, since 1974 at least, there are some people who don't know anything about it. When I talk about it, they have a really surprised look on their face like it is a whole new world. Most people are very open to hearing about it, and I get requests to send more information about it from the people in the audiences. In this article I will talk about some things I want people to know about self-advocacy.

Here is what Self-Advocates Becoming Empowered, the new national self-advocacy organization, believes about self-advocacy.

...There is always a risk factor when someone is making choices for themselves, but people still need the opportunity, even if they make a mistake.

We believe that people with disabilities should be treated as equals. That means that people should be given the same decisions, choices, rights, responsibilities and chances to speak up to empower themselves, as well as to make new friendships and renew old friendships, just like everyone else. They should also be able to learn from their mistakes like everyone else.

The self-advocacy movement was started by people with disabilities, especially people who had been in institutions and state schools, because they wanted their basic rights like everybody else. But before they could exercise their rights, they had to fight for the right to be heard and to have choices in their lives. They had to find out what basic rights they had, and then they had to begin to teach other people with disabilities, parents and service providers.

Self advocacy is for everyone. Some people say to me, "It is fine for you to speak for yourself, because you aren't as disabled as my son or daughter, or the people

I work with." I disagree with them. I say, "Have you taken the time to learn what that person wants or might need? Has the person heard about their rights? Is he or she facing an issue they need support with? What can the person say for himself or herself, and how can you help him or her express more? Or are you just assuming that they want what you want for them?"

A lot of times I find that people have not taken the time to ask, and have just assumed they knew what was best for the person. I had one parent say to me one time that she always made the decisions because it was easier than figuring out how to help her daughter communicate. I said to her that I didn't know what her daughter's disability was, but there had to be a way that she could actively participate in the choices about her life.

The first thing they would have to do is figure out a way for the mother and daughter to communicate with each other. Next would be to try to discover how the daughter could learn more about the choices she has, and then how she could make the choices. The daughter could be supported to make an informed

Kennedy, M., "Thoughts about self-advocacy," *TASH Newsletter*, Issue 3, March 1997, pp. 7–8. Reprinted with permission of TASH. For additional information on TASH, write: 29 W. Susquehanna Avenue, Ste. 210, Baltimore MD 21204; 410-828-8274 (voice), 410-828-6706 (fax), or visit our Web site at www.tash.org.

choice of some kind, even one the mother might not make or feel totally comfortable with. This wouldn't have to be a big choice. We know there is always a risk factor when someone is making choices for themselves, but people still need the opportunity, even if they make a mistake.

When people tell me that I am "higher functioning" than the people they are talking about, I feel like they are telling me that I don't have anything in common with other people with disabilities. It's like they are putting me in a whole different category and saying that I don't have any right to speak. It upsets me because I take it that they don't want to give anyone else the opportunities I have been given, and that what I say can be ignored because they see me as more capable. It is a way of dividing us and putting down those who have more severe disabilities or who haven't had the opportunities to experience different situations in life.

Instead, they should be looking at how much each person would be able to offer if they were just given the chance to voice their wants and exercise their rights. For example, I recently visited a group home and heard a staff person say, "How do you like the way I decorated the house? The manager said I could do whatever I want." That told me that the residents didn't have a say in how their home would be decorated, when they could have been involved in planning and picking out the decorations. This is a simple example but who knows how things would look if the residents had helped with the decorating? And how will those residents learn to make other de-

cisions if they can't be involved in how their home looks? I don't think she had even thought about involving them.

Later on she said to me, "We give choices." But even if that is true, it leaves the staff people in control.

The self-advocacy movement is here to say that things must be different. We are saying that we should have real choices, not just the choices that other people give us. Real choices means having the chance to choose the same things that other people, who don't have disabilities, have. No more and no less. Changing the words you use to refer to things is not enough. Calling everyone with a disability a self-advocate, or saying that everyone is given choices, are examples of just changing the words. To me, being a true self-advocate means being an active participant in a self-advocacy organization, speaking up for yourself, and making sure that your wants and needs are understood and valued. It also means understanding your responsibilities as a member of this society.

Self-advocacy has become popular, to the point that it has become a buzzword that people use without really knowing much about it. Some of the dangers of that are that agencies can use the word to make themselves look good, or that people will pick a select few of us to be on every committee, to give testimony, and so on, without looking for other people with disabilities who might have something to contribute. Then they can say that they have consumer involvement, without really having it, because the same "consumers" are doing everything.

Another danger of not really understanding self-advocacy is that people outside of the movement, like parents or agency representatives or public officials, tell us what self-advocates should be doing. They are always saying, "You should testify about this," or "you should be working on that," without realizing that we need to decide for ourselves what we should be working on and how much time we can spend on what we choose to do. It is hard for us because most of us have been taught that we should please other people, not disappoint them by saying no. Often the advisors (these are people without disabilities who support us in our self-advocacy work) have to help us set limits and see that it is okay to set our own priorities.

The self-advocacy movement is international. There are organizations in Britain, Australia, New Zealand, Canada, Sweden, and other countries. There is a new book about self-advocacy all over the world, and I recommend it highly. It is *New Voices: Self-Advocacy by People with Disabilities*, edited by Gunnar Dybwad and Hank Bersani, Jr. It has chapters by people from each of the countries that I mentioned. They talk about their philosophies of self-advocacy, in their own words, and about its history in their countries. There is a whole section on the United States, but I believe it is also important to see how people in other countries think about it.

The common thread, to me, is that people with disabilities want a fair shake in life. We want the same things as everyone else. We don't want our lives controlled by systems and the people who work in them. We know that everyone has to follow some rules, but it is impossible to have a meaningful life if you are al-

We are saying that we should have real choices, not just the choices that other people give us.

ways controlled by other people. I recently wrote a chapter on self-determination (Kennedy, pp. 45–6) where I talked about this issue in depth. I will quote some of the part where I gave suggestions:

"The system . . . needs to support the idea of teamwork and power sharing between people and their helpers. The system also needs to support the idea that people should be able to live how they want to, even if the professionals would live differently. The system is there to assist, offering guidance but not threatening us if we don't take the advice. This always means listening to us, really listening, and giving us feedback that is honest but respectful."

People involved in the self-advocacy movement help each other to advocate for things like power-sharing and system change. As a movement, we work on broad goals, like closing all the institutions in the country, but we don't forget the individual person with a disability who has problems in his or her own life. We support each other as much as we can, and because of this we have learned many lessons about listening and speaking up.

References

Dybwad, G., & Bersani, H. Eds. (1996). *New voices: Self-advocacy by people with disabilities*. Available through Brookline Books, P.O. Box 1047, Cambridge, MA 02238-1047. $29.95 Telephone 617-868-0360.

Kennedy, M. Self-determination and trust: My experiences and thoughts. In D. J. Sands and M. L. Wehmeyer, *Self-determination across the lifespan: Theory and practice*, pp. 45–46.

Available soon from Paul H. Brookes Publishing Co., P.O. Box 10624, Baltimore, MD 21285-0624. Stock X 238X, approximate price $35.00. Telephone 1-800-638-3775; fax 410-337-8539.

The preparation of this article was supported in part by the National Resource Center on Community Integration, Center on Human Policy, School of Education, Syracuse University, through the U.S. Department of Education, Office of Special Education and Rehabilitative Services, National Institute on Disability and Rehabilitation Research (NIDRR), through Contract No. H133D50037. No endorsement by the U.S. Department of Education should be inferred. The Center on Human Policy subcontracts with TASH for space in this newsletter.

 Article Review Form at end of book.

What do you think Diane Coleman means when she says, "The disability community is the canary in the coal mine?" Why do you think the disability rights advocates see a need to mount their protest against assisted suicide and euthanasia so strongly?

Not Dead Yet

"We don't want your pity or your lethal mercy. We want life!"

Nat Hentoff

I have covered—and sometimes participated in—a diversity of protest actions. Civil rights, anti-Vietnam War, anti-death penalty, and a number of union picket lines against bosses who underestimated us.

The most resilient and courageous groups I've gotten to know are composed of disability rights activists. They are aware that there is not much real concern about them among much of the populace. Many of us prefer not to look at—or think about—"defective people."

Yet the disability activists—male, female, black, white, Asian, gay, lesbian—do not brood. They act as resisters, not victims. And currently, a coalition of the disabled is engaged in a major campaign—on the streets, in hospitals, and in the media—to prevent their being swept into "assisted" suicide by the recent Ninth and Second Circuit Court decisions that legitimated Dr. Death, Jack Kevorkian, and made assisted suicide—and euthanasia—legal.

Dr. Jan Fawcett, who tried unsuccessfully to rescue one of her patients from the ministrations of Dr. Kevorkian, says: "Kevorkian created an atmosphere for her [the patient] where death was okay."

Affecting many more people, over time, than Kevorkian's ability to create despair are the combined high-federal-court rulings, which say that euthanasia and assisted suicide are okay.

All too aware that many doctors and hospital administrators have little respect for "the quality of life" of the disabled, these activists do not want—as one of them says—to see the disabled "march into the ovens."

The new coalition is called Not Dead Yet. A lead organizer is Diane Coleman, executive director of the Progress Center for Independent Living in Oak Park, Illinois. A lawyer with extensive experience in organizing and legal work in civil rights and disability rehabilitation research, she has been disabled, since birth. Due to

The disabled are the canary in the coal mine. If we're declared better off dead, who will be next?"

spinal muscular atrophy, Coleman has been in a wheelchair since the age of 11.

Coleman emphasizes: "The disability community is the canary in the coal mine. This assisted suicide–euthanasia issue is a test for our nation. If we as disabled, chronically ill, or terminally ill people are declared better off dead, who will be next?

"The risk of wrongful death of people with disabilities is tremendous because we simply are not getting the same suicide prevention that nondisabled people receive. Nondisabled people assume that our desire to die is rational. Doctors constantly and dramatically underestimate our quality of life compared to our own assessments."

During a recent hearing on assisted suicide before the House Subcommittee on the Constitution—headed by Republican congressman Charles Canady of Florida—Diane Coleman told of court decisions over the last decade that have allowed life-sustaining treatments to be withdrawn from persons "with substantial, *though not terminal,* disabilities. This trend is rooted in pervasive and largely unconscious societal prejudices against people with disabilities." [Emphasis added.]

Another organizer for Not Dead Yet is Woody Osburn, a full-time civil rights specialist with the Pennsylvania Coalition of Citizens With Disabilities. He is a quadriplegic.

"Americans with disabilities," says Osburn, "don't want your pity or your lethal mercy. We want freedom. We want *life!*

"Our deaths are being viewed as more desirable than providing services, such as in-home care, that would allow us to live as free and independent citizens. Instead, many of us are caged in nursing homes and other institutions or dependent on a family member—the two main circumstances that lead to assisted suicide."

I talked to another disability rights organizer involved in Not Dead Yet. Joe Ehman writes for a remarkably energizing and challenging publication, *Mouth: the voice of disability rights* (61 Brighton St.; Rochester, NY 14607-2656). He has written of his encounter with a decidedly biased view of his own "quality of life":

"A few hours after surgery, still delirious from the anesthesia and from post-surgical morphine and demerol, I had to hear from a social worker who wanted to force me to sign a Do Not Resuscitate order.

"I mustered my strength and screamed, 'I'm 30 years old. I don't want to die.' "

"Another nurse came into the room. She asked why I was verbally abusing a staff member."

"I responded that there was nothing in arm's reach to throw at the bitch."

Lucy Gwin, editor of *Mouth,* tells me that the following proclamation will soon be highly visible in many hospitals:

"That DNR order they want you to sign?
"DON'T SIGN IT,
"It's your own death warrant.
"What it means is: Do Not Resuscitate.
"Also, if they give you the wrong anesthetic, no doctor will lift a hand to save you.
"Just say NO to DNR.
"Tell them you're NOT DEAD YET."

Not Dead Yet is also distributing a leaflet that contains a quote from a *Time* magazine story of Kevorkian. He was asked: "How do you decide whom to help? Does the patient have to suffer from a life-threatening illness?"

"No, of course not," Kevorkian said. "And it doesn't have to be painful. But your quality of life has to be nil. I will argue with [my critics] if they will allow themselves to be strapped to a wheelchair for 72 hours so they can't move, and they are catheterized, and they are placed on the toilet and fed and bathed."

Kevorkian has become a Halloween mask, but there are many who agree with him when he says—as he did in a statement put before a Michigan circuit court in 1990—that "the voluntary self-elimination of mortally diseased and crippled lives can only *enhance* the preservation of public health and welfare."

Go gently into that good night, those of you in wheelchairs.

 Article Review Form at end of book.

What is the central argument presented by Congressman Henry Hyde, and endorsed by Hentoff, for preventing parents and medical personnel from allowing an infant with disabilities to die? Why do you think Hentoff presents the case of the Bloomington Baby?

Getting Rid of Damaged Infants

The infant with Down's syndrome was starved to death for his own good.

Nat Hentoff

For a long time, I've been reading medical journals to get leads on stories that usually do not appear in the regular press. For example, in 1982, I found this report in the *Archives of Internal Medicine:*

It is common in the United States to withhold routine surgery and medical care for infants with Down's syndrome for the explicit purpose of hastening death.

Put less delicately, these infants were killed because they were damaged and therefore their "quality of life" did not warrant their growing up. In addition, caring for them would cost a lot and place a heavy emotional burden on their parents.

That news item has led me to a number of stories, including this year's revelation of the degree to which this extinguishing of handicapped infants is still going on. I have been told that as a result of my current research, an influential member of Congress soon may hold a hearing on this continuing termination of children.

These are not fetuses. And this has nothing to do with partial-birth abortion. This column is about completely born infants. In *Roe* v. *Wade,* Justice Harry Blackmun, who wrote the majority opinion, ruled that fetuses are not "persons" under the Constitution and so—like blacks in the Dred Scott decision—have no rights. But, Blackmun added, once a child is born, he or she has the same rights we all do—equal protection of the laws and protection from summary execution.

After coming across that report in the *Archives of Internal Medicine* in 1982, I found further news in a 1983 report—which has not gone out of date—from the President's Commission for the Study of Ethical Problems in Medicine:

Decisions to forgo therapy [for handicapped infants] are part of everyday life in the neonatal intensive care unit. With rare exceptions, these choices have been made by parents and physicians *without review by courts or any other body.* [Emphasis added.]

Parents, I discovered, were advised by doctors—as it was euphemistically put—to "let the child go." Some parents resisted, but others said farewell to their babies. When they were asked why, they invariably answered, "Quality of life."

As I was writing this a week ago, I got a call from Martha Griswold, a California social worker who has a regular radio program on the disabled.

She is 67 and has bachelor's and master's degrees. When she was born with spina bifida—an incomplete closing of the spinal column—the doctor told her parents that she had only five weeks to live and they might as well get it over with.

She was on crutches for years, is now in an electric wheelchair, has a quick wit, and her life force is in fine shape.

By contrast, something terrible happened to an infant in 1982. As a result, a revolutionary law to save damaged infants was passed by Congress two years later.

The baby was born with Down's syndrome, which leads to mental retardation. The parents were told that he would not attain even "a minimally adequate quality of life." I've known Down's syndrome youngsters; one roomed with my younger son at school. But these parents agreed with their obstetrician and gave the order that the baby—which also had a deformed esophagus that could have been routinely corrected—not be fed.

The nurses in the special-care unit refused to starve the child to death, and the baby was moved to another part of the hospital where the parents had to hire private nurses. One of the defiant regular nurses, Linda McCabe, told me: "At least I wasn't part of the killing."

A pediatrician was so appalled at the starving of what came to be called the Bloomington Baby that he and two colleagues—ignoring the wishes of the parents—carried intravenous equipment to the baby's room, planning to feed the child. But it was too late. The process of dying could not be reversed.

This time the killing of an infant because of its prospective "quality of life" became a national story. A movement then began in Congress to pass the Child Abuse Prevention and Treatment Act. It would expand the definition of child abuse and neglect by penal-izing the "withholding of medically indicated treatment from disabled infants with life-threatening conditions." This did not mean that *every* damaged child would have to get care. Doctors would *not* have to intervene if treatment would merely prolong dying or if the infant were "chronically and irreversibly comatose."

As I covered the debate on the House floor, I was amazed and repelled to see some of the most prominent Democratic liberals arguing strenuously against the bill—Henry Waxman, Barney Frank, Charles Rangel, Geraldine Ferraro, Robert Kastenmeir, Gerry Studds, George Crockett, and Barbara Mikulsi, among them.

The fate of those children, these Democrats said, must be determined by their parents and doctors. Children, therefore, were mere property—with no rights of their own. I thought of the Bloomington Baby.

On the other side, the most powerful argument was given by Henry Hyde. He and I often disagree. Hyde is prolife, but as I've told him, if he were *consistently* prolife, he'd be against the death penalty.

But on this issue, Hyde was compellingly human as he said:

The parents who have the emotional trauma of being confronted with this horrendous decision—and seeing ahead a bleak prospect—may well not be, at that time and that place, the best people to decide. . . .

I suggest that a question of life or death for a born person ought to belong to nobody, whether they are parents or not. *The Constitution ought to protect that child.* [Emphasis added.]

Because they are handicapped, they are not to be treated differently than if they were women or Hispanics or American Indians or blacks. Their handicap is a mental condition or a physical condition; but by God, they are human, and nobody has the right to kill them by passive starvation or anything else.

Getting the bill passed involved a long, bitter fight. It was the staffers, especially in the Senate, who finally forged a winning coalition. They traded information with each other—the way the Supreme Court justices' clerks do—and provided strategic counsel to their bosses as to how to get enough votes.

 Article Review Form at end of book.

Why do McDermott and Varenne introduce the H. G. Wells character "Nunez" and his experience in the Country of the Blind? What do the authors mean when they say "culture *as* disability"?

Culture *as* Disability

Ray McDermott

Stanford University and Institute for Research on Learning

Hervé Varenne

Teachers College Columbia University

If a blind Man should affirm, that there is no such Thing as Light, and an Owl no such thing as Darkness, it would be hard to say, which is the verier Owl of the two.

—Samuel Butler (1970[1759]), *Characters*, ca. 1662

In 1904, in a short story called "The Country of the Blind," H. G. Wells sounded the anthropological instinct full force.[1] A man by the name of Nunez is on a peak in the Andes, falls to what should have been his death, and finds himself dropped miraculously into an isolated valley populated exclusively by congenitally blind persons. Nunez is not particularly nice, and he senses only opportunities. He can see, and they cannot. The world is his, for, he figures, "in the Country of the Blind, the One-eyed Man is King" (Wells 1979:129). Almost instantly, Nunez runs into trouble. The

Country of the Blind is of course wired for people who cannot see:

It was marvelous with what confidence and precision they went about their ordered world. Everything, you see, had been made to fit their needs; each of the radiating paths of the valley area had a constant angle to the others, and was distinguished by a special notch upon its kerbing; all obstacles and irregularities or path or meadow had long since been cleared away; all their methods and procedures arose naturally from their special needs. [Wells 1979:135]

"Everything, you see," says Wells, showing the difficulty of a seeing person explaining a Country of the Blind, where there was no word for see, nor any words for things that could be seen. If Wells had said, "Everything, you hear," or "Everything, you smell," he might have made more sense, but not to Nunez: "Four days passed, and the fifth found the King of the Blind still incognito, as a clumsy and useless stranger among his subjects" (1979:134). From bad, things get worse until the people of the valley decide on a definition of the problem and a solution. Their surgeon says that his eyes are diseased: "They are

greatly distended, he has eyelashes, and his eyelids move, and consequently his brain is in a state of constant irritation and destruction" (1979:142). The only solution is to cut them out of his head, and Nunez is forced to escape back up the mountain.

The story reads like much anthropology in this century. First, we are told of another culture, far away and isolated, and then we are asked to appreciate how smart and well adapted the people in the other culture are. It is the anthropologist's ideal setting for making two strong points: the first, that we are arrogant to think we know better than people in other cultures, and the second, that we are foolish to not appreciate how much is known by others in their own terms. We can state the anthropological instinct directly: *Not only is our wisdom not total, there is yet much to be learned from others.* H. G. Wells displays the point dramatically, and 90 years of ethnography have subsequently turned anthropological instinct into a principle of common sense in the progressive world.

The perfect unit for displaying such instinct and insight is what anthropologists call *culture,* a much-contested term that is generally taken to gloss the well-bound containers of coherence that mark off different kinds of people living in their various ways, each kind separated from the others by a particular version of coherence, a particular way of making sense and meaning. In the Country of the Blind, a One-eyed Man is confused and confusing. That is what it is like to be in another culture. With time, had he been a decent person, had he been an anthropologist, he could have learned their ways well enough to write an ethnography of their particular version of wisdom.

There is a downside to the instinctive use of the term *culture* as a container of coherence: The container leaks. Even a century ago, it was rare for a culture to be as isolated as H. G. Wells imagined. Conditions of the anthropologist's arrival were usually worked out in advance, if not by actual contact with the people being visited, then by the visitor and the visited having somehow been brought together by their respective places in the wider world order. Margaret Mead never fell down a mountain into a new tribe, for retinues of colonial officials, porters, and secretaries eased her way. Even H. G. Wells had to build a point of contact into his fiction: the people in the Country of the Blind, isolated for 14 generations before Nunez's arrival, spoke an old version of Spanish which, minus the visual vocabulary, Nunez could use to figure out where he stood.

There is a second problem. The coherence of any culture is not given by members being the same, nor by members knowing the same things. Instead, the coherence of a culture is crafted from the partial and mutually de-

pendent knowledge of each person caught in the process and depends, in the long run, on the work they do together. Life in culture, Bakhtin (1984[1940]) reminds us, is polyphonous and multivocalic; it is made of the voices of many, each one brought to life and made significant by the others, only sometimes by being the same, more often by being different, more dramatically by being contradictory. Culture is not so much a product of sharing as a product of people hammering each other into shape with the well-structured tools already available. We need to think of culture as this very process of hammering a world. When anthropologists instinctively celebrate the coherence of culture, they imply that all the people in the culture are the same, as if stereotyping is a worthy practice as long as it is done by professionals. Thick brush-stroke accounts of Samoans or Balinese, to stay with Margaret Mead, may give some hints as to what Samoans and Balinese must deal with in their daily life, but they can greatly distort the complexity of Samoans and Balinese as people. The coherence of culture is something many individuals, in multiple realities, manage to achieve together; it is never simply the property of individual persons.

The anthropological instinct has been perhaps most destructive when applied to the divisions and inequalities that exist inside a presumed cultural container, that is, the culture "of which they are a member," "to which they belong," or "in which they participate." The problem in assuming that there is one way to be in a culture encourages the misunderstanding that those who are different from perceived norms are missing something, that it is their doing,

that they are locked out for a reason, that they are in fact, in reality, disabled. If it is distorting to describe Samoans and Balinese without an account of the full range of diversity to be found in Samoa or Bali, imagine how distorting it can be in complex divided fields like the United States.

When culture is understood as the knowledge that people need for living with each other, it is easy to focus on how some always appear to have more cultural knowledge than others, that some can be a part of everything and others not, that some are able and others not. Before entering the Country of the Blind, Nunez thought that sight was essential to being fully cultured and that having sight in a world of people who cannot see would net him the cultural capital of a king. The anthropological instinct teaches us that he was arrogant to think he knew better and foolish to not learn from his masterful subjects. The instinct gives us an essential insight, and we can be thankful that anthropology has taken its place in the human sciences. But did Nunez really have to be locked so thoroughly out of the culture of those who could not see? Was it all his fault, or was he invited to look so bad? Need we think that the Country of the Blind had only one way to be, or that the blind and the sighted had to suffer conflict because of an irreducible biological or early enculturated difference? And what are we to make of his betrothed, the blind woman who enjoyed his illusions of sightedness and who could well understand his marginal position given that she too had been pushed aside by an appearance that included eye sockets that to the hand seemed to be full? In the Country of the Blind even a blind woman can be made disabled. In every society, there are ways of being locked out. Race, gender, or beauty can serve as the dividing point as easily as being sighted or blind. In every society, it takes many people—both disablers and their disabled—to get that job done. A disability may be a better display board for the weaknesses of a cultural system than it is an account of real persons.

Disabilities, their definition, their ascription, and their ties to social structure raise ultimate questions about cultural life which cannot be answered firmly in this article, but we can offer a reformulation of the problems involved. We do so in four sections. First, we claim that disabilities are approached best as a cultural fabrication, and to make our case we offer an account of an apparent disability, deafness, in a cultural context in which it does not count as a disability. Second, we focus on the recent popularity of disabilities in the United States as a good example of American culture at work.[2] Third, we identify three ways in which theories of culture and theories of disability have been similarly formulated with the materials of American culture, and we show their relevance to currently popular accounts of school failure. Fourth and finally, we offer a version of how two fairly new disabilities, learning disabilities and illiteracy, have been institutionalized as an active part of American education.

Above all, it must be clear by now that this article is not about disabled persons. It is about the powers of culture to disable. It is also intended to show how those now treated as disabled—from deaf and blind persons at one end of a continuum of abjection to the learning disabled at the other—are the most telling example of

such an elaboration. In cultural terms, the difficulties that people in wheelchairs (or city shoppers with carts, etc.) face with curbs and stairs tell us little about the physical conditions requiring wheelchairs or carts, but a great deal about the rigid institutionalization of particular ways of handling gravity and boundaries between street and sidewalk as different zones of social interaction. Consideration of how such small matters can be turned into a source of social isolation and exclusion is a good way to ask about the nature of culture *as* disability.

The Cultural Construction of Disability

Human psychology may well provide the keyboard, but it is society which plays the tune.

—Anthony Wilden, *System and Structure*, 1972

For the two centuries before our own, the people on Martha's Vineyard, a small island off the coast of Cape Cod, Massachusetts, suffered, or we might say, were privileged by a high rate of genetically inherited deafness, approximately 1 person in every 155. It is easy to use the word *suffered* to evoke sympathy from hearing persons for the plight of the deaf. It is a physical difference that can count, and it is not unusual for deaf people to suffer terribly because of the way it is made to count in various social settings. It is not clear that the people of Martha's Vineyard would share the horror with which most hearing Americans approach deafness. Although it was definitely the case that the Vineyard deaf could not hear, it is also the case that they had the means to turn not

hearing into something that everyone in the community could easily work with, work around, and turn into a strength. In Nora Groce's (1985) history, we are given a picture of deaf persons thoroughly integrated into the life of their community and the hearing thoroughly integrated into the communicational intricacies of sign. When surviving older members of the community were asked to remember deaf neighbors, they could not always remember who among them had been deaf, for everyone there spoke sign language, sometimes even hearing people with other hearing people.

The case of the Vineyard deaf raises questions about the nature of disability, questions that go beyond etiology to function and circumstance: *When does a physical difference count, under what conditions, and in what ways, and for what reasons?* When, how, and why: these are, of course, deeply cultural issues, and depending on how a physical difference is noticed, identified, and made consequential, the lives of those unable to do something can be either enabled or disabled by those around them. From Martha's Vineyard, there is good news: It is possible to organize a culture in which deafness does not have to isolate a person from a full round in the life of a community; not being able to hear can cut off behavioral possibilities that can be taken care of in other ways, and by everyone speaking sign, other possibilities can be explored. There is also bad news: Martha's Vineyard was not an island unto itself, but a peripheral area in a larger social field within which deafness was treated as an appalling affliction.

The easy use of the term *suffer* often carries an invidious comparison of the "disabled" with those seemingly "enabled" by the conventions of a culture. A more principled account of life inside a labeled/disabled community would show, for example, that the abjection with which so-called normals approach labeled/disabled people is one-sided and distorting. A recent advance in cochlea implants, for example, has deaf children hearing, a seeming advance to researchers, but the source of unrest in the deaf community. Outsiders to the deaf experience are surprised to find out that being able to hear is not as important as being a member of the deaf community. Similarly, sighted persons are surprised that life-long blind persons surgically given the "gift" of sight in their adult years are usually overwhelmed by the drabness of the seen world; "suffering" blindness is minimal compared to "suffering" the depression that follows the recovery of vision (Gregory and Wallace 1963).

On Martha's Vineyard, people had jobs to do, and they did them. That one person could do them faster or better than another was likely less important than that the jobs got done. In such a world, it was not important to sort out the deaf institutionally from the hearing. By almost every social measure—for example, rates of marriage and propinquity, economic success, and mastery of a trade—deaf persons were indistinguishable from hearing persons on Martha's Vineyard.

Unfortunately, deaf persons on Martha's Vineyard were not treated well by outsiders who could not sign, and the fortunes of the deaf declined as the island opened up to extensive tourism. That they could not hear was made worse by outsiders who pitied them, wrote them up in Boston newspapers, explained their origin in scientific tracts (one

popular claim: their deafness was a result of a melancholy suffered by their mothers), called for a remedy of their situation, and suggested a eugenics program for their erasure. An irony can be found in the fact that perhaps the people best able on Martha's Vineyard to read such reports were deaf. Although most Vineyarders went to school for only five years in the 1800s, by mandate of the state educational system, the deaf were supported through ten years of school, and when faced with a difficult reading and writing task, the hearing would often go to a deaf person for help.

In a study from inside deaf culture, Padden and Humphries state the case: "being able or unable to hear does not emerge as significant in itself; instead it takes on significance in the context of other sets of meaning to which the child has been exposed" (1988:22). It is one kind of problem to have a behavioral range different from social expectations; it is another kind of problem to be in a culture in which that difference is used by others for degradation. The second problem is by far the worse.

Making Disabilities in American Education

A fact is like a sack which won't stand up when it is empty. In order that it may stand up, one has to put into it the reason and sentiment which have caused it to exist.
—Luigi Pirandello, *Six Characters in Search of an Author*, 1922

For the past thirty years, the anthropology of education has been dominated by the question of how to talk with rigor and respect about children, particularly minority children, who fail in school. There must be something

wrong with their life, goes the mainstream story—how else to talk about their not having learned to read or gained the basics of elementary mathematics? Yes, there must be something wrong with their life, but is this saying anything useful? What if the very act of saying that there is something wrong with their lives, if improperly contextualized, makes their situation worse?

Two general modes of contextualization show up. The first answers the question of what is wrong with their life by focusing on what is wrong with them: the children and often their families. Much in the name of helping, of course, these answers specify nonetheless that something is in fact wrong inside the children, something wrong in their cognitive, linguistic, and social development. Often the very existence of the inquiry and explanation of what is wrong with their life makes things worse. They have to put up not only with missing out on certain developments that come easily to the middle class, they have to be doubly cursed and taunted by middle-class researchers explaining what they do not have (McDermott 1987). Instinctively anthropologists resist such interpretations.

The second contextualization instead answers the question of what is wrong with their life by focusing on what others do to make their life so seemingly, or at least so documentably, miserable and unproductive. Instead of focusing on what is wrong inside the child, the second effort focuses on what is wrong outside the child in the world we give them. This effort is an improvement over the blame-the-victim approach and has the advantage of self-criticism in the acknowledgment that the world given to them, the part that does not work for them in school, includes everyone involved in constructing "School" in America: school personnel, of course, and parents, and let us not forget the philosophers, curriculum designers, textbook publishers, testers, and educational researchers, including anthropologists, in other words, "Us."

American education has numerous made-to-order general categories for describing children in trouble, for example: deprived, different, disadvantaged, at-risk, disabled. The general categories in turn can invite finer distinctions. Children are said to be not just deprived, but cognitively, linguistically, or even culturally deprived. There seems to be no end to the ways that a child can be called culturally different, and over the last decade just about any recognizable behavior has been cited as an instance of a cultural difference. Also over the past decade, there has been an explosion of terms for the kinds of disabilities that can be ascribed to a child: attention deficit disorder is popular now, but we are never far from mentally retarded (sometimes "educably" so), dyslexic (and who can forget "mixed lateral dominance" and "strethosymbolia"), minimally brain damaged, emotionally disturbed, and so on.

Despite the plethora of categories, none of them should please the anthropologist, for none of them guarantees a balance point between showing how bad things are in the lives of children who need our help and showing how the problem is a product of cultural arrangements— *a product of our own activities*— as much as a product of isolated facts about the neurology, personality, language, or culture of any child. The facts, ma'am, are not just there to be described and the conditions alleviated. The "facts," as Pirandello warned, are filled with the "reason and sentiment" brought to the problem, the same reason and sentiment that leave the problem, once facted, once fabricated, once made the object of institutional expertise and budget lines, often falsely intransigent and unworkable. The urge to help invites an hysterical description of the problems, and American descriptions and explanations in turn leave the people who are in need of help actually worse off for our effort.

This article bears a strange title but one, we argue, appropriate to the situation. Culture, the great enabler, is disabling. *Culture* is generally taken to be a positive term. If there is anything people do naturally, it is that they live culturally, in groups, with goals, rules, expectations, abstractions, and untold complexities. Culture, as we say in our lectures, gives all we know and all the tools with which to learn more. Very nice, but every culture, we must acknowledge, also gives, often daily and eventually always, a blind side, a deaf ear, a learning problem, and a physical handicap. For every skill that people gain, there is another that is not developed; for every focus of attention, something is passed by; for every specialty, a corresponding lack. People use established cultural forms to define what they should work on, work for, in what way, and with what consequences; being in a culture is a great occasion for developing abilities, or at least for having many people think they have abilities. People also use established cultural forms to define those who do not work on the "right" things, for the "right" reason, or in the "right" way. Being in a culture is a great occasion for developing disabilities, or at least for having many people think that they have disabilities. Being in a culture may be the only road to enhancement; it is also very dangerous.

This article is not about disability as such but about the cultural fabrication and elaboration of disability. The examples that it develops are to tell us not so much about disabled persons or even about their situation in American culture, but about the workings of culture.[3]

At a second level, this article is about the development of disability as an institution and trope in American culture and particularly in American education. Over the past forty years, there has been developing in the United States a system of categorization which limits us to only two ways for a person to be. One way is to have been classified, occasionally remediated, and often mistreated as disabled. The other way is to be temporarily a half-step ahead of being classified, remediated, and mistreated as disabled. The cultural ascription of disability is an occasional and monumental event in most lives, and the members of our culture, at their worst and, horrors, *at their most cultured*, have been actively making the ascription of disability a constant event in the lives of an increasing number of persons.[4]

Disability has become a potent cultural fact for most American lives, and this is sometimes for the better and often for the worse. Decades ago, Americans sent their children to school, and some did well and others not. Those who did not do well lived their lives outside of school without having to notice any particular lack in themselves. With or without school, people proceeded to a life of recording, filing, repairing, and selling (albeit often for different wages). Now Americans are raising special kinds of children, who go to special schools specially designed by people with other special qualities. In the process, everyone acquires a long history of successes and failures, "special" achievements of all sorts, that become part of the self that others will know.

Three Ways of Thinking about Culture and Disability

There are numerous ways to think about the nature of culture and disability. Within the variety, there is enough order to show that approaches to using each term, *culture* and *disability*, differ along a continuum of assumptions about the world, its people, and the ways they learn. In the present section, we distinguish three approaches to how the terms are used, and we contrast them to highlight the range of concepts available to anyone working on any phenomenon requiring them. The three approaches are presented in the order of how much of the world they take into account.

The Deprivation Approach

This approach takes up the possibility that people in various groups develop differently enough that their members can be shown to be measurably distinct on various developmental milestones. It usually starts with a stable set of tasks and uses them to record varying performances across persons and cultures. Low-level performances by members of a group are taken as examples of what the people of that group have not yet developed (for example, certain versions of abstraction, syllogistic reasoning, metacontextual accounts of linguistic behavior, etc.). A crude version of this argument has it that:

We have culture, and you don't.

A Nunez version would have it that:

I have eyes, and you don't.

To unpack the assumptions underlying the argument, imagine that the world consists of a set of tasks, some of them difficult enough that some people are able to do them and others not. To make matters worse, there is a public assumption that, although society can care for those who lag behind, they are out of the running for the rewards that come with a full cultural competence.

By method and style of argument, this approach has been based mostly on psychometrics and has attracted the intuitive wrath of anthropologists who have argued that all groups, however interesting their differences, are essentially equivalent.

In the explanation of school failure, the possibility that some cultures routinely produce mature people with less development than adults in other cultures brought us the infamous cultural deprivation argument that had minority children failing in school because of impoverished and impoverishing experiences in their homes. From 1965 to 1980, much work went into making this position untenable in academic circles, but it has lived on in the common sense that most of us use to talk about school success and failure. Of late, much like the inherent intelligence and IQ bell-curve foolishness, it has seen a revival. Even anthropologists have produced a number of deprivationist descriptions, particularly in work with minorities in their own culture.

The Difference Approach

This approach takes up the possibility that the ways people in different groups develop are equivalently well tuned to the demands of their cultures and, in their various ways, are equivalent paths to complete human development. It relies less on predefined tasks and instead focuses on the tasks performed by ordinary people, well beyond the reach of the laboratory, as a matter of course in different cultures. If it is possible to describe the task structure of varying cultures, then it is possible to discern what abilities and disabilities cultures might develop (for example, quantity estimation skills among African farmers and Baltimore milk-truck dispatchers, calculation skills among African tailors, mnemonic strategies among Micronesian navigators using the skies for direction). A crude version has it that:

We have culture, and you have a different one.

Nunez does not have a difference theory, but H. G. Wells does, at least in relation to Nunez.[5]

To unpack the assumptions underlying the argument, imagine that the world consists of a wide range of tasks and that some achieve competence on one set of tasks and others do well on other sets of tasks. Despite a liberal lament that variation is wonderful, those who cannot show the right skills at the right time in the right format are considered out of the race for the rewards of the wider culture. This approach is favored among anthropologists and ethnographically oriented psychologists, particularly those working on school problems among minorities.

In explanations of school failure, this account maintains

that children from a minority cultural background mixed with teachers from a more dominant cultural background suffer enough miscommunication and alienation to give up on school, this despite the fact that they are, at least potentially, fully capable. This is by far the most popular language among anthropologists for theorizing about learning and schooling. It is closest to the anthropological instinct for talking about who are locked out of the system. Against a flood of deprivationist thinking in the early 1960s, the difference stand took shape to honor the lives of those who had been left out of the system and who were in turn being blamed for their failings. Where the deprivationist saw a poverty in the language development of black children, sociolinguists (e.g., William Labov, Roger Shuy) saw only a different dialect, grammatically as complex as any other language and lacking nothing but the respect of mainstream speakers of English. Where the deprivationist saw cognitive delays in the behavior of inner-city children, ethnographic psychologists (e.g., Michael Cole) showed how thinking was invariably complex once it was studied in relation to ongoing social situations. Where deprivationists saw immorality and the breakdown of the family among the poor, anthropologists (e.g., Elliot Liebow, Carol Stack) found caring behavior set against a breakdown in the opportunities available in the job market. Where deprivationists saw mayhem in classrooms, ethnographers (e.g., Frederick Erickson, Peg Griffin, Ray McDermott, Hugh Mehan) looked closely and saw tremendous order, some of it oppositional but an order nonetheless.

The gradual replacement of the deprivationist stand by a difference theory of why children from minority cultural groups fail in school represents a considerable achievement, but a temporary one. There is a delicate line that separates saying that minority children are missing enough of mainstream culture to be constantly in trouble at school and saying that minority children are missing culture period. This is a delicate tension in the cultural difference stand, and it has been interesting how much an ethnographer with an allegiance, by way of the anthropological instinct, to appreciating children from other cultures gradually accepts mainstream criteria for measuring minority children as culturally deprived and disabled by their experience at the bottom of the cultural hierarchy.

The Culture-as-Disability Approach

This approach takes up the possibility that every culture, as an historically evolved pattern of institutions, teaches people what to aspire to and hope for and marks off those who are to be noticed, handled, mistreated, and remediated as falling short. Cultures offer a wealth of positions for human beings to inhabit. Each position requires that the person inhabiting it must possess, and must be *known as possessing*, particular qualities that symbolize, and thereby constitute, the reality of their position *to others*. People are only incidentally born or early enculturated into being different. It is more important to understand how they are put into positions for being treated differently. Notice that, by this approach, no group stands alone, nor even in a simple relation to more dominant other groups, but always in relation to the wider system of which all groups, dominant and minority, are a part.

This approach starts with the question of why any culture would develop an assumedly stable set of tasks and a theory of cognitive development, development against which people of named different kinds might be distinguished, measured, documented, remediated, and pushed aside. On what grounds could experts have assumed that the complex worlds of individuals in multiple relationships with each other would stand still enough to be characterized by simplified accounts of either their culture, their cognition, or the ties between whatever culture and cognition are taken to be? One version of the grounds for simplicity is that such theorizing is part of wider-scale institutional and political agendas, in particular, that it has been handy for the governments of modern, ideologically rationalistic, class-divided, industrial, and information-based states to isolate individuals as units of analysis and to record the workings of their minds for public scrutiny and control. The contemporary nation state is above all a record keeper, much more than it is a container of culture or an organizer of learning (Thomas et al. 1988). A crude version of this approach has it that:

It takes a whole culture of people producing idealizations of what everyone should be and a system of measures for identifying those who fall short for us to forget that we collectively produce our disabilities and the discomforts that conventionally accompany them.

Neither Nunez nor H. G. Wells has such a theory. One cannot be disabled alone.

To unpack the assumptions underlying the argument, imagine that the world is not really a set of tasks although it is often made to look that way. Being in the world requires dealing with indefinite and unbounded tasks while struggling with the particular manner in which they have been shaped by the cultural process. In modern societies this has meant dealing with task definitions and display specifications that resist completion and lead to degradation. Competence is a fabrication, a mock-up, and people caught in America work hard to take their place in any hierarchy of competence displays. Being acquired by a position in a culture is difficult and unending work. The most arbitrary tasks can be the measure of individual development. Not only are cultures occasions for disabilities, but they actively organize ways for persons to be disabled.

By this last approach, culture refers to an organization of hopes and dreams about how the world should be. The same people, using the same materials and in ways systematically related to our hopes and dreams, also give us our problems. As Louis Dumont (1970[1960]) once starkly argued, racism is a correlate of liberal democracy: if "all men are created equal," then evidence of inequality requires the dehumanization of many. Without a culture we would not know what our problems are; culture, or better, the people around us in culture, help to define the situation-specific, emotionally demanding, and sensuous problems that we must confront. We might just as well say that culture fashions problems for us and, from the same sources, expects us to construct solutions. It is from life inside this trap that we often get the feeling that working on problems can make things worse.

Examples of the Acquisition of Persons by Culturally Fabricated Disabilities

The world's definitions are one thing and the life one actually lives is quite another. One cannot allow oneself, nor can one's family, friends, or lovers—to say nothing of one's children—to live according to the world's definitions: one must find a way, perpetually, to be stronger and better than that.

—James Baldwin, *The Evidence of Things Not Seen*, 1985

Instances of culture *as* disability may be ubiquitous, but analyses are rare. We have been tempted to focus on the cultural creation and management of apparent biological disorders (e.g., alcoholism, autism, and schizophrenia) and the fabrication and handling of disorders more obviously the product of people being hard on each other in social interaction (e.g., the inarticulate, the insecure, the anorexic, the depressed, the lying and conniving, the alienated, the foolishly omniscient, and the full range of virtually every body being insufficiently gendered to current biases). Each would require a complex analysis. Sadly but not surprisingly, the ethnography of schooling is rich with accounts of teachers, students, administrators, and researchers disabling each other in fully cultural ways. The following discussion offers only two examples, the learning disabled child and the illiterate adult.

Learning Disabilities (LDs): The Case of Adam, Adam, Adam, and Adam

1. Deprivation. The school world is a set of tasks, and people who share the LD label, because there is something wrong with them, cannot perform the tasks as quickly or as well as others.

2. Difference. The school world is a set of quite arbitrary tasks not necessarily well tied to the demands of everyday life (phonics, words out of context, digit-span memory), and people who share the LD label are restricted in various institutional circumstances to operating on tasks in ways that reveal their weaknesses. The performance of LD people on other kinds of tasks, or even the apparent same tasks in other circumstances, can reveal their strengths.

3. Culture *as* disability. The world is not a set of tasks, at least not of the type learned, or systematically not learned, at school, but made to look that way as part of political arrangements that keep people documenting each other as failures. Over the past 40 years, school performance has become an exaggerated part of established political arrangements, and by pitting all against all in a race for measurable academic achievement on arbitrary tasks, school has become a primary site for the reproduction of

inequality in access to resources. The use of the term *LD* to describe, explain, and remediate children caught in a system of everyone having to do better than everyone else is a case in point. Even if used sensitively by people trying to do the right thing for the children apparently disabled, the term has a political life that involves millions of people operating on little information about the consequences of their work. (See Coles 1987 for a social history of the category and demographics; see Mehan 1986, 1991, 1993, and Mehan et al. 1986 for a detailed and sophisticated account of how children are labeled.)

A group of us worked with Adam and his third- and fourth-grade classmates across a range of settings for over a year (Cole and Traupmann 1981; Hood et al. 1980; McDermott 1993). The settings included an oral test on experimental and psychometric tasks, classroom lessons, more relaxed after-school clubs, and one-on-one trips around New York City. We knew Adam well enough to notice differences in his behavior across the four settings that formed a continuum of competence, arbitrariness, and visibility:

The continuum is arranged from left to right and represents an increase of either:

Everyday life → After-school clubs → Classroom groups → One-to-one tests

1. task difficulty and cognitive competence (from mastery in everyday life events, at one end, to minimal performance on test materials, on the other);

2. the arbitrariness of the task and the resources the child is allowed to use in the task performance (from everyday life, where tasks are well embedded in ongoing relations among persons and environments and one can use whatever means available to get the job done, at one end, to tasks ripped from their usual contexts and isolated specifically to measure what a child can do with them unaided by anything other than his or her mind); or

3. the social visibility, and often measurability, of the task performance (from invisible as a problem of any kind in everyday life settings to painfully and documentably noticeable on tests).

How to understand the four Adams who show up in the different contexts? Our three approaches to culture and disability offer a framework for articulating Adam's situation.

By the deprivation approach, Adam is part of a group of people who display particular symptoms in the face of reading and other language-specific tasks. These are persons grouped together as LD. Adam is often described, by both diagnostic tests and school personnel, as having trouble paying attention and remembering words out of context. His symptoms are easily recognized, and his life in school is one of overcoming his disability. School is particularly difficult, because he is often embarrassed by what he cannot do that other children find comparatively automatic.

By the difference stand, Adam can be understood in terms of what he cannot do only if he is also appreciated for what he can do. One way to understand the continuum of scenes along which his behavior varies is that it moves from unusually arbitrary in its demands on the child to completely open to local circum-stance. At the test end of the continuum, one must face each question armed only with one's head; if Adam has to remember a string of seven digits, he cannot ask for help, look up the information, or even take time to write it down. At the other end of the continuum, in everyday life, whatever is needed to get a job done is allowable; if Adam has to remember a telephone number, he is unconstrained in how he can proceed. In focusing on what Adam can do, we can see that he is fine in most of his life, and it is only in response to the arbitrary demands of the school culture that he is shown to be disabled.

By the culture-*as*-disability approach, Adam must be seen in terms of the people with whom he interacts and the ways in which they structure their activities together. Such an approach delivers an account not so much of Adam but of the people most immediately involved in the production of moments for him to be recognized as a learning problem. It turns out that all the people in his class—the teachers, of course, and all the children as well—are involved at various times in recognizing, identifying, displaying, mitigating, and even hiding what Adam is unable to do; if we include his tutors, the school psychologists, the local school of education where he goes for extra help (and his teachers for their degrees), if we include the researchers who show up to study him and the government agencies that finance them, the number of people found contributing to Adam being highlighted as LD grows large. If we add all the children who do well at school because Adam and others like him fail standardized tests, then most of the country is involved in Adam being LD. We use the term *culture* for the arrangements that allow so many people to be involved in Adam's being LD, for it emphasizes that, whatever problems Adam may have in his head, whether due originally to genetic or early socialization oddities, these would have had a different impact on his relationships with others if the culture that he inhabits did not focus so relentlessly on individual success and failure. The culture that promises equality of opportunity while institutionalizing opportunities for less than half of the people to be successful in school is a culture that invites a category, LD, and its systematic application within the educational system. Adam is a display board for the problems of the system.

The Illiterate: The Case of Exterminating Literacy

1. Deprivation. The world is a text, and some people know how to read better than others. The illiterate are missing much of what they need to get around the world, and as a culture and an economy, we are being weighed down with unproductive workers who cannot read. That a high percentage of illiterate persons are in minority groups with a wide range of other problems shows what happens to people who cannot read and write in the modern world.

2. Difference. *Literacy* is a complex term covering a wide range of activities that differ from one context or culture to another. Its role in different societies—indeed, in our society—can vary quite remarkably, and it is not at all clear that it has positive or even uniform effects on a people, their ways of thinking, or their modes of production.

3. Culture *as* disability. *Illiteracy* is a recent term in our lives; it was introduced in England about a century ago and has been gathering increasing attention to the point where now just about any shift in the definition can leave different portions of the population outside its attributive powers, for example, the computer or mathematical illiterate. The circumstances of the application of the term *illiteracy* to persons then and now have been intensely political more than pedagogical or remedial (Donald 1983; Smith 1986). The fundamental and powerful assumptions of our culture are that:

- literacy is inherently good for the individual;

- literacy is good for a culture;

- literacy is difficult to acquire;

- literacy should be transmitted to illiterates in classrooms.

There is little comparative evidence to support any of these positions. Worse, and this is crucial, these positions may be least true in societies in which people believe them:

- the more people believe that literacy is difficult to acquire, the more they find reasons to explain why some read better than others and, correspondingly, why some do better than others in the economic and political measures of the society;

- the more people believe that literacy is cognitively and culturally transformative, the more they can find reasons to degrade those without such powers;

- the more people believe that literacy is best learned in classrooms, the more they

ignore other sources of literacy, and the more they insist on bringing back to school those who have already "failed" to develop school literacy.

Although literacy can help transform a social information processing system and can be taught in classrooms, the very insistence on the truth of these facts can arrange conditions by which neither is possible.

With the help of a union local in New York City, a few of us (Shirley Edwards, David Harman, and Ray McDermott) ran a literacy program for the pest exterminators who service the city's housing projects. Half the members of the union were not fully licensed, and they faced lower pay and job insecurity until they passed a written exam. The exam was written on an eleventh-grade level, and it would have been easy to find the men simply not knowing enough to ever work their way through the materials. If we had simply followed the deprivation approach, there was much at hand to guide our way. Standardized tests were in place, and experts could be hired to handle the many levels of reading ability or spoken-English competence to which curriculum might be addressed. As lower-level city workers, the exterminators could be understood as missing many of the skills that they would need to get through the test; because they came from a "culturally deprived culture"—yes, we have culture, but they don't—one could only wonder how they could get through the day.

In our organization of the literacy program, we instead took a difference approach, which, by the counterexample of the exterminators' success in the program, gradually grew into a culture-*as-*

disability stand. We assumed that the exterminators were not culturally deprived as much as they might be different from those with more education and that such differences were made most manifest on standardized tests. There was evidence that we were right, for the men had been working as exterminators for many years; if nothing else, we reasoned, they must know a great deal about exterminating. If we could appreciate what they can do, we might find a way to use their skills on a difficult paper-and-pencil test. To maximize their participation and to make the best use of their pest-control subculture, we hired exterminators who had passed their tests to teach those who had not. Yes, we have a culture, and so do they. The best way to initiate them to our test-taking culture, the reasoning goes, is on their own terms.

After weeks in the exterminator classrooms, we had more evidence that the men knew much more than anyone might have imagined, and even better, they were using it to help each other prepare for their exams. How could we have assumed otherwise? How could we have believed that they did not know? What is it about our culture that would have us believing that we knew better than they did? Were we, in effect, disabled when it came to seeing the knowledge base of the exterminators? One place to find an answer to this question is in the classrooms that enabled the exterminators to become book learners. They already knew a great deal about exterminating, but they had to organize their knowledge by its test relevance.

One practice test opened with the question, "Fumigants do not burn the skin. True or false?" Half the men answered "True", the other half, "False." A quick look around the room indicated that they all knew the answer; they all used fumigants in the field, and they had been careful not to have burned their hands off. Knowing that fumigants burn the skin is not the same as knowing the answer to the test question about whether fumigants burn the skin. The teacher addressed the problem directly: "Let me help you out with this one. Every time you get a question, true or false, if the question is false, the answer, automatically, is false. Why? Because fumigants burn the skin." His intervention is met with a chorus of affirmation. What is being taught is an approach to the test, not knowledge about the world. After answering incorrectly a question about the amount of pesticide in a particular application, "5 percent to 45 percent, true or false," a student was told, "You gonna go by the book, give or take 5 or 10 percent. Don't go by your own ideas." On the job, their ideas rarely had to be within "5 or 10 percent." Tests went by a different and, in terms of exterminator practice, a quite arbitrary standard of precision.

In the union classes, the men used "their" culture to run the classrooms, and they had a way of talking to each other that outsiders might not have managed well. They mobilized their community both in the classroom and beyond. Teachers and students who did not find it easy to operate in a classroom were found helping each other on lunch hours and weekends. Perhaps most exciting, they often said that it was not possible to fail at exterminating literacy forever. One could fail the big test, but one could take it over again and again. Every night they were told that the union would stick with them until they passed. By breaking through the constant threat of failure, they were reorganizing their access to school knowledge and simultaneously they were showing us how much we were the other half of their failure. As they become more visible as knowing people, our own surprise made more visible to us how much we had invested, even though we had organized the program to honor what they knew, in not seeing them as knowing people. They were not deprived independently of a school arranging for them to look that way. Nor were they different independently of the institutions making them different by keeping them at a distance from mainstream biases and expectations. For every disability and difference brought to the fore, there is a cultural, and invisible, order that is the background. The exterminators and their union subverted that background; they subverted the ritualized meritocracy that had everyone thinking they were different, or less than different. For a moment, they hid their possible difference in the privacy of their own assemblies and presented themselves as not different. They read and discussed the manual, and they passed the test; they subverted a system that claimed that "knowing how to take the test" is irrelevant to the testing itself.

By the dictates of the culture, in American education, everyone must do better than everyone else. Of course, this is both logically and social-structurally impossible. Failure is a constant possibility in American schools, and by the dictates of the normal curve, it absorbs about half the students along the way. Failure is always ready to acquire someone. The exterminators had for the most part been acquired by school failure. We, university people running the program, had been acquired by school success in exact proportion to the difficulties of those designated as failures: we above the norms and they below. It is not easy to get the threat of failure out of the classroom. The exterminators could handle whatever literacy came their way in the daily round: everyday literacy acquires its readers, and this includes the bug exterminators of New York City. Test literacy, on the contrary, is designed to acquire failures, that is, to identify and document illiterates, and this can also include the bug exterminators.

The story ends on a positive note. For a brief moment, their union made it possible for the exterminators to confront the tests successfully. Should a high rate of "success" threaten other aspects of social relationships on the job, then the test will be made more difficult and the old rate of failure will be reproduced. If social structuring processes in America must be fed by repeated identifications of failure in school and school-like institutions, then American education will continue acquiring people for its positions of failure. America will have its disabilities.

Conclusion

This essay has called on the ethnographic study of disabilities as a resource for rethinking the terms *culture* and *disability*. An analysis of the cultural construction of institutional occasions for the creation and display of various disabilities—deafness, learning disabilities, and illiteracy—reveals not broken persons but identifications neatly tuned to the workings of institutions serving political and economic ends through formal educational means.

In the ethnographic study of disability, the subject shifts from Them to Us, from what is wrong with them to what is wrong with the culture that history has made a Them separate from an Us, from what is wrong with them to what is wrong with the history that has made for all of us, from what is wrong with them to what is right with them that they can tell us so well about the world we have all inherited.

Notes

1. An earlier version of half this article makes up about a third of McDermott and Varenne, in press. To the people we thanked for help with the early effort, we want to add Douglas Campbell, Shelley Goldman, and Verna St. Denis for help with the present article. Thanks to Michael Cole for introducing McDermott to Nunez about ten years ago.

2. We work here with the distinction between United States and America as Varenne has developed it (1986, 1992).

3. Fortunately, the anthropological and comparative study of disability has developed its own literature of late. For rich examples and bibliography, see Ingstad and Whyte 1995 and Peters 1993. Gold and Duvall (1994) offer accounts of anthropologists working with disabilities in fieldwork.

4. There are almost 30,000 words in English for describing a person (D'Andrade 1985). Most are organized into contrast pairs, usually one with a positive and one with a negative connotation. For every word praising a person as able, there is another pointing to an absence; so goes good and bad, beautiful and ugly, hearing and deaf, smart and dumb, literate and illiterate, and so on. What one side of the contrast pair gives, the other side takes away; where one person has a possession, another has a poverty, that is to say, not just an absence of something valued, but an identifiable absence, more visible and louder than any presence. These are rich resources for keeping some people always in trouble for explicitly not having what others explicitly have, good materials for a culture constantly acquiring, sorting, and institutionalizing those who, for some moment at least, cannot be what is desired and required.

5. Wells may have been a better anthropologist in his fiction than in his relations with neighbors. In a response to James Joyce's *Portrait of the Artist as a Young Man*, Wells (1917) declared: "Like some of the best novels of the world it is a story of education; by far the most living and convincing picture that exists of an Irish Catholic upbringing." So far so good, but he continues: "the interest for the intelligent reader is the convincing revelation it makes of the limitations of a great mass of Irishmen," limitations that Wells is willing to specify for a page on his way to a political stand on why there is "excellent reason for bearing in mind that these bright-green young people across the Channel are something quite different from the liberal English in training and tradition." There is reason to be "absolutely set against helping them" (Wells 1917:160). Wells may have had the same feeling about Spanish surname diacritics.

References Cited

Bakhtin, Mikhail. 1984[1940]. Rabelais and His World. Indianapolis: Indiana University Press.

Balzac, Honoré de. 1899[1845]. The Peasants. G. B. Ives, trans. Philadelphia: George Barrie and Son.

Baldwin, James. 1985. The Evidence of Things Not Seen. New York: Henry Holt and Company.

Bourdieu, Pierre. 1977. Outline of a Theory of Practice. London: Cambridge University Press.

Butler, Samuel.1970[1759]. Characters. Cleveland: Press of Case Western Reserve University.

Cole, Michael, and Kenneth Traupmann. 1981. Comparative Cognitive Research: Learning from a Learning Disabled Child. *In* Aspects of the Development of Competence. W. A. Collins, ed. Pp. 125–154. Minnesota Symposium on Child Psychology, 14. Hillsdale, NJ: Erlbaum.

Coles, Gerald. 1987. The Learning Mystique. New York: Pantheon.

D'Andrade, Roy. 1985. Character Terms and Cultural Models. In Directions in Cognitive Anthropology. Janet Dougherty, ed. Pp. 321–343. Urbana: University of Illinois.

Donald, James. 1983. How Illiteracy Became a Problem. Journal of Education 165:35–51.

Dumont, Louis. 1970[1960]. Caste, Racism, and "Stratification": Reflections of a Social Anthropologist. *In* Homo Hierarchicus. Pp. 239–259. Chicago: University of Chicago Press.

Gold, Gerald, and Louise Duval, eds. 1994. Working with Disability. Anthropology of Work Review 15:1–35.

Gregory, Richard L., and Jean Wallace. 1963. Recovery from Early Blindness: A Case Study. Monographs of the Quarterly Journal of Experimental Psychology, Supplement 2. Cambridge, England: W. Heffer and Son.

Groce, Nora. 1985. Everyone Here Spoke Sign Language. Cambridge, MA: Harvard University Press.

Heath, Shirley Brice. 1983. Ways with Words. New York: Cambridge University Press.

—.1990. The Children of Trackton's Children. *In* Cultural Psychology. James Stigler, Richard Shweder, and Gilbert Herdt, eds. Pp. 296–319. New York: Cambridge University Press.

Hood, Lois, Ray McDermott, and Michael Cole. 1980. "Let's *Try* to Make It a Good Day"—Some Not So Simple Ways. Discourse Processes 3:155–168.

Hughes, Langston. 1959. Selected Poems. New York: Vintage.

Ingstad, Benedicte, and Susan Whyte, eds. 1995. Disability and Culture. Berkeley: University of California Press.

Lévi-Strauss, Claude. 1987[1950]. Introduction to the Work of Marcel Mauss. Felicity Baker, trans. London: Routledge and Kegan Paul.

McDermott, Ray. 1987. Explaining Minority School Failure, Again. Anthropology and Education Quarterly 18:361–64.

—.1988. Inarticulateness. *In* Linguistics in Context. Deborah Tannen, ed. Pp. 37–68. Norwood, NJ: Ablex.

—.1993. The Acquisition of a Child by a Learning Disability. *In* Understanding Practice. Seth Chaiklin and Jean Lave, eds. Pp. 269–305. New York: Cambridge University Press.

McDermott, Ray, and Hervé Varenne. In press. Culture, Development, Disability. *In* Essays on Ethnography and Human Development. Richard Jessor, Ann Colby, and Richard Shweder, eds. Chicago: University of Chicago Press.

Mehan, Hugh. 1986. The Role of Language and the Language of Role in Institutional Decision Making. *In* Discourse and Institutional Authority. Sue Fisher and Alexndra Todd, eds. Pp. 140–163. Norwood, NJ: Ablex.

—.1991. The School's Work of Sorting Students. *In* Talk and Social Structure. Deirdre Boden and Don Zimmerman, eds. Pp. 71–90. Berkeley: University of California Press.

—.1993. Beneath the Skin and between the Ears. *In* Understanding Practice. Seth Chaiklin and Jean Lave, eds. Pp. 241–268. New York: Cambridge University Press.

Mehan, Hugh, Alma Hertweck, and J. Lee Meihls. 1985. Handicapping the Handicapped. Stanford, CA: Stanford University Press.

Murphy, Robert F. 1987. Body Silent. New York: Holt.

Padden, Carol, and Tom Humphries. 1988. Deaf in America: Voices from a Culture. Cambridge, MA: Harvard University Press.

Peters, Susan, ed. 1993. Education and Disability in Cross-Cultural Perspective. New York: Garland Publishing.

Pirandello, Luigi. 1922. Six Characters in Search of an Author. *In* Naked Masks. Eric Bentley, ed. Pp. 211–276. New York: Dutton.

Smith, David M. 1986. The Anthropology of Literacy Acquisition. *In* The Acquisition of Literacy: Ethnographic Perspectives.

Bambi Schieffelin and Perry Gilmore, eds. Pp. 261–275. Norwood, NJ: Ablex.

Spindler, George, and Louise Spindler, with Henry Trueba and Melvin D. Williams. 1990. The American Cultural Dialogue and Its Transmission. Philadelphia: Falmer Press.

Thomas, George, John Meyer, Francisco Ramirez, and John Boli. 1988. Institutional Structure, Constituting State, Society, and the Individual. Beverly Hills: Sage.

Varenne, Hervé. 1984. Collective Representation in American Anthropological Conversations about Culture: Culture and the Individual. Current Anthropology 25:281–300.

—.1992. Ambiguous Harmony: Family Talk in America. Norwood, NJ: Ablex.

Varenne, Hervé, ed. 1986. Symbolizing America. Lincoln: University of Nebraska Press.

Varenne, Hervé, and Ray McDermott. 1986. "Why" Sheila Can Read: Structure and Indeterminacy in the Reproduction of Familial Literacy. *In* The Acquisition of Literacy: Ethnographic Perspectives. Bambi Schieffelin and Perry Gilmore, eds. Pp. 188–210. Norwood, NJ: Ablex.

Varenne, Hervé, and Ray McDermott, with Shelley Goldman, Merry Naddeo, and Rosemarie Rizzo-Tolk. n.d. Successful Failure: Education as Cultural Fact. Volume in preparation.

Wells, H. G. 1917. James Joyce. New Republic, March 10:158–160.

—.1979. Selected Short Stories. Baltimore: Penguin.

Wilden, Anthony. 1972. System and Structure: Essays in Communication and Exchange. London: Tavistock Publications.

Article Review Form at end of book.

WiseGuide Wrap-Up

- Exceptionality and disability can be interpreted as culturally determined phenomena; they exist within the context of a society, a time, and a place. Because exceptionality and disability are determined by a culture, they reflect the values of that culture.

- Individuals with disabilities and their families face many challenges, one of which is social acceptance. Like most others, people with disabilities seek to be productive, independent members of society. Many people with disabilities believe that, in a society in which their rights are not automatically guaranteed, they need to be their own advocates.

R.E.A.L. Sites

This list provides a print preview of typical **coursewise** R.E.A.L. sites. (There are over 100 such sites at the **courselinks**™ site.) The danger in printing URLs is that web sites can change overnight. As we went to press, these sites were functional using the URLs provided. If you come across one that isn't, please let us know via email to: webmaster@coursewise.com. Use your Passport to access the most current list of R.E.A.L. sites at the **courselinks**™ site.

Site name: The Family Empowerment Network
URL: http://www.downsyndrome.com
Why is it R.E.A.L.? You can use this site to join advocacy groups for disability issues, connect to a database for recreational and educational activities for children with disabilities, link up with a parent-to-parent support group or a sibling support project.
Key topics: families, parents, siblings, advocacy, recreation
Activity: Place a question about Down syndrome in the Family Empowerment Network Message Board and see how it is answered.

Site name: Our-Kids: Devoted to Raising Special Kids with Special Needs
URL: http://rdz.stjohns.edu/library/support/our-kids
Why is it R.E.A.L.? This site is designed to support parents and others who seek to help children with special needs. It connects users to a support group for parents and caregivers, recommends books, and lists Internet resources.
Key topics: families, parents, support groups
Activity: Find "Welcome To Holland," a brief essay by Emily Perl Kingsley about parenthood and disability.

Site name: Special Education Needs Network
URL: http://schoolnet2.carleton.ca/sne/
Why is it R.E.A.L.? This site is for families, teachers, schools, and professionals. Readers will find an online newsletter and a conference directory.
Key topics: Internet resources, resources, families
Activity: Find the newsletter and summarize one of the articles for your class.

Site name: The Family Village
URL: http://www.familyvillage.wisc.edu
Why is it R.E.A.L.? This site includes a disability awareness bibliography and descriptions of programs designed to change attitudes toward persons with disabilities.
Key topics: attitudes
Activity: Find the "Kids on the Block" program and learn how some have tried to change students' attitudes using puppets.

Site name: disAbility Information and Resources.

URL: http://www.eskimo.com/~jlubin/disabled.html

Why is it R.E.A.L.? This site connects people with disabilities to products and services, medical information, and job training programs.

Key topics: resources, assistive devices, medical information, travel, recreation, advocacy

Activity: Identify a vacation destination that is accessible to persons in wheelchairs.

....

section 2

Learning Objectives

After studying this section, the reader will:

- Possess knowledge about the growth of special education since 1975.

- Know the costs of special education and how the costs are shared among federal, state, and local governments.

- Understand the role of parents in placement decisions.

- Grasp the various issues. surrounding special education.

- Understand a variety of arguments supporting special education.

- Understand a variety of arguments against special education.

The Special Education Controversy

 **WiseGuide Intro**

In this section, we examine the issues surrounding the current special education controversy. Special education is the label given to an array of specialized services that schools are required to provide to students with disabilities. The legal mandate for these services is Public Law 94-142, which has been given the new name Individuals with Disabilities Education Act (IDEA). Since its initial passage in 1975, the number of students with disabilities has grown enormously, particularly in the category of learning disabilities. And with the growing number of classified children has come an enormous increase in the cost. Critics of special education believe that the benefits do not justify that cost; they particularly attack the label "learning disabled" as being ambiguous and leading to inappropriate placements in special education settings. Some look to the inclusion of students with disabilities in general education classrooms as a way to reduce the cost of special education.

In this section, we look at the special education controversy from a variety of perspectives. Douglas Fuchs and Lynn S. Fuchs, in "What's 'Special' About Special Education?", describe what they perceive as the value of special education. They contend that special education for students with learning disabilities does what it is supposed to do: it provides students who have learning disabilities with individualized education tailored to their specific needs. Chester E. Finn, Jr., in "Corrupted Intentions," presents a very different view of special education: he argues that special education is too costly, keeps funds from other educational programs, and exists to support special education professionals.

In "The Struggle To Pay For Special Ed.," Sam Allis looks at the dilemma of parents in small school districts whose neighbors are angry at the cost of educating a child with a severe disability. David O. Krantz, in "Funded Into Perpetuity," contends that money is not the true problem in special education; rather, he believes that the crisis of special education is its focus on special education professionals, rather than special education consumers, whose concern is outcomes.

Lisa Gubernick and Michelle Conlin, in "The Special Education Scandal," contend that children with discipline problems are being served in special education programs as if they had disabilities; they also argue that the current system allows parents to force school districts to pay for services that children do not need. Finally, in "Special Education Is Not a Scandal," Brent Staples defends special education as a valuable and necessary service for students whose brains function differently.

Questions

R8. What do the authors see as the effect of the inclusion movement on the field of special education? What evidence do the authors present of the value of special education?

R9. What does the author see as the goals of special education advocates? What is the relation between the civil rights movement and the special education movement, according to the author?

R10. How could the dilemma of the Maynard family, whose community must raise taxes to pay for their son's education in a special school, be avoided? What accounts for the increase in the number of students in special education, according to the author?

R11. What does the author view to be the reason why each level of government wants to pass the cost of special education on to the other? According to the author, what accounts for the growth of students in the learning disabilities category in California?

R12. What is the authors' purpose in beginning and ending their article with the case of the student who kicked his pregnant mother, set fires, and shoplifted? Who do the authors view as being the beneficiaries of special education?

R13. According to the author, what accounts for learning disabilities? What is the author's main defense of special education?

What do the authors see as the effect of the inclusion movement on the field of special education? What evidence do the authors present of the value of special education?

What's 'Special' About Special Education?

Douglas Fuchs and Lynn S. Fuchs

Douglas Fuchs and Lynn S. Fuchs are professors of special education at George Peabody College of Vanderbilt University. Nashville, Tenn.

On the day we began to write this article, Mark Wellman, former park ranger and professional rock climber, now a motivational speaker and paraplegic, was shown in his wheelchair modeling a milled wool and nylon jacket ($1,350) and wool trousers ($750) in a fashion supplement to the *New York Times*. One week earlier, Heather Whitestone, a talented and deaf 21-year-old, had won the Miss America contest, which was covered on national television. And last summer, 30 million moviegoers saw Tom Hanks play a mildly retarded everyman in *Forrest Gump*.

Such high-profile, positive images of people with disabilities are increasingly common. They symbolize a hard-won victory for those in the disability community who for many years labored for greater normalization, or inclusion, of persons with disabilities

in mainstream culture. These images, however, belie a troubling fact: special education is under fire from within and without, and the disability community, long known for its cohesiveness,[1] appears to be coming apart at the seams.

A Field Under Siege

Immoral. Special education's most strident critics are the "full inclusionists," a small but influential group of special educators and parents who advocate in behalf of children with severe mental retardation. Full inclusionists are adamant about the right of these children to make friends with nondisabled classmates—an objective unlikely to be met, they say, in separate placements. At the same time, they believe that general education historically has used, currently uses, and forever will use special education settings as dumping grounds for children it deems "unteachable" and that general educators typically consider children with severe mental retardation to be the least teachable. Hence, to ensure these children's place in the mainstream

and to preclude the stigmatization and warehousing purportedly inherent in separate programs, full inclusionists call for an end to all special education settings, which some have described as the moral equivalent of apartheid and even of slavery.[2]

Intellectually bankrupt. Some advocates of detracking,[3] in concert with special educators like Maynard Reynolds,[4] have focused less on the purported injustice of separate placements and more on what they see as the invalidity of special education's disability categories, tests, and instructional services. A typical salvo from this group announces that many disability categories—most notably, "learning disabilities"—are social constructions without scientific validity.[5] These categories are merely the inventions of parents lobbying for services for their children,[6] of classroom teachers seeking to unburden themselves of difficult-to-teach students,[7] and of special education administrators eager for more special-needs "clients" to bring in more teachers and dollars for their programs.[8] Given the absence of sound theory to undergird such constructs

Fuchs, D. & Fuchs, L. S., "What's 'special' about special education?," *Phi Delta Kappan,* 76(7), 1995, pp. 522–530. Reprinted by permission of the author.

as learning disabilities, say the critics, it should come as no surprise that many tests used to identify students with special needs are invalid for such purposes, leading to the labeling of many "false positives," those wrongly identified as disabled.[9]

The coup de grâce in this critique of special education's legitimacy is the contention that the enterprise flat out doesn't work. The professional literature is full of pronouncements like "[Special education] pulls students from general education classrooms and places them in small, segregated classes, in which they . . . are given watered-down curriculum and receive less rather than more instructional time."[10]

Whereas most detracking proponents do not join the full inclusionists in arguing for an end to special education placements, at least some of them would like to see the system considerably reduced in size.[11] These detracking proponents and some special educators recommend the transfer to general education of most, or all, children with learning disabilities, as well as the monies that until now have followed such children to special education programs. Some detracking supporters believe that general educators have the know-how to do better by these children, and special education dollars will help them to put this knowledge to work.[12]

Fiscally irresponsible. In New York City, downsizing special education is one of the few topics on which the schools' chancellor, Ramon Cortines, and the city's mayor, Rudolph Giuliani, can agree. How so? For the past 15 years, special education in the Big

Special education is under fire, and the disability community, long known for its cohesiveness, appears to be coming apart at the seams.

Apple has been administered under the terms of a 1980 consent decree issued by a federal judge in a class action lawsuit filed on behalf of José P., a Puerto Rican student with disabilities. Because of its court protection, special education has continued to grow, even as other parts of the school system have been decimated by budget cuts.[13] New York City currently spends $1.67 billion, or 22 cents of every school dollar, on special education. The special education system employs one-quarter of all school employees and provides services to 130,037 students, or 13% of the city's one million schoolchildren.[14] It spends about $18,700 per pupil, while general education spends only between $3,500 and $5,000 per pupil.[15] The board of education's budget director, Leonard Hellenbrand, has said that nondisabled students suffer as a result of the court-ordered increases in special education spending. "Kids that don't have court orders in their hands are dead meat," he said.[16] Squeezed by the lingering effects of a multi-year recession and the public's concern about government spending, politicians and school administrators across the country are increasingly vexed by special education's high cost.[17]

Visible and vulnerable. The media have echoed many of these criticisms and concerns. The *Wall Street Journal,* for example, editorialized. "The most common special-ed category is the youngster simply found to have a 'learning disability.' In lay terms, this description . . . could fit nearly anyone."[18] A writer in the *National Review* opined that "4 of the 5 million public-school special educa-

tion students have no mental or physical handicaps" and should not be receiving special education services.[19] And in a cover story titled "Separate and Unequal: How Special Education Programs Are Cheating Our Children and Costing Taxpayers Billions Each Year," *U.S. News & World Report* accused special education of being ineffective, being more interested in dollars than in students' welfare, and serving as handmaiden to a number of school systems engaged in racially biased practices.[20]

Demoralization. Full inclusionists, detracking advocates, politicians, school administrators, the media, and others have contributed to a Zeitgeist that sees special education as more harmful than helpful.[21] A few special education professors have been so persuaded by this view that they deserted their own departments for others or worked to diminish the visibility and importance of their own units by helping to reduce them to "programs," subsuming them under headings like "curriculum and instruction." Some even succeeded in eliminating special education as both a department and a program. Data from the Higher Education Consortium on Special Education (HECSE) may reflect this phenomenon. Of 45 universities granting doctoral degrees in special education and forming the HECSE group, 39 responded to a recent survey. In 1987, 36 of the 39 claimed to have special education departments; in 1992, the number was 25, a 31% drop in five years.[22]

Arguably, the Zeitgeist has also contributed to the attrition observed among special educators in elementary and secondary schools. It has been estimated that special educators nationwide leave the profession at a yearly rate of 7.3%—or about 17,500 individuals.[23] In several states, however, the rate has been estimated at 10% to 15%—in some districts, as high as 30% to 50%.[24] Although many factors contribute to a special educator's decision to leave teaching, stress, burnout, and job dissatisfaction are frequently mentioned as important causes.[25] Research shows that administrative support can blunt the effects of these harmful factors.[26] But overburdened administrators (many in court defending special education) have little time or opportunity to provide that kind of support.

Dissension. Of the just-mentioned criticisms of special education, none cuts to the quick like the charge that many disability categories, including learning disabilities, are bogus. Nationwide, 2.25 million students, nearly one-half of all students with disabilities, are certified as having learning disabilities.[27] If certain critics were to have their way and all students with a learning disabilities label were de-certified, special education's clientele would be reduced by almost 50%. Although it is not our aim to respond to all charges leveled at our field, we feel compelled to address a couple of them, and this is one.

Yes, 2.25 million children designated as having learning disabilities are a lot of children; yes, thousands—maybe hundreds of thousands—of these students do not have learning disabilities; and yes, those wrongly labeled, in our view, should be in mainstream classrooms, not in special education programs.[28] But those who would have us believe that there is no such thing as learning disabilities either 1) ignore considerable evidence[29] showing that students so labeled consistently perform significantly less well than low-

achieving nondisabled students on various academic measures or 2) downplay this reliable between-group difference, emphasizing instead the degree of overlap between the two groups.[30] To ignore or downplay the fact that the mean of the group with learning disabilities is significantly below that of the nondisabled low-achieving group is to fail to appreciate a pivotal point about inferential statistics: when groups differ significantly on a given measure—and especially when they do so consistently—we may assume that they represent *different populations.* To insist that learning disabilities is a phantom category also ignores findings from surveys of and interviews with general educators at elementary and secondary levels who tend to consider students with learning disabilities to be different from their nondisabled classmates.[31]

Many students with learning disabilities, then, have learning needs substantially different in amount or kind from those of nondisabled children. An important implication, we believe, is that the full-time placement of *all* students with learning disabilities in mainstream classrooms will result in the failure of some to obtain an appropriate education or one from which they will benefit. No doubt general education can be made more accommodating of student diversity through important innovations such as cooperative learning, but we believe that there are limits on just how resourceful and responsive the mainstream can become. See, for example, research by Rollanda O'Connor and Joseph Jenkins and by Karen Tateyama-Sniezek, which suggests that many children with learning disabilities may not benefit from coopera-

tive learning;[32] the work of Ruth McIntosh et al., of Naomi Zigmond and Janice Baker, and of others, which documents how infrequently general educators modify their instruction for special-needs students;[33] and Elfrieda Hiebert's summary of Reading Recovery research in the U.S., which draws attention to how little we know about the reading method's applicability to students with learning disabilities and, presumably, to those with other academic disabilities.[34]

We are not alone in viewing the mainstream as incapable of accommodating all children, all of the time; indeed, this is the perspective of a majority of the disability community. And it explains why parent and professional groups such as the Learning Disabilities Association, the National Joint Committee on Learning Disabilities, and the Division of Learning Disabilities of the Council for Exceptional Children,[35] as well as many other disability groups,[36] firmly, if not fiercely, support special education placements and consider full inclusion a threat to the provision of an appropriate education to each and every child with a disability. The emotions aroused and the discord provoked by full inclusion are reflected in the words of Bernard Rimland, a well-known advocate and parent of a son with disabilities: "I have no quarrel with [full] inclusionists if they are content to insist upon inclusion for *their* children. But when they try to force me and other unwilling parents to dance to their tune, I find it highly objectionable and quite intolerable. Parents need [placement] options."[37]

What's special about special education? Rimland and other supporters of special education placements notwithstanding, this is a critical time for the field. With the reauthorization of the Individuals with Disabilities Education Act (IDEA) before Congress, with many groups expressing profound dissatisfaction with special education services, with evidence that more than a few special educators are demoralized, and with a disability community that was formerly described as mutually supportive and synergistic[38] now squabbling so bitterly and pervasively, it seems timely to ask, What's special about special education? We will respond by identifying its unique resources (input), by discussing the impact of these resources on student performance (output), and by analyzing effective teaching practices that mediate between inputs and outputs. By "special education" we mean instruction for school-age children in resource rooms and self-contained classes. A discussion of day treatment and residential programs, as well as of special education's contributions to early intervention and school-to-work transitions, is beyond the scope of this article.

Input

Since the 1950s education policy has been intended to prohibit discrimination, both because discrimination is immoral and because it is believed to produce unequal opportunity for future social and economic rewards.[39] One often-used strategy to discourage discrimination has been to make comparable outcomes both the primary goal of schools and the ultimate test of equality of educational opportunity. According to this approach, most recently questioned by Charles Murray and Richard Herrnstein,[40] the purpose of education is to

minimize between-group differences in learning. Hence, policy makers permit the distribution of more resources to poorer-performing groups to compensate for the fewer resources they received in the past—a factor that might account for current inequalities in performance.

The IDEA reflects the strategy of weighting resources in favor of children with disabilities to help them perform as much like nondisabled children as possible.[41] Under IDEA, school districts must provide and pay for an appropriate education for every child with a disability, regardless of cost.[42] In 1985–86, state-reported expenditures for special education and related services were just under $16 billion—or $18.6 billion in constant 1989–90 dollars. Of this sum, $1.4 billion, $10.8 billion, and $6.4 billion came from federal, state, and local sources respectively. This works out to a national average per-pupil cost of approximately $7,800 in 1989–90 dollars, or about 2.3 times the cost of a regular education.[43]

Individualized instruction, smaller classes, and more highly trained teachers. School districts spend special education money on children from infancy through young adulthood because IDEA requires districts to ensure that all students receive a free and appropriate education. Students are identified through a multidimensional evaluation and are placed in a least restrictive environment in which they are as close as possible to nondisabled, age-appropriate peers and from which they will benefit instructionally. In addition, general and special educators develop an indi-

vidualized education program (IEP) for each special-needs student, which includes long- and short-term goals and the specification of necessary related services, such as interpreters, transportation, technological aids, and work/study coordinators.

To facilitate the realization of IEP goals, school districts grant special educators smaller classes than those assigned to general educators. In 1990–91, 297,490 full-time special educators were employed nationwide to work with 4,362,445 children between the ages of 6 and 21—in other words, 14.66 children per special education teacher. In addition, in the same year, 295,822 full-time teacher aides, psychologists, social workers, counselors, and occupational, physical, and recreational therapists worked with special-needs students between 3 and 21 years of age.[44]

Special educators not only have fewer students than do general educators, but they also tend to have more advanced degrees. According to the Schools and Staffing Surveys and Teacher Followup Surveys conducted by the National Center on Education Statistics, 54.6% of special educators have master's degrees, and 11.3% have educational specialist or doctoral degrees; for general educators, the percentages are 39.9% and 5.7% respectively.[45] The federal government has underwritten part of special educators' advanced training.

Research and development. The total amount authorized by Congress for education research and development in 1989, representing "basic" and "applied" activity, was $145.6 million,[46] two-tenths of 1% of the federal

> Special educators not only have fewer students than do general educators, but they also tend to have more advanced degrees.

government's total research and development expenditures of $62 billion in 1989.[47] Of the $145 million allocated to education research, special education's share was about 12%, with about $17 million going to the Division for Innovation and Development (DID).[48]

The bulk of the research funded by DID is problem-focused, intervention-oriented, and field-based. While he was still DID director, Martin Kaufman explained, "We are . . . intimately involved with the policy makers, . . . the professional associations representing teachers and administrators, [and] the parent groups, because it is their needs, not theory divorced from those needs, that drive us."[49] DID-funded research has produced a large armamentarium of teaching strategies and curricula for children and youth with disabilities, such as self-management procedures, mnemonic strategies, peer tutoring, Direct Instruction, and systematic formative evaluation. Quantitative syntheses of multiple—sometimes hundreds of—studies have demonstrated the effectiveness of these and other techniques and curricula, many of which were developed expressly for small-group and individualized instruction.[50] Furthermore, special education researchers have found innovative ways to bridge the divide between research and practice, providing many teachers with effective educational practices.[51]

Output

With more dollars per student to "buy" IEPs, with proportionately more teachers with advanced degrees, with smaller special education classes, and with a research and development program that has produced effective teaching strategies and curricula, the obvious question is whether such special inputs have translated into special outputs. That is, are we justified in speaking of special education's "value added"? Overall, we believe so.

Questionable grounds for skepticism. The aforementioned refrain, "Special education can't work," continues to resound in the professional literature and popular press for at least two notable reasons: critics give too much credence to the so-called efficacy studies and too little attention to more recent scholarly reviews of the literature and other evidence.

The efficacy studies, conducted during the past 60 years and involving mostly students with mental retardation, generally show special-needs students in mainstream classrooms performing as well as, or better than, their counterparts in special education programs. This result has led many to question the effectiveness and necessity of special education. What many critics have not understood, or have conveniently overlooked, is that nearly all of these investigations are seriously flawed—and flawed in precisely the same way: the researcher rarely assigned the disabled students at random to special education and mainstream classes. Rather, in almost every case, school personnel had assigned students to programs to suit their own pedagogic purposes long before the researcher showed up, with the consequence that the mainstreamed students were stronger academically from the study's start.[52]

Scholarly reviews. Scholarly reviews of the literature cast special education in a somewhat different light. Conrad Calberg and Kenneth Kayale, for example, undertook a meta-analysis of 50 independent studies of special classes (including resource rooms) versus regular classes. They concluded that "special classes were . . . significantly inferior to regular class placement for students with below average IQs, and significantly superior to regular class for behaviorally disordered, emotionally disturbed, and learning disabled children."[53] Paul Sindelar and Stanley Deno's narrative review of 17 studies explored the effectiveness of resource rooms. They used more stringent selection criteria than did Carlberg and Kavale, reviewing only investigations with relevant comparison groups. Nevertheless, their findings are consonant with those of Carlberg and Kavale: resource rooms were more effective than regular classrooms in improving the academic achievement of students with learning disabilities or emotional and behavioral disturbances. By contrast, there were no reliable differences between resource and mainstream classes with respect to the academic improvement of children with mild mental retardation. Moreover, as Sindelar and Deno noted, "one clear trend has begun to emerge: The most carefully designed studies have . . . obtained the most affirmative results [for special education programs]."[54]

Additional reviews of the efficacy studies by Nancy Madden and Robert Slavin[55] and by Gaea Leinhardt and Allan Palley[56] do not agree in all respects with the Carlberg/Kavale and the Sindelar/Deno reviews. But all four syntheses agree on this central point: for certain students, special education programs appear to promote greater academic achievement than do regular classrooms.

Time-series research. Douglas Marston compared the effectiveness of general education versus special education for students with learning disabilities in the Minneapolis Public Schools. To circumvent methodological problems inherent in the hoary efficacy studies, Marston employed time-series analysis. Such analysis eliminates the need for the random assignment of study participants by requiring them to serve as their own controls as they are measured repeatedly across multiple treatment conditions. Three Minneapolis elementary schools identified 272 nondisabled students in grades 4 through 6 who performed at the 15th percentile or below on a reading achievement test. Of this number 11 students were subsequently referred to and found eligible for special education services and spent a minimum of 10 weeks in both general and special education programs. Figure 1 shows each student's average gain per week (in terms of number of words read correctly) in each program.* The students nearly doubled their weekly rate of gain in special education: 1.5 words (SD < .57) in special education versus .60 words (SD < .35) in general education.[57]

With Pamela Fernstrom, we also conducted time-series analyses on the academic achievement of elementary and middle school students with learning disabilities in special and general education programs. Whereas Marston followed students as they moved from general education into special education, we did the reverse. To evaluate the effectiveness of a mainstream strategy, we tracked 21 students with learning disabilities from eight schools in middle Tennessee before and after they transferred to general education classes. Mathematics achievement

*Does not appear in this publication.

data were collected weekly for about 10 weeks while the students were in special education and about seven weeks after they reintegrated into mainstream classes. We found that students made modest but steady progress in special education, whereas they demonstrated no gain in general education.[58]

Teacher and parent surveys. Corroborating these research results are the opinions of many school personnel. Cherry Houck and Catherine Rogers asked a randomly selected statewide sample of Virginia's special and general education supervisors, principals, elementary and secondary mainstream teachers, and teachers of students with learning disabilities to respond to the assertion that " 'pull-out' [special education] programs do students with learning disabilities more harm than good." A total of 61.5% of respondents "disagreed" or "tended to disagree" with the statement; 29.7% "agreed" or "tended to agree"; and the remainder of the sample expressed no opinion.[59] Surveys of general educators in Southern California and northern Illinois[60] and in northwest Iowa[61] have reflected similar support for special education programs. Moreover, a recent Harris poll indicated that 94% of general educators believe that services for students with disabilities are better now than 12 years ago and that 77% of parents of children with disabilities are satisfied with special education services.[62]

Special education programs can and do work in certain places—make no mistake. However, it is equally clear that they do not work everywhere. For years, special education has been excessively concerned about compliance with federal law and insufficiently concerned about

educational outcomes.[63] Few would disagree with the statement that special education can and should be improved in many school districts. But to assert, as many today do, that it is broken everywhere is downright false—as false as it is to say that regular education is broken everywhere.[64]

Mediating Between Inputs and Outputs

What, if anything, is special about the successful special educator's approach to instruction? At least two features, we believe: the use of empirically validated procedures and an intensive, data-based focus on individual students. To illustrate these characteristics, we describe special educators' use of Curriculum-Based Measurement (CBM).

Curriculum-Based Measurement. CBM is a set of assessment methods developed by Stanley Deno[65] and, with DID funding, validated by many others over the past two decades. CBM specifies procedures for regularly measuring student performance within the local school curriculum to monitor progress toward end-of-year global literacy and numeracy goals. Research has provided teachers with valid methods for creating, administering, and scoring assessments across different curricula.[66]

The CBM methodology is used by special educators nationwide to develop effective, individualized instructional programs over time. With CBM, a special educator assesses student performance twice each week. The resulting database provides the teacher with two types of information useful for instructional decision making: proficiency indicators, which describe students' past, current, and future growth trajectories; and profiles of students' strengths and weaknesses in the curriculum. Whenever a student's growth trajectory suggests that the established end-of-year goal may underestimate his or her potential, the teacher raises the goal for that student. When the growth trajectory indicates that the student may fail to achieve the end-of-year goal, the teacher modifies the instructional program.

To identify promising strategies for enhancing instruction, the special educator relies on a CBM profile of a student's curricular strengths and weaknesses, the student's rate of overall growth (indexed by CBM), and a historical analysis of the instructional components of the student's program. Through this data-based, analytic process, the special educator tests alternative hypotheses about which instructional methods will produce the most satisfactory growth rates. Over time, an instructional program is fine-tuned for each student.

Special educators who use CBM to develop demonstrably effective instructional programs engage in the following practices. First, they use CBM to monitor the appropriateness of the goals they set and to keep those goals ambitious. Special educators who set and maintain ambitious goals facilitate superior achievement by their students.[67] Second, collecting CBM data routinely does little by itself to improve student growth. Rather, successful special educators use the data continually to revise and tailor their students' programs.[68] Third, when the CBM data reveal inadequate growth, effective special educators frequently obtain human or computer-generated expertise to help them develop important revisions to their existing instructional programs.[69] When special educators use CBM in these ways, they facilitate impressive academic gains among students with very serious learning difficulties—with effect sizes of .70 standard deviation units.[70]

Empirically validated and individualized. The CBM technology for tracking student growth toward broad literacy and numeracy goals and for connecting the assessment information with instructional decisions has been researched for two decades and reported in more than 100 empirical studies. Special educators can confidently use CBM to enhance learning outcomes with children who demonstrate persistent and severe learning problems.

The research and development activity associated with CBM is not unusual in special education. Many special education practices used nationwide have been developed and validated with similar care. Given the profound learning problems of many students in special education programs—and these students' demonstrated failure to profit from general education instruction—such empirically validated practices are necessary to promote meaningful academic growth.

Virtually all validated special education practices share one important characteristic: they focus the special educator's instructional decisions on the individual student. Individualized instruction is perhaps the signature feature of effective special education practice. It exemplifies a basic value and represents a core assumption of special educators' professional preparation; it requires teachers to reserve judgment about the efficacy of instructional methods until those methods prove effective for the individual student; it necessitates a form of teacher planning that incorporates ongoing, major adjustments and revisions in response to an individual student's learning patterns; and it requires knowledge of multiple ways to adapt curricula, modify instructional methods, and motivate students.

Can General Education Become Special Education?

Can teaching methods that focus instructional decisions on individual students and that have been empirically validated by special educators in special education settings be exported to mainstream classrooms to improve the outcomes of students with severe learning problems? This is a timely question, given the increasing popularity of full inclusion. We have explored this question by studying CBM's use in mainstream classrooms. Our attempts to encourage general educators to adopt special education's individual decision-making orientation have proved discouraging. We have found that the instructional adaptations that general educators make in response to students' persistent failure to learn are typically oriented to the group, not to the individual, and are relatively minor in substance, with little chance for helping students with chronically poor learning histories.[71]

Indeed, to make CBM more compatible with most general education settings, we have had to change CBM's traditional focus

> Special education programs can and do work in certain places—make no mistake. But it is equally clear they do not work everywhere.

orientation. With classwide decision making, general educators use CBM to create task-oriented motivational climates[72] and to identify appropriate content for peer-mediated instruction sessions within their classrooms.[73] In such settings, learning outcomes for low-, average-, and high-achieving students are considerably better than in classrooms without classwide CBM decision making (respective effect sizes = 1.14, .45, and .63). However, results in classrooms with CBM decision making are considerably less impressive for children with learning disabilities (effect size = .26). This stands in stark contrast to the aforementioned improvements observed among students with learning disabilities when an individual CBM decision-making orientation is used by special educators in special education settings (effect size = .70).

Many practices validated by special educators for use in special education settings, like CBM, do not transfer easily to most mainstream classrooms, where teachers have many students and often a different set of assumptions about the form and function of education. Focusing intensively on the individual student—as most special education practices require—means that teachers must conduct different instructional activities for different students at different times. This approach is simply impractical for classrooms of 25 to 35 students. Moreover, special education's most basic article of faith—that instruction must be individualized to be effective—is rarely contemplated, let alone observed, in most general education classrooms.

For sound reasons, mainstream teachers have important competing priorities: the good of the group and the extent to which

activities are engaging and maintain classroom flow, orderliness, and cooperation. These operational priorities (and a committed teacher) make general education a productive learning environment for 90% or more of all students. For the remaining children, however, a different orientation is required. Special education, with its emphasis on empirically validated practices and its use of data-based decision making to tailor instruction to the individual student's needs, has the capacity to effect better outcomes for this small minority of learners.

Coda

We are not apologists for special education. Many times we have tried to shake our field by its shoulders with regard to its assessment practices, state reimbursement formulas, reintegration efforts, and overidentification of students. But such concerns—as well as other legitimate problems raised by full inclusionists, detracking advocates, school administrators, and others—should not be construed as evidence that special education cannot work. It can and does work—it *is* special—in many places. And it is unique in ways that general education is not and probably never can be.

That special education isn't special everywhere is the fault of many, including those of us at colleges and universities who are responsible for preservice education. Parents, advocates, the courts, federal officials, and others should hold special educators' feet to the fire rather than seek special education's elimination or dramatic diminution by such means as moving all students with learning disabilities into regular classrooms full time. In many places special education (like gen-

eral education) requires change. Let's get on with it, but let's also not forget what's special about special education. If we do, many students will pay the price.

1. Joseph P. Shapiro. *No Pity: People with Disabilities Forging a New Civil Rights Movement* (New York: Times Books, 1993).
2. Dorothy K. Lipsky and Alan Gartner. "Capable of Achievement and Worthy of Respect: Education for Handicapped Students As If They Were Full-Fledged Human Beings," *Exceptional Children,* vol. 54, 1987, pp. 69–74; and Susan Stainback and William Stainback, letter to the editor, *Journal of Learning Disabilities,* vol. 21, 1988, pp. 452–53.
3. See, for example, Emily Dentzer and Anne Wheelock, *Locked In/Locked Out: Tracking and Placement Practices in Boston Public Schools* (Boston: Massachusetts Advocacy Center, 1990); and Margaret C. Wang and Herbert J. Walberg, "Four Fallacies of Segregationism," *Exceptional Children,* vol. 55, 1988, pp. 128–37.
4. Maynard C. Reynolds, "Classification and Labeling," in John W. Lloyd, Alan C. Repp, and Nirbhay N. Singh, eds., *The Regular Education Initiative: Alternative Perspectives on Concepts, Issues, and Models* (Sycamore, Ill.: Sycamore, 1991), pp. 29–41.
5. See, for example, Thomas M. Skrtic, *Behind Special Education: A Critical Analysis of Professional Culture and School Organization* (Denver: Love, 1991); and Christine E. Sleeter, "Learning Disabilities: The Social Construction of a Special Education Category," *Exceptional Children,* vol. 53, 1986, pp. 46–54.
6. Sleeter, op. cit.
7. Sam Dillon, "Special Education Soaks Up New York's School Resources," *New York Times,* 7 April 1994, p. 18.
8. Joseph P. Shapiro et al., "Separate and Unequal: How Special Education Programs Are Cheating Our Children and Costing Taxpayers Billions Each Year," *U.S. News & World Report,* 13 December 1993, pp. 46–49, 54–56, 60; and Wang and Walberg, op. cit.
9. See, for example, Reynolds, op. cit.
10. Wang and Walberg, p. 131.

11. See, for example, *Special Education: New Questions in an Era of Reform* (Alexandria, Va.: National Association of State Boards of Education, October 1991).

12. See, for example, Robert E. Slavin et al., "Neverstreaming: Prevention and Early Intervention as an Alternative to Special Education," *Journal of Learning Disabilities*, vol. 24, 1991, pp. 373–78.

13. Sam Dillon, "New York City Schools Monitor Contends That Special Education Cost Is Inflated," *New York Times*, 14 August 1994, p. 18.

14. Dillon, "Special Education."

15. Dillon, "New York City Schools."

16. Quoted in ibid.

17. Debra Viadero, "States Turn to Spec.-Ed. Programs for Budget Cuts," *Education Week*, 12 June 1991, p. 16.

18. "Special Ed's Special Costs," *Wall Street Journal*, 20 October 1993, p. A-14.

19. R. L. Wood, "A Different Sort of Handicap," *National Review*, 12 September 1994, pp. 58, 60.

20. Shapiro et al., op. cit.

21. Daniel P. Hallahan and James M. Kauffman, "Toward a Culture of Disability in the Aftermath of Deno and Dunn," *Journal of Special Education*, vol. 27, 1994, pp. 496–508.

22. Herbert J. Rieth, personal communication. 1 February 1994.

23. Sharon A. Bobbitt, Elizabeth Faupel, and Shelley Burns, *Characteristics of Stayers, Movers, and Leavers: Results from the Teacher Followup Survey, 1988–89* (Washington, D.C.: National Center for Education Statistics, 1991).

24. Paul Lauritzen and Stephen Freidman, cited in Judith D. Singer, "Once Is Not Enough: Former Special Educators Who Return to Teaching," *Exceptional Children*, vol. 60, 1993, p. 60; and Judy Smith-Davis, P. J. Burke, and M. M. Noel, cited in Singer, p. 59.

25. Lawrence H. Cross and Bonnie S. Billingsley, "Testing a Model of Special Educators' Intent to Stay in Teaching," *Exceptional Children*, vol. 60, 1994, pp. 411–21.

26. Peggy C. Littrell, Bonnie S. Billingsley, and Lawrence H. Cross, "The Effects of Principal Support on Special and General Educators' Stress, Jog Satisfaction, School Commitment, Health, and Intent to Stay in Teaching," *Remedial and Special Education*, vol. 15, 1994, pp. 297–310.

27. Office of Special Education Programs, *Fifteenth Annual Report to Congress on the Implementation of the Individuals with Disabilities Education Act* (Washington, D.C.: U.S. Department of Education, 1993).

28. For documentation of an urban school system's overidentification of low-achieving students as students with learning disabilities, see Jay Gottlieb et al., "Special Education in Urban America: It's Not Justifiable for Many," *Journal of Special Education*, vol. 27, 1994, pp. 453–65.

29. See, for example, Kenneth W. Merrell, "Differentiating Low-Achieving Students and Students with Learning Disabilities: An Examination of Performances on the Woodcock-Johnson Psycho-Educational Battery," *Journal of Special Education*, vol. 24, 1990, pp. 296–305.

30. See, for example, James E. Ysseldyke et al., "Similarities and Differences Between Low Achievers and Students Classified Learning Disabled," *Journal of Special Education*, vol. 16, 1982, pp. 73–85.

31. See, for example, Cherry K. Houck and Catherine J. Rogers, "The Special/General Education Integration Initiative for Students with Specific Learning Disabilities: A 'Snapshot' of Program Change," *Journal of Learning Disabilities*, vol. 27, 1994, pp. 435–53.

32. Rollanda E. O'Connor and Joseph R. Jenkins, "Cooperative Learning as an Inclusion Strategy: The Experiences of Children with Disabilities," unpublished manuscript, University of Pittsburgh, 1994; and Karen M. Tateyama-Sniezek, "Cooperative Learning: Does It Improve the Academic Achievement of Students with Handicaps?," *Exceptional Children*, vol. 56, 1990, pp. 426–37.

33. Ruth McIntosh et al., "Observations of Students with Learning Disabilities in General Education Classrooms," *Exceptional Children*, vol. 60, 1993, pp. 249–61; and Naomi Zigmond and Janice M. Baker, "Is the Mainstream a More Appropriate Educational Setting for Randy? A Case Study of One Student with Learning Disabilities," *Learning Disabilities Research & Practice*, vol. 9, 1994, pp. 108–17.

34. Elfrieda H. Hiebert. "Reading Recovery in the United States: What Difference Does It Make to an Age Cohort?," *Educational Researcher*, December 1994, pp. 15–25.

35. "Position Paper on Full Inclusion of All Students with Learning Disabilities in the Regular Education Classroom," Learning Disabilities Association, Pittsburgh, January 1993; "A Reaction to 'Full Inclusion': A Reaffirmation of the Right of Students with Learning Disabilities to a Continuum of Services," National Joint Committee on Learning Disabilities, Baltimore, January 1993; and Division of Learning Disabilities, *Statement on Inclusive Schools and Communities* (Reston, Va.: Council for Exceptional Children, April 1993).

36. See Douglas Fuchs and Lynn S. Fuchs, "Inclusive Schools Movement and the Radicalization of Special Education Reform," *Exceptional Children*, vol. 60, 1994, pp. 294–309.

37. Bernard Rimland, "Inclusive Education: Right for Some," *Autism Research Review International*, vol. 7, 1993, p. 3.

38. See, for example, Joseph P. Shapiro, op. cit.

39. James M. Kauffman, "Historical Trends and Contemporary Issues in Special Education in the United States," in Kauffman and Daniel P. Hallahan, eds., *Handbook of Special Education* (Englewood Cliffs, N.J.: Prentice-Hall, 1981), pp. 3–23.

40. Charles Murray and Richard J. Hernstein, *The Bell Curve* (New York: Free Press, 1994).

41. Kauffman, "Historical Trends."

42. Barbara D. Bateman and Cynthia M. Herr, "Law and Special Education," in Kauffman and Hallahan, pp. 330–60.

43. Stephen Chaikind, Louis C. Danielson, and Marsha L. Brauen, "What Do We Know About the Costs of Special Education? A Selected Review," *Journal of Special Education*, vol. 26, 1993, table 5, p. 361.

44. Office of Special Education Programs, op. cit.

45. Erling Boe, personal communication, 21 October 1994.

46. *Research and Development Activities* (Washington, D.C.: U.S.

Department of Education, Exhibit A-11-44A, 18 December 1989).

47. James W. Guthrie, "Education R & D's Lament (and What to Do About It)," *Educational Researcher*, March 1990, pp. 26–34.

48. "Fact File: Higher Education Funds Requested in Fiscal 1991 Budget," *Chronicle of Higher Education*, 7 February 1990, p. A-31.

49. Quoted in Barbara McKenna, "Special Education Research Priorities Focus on Action," *Educational Researcher*, June/July 1992, p. 27.

50. For more on these review articles, see Douglas Fuchs and Lynn S. Fuchs, "Special Education Can Work," in James M. Kauffman and Daniel P. Hallahan, eds., *Assessment and Treatment of Students with Behavior Disorders* (Hillsdale, N.J.: Erlbaum, forthcoming).

51. See, for example, Frank M. Kline, Donald D. Deshler, and Jean B. Schumaker, "Implementing Learning Strategy Instruction in Class Settings: A Research Perspective," in Michael Pressley, Karen Harris, and John Guthrie, eds., *Promoting Academic Competence and Literacy in School* (San Diego: Academic Press, 1992), pp. 361–406.

52. For a discussion of critics' misuse of the efficacy studies, see Hallahan and Kauffman, op. cit.

53. Conrad Calberg and Kenneth Kavale, "The Efficacy of Special Versus Regular Class Placements for Exceptional Children: A Meta-Analysis," *Journal of Special Education*, vol. 14, 1980, p. 295.

54. Paul T. Sindelar and Stanley L. Deno, "The Effectiveness of Resource Programming," *Journal of Special Education*, vol. 12, 1979, pp. 17–28.

55. Nancy A. Madden and Robert E. Slavin, "Mainstreaming Students with Mild Handicaps: Academic and Social Outcomes," *Review of Educational Research*, vol. 53, 1983, pp. 519–69.

56. Gaea Leinhardt and Allan Pallay, "Restrictive Educational Settings: Exile or Haven?," *Review of Educational Research*, vol. 52, 1982, pp. 557–78.

57. Douglas Marston, "The Effectiveness of Special Education: A Time-Series Analysis of Reading Performance in Regular and Special Education Settings," *Journal of Special Education*, vol. 21, 1987–88, pp. 13–26.

58. Douglas Fuchs, Lynn S. Fuchs, and Pamela Fernstrom, "A Conservative Approach to Special Education Reform: Mainstreaming Through Transenvironmental Programming and Curriculum-Based Measurement," *American Educational Research Journal*, vol. 30, 1993, pp. 149–77.

59. Houck and Rogers, op. cit.

60. Melvin I. Semmel et al., "Teacher Perceptions of the Regular Education Initiative," *Exceptional Children*, vol. 58, 1991, pp. 9–23.

61. Robert D. Coates, "The Regular Education Initiative and Opinions of Regular Classroom Teachers," *Journal of Learning Disabilities*, vol. 22, 1989, pp. 532–36.

62. Cited in James M. Kauffman, "Restructuring in Sociopolitical Context: Reservations About the Effects of Current Reform Proposals on Students with Disabilities," in Lloyd, Repp, and Singh, pp. 57–66.

63. Thomas Hehir, "Special Education: Successes and Challenges: A Memo from the Director of the U.S. Office of Special Education Programs," *Teaching Exceptional Children*, Spring 1994, p. 5.

64. Daniel Tanner, "A Nation 'Truly' at Risk," *Phi Delta Kappan*, December 1993, pp. 288–97.

65. Stanley L. Deno, "Curriculum-Based Measurement: The Emerging Alternative," *Exceptional Children*, vol. 52, 1985, pp. 219–32.

66. See Mark R. Shinn. *Curriculum-Based Measurement: Assessing Special Children* (New York: Guilford, 1989).

67. Lynn S. Fuchs, Douglas Fuchs, and Carol L. Hamlett, "Effects of Alternative Goal Structures Within Curriculum-Based Instruction," *Exceptional Children*, vol. 55, 1989, pp. 429–38.

68. Ibid.

69. Lynn S. Fuchs, Douglas Fuchs, Carol L. Hamlett, and Pam M. Stecker, "Effects of Curriculum-Based Instruction and Consultation on Teacher Planning and Student Achievement in Mathematics Operations," *American Educational Research Journal*. vol. 38, 1991, pp. 617–41.

70. Ibid.

71. Lynn S. Fuchs, Douglas Fuchs, Carol L. Hamlett, Norris B. Phillips, and Kathy Karns, "General Educators' Specialized Adaptations for Students with Learning Disabilities," *Exceptional Children*, in press.

72. Eric M. Anderman and Martin L. Maehr, "Motivation and Schooling in the Middle Grades," *Review of Educational Research*, vol. 64, 1994, pp. 287–309.

73. Lynn S. Fuchs, Douglas Fuchs, Carol L. Hamlett, Norris B. Phillips, and Johnell Bentz, "Class-wide Curriculum-Based Instruction: Helping General Educators Meet the Challenge of Student Diversity," *Exceptional Children*, vol. 60, 1994, pp. 518–37.

Article Review Form at end of book.

What does the author see as the goals of special education advocates? What is the relation between the civil rights movement and the special education movement, according to the author?

Corrupted Intentions

Reforming special education

Programs designed to help handicapped children may be doing more harm than good.

Chester E. Finn, Jr.

Mr. Finn is a former assistant secretary of education and is John M. Olin Fellow at the Hudson Institute.

Conservatives talk a good game about lifting Uncle Sam's heavy hand from the back of American education and restoring control of schools to parents and communities. It's high time they tackle the "special" education of disabled students. For more than two decades, this program has embodied all that Newt Gingrich and the feisty freshmen say they abhor: onerous, unfunded federal mandates; extra benefits and rights for government-designated populations; opportunities for activists and lawyers to hustle more taxpayer-financed largesse; and, most of all, the smug assumption that Washington knows best how to run the nation's schools.

The special-education program does not even work very well. And it costs real money: about $3.25 billion in federal funds each year, plus billions from Medicaid and other programs that help pay for services it mandates.

Yet today it's not even on the reformers' list. Special education has been exempted from all known block-grant schemes. Bills to abolish the Education Department would transfer it intact. The pending 1996 appropriation scarcely nicks it. Although the main statute awaits reauthorization, nobody on Capitol Hill suggests more than mere tinkering. Sub-committee chairmen Bill Frist and "Duke" Cunningham handle it with kid gloves.

The reason for such caution is, to put it gently, non-substantive. Everyone knows there's reason to revamp the entire program, recently described by a House staffer as "an incredible case of . . . micro-managing local school districts." Still, it's assumed throughout political Washington that any attempt to change it would be suicidal.

The special ed-ifice rests on two pillars. One is civil-rights legislation that since 1973 has barred discrimination against the handicapped. The other is the federal aid program, first enacted in 1975, which declares that every disabled youngster must be provided a "free appropriate public education" tailored to his unique needs—whatever that entails.

The statute does not say this should be done within available resources or that Uncle Sam will pay for it. At its peak, Washington covered about 12 per cent of the cost. Today, the federal share is around seven per cent. States and localities are saddled with a bill of at least $30 billion, perhaps as much as $50 billion.

States do not have to participate—but then they would forfeit their federal monies. Faced with no-escape civil rights laws and court decisions that use the "equal court decisions that use the "equal protection" clause to mandate extra educational services for disabled youngsters, it is no surprise that the federal program now rules from ocean to ocean.

As one might expect, both the civil-rights measures and the special-education program began as remedies for *bona fide* wrongs. Many handicapped youngsters did not attend school at all in the early 1970s. "Compulsory attendance" laws often exempted them. Horror stories told of kids shut in attics and cellars.

In response, a rash of successful lawsuits secured handicapped youngsters the right to public education almost everywhere. By 1975, only two states had not provided schooling for most such children. But leaving this to the states was too slow and patchy for the advocates. Why have fifty programs with different provisions when Uncle Sam could create a single big one—and dangle the federal dollar to draw everyone into its web?

Today's special-education program is complex, as might be expected of anything that serves five million-plus youngsters. Each state must have a comprehensive plan for serving all disabled persons aged 3 to 21, whether they're in school, home, hospital, or jail. The more such people the state finds, the more federal dollars it gets.

School systems must provide all the services spelled out in each child's individual education plan, even if that means hiring more staff, paying tuition to private schools, or arranging for "clean catheterization." In practice the special-education program has first claim on the district's entire budget.

Disabled students must be educated in the "least restrictive environment," which means placed whenever possible in regular classrooms. Such "inclusion" works well for some but can lead to chaos when a teacher must cope with youngsters who have severe emotional and behavioral problems.

Yet the teacher does not have much say. Parents have sweeping "due process" rights to shape their disabled child's educational program, and a thriving legal practice is eager to help them exploit those rights. (Since the school system must pay parents' legal fees, it's no surprise that administrators are apt to cave quickly to their demands).

A double standard applies to discipline. It's nearly impossible to suspend or expel a disabled child. Even moving him out of the classroom requires parental consent or a court order. Although one federal law requires states to suspend a gun-toting student for a full year, if he is disabled another statute limits even his placement in an "alternative setting" to 45 days. (For other weapons, the limit is ten days). Says Fairfax County's school superintendent Robert Spillane, "Any student who is classified as disabled is now literally able to get away with anything."

Just as the birth of special education followed the familiar civil-rights scenario, its evolution also hewed to a well-thumbed script. Non-discrimination evolved into affirmative action for the disabled. (The Americans with Disabilities Act is a vivid example.) A once small and discrete population of "victims" has grown—and its boundaries blurred—as more groups see advantages in joining it. Reverse discrimination sets in as non-victims find themselves denied benefits. Huge bureaucracies stretch their tentacles. Lawyers grow rich. Activist organizations get new grants.

The corruption of good intentions begins with special ed's bizarre incentives, particularly the impulse to grow.

How many disabled youngsters there are in the land depends, of course, on how "disability" is defined. The special-education population has swollen as more students have been classified with "learning disabilities." About a hundred thousand youngsters are now added to that category each year and today the "L.D." population makes up half of all children in special education, up from barely a fifth in the late 1970s. Indeed, the ballooning of that population accounts for virtually the entire growth of special education—from 8.5 to 12 per cent of public-school enrollments. (In New Jersey it's reached 16 per cent, in Massachusetts 17 per cent.) And the numbers keep rising. Between 1992–93 and 1993–94, public-school enrollments grew 1.4 per cent, but the special ed rolls added 4.2 per cent, the biggest increase ever.

The children we now term "learning disabled" were not kept in attics before Washington intervened. Mostly they are kids who, in an earlier time, were said to misbehave a lot or to have a short attention span. Many did poorly in school and some were nuisances in class. Teachers and parents both had reason to welcome an alternative approach. For the teacher, special education became an easy place to send the kid who disrupted her lessons. From the parents' standpoint, it got them off the hook—Gee, Officer Krupke, my kid's not naughty, he's disabled!—while opening the door to a trove of services and rights unavailable to the family next door (whose kid was simply naughty).

By the early 1990s, one in eight of New York City's one million students was classified as disabled; nearly a quarter of the school budget went into special education; and a fourth of the system's employees worked within its sprawling bureaucratic empire.

Such growth served diverse interests: special-education bureaucrats, of course, whose domain and power grew; teachers who could off-load classroom pests; school-system budgeteers who got extra money as their special-ed population grew; superintendents who could boost scores by excluding more pupils from state tests; parents who could claim added services for their kids via this route; and litigious lawyers and advocacy groups whose living this is.

The program's growth created problems even beyond its soaring costs. New forms of segregation emerged as many minority youngsters (mostly boys) found themselves "sent to special ed" in urban school systems. Traditional civil-rights groups began to protest. Parents who sought extra help for their children didn't necessarily want them in separate classrooms. Most avant garde special educators fervently believe in "mainstreaming." Yet inclusion has produced its own backlash: classrooms disrupted and students shaken by the erratic behavior of disturbed classmates.

As for the putative beneficiaries, there's scant evidence that special education does them much good. A University of Pittsburgh team, for example, found that "general education settings produce achievement outcomes for students with learning disabilities that are neither desirable nor acceptable." The federal Education Department admits that "[A]chievement for students with disabilities remains less than satisfactory. . . . Results for students with learning disabilities and emotional disabilities are particularly poor."

There are five solid reasons why Congress ought to place the overhaul of special education high among its priorities:

- It's a burdensome, costly, and growing unfunded mandate-*cum*-entitlement.

- It establishes a class of people who are entitled to benefits that others do not receive while creating incentives to expand that class.

- It impedes other promising reforms. Because the special-education empire is threatened by anything that cuts red tape, its lobbyists oppose charter-school bills, standards-based accountability, and vouchers.

- Its cost-benefit ratio is dubious. This is a sensitive topic, as only a churl would skimp on disabled children. Yet in weighing society's overall human capital investment, it's appropriate to ask whether the next million dollars are better spent on more services for a few handicapped youngsters or on physics and math for a large number of kids who are apt in the future to be mainstays of the country's economic strength.

- It fans the flames of victimhood and Washington-knows-best while making it easier for educators and parents to avoid responsibility for their students' achievements.

Even the education establishment is no longer of one mind. The American Federation of Teachers is troubled by the burdens that special education places on teachers. School boards are aggrieved by its soaring costs. Principals find school safety threatened by its double standards.

Desirable reforms are easy to sketch. Distribute federal block-grants via a formula that doesn't create perverse incentives. Permit states to close the program's open-ended entitlement and weigh special-education services against competing priorities. Roll back the rules (and bureaucracies) that substitute Washington's judg-

ments for those of teachers, parents, and school boards. Eliminate the double disciplinary standard. Restore the civil-rights protections to prohibitions against individual discrimination, not group benefits. Exempt innovative programs like charter schools. Quit paying lawyers' fees. Experiment with vouchers for parents.

Easily described, yes, but not easily done as long as the entire topic is avoided on Capitol Hill. Not even the intrepid House freshmen, in their bill to abolish the Education Department, were willing to touch special education. No presidential candidate has gone near it.

As for the Clinton team, its special-education bureau is headed by a long-time activist, and its civil-rights office by a litigious and enterprising enforcer. Between them, the Education Department grows ever more intrusive. A recent "monitoring report" on South Carolina's program faulted the state for not screening prison inmates to see if they need special-education services. They held an Alabama district to be discriminatory because resource classes for L.D. youngsters were held in a trailer.

They even hassle their own agency. They're pressing the National Assessment of Educational Progress to divert scarce resources into costly accommodations to enable more disabled youngsters to take its tests (though nobody expects such data to be comparable). Until members of Congress complained, they sought to restrict the government's popular "blue ribbon" schools competition to the handful of buildings that are fully "accessible."

Insofar as the program's excesses are buttressed by zealotry, its reform prospects are slim. But what about cowardice? Will political calamity truly befall all agents-of-change in this domain?

Perhaps not. The special-education population is about the same size as the Hispanic enrollment in U.S. public schools (and about as large as the total private-school enrollment). No member of Congress has high concentrations in his district, though none is without some such constituents. Every community and state has its own built-in special-education lobby. That is why some state laws go farther than the federal program and why today, even if Uncle Sam were to fold his tent, disabled youngsters would not be shut in closets or barred from school.

The governors have already signaled that they'd like to have more decisions returned to the states. So have state school superintendents. Allying those two powerful groups with teacher unions and school boards would yield some political "cover" for skittish Congressmen. If special-education reform were also harnessed to changes that benefit masses of non-disabled youngsters —e.g., vouchers, real block grants, or safer schools—such a coalition might wield serious clout.

Of course, the specter of tiny wheelchairs circling the Capitol in protest cannot be dismissed. Special-education advocates are expert at lathering the parents of disabled children into paroxysms of outrage and entreaty. And many of the kids tug at the heartstrings—and the TV screen.

The activists know this well and can be as cynical in using such assets as are partisans of other causes. That's why special education is a test of Congressional consistency and resolve. The reason to reform U.S. education, after all, is not to placate its producer interests and their lobbyists but to strengthen its quality for all children, disabled and non-disabled alike. Exempting one bloated bureaucratic remnant of the early Seventies from the norms of the late Nineties does nobody much good.

 Article Review Form at end of book.

How could the dilemma of the Maynard family, whose community must raise taxes to pay for their son's education in a special school, be avoided? What accounts for the increase in the number of students in special education, according to the author?

The Struggle to Pay for Special Ed.

Congress and the states have mandated help for the learning disabled but haven't put up the funds.

Sam Allis
Boston

Two years ago, the Maynard family of rural Union County, South Dakota, received a Christmas card that read, "A 1995 New Year's wish for you and your family: death and destruction." Since 1992, the family had been getting hate mail from their neighbors. At one point, the family's youngest son, Casey Maynard, then 5, was told by a preschool playmate that the Maynard's house was going to be burned down. "Mommy, why do they hate my brother?" he asked his mother.

His older brother Jonathan, now 21, is autistic and attends a private school in Connecticut. The annual tab, including as many as eight trips a year for his family to visit him, is about $125,000. And the cause of the community outrage was that the money for Jonathan's special education comes, under the legal requirements of the Individuals with Disabilities Education Act, from the budget of the local school district. There was an 80% increase in

the school budget, a quarter of which accounted for Jonathan's special-education needs, causing property taxes to shoot up some 55% in 1992.

School board meetings were scary for the Maynards. "It was like walking into a Klan meeting," recalls Cathy Maynard, Jonathan's mother. "People we lived beside for generations will no longer talk to us. We didn't choose the role. We did what any good parents would do."

While the venom facing the Maynard family is rare, the conflict that spawned it is not. Federal and state laws require educational help for children with a wide range of physical, cognitive and emotional disabilities. But having passed the bills that mandate this help, Congress and state legislatures across the country have been parsimonious with the money to pay the added costs. This leaves the financial burden on the localities and produces intense conflict between parents and school officials.

Parents of special-ed. children, for example, often suspect that schools try to deny their

kids the help they need, and to which they are legally entitled, in order to save money. School officials counter that onerous regulations force them to spend more time worrying about potential lawsuits than about education. They also fume at parents who solicit bogus diagnoses of learning disabilities so their children will get more attention.

"There is no fault," observes Dr. Melvin Levine, a North Carolina-based pediatrician and a nationally recognized expert on attention deficit disorder, one of the most common diagnoses requiring special help. "It's existential." Advances in medicine and psychology have vastly improved the identification of disabilities of all sorts in children. Technology is saving youngsters who 20 years ago would have perished at birth but today survive with profound learning problems. Children damaged by being born to drug-addicted mothers have added to the burden.

Last year 1 in 8 kids in the public school population, 5.4 million, were in special ed., up from

4.8 million five years earlier. In New York City the number of special-education kids has soared from 40,000 to 165,000 in the past two decades, even as total enrollment has declined by 100,000. Boston's special-ed. budget has almost doubled in the past eight years, from $65 million to $116 million, and now consumes almost a quarter of the total budget. Special-ed. spending nationally has doubled during the past 25 years to $30 billion, according to a yet unpublished report by the Washington-based Council for Educational Development and Research.

The federal special-ed. law enacted in 1975 was supposed to cover 40% of these costs. No such luck: last year the federal share of national spending for special education was a mere 7%. Every state now has its own special-ed. law as well, and support at that level varies. Massachusetts, which has one of the highest percentages of special-ed. students of any state in the country (11.1%), picked up only 17% of the costs last year. One way to reduce the burden, many believe, is to bring youngsters now taught in separate settings into regular classrooms. Under this inclusion approach, the special-education dollars follow the children. At Boston's Patrick O'Hearn Elementary School, for example, 20 of its 66 special-ed. children have significant handicaps that could gain them private placement. Yet they are taught in regular classrooms at great savings to taxpayers.

But inclusion is no fiscal panacea. O'Hearn principal William Henderson, himself legally blind, warns that it could be more expensive in the short run to carry out properly. Teachers must be retrained to work with special-ed. children, and additional staff will be needed to help. "Anything less is dumping," he says. Inclusion is also more manageable in elementary school, where the emphasis is on child development, than in high school, where students are judged by performance. "High school inclusion has little or no relevance in the lives of the severely disabled," says one high school special-ed. director in a Boston suburb. "The kids are often miserable because they have no friends except their tutors. I think parents are beginning to realize this."

Thomas Payzant, superintendent of the Boston school system, believes inclusion can be cost effective there only if he has control of the referrals for special-ed. evaluations now initiated by parents, teachers and other agencies. "We've gone from one extreme to the other in the last 25 years," says Payzant. "Now, if anything comes up, you refer the child. We have to get control of the front end, and we don't have that now."

Many referrals involve such learning disabilities as attention deficit disorder. North Carolina's Dr. Levine says that the methodology used is often "ridiculous" and that ADD misdiagnoses abound.

Ultimately, he says, special ed. is a resource-allocation issue. "We have to be honest," he argues. "Why can't a community say, 'Long-term therapy works, but we can't afford it'?"

As special-education budgets mushroom, some experts are looking for ways to soften the mandates. Edward Moscovitch, author of *Special Education, Good Intentions Gone Awry*, has one proposal. "I would have an ironclad provision that if a child is making reasonable progress in school, he doesn't get special ed., regardless of the disabilities," he says.

The good news is that huge strides have been made to improve the plight of special-needs students. "The question now being asked is how can we do it, as opposed to should we do it," says Judith Heumann, U.S. Assistant Secretary of Special Education and Rehabilitative Services.

The bad news is that the Maynards plan to move away from the farm that has been in their family for 120 years as soon as Jonathan has completed his program in Connecticut. "It's not getting better. We can't possibly bring him back," says Cathy Maynard. "We're lepers in our own community."

-With reporting by Julie Grace/Union County and Ann M. Simmons/Washington

 **Article Review Form at end of book.**

What does the author view to be the reason why each level of government wants to pass the cost of special education on to the other? According to the author, what accounts for the growth of students in the learning disabilities category in California?

Funded into Perpetuity

The real special education crisis is not rising costs, but student outcomes

David O. Krantz

David O. Krantz is the co-author of "A Failure of Vision," a white paper on special education funding written for the California legislature, and is a member of the board of directors of the CAC Network, a statewide organization that supports special education community-advisory committees. A former elementary teacher and school psychologist, he is the executive vice president of Consulting Psychologists Press Inc. in Palo Alto, Calif.

A more apt headline for *Education Week's* page-one story "States Rethink How to Pay for Special Education" (*Nov. 27, 1996*) might have been: "States Think of New Ways Not to Pay for Special Education." Evidently, officials have decided that if they can't fix the problems in special education, they can make it go away by a process of attrition.

Among the many problems now widely acknowledged as af-

flicting special education is the fact that fully half of the 5 million or so enrolled students, those in programs for the learning-disabled, do not receive an adequate education. To be fair, this singular failure is offset by the equally spectacular achievement of literally unlocking the doors of public education for hundreds of thousands of children who otherwise would have been denied such access.

But the fact that there was no mention of parents in the article on special-education costs is testimony to their continuing low status in the field. That the consumers of special education services are not participating in any meaningful way in the "rethinking" mentioned means that any new funding method is likely to preserve the status quo while perpetuating its attendant and profound problems.

As a consumer of special education services, I can see that the debate on funding is not guided by any real desire to reform special education. It is being driven by open challenges among educators on the sanctity of special education funding. In a era of declining resources, brought about by diminished confidence in the leaders of our educational enterprise, the money set aside for special education has become an all too tempting target.

Elegant rationales for sharing this money with other programs are being offered, chief among these the so-called need for more "flexibility." For the consumer skilled at reading between the lines, "flexibility" does not mean better education, it means less accountability. "Flexibility" is a code word that springs from a desire to escape the special education mandate. But the mandate did not dictate the rigid programs from which officials now seek relief. These programs, which evidently have become unmanageable in terms of cost, are entirely the invention of education bureaucrats.

The heart of the debate about funding is the sad fact that no one wants to pay for special education.

Indeed, the "rethinking" article depicts states and districts at each other's throats in a vigorous struggle to avoid special education costs. The reason for this is that many of our public officials do not now and never really have fully embraced their responsibility to educate all children.

The truth of this observation is demonstrated by the public confession last year, in the form of a judicial consent decree, by one of the largest special education programs in the nation to charges that it "pervasively and continuously failed to . . . serve the educational needs of children with disabilities" (*Chanda Smith* v. *Los Angeles Unified School District* Consultant's Report). It is noteworthy that this finding follows by more than 20 years the passage of the special education mandate, Public Law 94-142.

Is there enough money for special education? According to the article, special education policymakers do not seem to understand what causes special education costs to increase, or even if they really are increasing.This is not surprising. Here in California, we managed in a recent year to spend between $2.7 billion and $3.1 billion (the exact figure is not known) on special education, without the benefit of what would pass for a budget document.

It is hard to believe that policymakers don't know what causes special education costs to increase. Conceivably, they don't want to know. Among those who believe costs are skyrocketing, the fact that special education staffing over the past 20 years has grown at approximately twice the rate of the student population seems to have escaped attention.

Likewise, officials seem unable to understand the relationship between growth in programs and poorly conceived eligibility standards, so notoriously bad that children "qualified" for services in one state or location frequently won't be in another. This problem is compounded by the near-total absence of exit criteria. Only a tiny fraction of those growing numbers who enter special education ever leave. The consequences of this reality seem not to have been calculated.

Although rarely acknowledged, events outside special education can have a profound effect on enrollments. For example, while class size here in California was growing to one of the largest student-teacher ratios in the nation, we were charting a disastrous course toward a single method of teaching reading (whole language). In this same period, enrollments in programs for the learning-disabled increased by over 60,000. Officials in California have not made this connection, possibly because it would mean taking responsibility for mistakes made in regular education and then acknowledging these mistakes as chief causes for otherwise mysterious epidemics of learning disabilities.

Educators would have us believe that millions of children have trouble learning in school because of innate defects or disorders, not because of the way they are taught.These same officials prefer to believe that it is the children who cause special education costs to rise, rather than the way in which they have devised and manage the system.

However, once established, special education programs inevitably become "entitlements,"

> Educators would have us believe that millions of children have trouble learning in school because of innate defects or disorders, not because of the way they are taught.

not for children, many of whom pass through these programs untouched by a successful learning experience, but for the numerous professionals assembled to staff them. Such programs are funded into perpetuity, without regard for educational outcomes.

One way to determine if there is enough money for special education is to observe with our own eyes what districts actually do with their financial resources. Over the past few years, two California districts have together spent well over $1 million to, in one case, prevent the full inclusion of a child (the district lost) and, in the other, retaliate against a teacher who advocated for a child in need of special education services (a case that is on its way to the U.S. Supreme Court). These are not isolated examples. There appears to be plenty of money for special education but not necessarily for special education children.

If consumers were invited to the table to discuss special education funding, we would argue that the issue is not about limited funds. It is about what we are getting for the money. One measure is provided by the high-school graduation rate, which recently stood at a mere 30 percent for the more than 500,000 students with disabilities here in California.

Special education consumers have a clear understanding of what needs to change in special education. If our voice were heard, the focus would be on solutions to deeply entrenched and intractable problems. For starters, we would articulate the need to connect the funding for special education interventions to educational outcomes—a concept that appears beyond the grasp of our education leaders.

Last year, the steering committee of the California Coalition of Special Education Parent Groups sent a white paper to the California legislature that provided an analysis of special education funding written from the consumer perspective. Among the suggestions contained in this 30-page document is one to connect educational outcomes to funding by direct reimbursement of individualized-education-plan teams. Full reimbursement for actual costs would be conditional on agreement among members of the IEP team, including parents, that the program has met its educational objectives. A compelling advantage of this idea is elimination of the many layers of bureaucracy that stand between funding and the learner.

Dismayed state officials in California have ridiculed the idea as unworkable—one indication that we are on the right track. But the real reason for their anxiety is unstated. If adopted, this modest proposal would be a first step toward dismantling the special education bureaucracy. This is not what planners currently have in mind as they "rethink" special education funding.

 Article Review Form at end of book.

What is the authors' purpose in beginning and ending their article with the case of the student who kicked his pregnant mother, set fires, and shoplifted? Who do the authors view as being the beneficiaries of special education?

The Special Education Scandal

Back when Congress passed laws mandating special services for handicapped children, those services cost $1 billion a year. Twenty years later it's an unmonitored mess, costing hapless taxpayers some $60 billion a year.

Lisa Gubernick and Michelle Conlin

Jeremy Wartenberg kicked his pregnant mother. He set fires, lied and shoplifted. He swore at his teachers and threatened to kill his classmates. During his first year at the Capistrano Valley High School in southern California he failed every course from math to gym.

Diagnosed as needing special education services, Wartenberg was pulled out of his regular classes and given special tutoring at taxpayer expense. But Capistrano Unified School District administrators believed that he suffered no substantial learning disabilities, and they wanted to put him back in the regular classroom full time.

Unfair, insisted his forgiving parents, who enrolled him at a $20,000-a-year private school and hit the public school district up for the tab. After years of court wrangling, the school district ended up paying for everything—three years of private school tuition and legal fees for both sides, totalling $500,000. As we will see later, the money appears to have been wasted.

An eighth-grader in Jasper, Ala. entered the lunchroom a few years back, turned off the gas on the stove, blew out the pilot light and then turned the stove back on and waited for the place to explode—twice. It didn't, but the school expelled him. No way, said the parents: Their boy should have been identified as needing special education services. The hearing officer hired by the state agreed, the would-be demolition expert went back to class, and the school board was out over $20,000 in legal fees.

Such horror stories of wasted public funds are legion. The federal special education law, first passed more than two decades ago, was supposed to make public school education more accessible for blind, deaf and paraplegic children, as well as those with learning and emotional problems.

The idea was fairly simple: Under what's now called the Individuals with Disabilities Education Act, children with disabilities would be given tutors or other special help. Cost? Originally the program cost roughly $1 billion a year—a reasonable price for bringing millions of children into the mainstream.

Sadly, the program has become a costly failure. Worse, it can be a scandalous waste of money that might otherwise be used to improve public education.

Today so-called special education is costing taxpayers about $60 billion a year—the split is roughly $3 billion from the federal government, $57 billion from states and local districts. Of every dollar spent on education in the U.S., 20 cents goes to these programs. Per pupil, about twice as much is spent on the 5 million special education students than on the 52 million regular students.

These students impose an additional burden: Once a child is labeled as needing special education—regardless of whether for visual disabilities or "behavioral disorders"—he can't be expelled by the public school system, no matter how disruptive his behavior.

Is your kid's report card looking grim? Maybe he has "visual processing disorder," otherwise known as dyslexia. Maybe he gets into too many fights in class. Could be attention deficit disorder. Sign right up for special education—the taxpayers will foot the bill, including any legal fees you run up in winning the kind of schooling you want for your child.

"When we think of handicapped, we envision wheelchairs," says James Fleming, superintendent of the Capistrano Unified School District. "But the good intentions of this law have created chaos and anarchy in the administration of special education."

Fleming has had to battle lawyers who have demanded karate lessons for a kindergartner with an immune system disorder and school-paid trips to Disneyland for a child who was depressed. One attorney argued that a child who had seizures as the result of an operation to remove a brain tumor should be entitled to horseback riding lessons as rehabilitative therapy.

In an Austin, Tex. suburb, the mother of an emotionally disturbed child fought bitterly with the school that placed him in a special education class so he could be taught without disturbing the regular students. The mother disapproved of the teaching and wanted a new program

created, so she demanded her boy be pulled out of school.

Sad to say, a state-appointed officer agreed with the mother. The kid wound up with a private teacher plus an aide to restrain him when he got out of hand. Taxpayers also ended up with a $75,000 tab to cover the boy's six-month stay in a treatment center, plus $97,000 for the school's and the mother's legal fees.

Who profits? You guessed it. "Special education has become an ambulance—and the lawyers are chasing it," says Raymond Bryant, director of special education for Maryland's Montgomery County public schools.

Joan Honeycutt, a Tustin, Calif.-based attorney whose practice is almost exclusively special education cases, strikes fear in the pocketbooks of local school administrators. "At this point, when I see her name on a case, I just say, 'Fine, where do you want your kid to go?'" says Peter Hartman, superintendent of the 32,000-student Saddleback Unified School District in southern California. Honeycutt blames intransigent administrators for the problem. "They don't want to negotiate," she says. "They just want to be nasty."

Congress gave each state control over the process for determining if a child is eligible for special education, but most states follow the same general pattern: Once a parent decides his child might need special education, he informs the school district, which must test the child, generally within 50 days. Miss the deadline and the parents can take the case straight to a due process hearing, at which a third party listens to both sides and determines if the child is eligible.

> **"When we think of handicapped, we envision wheelchairs. But those good intentions have created chaos and anarchy."**

Next, parents, administrators and teachers meet to determine what kind of program the child needs. If the parents object, the case goes to a second hearing, which is not part of the judicial system per se; if the parents don't like that ruling, they can sue in local court. Discouraged by the waste of time and money, many school administrators simply surrender rather than fight. Robert Spoonemore, superintendent of Pflugerville Independent School District just outside of Austin, Tex., says: "Schools are now guilty until proven innocent."

No surprise that many smart, affluent parents use special education laws to demand special privileges for their kids. In one recent California case, parents with a multi-million-dollar land development operation wanted the local school system to pay for an $80,000-a-year residential school for their troubled child. "When we see parents who get involved with due process hearings, it's usually the ones who have the financial resources," says John Whritner, superintendent of the Greenwich, Conn. public schools.

"This is what gets stamped as justice, but it's robbing money from regular students," says Saddleback Unified School District's superintendent, Peter Hartman.

And while the U.S. Department of Education does some tracking of the performance of kids in special education, it monitors specific programs only sporadically. "There is this perception that the more money spent, the more services provided, the better off the child is, but no one knows," says Janet Beales, who has done several analyses of the special education system for the Los Angeles-based Reason Foundation, a market-based think tank.

The federal special education law is currently up for reauthorization, giving Congress a chance to curb its abuses. For starters, Congress could put a cap on special education spending. At the state level, New York Governor George Pataki has already advocated making such a change. This would eliminate such outrages as the one described in the box at right.*

A sharper line should be drawn between disability and disciplinary problems. Public schools should have the right to expel disruptive students regardless of whether or not they're disabled. Even the teachers' unions want the right to throw disruptive kids out.

Remember Jeremy Wartenberg, the kid who kicked his

*Does not appear in this publication.

pregnant mother and cost taxpayers $500,000 in special education money? In the last four years he's had a half-dozen convictions, on charges ranging from assault with a deadly weapon to petty theft to vandalism. He was sentenced to more than two years in prison.

 Article Review Form at end of book.

According to the author, what accounts for learning disabilities?
What is the author's main defense of special education?

Special Education Is Not a Scandal

While politicians and administrators work to dismantle the system, many disabled children who would once have been shut out of school are actually flourishing.

Brent Staples

Brent Staples writes editorials on politics and culture for The New York Times.

Before Congress intervened, public schooling for disabled children ranged from dismal to truly barbaric. As recently as the 1970's, they could be found strapped into their chairs and screaming, in conditions reminiscent of the Dark Ages. The picture changed with the Education for All Handicapped Children Act of 1975—since renamed the Individuals With Disabilities Education Act—which ordered the states to provide disabled children with "a free, appropriate public education." The effort to comply has been hellishly expensive, and disabled students still fail or drop out more often than they succeed.

But even with its problems, special education is spectacularly better than in the bad old days. Children who would once have been institutionalized or shut out of school are now educated under conditions that are enviable—even by affluent suburban standards. In New York City, for example, classes for regular students routinely exceed 35 students, with an overtaxed teacher who finds it difficult enough to learn the students' names. Depending on the disability, special-education classes can have as few as six children, tended by a teacher and as many as two teacher's aides. Children for whom public special education is judged to be inadequate—or whose parents have sued the school for failing to follow Federal law—are frequently sent to excellent private schools, with tuition and transportation costs paid by the state.

Faced with skyrocketing costs and wildly uneven results, nearly two-thirds of the states are sketching out plans to limit special-education spending. Most hope to save money by pushing disabled children out of the small, specialized classes that many of them need to succeed and into crowded, ill-equipped classrooms where they will compete with nondisabled peers. The process—often called mainstreaming or inclusion—is being justified by the civil rights notion that segregation of any kind is damaging and that diversity is an indisputable social good.

Researchers have yet to prove that mainstreaming is beneficial—or even that it does no harm. Still, educators who have watched children flourish in specialized settings are being urged to send them into regular classes. By dragging these children indiscriminately into the mainstream, we may actually be discarding them again—only this time in full public view.

About five and a half million children—between 11 and 12 percent of the school population—are categorized as disabled. The U.S. Department of Education estimates the cost of educating them at about $30 billion annually, up from about $1 billion 20 years ago. In New York City alone, the annual tab is $2 billion—22 percent of total education spending—to educate less than 13 percent of the children, with about three times as much spent on each full-time special-education student as on each general-education child.

Small, specialized classes cost more but are not the main problem. For starters, the special-education bureaucracy is many times larger than it needs to be.

A vast sum—probably hundreds of millions of dollars a year—is eaten up by Federally mandated evaluations that must be repeated far too often. The evaluations and the plans derived from them are useless in the classroom but have become a boondoggle for child-development specialists.

Federal record keepers list about a dozen disabilities in all, including visual and hearing impairments, autism, mental retardation, serious emotional disturbance and traumatic brain injury. The largest and most controversial group are those labeled learning disabled. These children make up slightly more than 50 percent of the special-education total—and their numbers have risen significantly over the last decade. The term learning disabled encompasses a wide range of problems but generally describes intelligent children who suffer no emotional impairment but find reading almost impossible without specialized instruction.

Conventional wisdom has it that human beings are neurologically wired to read and learn to do it automatically. But an ongoing, comprehensive study by the National Institutes of Health is telling a far different story. Begun in the 1960's, the N.I.H. study shows that 4 in 10 children have trouble learning to read. About half of these children have such grave difficulty that they fall behind early in school and stay behind.

In the most extreme cases, children appear to have abnormal activity in the parts of the brain that process phonemes—the basic sounds that correspond to the letters of the alphabet. The simplest rules of language elude them. When asked for a word that rhymes with "cat," for example, they have no idea what the question means. They stumble over words like "it" and "the." The disorder affects children of all cultural backgrounds and intelligence levels. It strikes those who were read to as infants as well as those who grew up without a book in sight.

One of the strongest arguments against mainstreaming such children is that less than a quarter of American teachers know how to teach reading to children who do not get it automatically. Successful mainstreaming would take a huge retraining effort, in addition to fundamental changes at teachers' colleges.

Learning-disabled children tend to do poorly in public schools, and often their problems go undiagnosed. Ashamed of failure, they act out in class, become truant and eventually drop out. The luckiest children are those whose disabilities are detected early and who are sent to special private schools where teachers drill them in the fundamentals of language. The children are walked through the alphabet again and again, learning to connect the letters to the sounds, the sounds to the syllables, the syllables to words and so on. The method—called phonics—was popular until the 1970's, when the "whole language" craze erupted. Whole-language enthusiasts taught that children were naturally disposed to reading and writing and learned those skills just as they learned to speak. Students were encouraged to wander through books and stories—making up "creative" spellings when they needed to.

Whole language made reading and writing fun for children who grasped them automatically. But it jettisoned the drill-and-practice component that 40 percent of American children need to learn reading. It should come as no surprise that the number of children described as learning disabled exploded during the 1980's.

Policy makers routinely see learning disabilities as either fictional—cooked up by the schools in search of increased state subsidies—or as "minor" disorders that warrant less concern than, say, blindness or deafness. But studies based on Government data show that about 43 percent of learning-disabled children leave school without diplomas and that an enormous number of them end up in jail soon afterward. Fewer than 2 percent of them go on to four-year colleges—as compared with about 28 percent of students who are visually impaired and 15 percent of the deaf.

The myth of mildness has led to many questionable assumptions, among them the idea that learning-disabled children can be successfully educated in regular classes as long as they are allowed occasional trips to a specialist. But a child who leaves class several times a week for special reading instruction will miss math, science or whatever is offered while he is away. Depending on the number of absences, the missing lessons could loom large in the child's education. Add in travel time and the ordinary shock of dislocation and the school day evaporates. In addition, school administrators watching their budgets are notoriously stingy with expensive special services, no matter how emphatically teachers or clinicians recommend them. As those services become optional, they will be withheld.

The clearest case against this approach is that of Shannon Carter, a special-education student who won a landmark decision in the Supreme Court four years ago. The public schools of

Florence County, South Carolina, had labeled Shannon lazy and unmotivated and allowed her to reach ninth grade with an undetected learning disability that had left her nearly illiterate. As she prepared to enter 10th grade, Shannon was actually reading at a fifth-grade level—and falling behind in virtually every subject. Distraught, Shannon attempted suicide. She was finally found to have a learning disability. School officials offered the typical mainstream formula of full-time regular classes with a few hours of special education a week. The Carters were dissatisfied and subsequently removed her from public school and placed her in a private academy, where she jumped several grade levels and graduated reading on par.

The family sued for the cost of tuition. Ruling unanimously for the Carters, the Supreme Court warned public schools that they had only two choices: educate learning-disabled children in accordance with the law or foot the bill for private-school tuition. Instead of strengthening special-education programs, the states have embarked on a campaign to define learning disabilities out of existence.

On children's television, the kid in the wheelchair has become a kind of mascot, beloved by all in his gang. But imagine a real-life classroom where all of the children are nondisabled except the one who drools uncontrollably, who hears voices or who can't read a simple sentence when everyone else can. Diversity is a noble ideal. But many disabled children would be marginalized and ridiculed in the mainstream.

The mainstreamers argue that special education was never intended as a permanent place for any except the most profoundly handicapped students. For most children, it was supposed to be an educational pit stop where they developed the skills they needed for full participation. This is true as far as it goes. But the central goal was always to educate children who had traditionally been viewed as ineducable. Integration was an important but distinctly secondary objective.

The danger for disabled students lies less in the specialized classes that allow at least some of them to succeed than in the widespread expectation that they cannot learn and are supposed to fail. Society needs to worry a good deal more about what these children are taught and a good deal less about who sits next to them in class.

 **Article Review Form at end of book.**

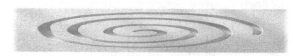

WiseGuide Wrap-Up

- Twenty years after the federal law that established the right of all children with disabilities to a free and appropriate education, special education is the focus of fierce debate. Because of rising costs and questions about its efficacy, the value of special education is currently being challenged.

- A major outcome of the debate about special education is increased support for the notion of inclusive education.

- This approach is based on the idea that students, regardless of their disability, should be educated in classrooms with their same-age peers and receive support services in the classroom.

R.E.A.L. Sites

This list provides a print preview of typical **coursewise** R.E.A.L. sites. (There are over 100 such sites at the **courselinks**™ site.) The danger in printing URLs is that web sites can change overnight. As we went to press, these sites were functional using the URLs provided. If you come across one that isn't, please let us know via email to: webmaster@coursewise.com. Use your Passport to access the most current list of R.E.A.L. sites at the **courselinks**™ site.

Site name: Office of Special and Rehabilitation Services

URL: http://www.ed.gov/offices/OSERS/

Why is it R.E.A.L.? This site describes the Office of Special and Rehabilitation Services, and its functions; OSERS oversees the Office of Special Education Programs, Rehabilitation Services, and the National Institute on Disability and Rehabilitation Research.

Key topics: law, rehabilitation services, research, government, Individuals with Disabilities Education Act

Activity: Find the text of the IDEA and identify which disabilities are covered by it.

Site name: The Office of Special Education Programs

URL: http://www.ed.gov/offices/OSERS/OSEP/index.html

Why is it R.E.A.L.? This web page describes this federal government agency and the special-education–related programs that the agency funds.

Key topics: government

Activity: Find the programs funded by OSEP and identify their purposes.

Site name: The Eighteenth Annual Report to Congress

URL: http://www.ed.gov/pubs/OSEP96AnlRpt/

Why is it R.E.A.L.? This site gives you the text of the 18th annual report to Congress on the implementation of the Individuals with Disabilities Education Act. This report identifies the successes and failures of special education in the United States as of 1996.

Key topics: government, Individuals with Disabilities Education Act, law

Activity: In the text of the report, identify the positive results of IDEA, as reported by the Office of Special Education Programs.

Site name: The Federal Resource Center for Special Education

URL: http://www.dssc.org/frc/index.htm

Why is it R.E.A.L.? This web page describes IDEA, discusses trends in special education, and presents news related to special education services around the country.

Key topics: Individuals with Disabilities Education Act, law

Activity: What are the current issues that are "In The News"?

....

Site name: The National Center to Improve the Tools of Educators

URL: http://darkwing.uoregon.edu/~ncite/index.html

Why is it R.E.A.L.? This site describes the National Center, whose function is to help writers, curriculum developers, and publishers create materials to serve students with disabilities, with particular emphasis on technological tools for instruction.

Key topics: technology, curriculum

Activity: Find the "Learning to Read/Reading to Learn" campaign. What is it about?

....

section

3

Learning Objectives

After studying this section, the reader will:

- Understand the purposes of vocational education and vocational rehabilitation for persons with disabilities.

- Identify ways in which special education teachers can promote vocational education and vocational rehabilitation for their students.

- Know how special education, vocational education, and vocational rehabilitation programs can collaborate with each other and with families.

- Know the various ways in which the workplace is likely to change in the future and how students with special needs should be prepared to join it.

- Understand how changes in the workplace will affect the role of special needs personnel.

- Know how special educators can help students with disabilities prepare for the transition to college.

The Transition to Adulthood Challenges for the Exceptional Individual

 **WiseGuide Intro**

One of the most difficult transitions for students with disabilities is from high school to the adult world. For some, this is the transition from school to work. For others, it is the transition from school to college. In both transitions, students with disabilities are forced to confront the real-life implications of their disabilities in an environment that is less familiar and where new demands are placed on them.

In part, the difficulty students have in making the transition is due to the supervision and attention students receive in high school. In the workplace and in college, the worker or the student is expected to function more independently. For some students, going to college also means moving away from home and taking greater responsibility for their own life. We know that many students with disabilities do not go to college and some who do drop out before completing their degree. We also know that the unemployment rate among individuals with disabilities is far higher than the unemployment rate of the nondisabled. Consequently, special educators must pay special attention to their role in preparing their students for the transition to adulthood.

In "Preparing Students for Transition," Carol A. Dowdy and Rebecca B. Evers describe vocational education and vocational rehabilitation for individuals with disabilities; they examine referral, eligibility, assessment, services, and curricula of each.

The next two articles are focused on the workplace of the future. In "Beyond 2000: Preparing Individuals from Special Populations for the Next Millennium," Jerry L. Wircenski and Michelle D. Wircenski predict how the workplace of the future will look and they discuss the implications of these changes for the preparation of students with disabilities. In "Meeting the Needs of Special Populations in the 21st Century," Patricia S. Lynch and Judy Reimer explore how changes in the workplace affect the function of special educators.

Finally, Barbara C. Gartin, Phillip Rumrill, and Riqua Serebreni, in "The Higher Education Transition Model," present an approach for the preparation of students with disabilities for college life, focusing on the academic development and psychosocial adjustment of the students in their new environment.

66

Questions

R14. What is the role of the special education teacher in preparing students for vocational education and rehabilitation? What are the different purposes of vocational education and vocational rehabilitation for the student who is disabled?

R15. According to the authors, what is the largest trend that we can expect in the workplace of the future? What role do the authors see for business in the preparation of individuals with disabilities for the world of work?

R16. The authors note an advance in the access to services and the participation in career education among special education populations. Given these developments, why do they advocate change? How does the inclusion of students with special needs into school-to-work programs affect the work of special needs personnel?

R17. How can special educators prepare students with disabilities for the psychosocial adjustment to college? Why do you think the authors stress college and community orientation so strongly?

What is the role of the special education teacher in preparing students for vocational education and rehabilitation? What are the different purposes of vocational education and vocational rehabilitation for the student who is disabled?

Preparing Students for Transition

A teacher primer on vocational education and rehabilitation

**Carol A. Dowdy
and Rebecca B. Evers**

Carol A. Dowdy, EdD, is an associate professor of special education at the School of Education at the University of Alabama. Rebecca B. Evers, EdD, is an assistant professor of special education in the Center for Pedagogy at Winthrop University in Rock Hill, South Carolina. Address: Carol A. Dowdy, School of Education, University of Alabama, UAB Station, Birmingham, AL 35243.

The reauthorization of the Individuals with Disabilities Education Act (IDEA) of 1990 mandates the provision of a coordinated set of transition activities within an outcome-oriented process for all secondary students who have an Individualized Education Program (IEP). School should incorporate these services into each student's IEP through a process of formal transition planning that includes the designation of interagency responsibilities and/or linkages when appropriate. In the planning stage, educators and other agency and program personnel can coordinate secondary school coursework, related activities, work experiences, responsibilities at home, and community participation to maximize a student's readiness for postschool settings. Certainly, the degree to which students access and succeed in postsecondary settings is to a large extent a result of their secondary programming (DeStefano & Wermuth, 1992). The effectiveness of the secondary programming may depend on the teacher's ability to effectively collaborate with personnel from the community, other agencies, and vocationally oriented programs.

The purpose of this article is to provide information that will facilitate the special education teacher's linkages with two important employment-oriented programs: vocational education and vocational rehabilitation. We provide an overview of each program and address the referral process, eligibility, the range of services and programs available, preparation of students for entry into vocational education and vocational rehabilitation, and tips for interagency collaboration.

Program Overviews

Vocational education is a program available in public school settings to develop specific occupational skills for secondary students in general and special education. Vocational rehabilitation is a program that assists eligible adults with disabilities in employment and integration into society to the maximum extent possible.

Although differences exist between vocational education and vocational rehabilitation, both programs have much to contribute to the successful transition of students with disabilities. Teachers should know about these two programs so they can

- Refer students appropriately;
- Describe services and programs available to students;
- Prepare students to successfully participate; and
- Collaborate effectively with personnel in vocational education and vocational rehabilitation programs.

Next, we describe the mission and goals of each program, the basic administrative patterns, and the current utilization of services and outcome data for students with disabilities.

Vocational Education

The purpose of vocational education is to provide opportunities for persons to develop occupational competencies through sequential educational instruction and training appropriate for their abilities and needs. Cobb and Neubert (1992) described the following five broad goals for secondary vocational education:

a. acquisition of personal skills and attitudes;

b. communication and computational skills and technological literacy;

c. employability skills;

d. broad and specific occupational skills and knowledge; and

e. foundations for career planning and lifelong learning. (p. 93)

The overall goal of placing students in vocational education is to develop fundamental, academic, and employability skills for the world of work in a vocational area of their interest.

Traditionally, vocational education has been seen as the most realistic method of assisting persons in making the transition from education to employment. Ensuring free and equal access to vocational education programs for individuals with disabilities has been incorporated in landmark legislation. The Education for All Handicapped Children Act of 1975, IDEA, and the Rehabilitation Act of 1973 (Section 504) mandate that educational programs and facilities, including vocational education and training programs at the secondary and postsecondary levels, may not discriminate against persons with disabilities solely on the basis of their disability. Further, institutions may not discriminate in recruitment and admissions practices or provision of reasonable support services, accommodations, and modifications to the course requirements and facilities.

Typically, vocational education in secondary public schools is administered by individual states through a department of vocational education. States may apply for funds through the U.S. Department of Education's Office of Vocational and Adult Education. The provisions of the 1990 Carl C. Perkins Vocational Education and Applied Technology Act eliminated previously set aside funds; now funds are directed to school districts where special populations are highly concentrated. For example, within school districts, 70% of the allocation is based on the number of economically disadvantaged students, 20% on the number of students with disabilities, and 10% on the overall number of students enrolled in vocational education. For postsecondary schools, the allocation is based on the number of economically disadvantaged students who are eligible under Pell Grants. The responsibility for determining how monies are spent falls to the local vocational and community college administrators.

Another important legislative action with a significant impact on the administration of vocational education programs is the reappropriation of the Perkins Act. Congress and the U.S. Department of Education are negotiating the renewal of the Perkins Act to take effect mid-1997. The U.S. Department of Education is attempting to increase the support services (e.g., Braille tests and teachers' aides) provided to special populations in vocational education classes. Vocational education administrators, however, believe that an expansion of support services will deplete program improvement funds and reduce the overall quality of vocational education programs ("Congress Blocks," 1994). In addition, some members of Congress wish to combine vocational education and job training programs while converting them to state block grants ("House, Senate," 1995). The new laws would supersede the Perkins Act.

Despite federal policy aimed at increasing the participation of students with disabilities in vocational programs, local implementation has resulted in the shrinking of programs and services (Kochlar & Deschamps, 1992). Specifically, the results may be (a) the elimination of special needs positions at the state and local level, (b) a shift of vocational education dollars to academics, (c) the elimination of vocational assessment and evaluation services, and (d) a shift of secondary vocational education funds to postsecondary programs (where there is no legal requirement to provide special education services under IDEA). This trend is all the more alarming in view of the proposed conversion to state block grants of many programs that currently are federally funded.

Vocational Rehabilitation

The purpose of vocational rehabilitation (VR) is to empower individuals with disabilities to achieve gainful employment consistent with their strengths, priorities, concerns, resources, and informed choices. This purpose is stated in the Rehabilitation Act of 1973 (amended in 1992 and 1993), which guides vocational rehabilitation services much as IDEA guides the special education service delivery system. The purpose of the Act is to assist states to deliver a comprehensive, coordinated vocational rehabilitation program designed to empower individuals with disabilities to maximize employment, economic self-sufficiency, independence, and inclusion and integration into society. These goals are pursued through comprehensive, state-of-the-art vocational rehabilitation programs, independent living centers, research, training, demonstration projects, and the guarantee of equal opportunity.

The legislation focuses on promoting meaningful and gainful employment and independent living in individuals with disabilities, especially individuals with severe disabilities (see Section 2(b)(1)(2)).

The Act mandates the following principles:

- Individuals with disabilities are presumed to be capable of engaging in gainful employment and benefiting from VR services;

- Opportunities for employment must be provided in integrated settings;

- Individuals with disabilities must be active participants in their own rehabilitation programs, making meaningful and informed choices in the selection of personal vocational goals and VR services they receive;

- Families or other natural supports can play a significant role in the VR process;

- Individuals with disabilities and their advocates are full partners in the VR program and must be involved in a meaningful manner and on a regular basis in policy development and implementation. (Section 100 (a)(2))

The federal government provides VR leadership and technical assistance to the states. It also provides 78% matching funds to the states for program implementation. Each state agency offers direct assistance to individuals with disabilities through local VR officials and individual counselors assigned to specific geographical areas or specific areas of disability.

Anyone who is familiar with an individual with a disability—or the individual him- or herself—can make a referral to vocational rehabilitation. After the appropriate VR counselor is identified, an initial interview is held to gather information about the disability and the person's work history. This begins the process necessary to determine the individual's eligibility for VR services. The assessment process will be described later in more detail; however, it includes assessing the individual's education and training, strengths, interests, work history, vocational rehabilitation needs, and employment goals (Dowdy & McCue, 1994). When eligibility is approved, the counselor and the individual (or the representative of the individual) develop an Individualized Written Rehabilitation Program (IWRP). According to the 1992 amendments to the Vocational Rehabilitation Act, each IWRP shall

a. be designed to achieve the employment objective consistent with the unique strengths, resources, priorities, abilities, capabilities, and concerns of the individual;

b. include the long-term goals determined by assessment;

c. include the degree to which the goals can be accomplished in integrated settings;

d. identify the short-term rehabilitation objectives related to the long-term goals;

e. include the specific services to be provided by VR and the dates of services anticipated;

f. include technological services if appropriate;

g. include specific on-the-job and related personal

assistance services to be provided;

h. include the need for post-employment services;

i. include how the services will be provided through cooperative agreements with other agencies or through VR personnel; and

j. include evaluation procedures and criteria for determining if the goals have been met.

The IWRP must also document that the individual was informed about choices and involved personally in determining goals, objectives, services, and service providers. The IWRP, which is signed by the individual or the individual's representative, must be reviewed and updated annually with any changes approved by all parties.

The 1992 amendments to the Act mandate collaboration with community agencies and specifically refer to special education services. Although there is no age criterion in the VR program, the typical age to begin services is 16. The 1992 amendments to the Act include the same definition of transition services as that used in IDEA, so VR counselors are also provided legislation to work with school personnel to agree on a coordinated set of activities needed for successful transition. Both agencies mandate that this program be based on the individual's choices, needs, and interests.

Referral and Eligibility

Vocational Education

Procedures for students to enter vocational classrooms and programs vary among school districts. Students may elect to take vocational courses or be so advised by guidance counselors in comprehensive high schools. In the case of students with disabilities, decisions regarding vocational programs may be part of the annual IEP meeting or written into the Transition Plan.

The legislative support for vocational education of students with disabilities provided through various federal acts may have affected the inclusion of students with disabilities in vocational education programs. Students with disabilities have had difficulty in completing high school as well as vocational education courses (U.S. Department of Education, 1994b; Wagner, 1991). However, these data should be interpreted carefully, because enrollment in general has decreased for vocational education (U.S. Department of Education, 1994a). More than half of the vocational teachers surveyed indicated that the status of vocational education was a serious problem in their school, and 47% responded that maintaining vocational enrollments was also a serious problem. This may be a direct result of increased pressure on nondisabled students to take more academically oriented high school programs. As states have raised graduation requirements to include more mathematics, science, and other academic classes, and as college admission standards have increased the requirements for foreign languages, mathematics, and science, the number of elective credit hours available for high school students to select vocational education has been reduced.

Further, gender and ethnic background appear to have an effect on accessibility to vocational education (Wagner, 1991). Although young men and women with disabilities were equally likely to have enrolled in vocational courses, young men spent significantly more time than young women in occupationally oriented courses (Wagner, 1991). These differences were apparent regardless of disability category. Similarly, Wagner (1991) found that White students were significantly more likely to have taken occupationally oriented courses than were African-American students.

Another major factor determining accessibility of vocational programs has to do with the structure of most secondary vocational programs. Enrollment in vocational programs at most high schools is reserved for juniors and seniors (Cobb & Neubert, 1992) and, in most secondary schools, the vocational education classes are considered electives (P. L. Sitlington, personal communication, September 16, 1994). If students with disabilities have dropped out in or before 10th grade (Wagner, 1991; Zigmond & Thorton, 1985) or have not had time in their programs for electives, then these programs are accessible too late in the students' school careers to have a beneficial effect on their school progress.

Vocational Rehabilitation

As noted, an individual with a disability can self-refer to a vocational rehabilitation agency, or any person familiar with the individual who has a disability can make the referral. High school teachers account for a large number of referrals to the VR agency. Each high school teacher should contact the local VR agency and determine the counselor assigned to the region or high school. It is helpful to keep an ongoing relationship with the VR counselor by inviting him or her into the classroom to meet all students. If possible, the teacher should hold an additional meeting where VR counselors can meet with parents of students with disabilities. As soon as the referral is made, the counselor will hold an interview to begin the assessment process. During this process, information is gathered to assist the counselor in determining eligibility.

Eligibility in the vocational rehabilitation system is different from the eligibility process in the vocational education system. In the VR system, the presence or diagnosis of a learning disability does not automatically entitle one for services (Abbott, 1987). However, the 1992 amendments to the Rehabilitation Act have made eligibility for VR services much more accessible to individuals with disabilities.

The amendments state that an individual must

(1) have a physical or mental impairment that results in a substantial impediment to employment;

(2) be able to benefit from vocational rehabilitation services in terms of employment; and,

(3) require vocational rehabilitation services to prepare for, enter, engage in, or retain gainful employment. (Section 102(a)(1))

The VR counselor is solely responsible for reviewing assessment data and determining eligibility for VR services. Counselors first look at the current assessment data available, and if those data are not sufficient, additional testing can be requested. Frequently, counselors rely on other agencies such as the education agency to obtain information. Important sources of information might include school history, medical and developmental his-

tory, psychological and neuropsychological testing, opinions from teachers and past employers, interviews with parents, vocational evaluations, and situational assessments (McCue, 1994).

The counselor is required to determine eligibility within 60 days after the individual has applied for services. The 1992 amendments to the Rehabilitation Act state that individuals are presumed to be able to benefit from VR services in terms of employment unless the state VR agency can demonstrate by clear and convincing evidence that the individual is not capable of benefiting. These changes in legislation have brought significant increases in VR acceptance rates. In the first 6 months of 1995, 75.7% of all applicants to VR were determined to be eligible. This represents a significant increase over the years prior to 1992 (Mars, 1995). With this tremendous increase in eligibility, counselors may have increasingly large caseloads, which may create an impasse to service delivery in the system. If an individual feels that his or her rights have not been protected or that he or she has not been treated fairly by the vocational rehabilitation system, that person is entitled to a fair hearing by an impartial hearing officer, and/or assistance from the Client Assistance Program (CAP) located in each VR state agency.

In approximately half the states, the VR agencies have determined that all eligible individuals cannot be served due to limited funds, and agencies have initiated an order of selection that provides services first to those individuals determined to be most severely disabled. The criteria for determining severity are established by each state within the guidelines of the 1992 amendments to the Act. An individual

with a severe disability is defined as an individual

(1) who has a severe physical or mental impairment which seriously limits one or more functional capacities such as communication, self-care, mobility, self-direction, interpersonal skills, work tolerance or work skills in terms of employment outcomes;

(2) whose vocational rehabilitation is expected to require multiple vocational rehabilitation services over an extended period of time;

(3) who has one or more physical disabilities resulting from such conditions as mental retardation, mental illness, Multiple Sclerosis, Muscular Dystrophy, Neurological Disorders (including strokes and epilepsy), paraplegia, quadriplegia, specific learning disabilities, or a combination of disabilities based on a valid evaluation of functional limitations and vocational potential. (Section 7(15)(a))

Once eligibility has been determined, the individual, the counselor, and family members or significant others get together to write the IWRP. Following is a discussion of the options that might be available to an individual through the vocational rehabilitation agency and the vocational education programs.

Services/Curricula

Vocational Education

Assessment. One of the most important services available in vocational education is assessment. The purpose of a vocational assessment is to collect and analyze information that will facilitate the development of goals and objectives for transition planning, including vocational program planning. This assessment should be a comprehensive, ongoing process, and data should be collected throughout the student's high school career. To assure appropriate placement in 9th-grade programs, assessment should begin during the 8th-grade year. Additional assessments should be completed at other strategic decision-making times, such as the beginning of 10th grade. Assessment should include a comprehensive profile of the student's strengths and limitations as well as interests and transition goals. The following components should be included in a vocational education assessment of students with mild disabilities (see Table 1 for an outline of assessment tools for both vocational education and vocational rehabilitation).

1. *Cumulative Data Review:* To begin, information may be obtained by reviewing cumulative records kept in a student's special education folder: attendance records, transcripts, teacher observations, recent psychological and medical evaluations, and current IEPs and Multidisciplinary Staffing Reports.

2. *Career Interest Inventory:* The purpose of career interest inventories is to gain information about the activities a person does or does not like to do and to assess occupational preferences. Information can be obtained using normed interest tests or informal activities with commercially available workbooks that have self-report inventories and checklists (see Brolin, 1995, and Cronin & Patton, 1993, for

comprehensive listings of publishers and products).

3. *Aptitude and Ability Testing:* In testing a student's aptitude, the purpose is to assess the person's capacity to learn a new activity. Certainly, information from psychological tests can be used here but, more importantly, tests designed to measure specific aptitudes such as mechanical and clerical should be administered.

To test a student's natural and/or acquired ability to perform various activities, assessment should include measuring the student's abilities in reading, mathematics, language, and daily living skills. Further, testing may include fine/gross motor coordination, dexterity, and tool usage. Again, information from psychological evaluations as well as the school district's group tests may be used. Situational evaluations and parent and teacher observations can provide valuable information regarding a student's ability to perform specific tasks. Finally, commercially prepared tests are available to test a student's ability to perform specific occupational skills.

4. *Interviews:* Interviews of the student, parents, and teachers can provide important information for planning. When talking with the student, the interviewer should collect information regarding current interests, hobbies, part-time or summer jobs held, and types of chores or tasks performed at home and school. Certainly, the classes and teachers liked the most and the least would provide insight regarding possible career interests. Students should be questioned about their ability to discuss

how their disability affects their lives. Finally, the interview should include some discussion of future personal goals and dreams (see Figure 1 for a sample student interview form).

When interviewing the parents, the interviewer should collect information regarding the strengths, limitations, and educational needs of their adolescent (see the sample parent interview form in Figure 2). During the teacher interviews, questions should focus on the student's functioning in the classroom, including functioning in both the cognitive and affective domains. If a vocational placement is being considered, information regarding the student's work-related behavior is critical, such as motivation, organizational skills, attention span, classroom conduct, and frustration level (see Figure 3 for a sample teacher interview form).

The above activities will provide the foundation of information necessary for beginning transition planning for most students with mild disabilities. However, in some cases, students may have difficulty expressing or identifying their interests and abilities. Additional information may be collected by using instruments and inventories designed to assess learning styles, values, career maturity, and job readiness.

Also, for students who have severe academic deficits and moderate to severe physical/mental disabilities, work samples and work evaluation systems may be used. Such testing requires a person trained as a vocational assessment specialist or trained to use the instruments selected.

Finally, for students who have extremely limited mental, physical, or emotional abilities,

Table 1 Description of Instruments Used in Vocational Assessments

Instrument	Type	Assessor	Population	Description
Wide Range Interest Opinion Test (Jastak & Jastak, 1979)	Interest	Teacher, teacher aide	Ages 5–Adult; all but most severe disabilities	150 questions, untimed & forced-choice; uses pictures; results provide both high- & low-interest choices
Janus Job Planner (Jew & Tong, 1987)	Interest	Student	High school to adult	Workbook; paper-and-pencil activities
Talent Assessment Program (TAP; Talent Assessment, Inc., n.d.)	Aptitude	Trained paraprofessional	Grade 8 to adult; all but multiply disabled	Scores given for visualizing structural detail; sorting skills (size/shape, color, texture); use of small/large tools; and memory
Armed Services Vocational Aptitude Battery (Department of Defense, n.d.)	Aptitude	School counselor	High school to adult; requires sixth-grade reading	Comprehensive data regarding aptitude for specific occupations
Practical Assessment Exploration System (PAES; Talent Assessment, Inc., n.d.)	Work sample	Teachers, paraprofessionals	Middle school to adult; all populations of disability	Simulated work situations; used for both evaluation and assessment of job-related skills
Vineland Adaptive Behavior Scales (Sparrow, Balla, & Cicchetti, 1985)	Functional skills	Parents, teachers	All populations with disabilities	Interview and survey format to determine skill level in four domains; communication, daily living skills, socialization, & motor skills
Prevocational Assessment & Curriculum Guide (Mithaug, Mar, & Stewart, 1978)	School & work skills	Teachers, paraprofessionals	All populations	Assesses 46 school & workshop expectations in 9 areas; curriculum guide assists writing instructional goals

for whom the appropriate placement might be day training in a community setting or supported and/or sheltered employment, interviews, paper-and-pencil assessment, and work samples may not present an accurate measure of competency. The assessment of these students should include evaluation of functional living skills and job simulations. Although the assessment of functional living skills can be conducted in a classroom, the job simulations and production work samples should be conducted outside the school setting.

After completing the assessments, a report should be prepared for the transition planning meeting. Presenting the information in a format that will facilitate the planning process is vital. In addi-tion, this information will assist in planning service delivery to support the student who is enrolled in a mainstream vocation class.

Curricula. The curriculum of typical high school vocational programs usually encompasses several components. Specific skill instruction would include auto-motive, wood, or metal work; cooking, sewing, or childcare; and computer keyboarding or book-keeping. Work-training programs are conducted in cooperation with local business, and student voca-tional organizations are there to provide needed assistance and support.

Vocational Rehabilitation

Assessment. The 1992 amend-ments to the Rehabilitation Act specifically state that the VR assess-ment process must be comprehen-sive enough to determine eligibil-ity, provide a diagnosis, identify vocational rehabilitation needs, identify any needs for technology services, and develop the IWRP. For VR purposes, it is important to determine the strengths, abilities, resources, and needs of an individual. Assessment should also determine the need for supportive employment. To deter-mine eligibility, the counselor must have a comprehensive assessment of all areas suspected to pose a vo-cational limitation. Areas of assess-ment might include interests, interpersonal skills, personality, ed-ucation achievements, intelligence, and related functional capacities; vocational attitudes; personal and social adjustments; and employ-ment opportunities. In addition,

DIRECTIONS: *Interview the student and record responses.*

A. ATTITUDE TOWARD DISABILITY

1. Tell me about your disability.
2. Are you in a special education program? Which one? Why
3. How do you feel about this program? Is it helpful?

B. INTERESTS IN LEISURE ACTIVITIES

1. What do you do in your spare time? Sports? Hobbies? Church? Extracurricular clubs at school?
2. What chores do you do at home?
3. Do you have friends? What do you and your friends do together?
4. On a perfect Saturday, what would you do?

C. FAMILY RELATIONSHIPS

1. What do you like best about your family?
2. Who usually helps you with schoolwork or other problems?
3. Is there anything that causes difficulties for you at home?

D. FUNCTIONAL SKILLS

1. If you had a job, how would you get to work?
2. Who selects your clothes?
3. Do you shop alone for your personal things?
4. Do you have an allowance or personal money from a job?
5. If you were home alone at dinner time, what would you eat and what would you do to prepare this meal?
6. If you had $1000, what would you buy?

E. EDUCATIONAL INTERESTS

1. What classes would you like to take? Would you like to include vocational classes?
2. Of all the classes you have taken, which one(s) was the best? Why?
3. Do you want to go to school after high school? Where?
4. What do your parents want you to do after high school?

F. WORK AND CLASS PREFERENCES

1. What teachers do you like best? Why? Least? Why?
2. Do you like to work alone or in a group?
3. When you work, do you like to sit most of the time or move around?
4. Do you prefer to work inside or outside?
5. Do you like to work on a computer?
6. Do you like to help people? Or work with things?

G. OCCUPATIONAL AND CAREER AWARENESS

1. Name as many jobs as you can. (time limit: 2 minutes)
2. Where do you begin to find a job?
3. What are some reasons people get fired?
4. What should you do when you are going to be absent or late to work?

H. FUTURE PLANS

1. What will you be doing during the next year, in 5 years, in 10 years toward the following postschool outcomes?

   Employment:

   Education:

   Living arrangements:
2. Will you need help meeting your goals? Which one(s)?
3. Where would you get the help you need?
4. What concerns you most about the future?

Figure 1. Sample student interview form. (This form may be photocopied for noncommercial use only. Copyright © 1996 by PRO-ED, Inc.)

DIRECTIONS: *Interview the parent who is the primary caregiver and record his or her responses.*

A. ATTITUDE TOWARD CHILD'S DISABILITY

1. Tell me about your child's disability. What are your child's strengths? Limitations?
2. Is your child in a special education program? Which one? Why?
3. How do you feel about this program? Is it helpful?

B. FAMILY RELATIONSHIPS

1. What are your family's strengths?
2. Who usually helps your child with schoolwork or other problems?
3. Is there anything that causes difficulties for your child at home?
4. Tell me about your child's relationships with other family members.

C. EDUCATIONAL PLANS

1. What classes would you like your child to take? Would you like to include vocational classes in your child's program? Which ones?
2. What skills would you like your child to learn in school?
3. What area of your child's education needs the most improvement?
4. What do you see your child doing after high school? Select one and explain your rationale.

   College/junior college

   Military

   Trade school

   Skilled employment

   Semi-skilled employment

   Other

D. LEISURE ACTIVITIES

1. What does your child do in his or her spare time? Sports? Hobbies? Church? Extracurricular clubs at school?
2. What chores do you assign for your child to do at home? Does your child complete these chores to your satisfaction?
3. Does your child have friends? What activities do they do together?
4. On a perfect Saturday, what would you and your child do together?

E. FUNCTIONAL SKILLS

1. If your child had a job, how would he or she get to work?
2. Who selects your child's clothes?
3. Do you allow your child to shop alone for personal things? Gifts?
4. Does your child have money for personal use? From an allowance or a job? Is your child allowed to manage his or her personal money?
5. If your child were home alone at dinner time, could he or she prepare a meal?

F. FUTURE PLANS

1. What will your child be doing during the next year, in 5 years, in 10 years toward the following postschool outcomes?

   Employment:

   Education:

   Living arrangements:

2. Will your child need help meeting his or her goals? Which one(s)?
3. Where would you and your child get the help you need?
4. What concerns you most about your child's future?
5. Name three jobs that you think your child could succeed at and would enjoy.

Figure 2. Sample parent interview form. (This form may be photocopied for noncommercial use only. Copyright © 1996 by PRO-ED, Inc.)

DIRECTIONS: *Interview teachers who have had this student in their classroom or extracurricular activities.*

A. COGNITIVE DOMAIN

Ask the teacher to discuss the student's cognitive abilities as related to instructional demands and academic tasks in the classroom. For example, does the student's disability have an impact on his or her ability to complete academic tasks such as homework? To understand lectures? To participate in group discussions? Does the student require support from special education personnel to complete tasks?

B. AFFECTIVE DOMAIN

Ask the teacher to discuss the student's ability to cope with stressful situations within the classroom, how the student relates to peers, general level of confidence and demeanor, and attitude toward school.

C. STUDENTS WORK AND/OR CLASSROOM BEHAVIOR

Ask the teacher to discuss the student's work habits. For example, is work handed in on time? Does student exhibit inappropriate behaviors that distract the classroom? Does the student work best in groups or alone? Is student able to concentrate and remain on task?

D. STUDENT'S LEARNING STYLE EXHIBITED IN CLASSROOM

Ask the teacher to discuss observations of the student's learning style. For example, does the student appear to learn better from demonstrations and models, from lectures, or from written text?

E. LIST THREE JOBS YOU THINK THE STUDENT WOULD ENJOY AND SUCCEED IN

1.

2.

3.

F. OBSERVED ATTITUDE TOWARD STUDENT

Ask the teacher to rate how the majority of students in the classroom relate to the student with disabilities.

_____ Accepting

_____ Accepting with reservations

_____ Question placement of student in class

_____ Would prefer not to work with student

_____ Refuse to work with student

Figure 3. Sample teacher interview form. (This form may be photocopied for noncommercial use only. Copyright © 1996 by PRO-ED, Inc.)

psychiatric and psychological records, medical information, and other information such as recreational, cultural, and environmental data pertinent to rehabilitation needs for employment must also be assessed (Dowdy, in press). The vocational assessment services described in the vocational education assessment process are equally important in assessment for VR purposes.

The 1992 amendments to the Rehabilitation Act specifically mandate the use of situational assessment to provide a realistic appraisal of work behavior. Situational assessment assesses an individual's work attitudes, work tolerance, work habits, and social behaviors while on a simulated or real job site. It is important for the evaluator to modify areas of difficulty or provide accommodations to facilitate success on the job during this assessment (McCue et al., 1994).

When the assessment is complete, other considerations are useful in preparing students for either vocational education or vocational rehabilitation. Students should be provided a thorough discussion of the results. Ultimately, students should be able to describe their strengths and limitations, as well as the accommodations they need for success in classroom and work environments. This preparation is particularly important in VR, where client choice is mandated. Clients should be able to communicate their goals and view professionals and their families as "consultants" as they make their life choices (Pramuka, 1994).

Services. Under the 1992 amendments to the Rehabilitation Act, vocational rehabilitation services are defined as any service or goods necessary to prepare an individual with a disability for employment. Services include but are not limited to the following:

1. Assessment for determining eligibility or vocational rehabilitation needs, including

assessment of rehabilitation technology needs if appropriate;

2. Counseling and work-related placement services, including assistance with job search, placement, retention, and any follow-up or follow-along needed to assist in maintaining, regaining, or advancing in employment;

3. Vocational and other training services, including personal and vocational adjustment, books, or other training materials. Training in higher education institutions cannot be paid for unless maximum efforts have been made to obtain grant assistance from other sources;

4. Physical and mental restorative services such as corrective surgery, eye glasses, and diagnosis and treatment for mental and emotional disorders;

5. Occupational licenses, equipment, tools, and basic stocks and supplies;

6. Transportation needed to participate in any vocational service;

7. Technological aids and devices; and

8. Supported employment services. (Section 103 (a))

Student Classroom Preparation

Vocational Education

Students with disabilities may experience difficulties in vocational classes that are similar to those they experience in academic classes. As in academic classes, students will be called on to use math, reading memorization, note-taking, and test-taking skills. In addition, students will need to maintain high levels of motivation and on-task behaviors in workshop settings. As much of the work in vocational classes must be completed in the workshop where special machinery and tools are available, students may have few opportunities to obtain help through traditional home, peer, or special education networks. Therefore, students with disabilities may benefit from instruction in independent learning strategies, including problem solving, time management, self-questioning, and mnemonic strategies.

Task analysis is known to be helpful in other learning situations and can be a "power tool" in vocational settings for students with disabilities. Some students can be overwhelmed by the size and scope of projects requiring several steps to complete. Helping students break the project into the tasks and subtasks for each class session will allow them to understand what is to be done daily in order to meet long-range deadlines. Further, in the workshop setting, requiring self-monitoring of on-task behaviors and adding a timeline to the task analysis will help students plan and manage their work. Finally, the task analysis should include a checklist for students to verify that they have completed all steps required in the correct sequence.

Support for the student can equal support for the vocational teacher as well, particularly if the special and vocational educators work together as a collaborative team. The special educator can perform a number of helpful tasks in the vocational workshop; examples include the following:

- Spend some time in the workshop setting, becoming familiar with the instructional and setting demands of the vocational class;

- Provide textual materials and worksheets in the format needed by students (e.g., taped lectures, Braille, highlighted passages);

- Videotape lectures and demonstrations so that students can review procedures for clarification;

- Review task analysis/timeline with students daily;

- Demonstrate procedures as the vocational teacher lectures;

- Write notes and outlines on the board or overhead while the vocational teacher demonstrates/lectures; and

- Circulate among students while they are working to monitor on-task behavior, offer assistance, and answer questions. This may be particularly useful when students are involved in the more academically oriented tasks of completing worksheets or taking tests.

In order to improve the opportunities for students with disabilities to access and be successful in vocational education courses, special educators should be aware of the situational factors that will affect students in these settings. *Instructional demands*, as defined by Evers and Bursuck (1993), are those prerequisite skills necessary for successful completion of a class. They include both academic skills (such as reading and math) and social behaviors (such as attending to task and working independently). Deshler, Putnam, and Bulgren (1985) defined *setting demands* as the teacher's expectations for students to effectively manage the information presented as well as the procedures the teacher uses to evaluate the students' academic progress. Table 2 briefly outlines the instructional and setting demands found in vocational classrooms.

Vocational Rehabilitation

Several areas of preparation are important for success in the vocational rehabilitation process. First, students must understand the reason they are being referred to a vocational rehabilitation counselor, the process for receiving services, and what services are available. For example, a student may antagonize a counselor by blunt demands such as "I want VR to pay for college" or "Find me a job!" They need a thorough understanding of the agency's mission and how they might benefit from working with the vocational rehabilitation counselor in terms of employment.

Students should also be trained in the area of metacognitive skills. It is important for students to compensate for their limitations and be able to state their strengths and limitations, plan, organize, set goals, and monitor progress toward their goals. VR counselors respect an individual's right to participate as a partner in the rehabilitation process. Self-advocacy and self-evaluation are important skills for this interaction. Counselors may ask an individual to visit a campus and obtain specific information or visit job sites and analyze job requirements in

terms of their own strengths and limitations. Teachers must begin to foster these skills in self-determination as part of the secondary curriculum.

Students also need to know about the world of work. They need an understanding of what it is to be a good employee and of the job market in their area in order to match their skills with available job openings. Teachers can find creative ways to incorporate information and experiences in work and independent living into existing courses, for example, math and economics.

Collaboration

Collaboration between families and agencies or programs such as special education, vocational education, and vocational rehabilitation is mandated by legislation. These individuals must work together throughout the design of the transition component of the IEP; if one of the responsible parties fails to follow through as designated by the IEP, another service delivery agency must be identified. Some suggestions to facilitate this collaborative process include the following:

1. Personnel from these agencies should be educated regarding the key components for the transition process for school-age students with disabilities.

2. Personnel should be informed of the transition services available in the local district, including the referral and eligibility process for each.

3. A local resource manual should be developed and continually updated to provide ready access to program overviews and important telephone numbers.

4. Agency personnel should be encouraged to meet students and families early in the transition process, possibly through classroom visits or specially scheduled meetings.

5. Procedures should be implemented to facilitate the authorized sharing between agencies of information on students. Too often, the "bureaucratic red tape" creates log-jams in the transition process.

6. Agency personnel should suggest information that could be taught in the special education classrooms to facilitate the transition process. Special education teachers should share their goals and needs for students with agency personnel.

7. Agency personnel participating in developing IEPs should consult before scheduling IEP and other types of meetings.

8. Students and families should be encouraged to contact a transition team member regarding their relative satisfaction with services provided.

9. Team members should maintain regular contact with one another regarding student progress and the status of transition services.

Conclusion

With an understanding of the services available and the processes involved in vocational education and rehabilitation, teachers can serve as the critical liaison between these programs and the students and their families. To adequately prepare students for their interaction with these pro-

Table 2 Instructional and Setting Demands in Vocational Classrooms

Report	Demands	
	Instructional	**Setting**
Greenan (1983)	28 mathematical 27 communication 20 interpersonal 40 reasoning skills	
Elrod (1987)	Basic math skills Reading ability of seventh to ninth grade	
Okolo (1988)		High levels of independence: self-monitoring, appropriate work habits, ability to stay on task
Okolo & Sitlington (1988)	Teacher lecture; note taking needed; independent use of text and workbooks	Independent work in labs/workshops
Evers & Bursuck (1993, 1994)	Teacher lecture; note taking required; use of texts and workbooks; requires some basic math and some geometry skills; homework assignments given; tests/quizzes for 20%–30% of grade	High levels of independent work required; specific projects with a specfic order of completion required; requirements for vocational education teachers identical to those of academic teachers

grams, teachers may add employment-related and living skills to their existing curriculum or incorporate the teaching of these skills into more traditional high school content areas. Equally important for special education teachers is building a partnership with professionals in these programs to facilitate the transition process for their students with disabilities.

References

Abbott, J. (1987, February). *Accessing vocational rehabilitation training and employment programs.* Paper presented at the annual meeting of the ACLD, San Antonio, TX.

Brolin, D. E. (1995). *Career education: A functional life skill approach.* Englewood Cliffs, NJ: Merrill.

Carl Perkins Vocational Education and Applied Technology Act Amendments of 1990, Pub. L. 101-392.

 Article Review Form at end of book.

According to the authors, what is the largest trend that we can expect in the workplace of the future? What role do the authors see for business in the preparation of individuals with disabilities for the world of work?

Beyond 2000

Preparing individuals from special populations for the next millennium

Jerry L. Wircenski and
Michelle D. Wircenski

University of North Texas

Abstract

This article begins with a look at the previous 20 years of programming and services for individuals from special populations. Following a review of the past is an examination of the workplace of the future and some suggestions for planning for the journey ahead. The article concludes with a discussion of the role of special populations personnel in shaping the future.

A Glance Over Our Collective Shoulder

As we look back at the previous 20 years of programming and services for individuals from special populations, we have seen the de-velopment and implementation of the following:

- equal access to vocational programs;

- individuals from special populations in inclusionary settings (full participation for all students);

- set-aside funds allocated for targeted special population groups;

- special populations representatives on national and state advisory councils for vocational education;

- vocational assessment processes for special populations;

- special services provided to meet the needs of individuals with special needs;

- counseling services to facilitate the transition from school to post-school employment;

- curriculum modification strategies;

- vocational education goals and objectives included in individualized education programs (IEPs), individualized vocational education plans (IVEPs), and individualized transition plans (ITPs);

- interagency collaboration; and

- cooperative planning and implementation by educators across grade levels and disciplines to meet the needs of individuals from special populations.

Across this nation exemplary school districts, administrators, teachers, parents, support person-nel, business and industry person-nel, students, and others have implemented programs and ser-vices for individuals from special populations in an attempt to ade-

Wircenski, J.L., & Wircenski, M.D., "Beyond 2000: Preparing individuals from special populations for the next millennium," *Journal for Vocational Special Needs Education* 19(3), 1997, pp. 128–131. Reprinted by permission of National Association of Vocational Education Special Needs Personnel, and the author.

quately prepare them for the work place. However, much more needs to be done if students from special populations are to make successful transitions from educational environments to the work place of the future.

Peering into the Future

The work place of the future will present great challenges for everyone. Pritchett (n.d.) has provided a glimpse into what the future may look like:

- An estimated two-thirds of U.S. employees work in the services sector, and *knowledge* is becoming our most important *product*.

- Communication technology is radically changing the speed, direction, and amount of information flow, even as it alters work roles all across organizations. Since 1987, homes and offices have added 10 million fax machines while e-mail addresses have increased by over 26 million.

- Less than half the work force in the industrial world will be holding conventional full-time jobs in organizations by the beginning of the 21st century. Those full-timers or insiders will be the new minority. Every year more and more people will be self-employed. Many will work temporary or part-time, sometimes because that's the way they want it, sometimes because that's all that is available.

- There has been more information produced in the last 30 years than during the previous 5,000 years. The information supply available to us doubles every five years.

- The cost of computing power drops roughly 30% every year and microchips are doubling in performance power every 18 months. Computer power is now 8,000 times less expensive than it was 30 years ago.

- The first practical industrial robot was introduced during the 1960s. By 1982, there were approximately 32,000 robots being used in the U.S. Today, there are over 20 million.

- In 1991, nearly one out of three American workers had been with their employer for less than a year, and almost two out of three for less than five years. The U.S. contingent work force, consisting of roughly 45 million temporaries, self-employed, part-timers, or consultants, has grown 57% since 1980. Going, if not gone, are the 9–5 workdays, lifetime jobs, predictable hierarchical relationships, corporate culture security blankets, and, for a large and growing sector of the work force, the work place itself, replaced by a cybernetics work space.

- Constant training, retraining, job-hopping, and even career-hopping will become the norm.

Business and industry will see drastic changes in the future which will affect the current work force as well as those who will enter it within the next several years. The National Institute of Corrections (1995) identified a changing scenario for the work force beyond 2000. The number of workers will fall with the number of young workers aged 16 to 24 dropping by almost two million, or eight percent, by 2000. The average age of workers will rise. The number of workers between the ages of 35 and 54 will increase by more than 25 million by 2000, and the mandatory retirement will rise to 70. Americans will be, on average, a good deal older in the century ahead; perhaps age will replace race as the great dividing line in our society (Kramer, 1997).

The *landscape* of the future labor force will look very different from the present scenario. More women will be on the job. By 2000, about 47 percent of the work force will be women, and 61 percent of all American women will be employed. One-third of new workers will be people of color. Over the next several years, almost a third of all new entrants will be people of color-twice current rates. There will be more immigrants than any time since World War I. Between 1970 and 1980, the foreign-born population of the U.S. increased by about 4.5 million, and approximately 450,000 more immigrants are expected to enter this country yearly through the end of the century. Immigration at this rate would add about 9.5 million people to the U.S. population and four million people to the labor force (National Institute of Corrections, 1995).

The new jobs will require higher skills. Whatever the occupation, technological innovation has already made it necessary for workers to continuously update and adapt their skills. People will change careers on average every 10 years. Even lower-skilled occupations will require workers who can read and understand written instructions, add and subtract and express themselves clearly. This will be a challenge for educators, as 23 million adults over the age of 18 are functionally illiterate and an additional 46 million are considered to be marginally illiterate at this point in time (National Institute of Corrections, 1995).

Most new jobs will be in the services and information sector. About half of all service workers will be involved in collecting, analyzing, synthesizing, structuring, storing or retrieving information as a basis of knowledge by the year 2000. Half of these people will be working at home (National Institute of Corrections, 1995).

The challenges for business and industry will be enormous. Not only will employers need to find ways to keep well qualified people on their payroll, they also face the challenge of helping others become more qualified to perform well. Unless educational and cultural gaps can be closed, many of the new workers will be ill-equipped to meet the advancing skill requirements of the new economy.

Unless our nation's students are better equipped to enter a changing work place, their financial future, as well as that of our nation's, is likely to remain bleak. Experts on the economy are concerned by the growing gap between the capabilities of high school graduates, especially those not bound for college, and the skills, knowledge, and habits that employers are requesting. More than half of our nation's youth leave school without the knowledge or foundation required to find and hold a good job. The concern of business and industry is well founded:

- only one-third of employers think that recent high school graduates show the capability to read and understand verbal and written instructions;

- only one-fourth report that high school graduates are capable of completing mathematical functions;

- requirements for entry-level workers in U.S. businesses are likely to increase, not remain static, if American industry is to compete globally;

- trying to increase productivity to better compete with Japan, Germany, and other economic powers, more decisions and responsibilities are moving to the factory floor; and

- entry-level workers are increasingly expected to think on their feet, solve problems that require several steps, and apply their knowledge and skills in new contexts (O'Neil, 1992, pp. 6–7); and,

- two-thirds of personnel officers at some of America's biggest firms said that they must screen more applicants now than five years ago to find qualified candidates for entry-level jobs.

"What you earn depends on what you learn", the mantra of the current administration in Washington, emphasizes the importance of all Americans being prepared for increasing global competition. Kramer (1997) stated that job training has to be reworked so that we have a national policy that covers all workers. In a knowledge-based economy, rapid and continuous growth depends most on innovation and worker competence.

President Clinton talks about "collapsing overlapping and outdated training programs into a G.I. Bill for America's workers" (Kramer, 1997, p. 62). Shapiro cited that

Since better-trained workers are usually more productive, markets should provide all the incentives for companies to make economically efficient training decisions. . . . If McDonald's trains a burger flipper to use a computer to monitor inventory, the employee's new skills may enable him to win a better position with Red Lobster or K-Mart, and the competitor reaps the benefit of McDonald's training investment. (Kramer, 1997, p. 62)

Planning Now for the Future: Preparing for the Journey Ahead

In an address to educators, Don Norris (1997), representing the Department of Education, reviewed the top 10 national education priorities of the Department as follows:

1. Set rigorous standards for all students.

2. Put a talented teacher in every classroom.

3. Teach students to read independently by the third grade.

4. Expand Head Start programs to meet the needs of children at a young age.

5. Expand school choice as a part of establishing accountability as a bottom line issue.

6. Ensure safe, disciplined, drug-free schools for all students.

7. Modernize school buildings across the country.

8. Open doors to post secondary education/college for everyone.

9. Help adults receive training through comprehensive grants that will allow them to seek all of the skills training and services that they need in order to prepare for the work place.

10. Make all students technologically literate.

11. Have libraries across the nation hook up and into technology for easy access of information and resources for all students.

These will become major goals across the country as schools strive to create more effective environments in which students can learn and achieve. In addition, a strong focus must continue to be made on methods of preparing all students for the global work force of the future. Charner and Hubbard (1995) conducted an analysis of 14 communities to identify key elements that are critical to this process. These elements include:

- Leadership from executives of educational systems;

- Leadership from program deliverers (e.g., instructors, counselors);

- Professional development for teachers and other staff;

- Cross-sector collaboration;

- Student self-determination;

- School-based curriculum and instruction;

- Work-based learning strategies;

- Integrated career information and guidance system;

- Progressive system that starts before grade eleven;

- Articulation with postsecondary institutions;

- Creative financing; and

- Application of research.

The Role of Special Populations Personnel in Shaping Future Directions

It is essential that educators not "throw the baby out with the bath water." Many of the initiatives which have been established and implemented in the past will need to be continued in the future, with appropriate changes as technology emerges.

The following components of successful programs and services should be embraced and implemented by all educators who have as their goal the preparation of individuals from special populations for the work force of the next millennium:

1. Career development and counseling services should be provided for students in a developmental, progressive direction beginning in elementary grades and continuing through post-high school options. These services should include levels of awareness, orientation, exploration, and preparation. Comprehensive vocational assessment services must be a part of this process. A career pathway should be identified no later than the ninth grade, with an accompanying four to six year plan of coherent courses.

2. Building a strong foundation of basic skills will continue to be of primary importance. The identified foundation skills and competencies from the Secretary's Commission on Achieving Necessary Skills (SCANS) should remain as a top priority in preparing individuals from special populations for the work place. The SCANS skills include foundation skills such as basic skills, thinking skills, and personal qualities. The SCANS competencies include proficiency in managing resources, interpersonal skills, information, systems, and technology. A Certificate of Initial Mastery (CIM) or Certificate of Advanced Mastery (CAM) should be documented for each student and made a part of their portable Career Portfolio which follows them wherever they go after completion of high school.

3. Work-based learning experiences for all students will be essential in the future. Every student should have some type of work experience, paid or unpaid, by the time they finish their formal educational experience. The use of work place mentors should augment these activities so that students can begin to relate their learning in school with the application to real life.

4. School-based learning experiences for all students should be implemented in all districts for all students. The combination of academic content should be taught through a contextual approach so that learning becomes meaningful for students. Examples of school-based learning experiences include the integration of academic and vocational curricula, contextual examples used in all classes by all instructors, career pathways for students during the high school years, and seamless articulation between levels (elementary to junior high, junior high to high school, high school to junior college/university).

5. Integrated curricula should become the norm in all schools for all students. In order for this to occur, general education instructors must become more work-based in their presentation of academic

content. This will mandate the collaboration of vocational and academic instructors to share contextual examples and real world applications. Shadowing and visitations to business sites will have to become commonplace. Curricula will have to be aligned between courses at the same level and among levels. Business, industry and community involvement will have to be woven into the fabric of curriculum. Professional development will have to be continuous, as technological changes will always reconfigure the current *state-of-the-art*.

6. Full participation for all students must become the norm in the future. All teachers will have to be trained to effectively relate to the blended classrooms of the future. *Mainstreaming* led to *inclusion* which is now heading toward *full participation* of all students in regular class environments with appropriate support services provided on-site as opposed to pull-out or pull-aside models. All educators will have to establish a philosophical base consistent with full participation models. Collaboration will be a continuous part of this delivery system. Preservice teacher education programs should integrate this reality into courses and practice teaching so that new additions to faculties in the public schools are prepared to work with all students.

7. There should be a strong focus on the development and utilization of a full range of support services delivered through a multidisciplinary site-based or district-based approach, including community and business/industry input and participation. We are beyond the time when the appropriate support services necessary for a specific individual to succeed in an educational environment are selected from a small range of available services within a single school. In order to create a world class work force, we must prepare individuals in more expansive environments, including all of the services available in the district and the geographic area.

8. Business and industry should be involved in all school-based operations. A multitude of contributions can be made by representatives from these arenas. Suggested activities include providing opportunities for students and educators to shadow, explore and interview workers; serving as work place mentors to individual students or groups of students (from face-to-face mentoring to cyber-mentoring using technology); hosting educational meetings at industrial/business settings followed by industry tours; participating in career days and career fairs; sharing trainers to co-teach in classes; offering industrial sites for field trips; making industrial sites for parent and educator professional development experiences; and providing grants (e.g., money, equipment, incentives for students, rewards for teachers, adopt-a-student, adopt-a-program, adopt-a-school, adopt-a-district).

9. Create strong linkages between all levels of education (elementary school through post secondary options).

10. Continuous professional development for educators, business/industry, and community members.

11. Continuous evaluation (summative and formative) procedures (internal and external sources) to determine the extent of success based on established criteria.

In addition to the aforementioned program components which many schools have implemented in the past, other enhancing elements should be added in the future in order for individuals from special populations to be adequately prepared for the next millennium. These elements include:

1. Search for, learn about, and incorporate into classrooms new research on learning systems and the effect of teaching strategies on different learners. As individuals enter the reality of learning organizations, they must be prepared to learn quickly and efficiently as industry rushes to keep up with technological changes.

2. Prepare learners to live and work in a diversified, global society. Students should be taught diversity skills so that they will be prepared to work with others, recognizing and valuing the differences that others bring to any group setting.

3. Create lifelong learners. There is no doubt that in the future individuals who expect to work in a rapidly changing society must expect to

continually upgrade skills and learn new technologies. The American Society of Training and Development published a report which identified knowing how to learn on the job as the most basic of all occupational skills (Hofstrand, 1996).

4. Become leaders in studying what the research tells us about successful programs for individuals from special populations and what research indicates should be done in the future. In any change model, systematic change occurs as an innovation which is infused into existing practices through innovative delivery practices so that the innovation is fully assimilated into the organization. Special needs personnel need to keep on the cutting edge of research results in work force preparation and special populations and focus on the five characteristics of any new innovation. These characteristics include:

   a. *Relative advantage.* The degree to which an innovation is perceived as better than the idea it supersedes;

   b. *Compatibility.* The degree to which an innovation is perceived as being consistent with existing values and past experiences;

   c. *Complexity.* The degree to which an innovation is considered easy to use and understand;

   d. *Triability.* The degree to which an innovation may be experimented with on a trial basis; and

   e. *Observability.* The degree to which the results of an innovation are visible to others (Rogers, 1983).

5. Follow legislative changes, especially as they affect funding and collaborative planning among various work force preparation individuals, institutions and agencies. Changes will constantly occur in the future. It is difficult at any one point in time to accurately predict these changes. Therefore, it is a responsibility for special needs personnel to actively become involved in the process of legislative change, interpret these changes in relationship to special populations, and share the interpretation of legislative mandates and guidelines with others.

Our journey is not over. Not even close. A new generation of individuals from special populations has entered the educational arena. As other organizations change to meet the demands of a global, competitive marketplace, so must educational institutions change in order to prepare workers of the future for this marketplace. Special needs personnel cannot return to our roots. We must forge on if our students are to be successful in dealing with all the tomorrows in their lives. Progress keeps picking up speed. The complexity of our world keeps increasing; the rate of change keeps accelerating. It's im-

portant for us to get clear on or thinking. . . . to accept the reality of what lies ahead. Let's just accept the fact that our careers will be lived out in a state of constant transition. We will constantly be confronted by the new, and often by the unexpected (Pritchett, 1996, p. 19).

References

Charner, I., & Hubbard, S. (1995, November). *Summary of findings from National Institute for Work and Learning/Academy for Educational Development.* Paper presented at the meeting of the Joint National Conference on Transition from School to Work, Orlando, FL.

Hofstrand, R. (1996). Getting all the skills employers want. *Techniques, 51.*

Kramer, M. (1997, January 20). Job training has to be reworked. *Time,* 149, 62.

Norris, Don. (1997, March) *Strategic initiatives.* Remarks presented at the George Washington University Higher Education Association Luncheon, Washington, D.C.

O'Neil, J. (1992). Preparing for the changing work place. *Educational Leadership,* 49, 6–9.

Pritchett, P. (n.d.). *New work habits for a radically changing world: 13 ground rules for job success in the information age.* Dallas, TX: Pritchett & Associates.

Pritchett, P. (1996). *MINDshift.* Dallas, TX, Pritchett & Associates.

National Institute of Corrections. (1995). *Cultural diversity training for trainers prepared for Texas Commission on Law Enforcement Officer Standards and Education.* Longmont, CO: Author.

Rogers, E. (1983). *Diffusion of innovations.* New York: Free Press.

U.S. Department of Labor. (1994). *Secretary's commission on achieving necessary skills.* Washington, DC: Author.

 Article Review Form at end of book.

The authors note an advance in the access to services and the participation in career education among special education populations. Given these developments, why do they advocate change? How does the inclusion of students with special needs into school-to-work programs affect the work of special needs personnel?

Meeting the Needs of Special Populations in the 21st Century

The role of vocational special needs personnel

Patricia S. Lynch and Judy Reimer

Department of Educational Psychology
Texas A&M University

Abstract

Education in the United States is currently undergoing major changes and reforms. Special needs personnel must ensure that special populations are considered and included in these changes and reforms. This article presents an overview of current trends and issues that impact vocational and employment training for special populations, discusses the implications these trends and issues have for vocational special needs personnel, and provides a vision for the future education of special populations.

As we move toward the 21st Century, the field of education is undergoing significant reform efforts and changes. The previous emphasis on the basic academic skills of reading, writing, and mathematics has not proved successful in preparing youth for today's work force. The new push in education is to prepare students for the world of work: to produce workers who can problem solve, think critically, and compete in a global community. An additional goal is to engage all youth in the lifelong acquisition of knowledge, skills, and attitudes necessary to pursue meaningful, challenging, and productive career pathways. Achievement of these goals will be assessed in terms of standards met and student outcomes; all students, including those who are members of special populations, are to be included both in career preparation and standard and outcome assessment. Vocational special needs personnel and their professional organizations will have a critical role in the educational and vocational preparation of individuals with special needs for this new work force.

Trends and Issues in Career and Technology Education

In determining the role of vocational special needs personnel and special needs professional organizations, particular issues related to special populations must be considered. A brief discussion of some of the educational trends

Lynch, P.S., & Reimer, J., "Meeting the needs of special populations in the 21st century: The role of vocational special needs personnel," *Journal for Vocational Special Needs Education, 19*(3), 1997, pp. 99–102. Reprinted by permission of National Association of Vocational Education Special Needs Personnel.

which impact the education and training of special populations follows.

The Increase of Special Populations

As the United States becomes more pluralistic, the backgrounds of students in vocational, as well as all, classrooms are increasingly diverse. In many urban areas, children and youth from ethnically diverse backgrounds comprise a majority of students served in classrooms (Pazey, 1993). There are rising numbers of students from low-income and disadvantaged backgrounds, as well as students with limited English proficiency. Educators have to deal with issues of teen pregnancy, gang involvement, homelessness, drug and alcohol abuse, violence and delinquency, and other situations that place students at-risk of failure on a daily basis (Price & Edgar, 1995).

In addition, the numbers of students with disabilities, including those with severe disabilities, is steadily growing (NCRVE, 1994; Smith, 1996); while special education in the past typically functioned as a separate system, it is increasingly being integrated into the general education system, thus adding to the diversity in classrooms (Pazey, 1993). Numbers of students with emotional and behavioral problems, some related to disability and some to at-risk environments, are also increasing. These students present a particular challenge to educators, many of whom are not trained to deal with these characteristics.

The Changing Work Force

The characteristics and needs of the work force are also changing. As society moves from an industrial emphasis toward one of information and service employment, today's job market requires that all high school graduates have both academic knowledge and work place skills and training. Educational requirements for better jobs are increasing; businesses need workers with greater intellectual and interpersonal skills (NCRVE, 1994; Perlman & Hansen, 1990a). Jobs of the future will demand workers who can problem solve, think critically, and work in groups, and who will seek to continually improve work processes.

The impact and use of technology will continue to expand and gain importance in the work force. All workers will require basic computer literacy skills. Technology provides greater opportunities for workers with disabilities to perform job tasks; at the same time, technology is also replacing certain jobs typically held by persons with disabilities (Perlman & Hansen, 1990b). One major concern with technology and disability is the gap between research and practice. "The economics of assistive devices makes for a strong deterrent to the manufacture of new technology that could be beneficial to people with disabilities" (NCRVE, 1994, p. 16). The difference between what is technologically possible and what is economically feasible can be very frustrating to special needs personnel.

Legislative and Policy Issues

Legislation supports the increased participation of members of special populations in vocational training and employment. Under the Carl D. Perkins Vocational and Applied Technology Education Act, programs receiving Perkins funds are required to ensure the full participation of special populations. Local recipients of funds must describe how they plan to meet the needs of special populations in their vocational programs (Coyle-Williams, 1991). The Americans with Disabilities Act of 1990 prohibits discrimination toward persons with disabilities in the work place and requires employers to make reasonable accommodations to make their facilities and jobs more accessible.

The Goals 2000: Educate America Act of 1993 provides educational goals for all students in the United States, including a minimum drop-out rate of 90%. The School to Work Opportunities Act of 1994 seeks to provide all students with opportunities to participate in education and training programs that prepare them for jobs in high-skill, high-wage careers and improve their opportunities for further education. The law also specifically mentions increasing opportunities for members of special population groups. The Individuals with Disabilities Education Act (IDEA) promotes academic and career development by requiring Individualized Education Plans (IEPs) for all youth with disabilities age 16 and older that include transition plans. The characteristics of effective transition programs outlined by IDEA are similar to those emphasized by the School to Work Opportunities Act.

While federal legislation has developed high educational goals for all students, the federal role in implementing and evaluating these goals is decreasing and moving to the states. In terms of program administration, the trend is toward decentralization in service agencies as well as in education. This allows states and local communities to use funds as they deem most appropriate to meet the needs of their particular populations. The development of community-based social services programs is also facilitated through decentralization (NCRVE, 1994). Opportunities will be provided to design programs which target specific local concerns and which can help meet the education and training needs of special populations.

Standards and Outcome-Based Learning

The focus on student achievement is moving from standardized test scores to more authentic assessment measures as a means of accountability (NCRVE, 1994). Measures such as multiple choice examinations are being replaced with measures such as portfolios of accomplishments and exhibitions (Grubb, 1996). Student outcomes such as graduation, participation in vocational preparation and postsecondary programs, and employment are being used to assess educational and vocational programs. In addition to their use for accountability, performance measures are being linked to program improvement efforts. Data regarding special population groups are often disaggregated and examined separately, but they must be considered in efforts to meet the needs of all students.

Implications for Special Needs Personnel

What do these trends imply for special needs personnel? In the past, we often have focused on special populations groups, advocated for them through professional organizations, and worked to meet their individual needs. As the focus in education moves to address needs of all students, the role of special needs personnel

must expand. No longer can we be concerned solely with special populations, but we must become a part of education as a whole. As special populations are included in general education, special needs personnel need to include themselves in policy decision-making, implementation, and evaluation of an inclusive school-to-work education system.

Collaboration

One of the most important roles of special needs personnel and their professional organizations, is to foster collaborative efforts. DeFur and Taymans (1995), in assessing competencies needed for transition specialists, found that the top three ranked competency domains primarily reflected "skills related to coordination, communication, and collaboration of transition services" (p. 46). We cannot meet the needs of our clientele on our own. Special needs personnel need to expand their networks to include general educators, administrators, service agencies, business and industry, parents, and students themselves; not only do we need to join the efforts of others as they seek to reform education, but we need to encourage them to join our efforts. Membership in our professional organizations need to expand from that of persons interested in serving a particular special population to a comprehensive group of professionals who seek to meet the individual needs of all students in a collaborative manner.

Advocacy

One very important role of the special needs professional is to serve as an advocate for special populations. We have operated in separate systems for so long, that the general education population

and community often are not aware of the needs of special populations or of how to include them in mainstream programs and activities. Often, part of the blame lies with us, as we protectively keep our students separate because only we have the expertise needed to educate and train them. Now we need to work toward empowering nonspecial needs personnel to include special populations in their programs, providing support and encouragement. As we provide inservice training, we need to advocate for the inclusion or maintenance of training regarding special populations in preservice teacher training programs. We need to advocate for programming that examines the needs of culturally and linguistically diverse populations. It will be up to the special needs profession to ensure that all really does mean all, to ensure full participation of special populations in school-to-work opportunities.

We also need to serve as advocates in the work place and the community. Special populations have been segregated in education settings, but even more so in employment and community settings. Special needs personnel can provide training/education and awareness programs for businesses and communities. Empowerment of employment and community leaders and their meaningful involvement in school-based school-to-work programs will greatly facilitate these activities.

Advocacy in governmental legislation and policy issues is another important aspect of the role of the special needs professional. With the decentralization of funding and policy-making, special needs personnel will need to ensure that full participation of special populations occurs at the local level. Through professional organizations, the voices of special population groups needs to be heard not only at the local level, but at state and national levels.

Professional Development

One goal of the School-to-Work movement is to foster the idea of lifelong learning. Special needs personnel need to realize that we, too, are lifelong learners. With all the reform efforts and changes, it is imperative that we continue to learn and to keep up with current trends and best practices. We do this primarily through belonging to professional organizations, attending workshops and conferences, joining electronic news groups, and networking with colleagues. How can we facilitate the implementation of best practices if we are not knowledgeable of them ourselves? How can we ensure the needs of our students are met if we are not sure of current legislation and policy? Professional development activities are more important than ever, and they are crucial in our constantly changing field if we are to have any impact on the education and training of special populations.

Research and Dissemination

Finally, as we continue to strive to meet the needs of special populations in the most appropriate and most cost-effective manner, we need to conduct research to guide us toward best practices. As society looks for educational outcomes and measures of accountability, special needs personnel will need to determine the most appropriate outcomes and measures for assessing achievement of special populations. Johnson and Rusch (1993) found that "little empirical evidence exists to support relation-

ships between identified best-practices and post-school outcomes" (p. 13). With an increased emphasis on accountability, this evidence needs to be documented.

As research is developed, it will be particularly important to disseminate findings. Often there is a large gap between research and practice: we need to attempt to close that gap. It is important to ensure that research related to special populations reaches a broad audience. As we address the needs of all students, all educators need information regarding the best way to meet these needs. Special needs personnel need to take the responsibility to ensure that all educators, administrators, employers, and communities have the skills and knowledge needed to include special populations in school-to-work opportunities for all students.

A Vision for the Future

Our vision for students who are members of special populations is that they are happy, motivated, and excited about learning; that they are learning more problem solving and critical thinking skills daily; and that they are able to apply school-to-work skills successfully on performance assessments. Teachers' and students' conversations will demonstrate that they respect each other and that there are high expectations for learning and achievement. Attendance rates will be high and drop-out rates nonexistent. The goal in terms of vocational education is that all of our students will graduate with the skills necessary to enter either postsecondary education programs, postsecondary training programs, or the job market in their chosen career cluster/career pathway.

With a focus on this vision, programs for special populations will have the following elements:

1. a collaborative team of general, special, and career/technology educators;

2. frequent school-to-work training and staff development opportunities that focus on work place competencies;

3. full access to and connections with all personnel, services, and activities for all teachers and students;

4. administrators, counselors, and assessment personnel available to provide needed assistance and support;

5. an advisory committee representing a diverse, cross-section of community, business and industry, administration, parents, educators, and student leaders who are willing to participate actively in the program;

6. a transition-specific and competency-based curriculum which integrates technology with all curricular concepts and topics;

7. academic instruction and learning strategies presented through work place contexts;

8. student competencies demonstrated through activity-based, applied learning activities, with teachers serving as facilitators;

9. dynamic partnerships between education and business and industry;

10. high expectations for students in terms of attendance and effort standards;

11. a large proportion of community-based learning opportunities; and,

12. student mastery of curriculum objectives demonstrated through performance-based, authentic assessments.

Summary

Although special populations have achieved many gains in access to services and participation in career and technology education, special needs personnel cannot yet afford to sit back on their laurels and enjoy the progress that has been made. The drop-out rate of African American and Hispanic youth, many of whom are from economically and educationally disadvantaged backgrounds, continues to be a significant problem (Pazey, 1993). Despite considerable gains in level of education, persons with disabilities are still twice as likely to be unemployed as the nondisabled population (National Council on Disability, 1996). Given the changes in the clientele being served, policies and legislation, and characteristics of the work force, the need for action by vocational special needs personnel and the importance of professional organizations such as the National Association for Vocational Special Needs Personnel (NAVESNP) are greater than ever. Through networking and the services and information provided by our professional organization, we need to collaboratively work toward ensuring that all truly does mean all students, including special populations, and that our students are significantly and meaningfully included and involved in career and technology programs, the work force, and the community.

References

Americans with Disabilities Act (ADA) of 1990, 42 U.S.C.A. 12101 *et seq.* (West 1993).

Carl D. Perkins Vocational and Applied Technology Education Act of 1990, 20 U.S.C.A. 2416 *et seq.* (West 1990).

Coyle-Williams, M. (1991). The 1990 Perkins Amendments: No more "business as usual." *TASPP Brief.* Berkeley, CA: National Center for Research in Vocational Education. (ERIC Document Reproduction Service No. ED 337 634)

DeFur, S. H., & Taymans, J. M. (1995). Competencies needed for transition specialists in vocational rehabilitation, vocational, education, and special education. *Exceptional Children, 62,* 38–51.

Goals 2000. Educate America Act. (1993). Public Law 102-227.

Grubb, W. N. (1996). The new vocationalism. What it is, what it could be. *Phi Delta Kappan, 77,* 535–546.

Individuals with Disabilities Education Act (IDEA) of 1990. 20 U.S.C.A. 238 *et seq.* (West 1990).

Johnson, J. R., & Rusch, F. R. (1993). Secondary special education and transition services: Identification and recommendations for future research and demonstrations. Career Development for *Exceptional Individuals, 16,* 1–18.

National Center for Research in Vocational Education. (1994). Shaping the future of vocational education. *NCRVE Change Agent,* 4(1). (ERIC Document Reproduction Service No. ED 378 377)

National Council on Disability. (1996). *Achieving independence: The challenge for the 21st century. A decade of progress in disability policy setting an agenda for the future.* Washington, DC: Author.

Pazey, B. (1993). *America 2000 and special education: Can the two be merged?* (ERIC Document Reproduction Service No. ED 360 773)

Perlman, L. G., & Hansen, C. E. (Eds). (1990a). *Employment and disability: Trends and issues for the 1990s. A report of the 14th Mary E. Switzer Memorial Seminar.* Alexandria, VA: National Rehabilitation Association. (ERIC Document Reproduction Service No. ED 341 186)

Perlman, L. G., & Hansen, C. E. (Eds). (1990b). *Vocational rehabilitation: Preparing for the 21st century. A report of the 14th Mary E. Switzer Memorial Seminar.* Alexandria, VA: National Rehabilitation Association. (ERIC Document Reproduction Service No. ED 385 044)

Price, L., & Edgar, E. (1995). Developing support systems for youth with and without disabilities. *Journal for Vocational Special Needs Education, 18,* 17–21.

School to Work Opportunities Act of 1994, 20 U.S.C.A. 6101 *et seq.* (West 1996).

Smith, T. M. (1996). *The condition of education 1996,* NOES 96-304. Washington, DC: U.S. Department of Education. National Center for Education Statistics.

About the Authors: Patricia S. Lynch is Visiting Assistant Professor in the Department of Educational Psychology, Texas A & M University and is President-Elect of the National Association of Vocational Education Special Needs Personnel (NAVESNP). Judy Reimer is a doctoral student studying career development education in the Department of Educational Psychology at Texas A & M University. Correspondence regarding this article should be addressed to Dr. Patricia Lynch, Special Education Program, Department of Educational Psychology, Texas A & M University, College Station, TX 77842-4225. Phone: 409/845-9462.

 Article Review Form at end of book.

How can special educators prepare students with disabilities for the psychosocial adjustment to college? Why do you think the authors stress college and community orientation so strongly?

The Higher Education Transition Model

Guidelines for facilitating college transition among college-bound students with disabilities

Barbara C. Gartin
Phillip Rumrill
Riqua Serebreni

Barbara C. Gartin (CEC Chapter # 136), Associate Professor, Department of Curriculum and Instruction, University of Arkansas, Fayetteville. Phillip Rumrill, Assistant Professor, Rehabilitation Counseling Program, Department of Educational Psychology, University of Wisconsin–Milwaukee. Riqua Serebreni, Program Coordinator, Campus Access, University of Arkansas, Fayetteville.

There are four difficulties commonly experienced by students with disabilities when they make transitions from school to college or other postsecondary institutions (Cordoni, 1982; Dalke & Schmitt, 1987; Evenson & Evenson, 1983; Rosenthal, 1989) (see box "Transition Dilemmas").

Special educators can take proactive steps to improve their students' prospects for college success. This article presents the Higher Education Transition Model, which can be used to facilitate college transition for students with disabilities, and suggests implementation guidelines for special education teachers.

Higher Education Transition Model

The Higher Education Transition Model is a three-part framework for use in facilitating college transi-

tion among students with disabilities (Serebreni, Rumrill, Mullins, & Gordon, 1993). The model encompasses (a) psychosocial adjustment, (b) academic development, and (c) college and community orientation as essential elements of successful transition to higher education settings. For successful transition to occur, all three elements must be in place. They not only coexist, but they interact to bring balance in the process of adjusting to college life.

Psychosocial Adjustment. For many students (with and without disabilities), college experiences form the bridge between adolescence and adulthood. Accordingly, meeting people, making friends, and forming social networks comprise an integral component of the higher education transition process. Psychosocial adjustment tasks of higher education transition include moving from dependence to independence, participating in social and recreational activities, and establishing and maintaining adult relationships.

Academic Development. To make successful transitions to higher education, students must develop the academic skills needed to meet the challenges of college classes. Academic development tasks of the higher education transition process include establishing effective study and time management strategies, acquainting oneself with course requirements and professors' expectations, choosing fields of study and career paths, and becoming aware of campus resources (role of advisement, career-related student employment opportunities, student professional organizations, student study groups, etc.).

College and Community Orientation. Becoming aware of one's new environment and its resources is the third essential element of higher education transition. Summer orientation programs offer cursory introductions to campus life and are very beneficial to incoming students, but students must explore in depth the campuses they have chosen and become familiar with the communities in which those campuses exist. The college or university becomes the student's second home for the next 4 years, and he or she must acclimate to the new community and its resources. These resources include public services, health care facilities, employment opportunities, transportation systems, cultural

Table 1	Higher Education Transition Model	
Essential Curricular Elements	**Instructional Objectives**
Psychosocial Adjustment	1. Self-advocacy skill development
	2. Handling frustration
	3. Social problem-solving
	4. College-level social skills
	5. Mentor relationships
Academic Development	1. College entrance exam preparation
	2. Test-taking strategies/accommodations
	3. Career awareness
	4. Goal setting
	5. Academic remediation
	6. Career preparation
	7. Learning strategies/study skills
	8. College services
	9. Transition to college
College/Community Orientation	1. College-level linkage
	2. Buddy systems
	3. College choices
	4. College resources/activities
	5. College orientation program
	6. Campus support groups
	7. Community services assessment

activities, restaurants, movie theaters, laundromats, and recreational facilities.

Guidelines for Secondary School Personnel

To increase the likelihood of successful transitions for college-bound students with disabilities, special educators and counselors can use the Higher Education Transition Model both in the development of high school curriculums and in preparation of transition plans for college-bound students. By addressing the three elements of the model (discussed previously) in planning information dissemination and skill training, special educators and counselors can provide students with disabilities appropriate edu-

cational experiences that will lead to successful postsecondary transitions. Table 1 presents an outline of the model and recommendations for implementation.

Psychosocial Adjustment

Promoting psychosocial development is not the exclusive responsibility of secondary educators. Teachers at all levels must help students with disabilities to develop the self-advocacy and socialization skills they will need in college. The following guidelines may help teachers promote these skills.

1. Focus instruction on the development of *self-advocacy* skills which will allow students with disabilities to better express their personal needs, to propose options for meeting those needs, and then to defend their selections of coping strategies.

2. Initiate programs to assist students with disabilities in developing the ability to handle frustration and to turn aggression into assertive action through *assertiveness training.* Role playing and direct instruction in advocacy skills often provide the student with valuable information concerning alternative behavioral actions.

3. Include group activities within curriculums to allow students opportunities to discuss difficult social situations and to solve problems of personal concern. Use *cooperative learning* and *peer tutor* programming whenever possible. Direct instruction in social skills and subsequent try-out opportunities often provide the students with alternative social strategies and increase their skills in social situations.

4. Include college settings and situations as discussion *scenarios* to aid in the transfer and generalization of communication and social skills.

5. Include information concerning the purpose and development of *student/mentor* relationships, which are often helpful to students in higher education settings.

Academic Development

The Higher Education Transition Model's academic development framework is based on Sandperl's (1989) academic model, which includes individualized assistance, writing consultation, tutoring, individual educational evaluations, and examination accommodations. Within the public school context, special education teachers and school counselors can assist in the preparation of students

with disabilities for success in college by (a) assessing students' academic histories, abilities, and potential for college success; (b) monitoring students' performance in college preparatory courses; (c) teaching study strategies and technology skills; and (d) providing technical assistance to college disability services personnel. The following guidelines will assist special education teachers, secondary teachers, and counselors in preparing students with disabilities for the academic rigors of higher education.

1. Provide information concerning *standardized college entrance examinations* such as the American College Test (ACT) or Scholastic Achievement Test (SAT), as well as information on the courses and materials available for preparing students for these examinations. For example, students with disabilities should be encouraged to enroll and participate in standardized testing situations such as the Pre-Scholastic Achievement Test (PSAT) in preparation for college entrance examinations. Also, those requiring accommodations or alternative conditions should be informed of request and documentation procedures.

2. Provide information concerning procedures for requesting *in-class accommodations.*

3. Encourage students with disabilities to participate in "summer camps," college day, museum tours, and sports events, in an effort to acquaint them with *social and cultural opportunities* available on a campus.

4. Assist in the evaluation of the appropriateness of career goals by providing opportunities for participation in occupational information groups, vocational assessments, and *career day programs.*

5. Assess transcripts of students with disabilities yearly to determine if they are enrolled in coursework appropriate for admission to postsecondary programs and institutions of higher education. The *prevention of academic deficiencies* is of great importance when students are enrolling in institutions with specific requirements and minimum admission standards.

6. In addition to the prevention of academic deficiencies, monitor students' performance in college preparatory courses to determine the appropriateness of the course in relation to the students' long-term career plans and to determine the appropriateness of *career choices* in relation to the students' demonstrated proficiencies.

7. Teach *study and research skills* to students with disabilities who plan to attend college. Introduce the use of taped texts, electronic notetakers, and a variety of electronic editing and communication formats that can assist with the completion of course requirements.

8. Routinely use in-class accommodations similar to those accommodations routinely used at colleges and universities. For example,

encourage the use of study guides and study groups whenever possible, as well as the use of *electronic technology,* taped texts, and computers.

9. Provide information concerning the services needed by the student to *disability services personnel* at the college or university to which the student applies.

10. Introduce students with disabilities to the disability services personnel on the campus where the student plans to attend, so that the student can *obtain assistance* in making a successful transition to the postsecondary environment.

College and Community Orientation

Just as psychosocial adjustment and academic development are integral aspects of the Higher Education Transition Model, students with disabilities must also be introduced to the context in which college transition occurs. That is, structured opportunities for students to "get to know" college campuses and communities are important college transition activities. The following proce-

dures will facilitate the important college and community orientation process.

Realizing Potentials
As the higher education option continues to be a viable postsecondary choice for students with disabilities, special educators and counselors can use the Higher Education Transition Model to improve their students' prospects for college success by creating successful transitions from high school to college. Educational experiences based on the components of the Higher Education Transition Model can assist students by helping them realize their full potential and establish higher education as a gateway to adulthood and independence.

1. Encourage students with disabilities to *"link"* with the colleges and universities as early as possible. Science fairs, band camps, sports camps, and other special events such as Black America Week, International Month, and Women's Issues Week can provide opportunities for establishing the linkage.

2. Advocate for students with disabilities by helping *facilitate friendships* among students with disabilities and other students. Teachers and counselors can provide formal introductions and informal activities for the inclusion of all students with similar interests.

3. Provide students with disabilities opportunities to review college catalogues, obtain scholarship information, and attend *College Day Programs.*

4. Whenever possible, acquaint students with postsecondary campuses through *tours* of the campus and information concerning the library, computer labs, dorms,

parking, student union, stadium, arena, and other campus facilities.

5. Urge students to attend the *college orientation program.* Orientation programs provide students with information about college or university rules and procedures. Early orientation provides the opportunity to meet with advisors and to register for courses before required classes become filled. Early orientation also provides the opportunity for the student to request services from disability services personnel and to alert faculty to class accommodations that will be needed.

6. Prepare students with disabilities to participate fully in campus life. Encourage students who will live on campus to use the telephone to talk with friends and family, but to stay on the campus and participate in dorm and *campus activities* whenever possible. Participation in campus activities will assist the student in developing a campus support network and a circle of friends.

7. Teach strategies for accessing *community services,* such as how to provide for medical needs, banking, shopping, entertainment, and other consumer activities. Involve the *parents* in these educational components; their involvement is critical to the success of the student's transition.

Planning for Higher Education

The process of transition from youth to adulthood has received considerable attention in recent educational and social science literature. Organized initiatives in special education and vocational rehabilitation support the notion that transition planning is necessary for students with disabilities to ensure that their educational experiences will culminate in outcomes that maximize independence and self-sufficiency (Halpern, 1985; Will, 1983).

These initiatives are based on the assumption that students with disabilities require more assistance and support than their nondisabled peers to progress through the often traumatic years of adolescence and early adulthood.

Legal Status

Transition planning is especially important in view of the fact that there is a change in the legal status of students with disabilities when they leave high schools, which are structured under Public Law 94-142 and Public Law 101-476, and enter postsecondary institutions, which are structured under Section 504 of the Rehabilitation Act of 1973 (Scott, 1991) and the Americans with Disabilities Act.

Students with disabilities graduating from high school move from a protective environment in which school personnel are legally responsible for identifying and providing appropriate services under Public Law 101-476 to an environment in which the students are expected to request specific accommodations and provide documentation of their disabilities under Section 504 and the Americans with Disabilities Act (Fairweather & Shaver, 1990).

School-to-work transition programs integrate educational and vocational rehabilitation services, thereby providing students with disabilities with additional support according to individual needs (Turner & Szymanski, 1990).

State of the Art

Unfortunately, the school-to-work transition approach has not yet been fully applied to the transition from public school special education services to institutions of higher education. In that process, students with disabilities often encounter inadequate vocational rehabilitation services and universities and colleges ill-prepared to meet their transition needs.

In other words, choosing to attend college rather than going directly to work after high school may place students with disabilities at a disadvantage, because formalized transition policies have not been established to address the higher education option.

References

Cordoni, B. K. (1982). Post-secondary education: Where do we go from here? *Journal of Learning Disabilities, 15,* 265–266.

Dalke, C., & Schmitt, S. (1987). Meeting the transition needs of college-bound students with learning disabilities. *Journal of Learning Disabilities, 20,* 176–180.

Evenson, T. L., & Evenson, M. L. (1983). An innovative approach to career development of disabled college students. *Journal of Rehabilitation, 49*(2), 64–67.

Fairweather, J. S., & Shaver, D. M. (1990). A troubled future? Participation in post-secondary education by youths with disabilities. *Journal of Higher Education, 61*(3), 332–348.

Halpern, A. S. (1985). Transition: A look at the foundations. *Exceptional Children, 51*(6), 479–486.

Rosenthal, I. (1989). Model transition programs for learning disabled high school and college students. *Rehabilitation Counseling Bulletin, 33*(1), 54–66.

Sandperl, M. (1989). *Toward a comprehensive model of learning disability service delivery.* Paper presented at The Next Step, An Invitational Symposium on Learning Disabilities in Selective Colleges, Cambridge, MA.

Scott, S. (1991). A change in legal status: An overlooked dimension in the transition to higher education. *Journal of Learning Disabilities, 24*(8), 459–466.

Serebreni, R., Rumrill, P. D., Mullins, J. A., & Gordon, S. E. (1993). Project Excel: A demonstration of the higher education transition model for high-achieving students with disabilities. *Journal of Postsecondary Education and Disability, 10*(3), 15–23.

Turner, K. D., & Szymanski, E. M. (1990). Work adjustment of people with congenital disabilities: A longitudinal perspective from birth to adulthood. *Journal of Rehabilitation, 56,* 19–24.

Will, M. (1983). *OSERS programming for the transition of youth with disabilities: Bridges from school to working life.* Washington, DC: Office of Special Education and Rehabilitation Services. (ERIC Document Reproduction Service No. ED 256 132).

 Article Review Form at end of book.

WiseGuide Wrap-Up

- The transition from high school to the adult world can be difficult for all students, but students with disabilities face even greater challenges. Whether they go to college or into the workforce, they are forced to face new demands, typically with fewer supports to help them.

- One of the most important responsibilities of special educators who work with adolescents is to prepare their students for adulthood. Vocational education and vocational rehabilitation are important in easing the difficulty of this transition.

R.E.A.L. Sites

This list provides a print preview of typical **coursewise** R.E.A.L. sites. (There are over 100 such sites at the **courselinks**™ site.) The danger in printing URLs is that web sites can change overnight. As we went to press, these sites were functional using the URLs provided. If you come across one that isn't, please let us know via email to: webmaster@coursewise.com. Use your Passport to access the most current list of R.E.A.L. sites at the **courselinks**™ site.

Site name: Challenge 2000

URL: http://www2.interaccess. com/netown/

Why is it R.E.A.L.? This web site focuses primarily on helping persons with disabilities gain access to employment, but it additionally is concerned with recreation and leisure activities and artistic and creative outlets.

Key topics: families, recreation, employment

Activity: Identify which employers are "proactive" Equal Employment Opportunity (EEO) employers.

....

Site name: School-to-Work Outreach Project

URL: http://www.ici.coled.umn.edu/schooltowork/

Why is it R.E.A.L.? This is the web site of the School-to-Work Outreach Project, funded by U.S. Dept. of Education. The project is designed to enhance job opportunities for individuals with disabilities and it includes model programs and exemplary practices.

Key topics: employment, vocational education

Activity: Select one exemplary school-to-work model program and describe it to your class.

....

section

4

Exceptionality and Cultural Diversity

The topics of exceptionality and cultural diversity are related in American schools for a number of reasons. First, in the United States, students in both general education and special education come from a wide variety of ethnic, cultural, and language backgrounds. This diversity may be one of our greatest assets as a society; however, it also presents challenges for teachers and, in particular, for special education teachers whose students have specific learning difficulties. Second, data show that, in the United States, minority groups such as African Americans and Hispanics are overrepresented in special education classes. How does this pattern emerge? Researchers and policy-makers have looked at the referral, testing, and placement processes, all of which contain a degree of bias.

In this section, three articles are included that examine these issues from different perspectives. In "The Overrepresentation of African American Children in Special Education," Charles J. Russo and Carolyn Talbert-Johnson examine the legal background of special education with specific attention to litigation relating to test bias and the placement of African American students. They make seven recommendations for change in the system to promote equity in American education.

The two next articles pertain to language-minority students. Russell Gersten and John Woodward, in "The Language-Minority Student and Special Education: Issues, Trends, and Paradoxes," look at the difficulties faced by students for whom English is not their native language and problems faced by their teachers. Such students sometimes are referred to special education because of their teachers' needs to find an alternative to the general education classroom. The authors examine the different models of instruction for language-minority students and make an attempt to bring together the approaches to instruction found in bilingual education and special education.

A teacher describes her experiences in "Conversations with a Latina Teacher about Education for Language-Minority Students with Special Needs," by Candace S. Bos and Elba I. Reyes. The experiences are those of Reyes in her work as a bilingual special education teacher. Her work with students informs her conclusions regarding how best to teach this population and how to promote the transition from a first to a second language. She describes a way of blending a more cognitive, interactive teaching approach with a more skills-oriented direct instruction approach that she has found to be effective.

Learning Objectives

After studying this section, the reader will:

- Understand the issue of overrepresentation in special education settings of students from ethnic and language-minority backgrounds.

- Know how legislation and litigation in education have affected students of minority backgrounds.

- Comprehend the issues surrounding test bias and the impact of test bias on the placement of students of minority backgrounds in special education.

- Identify ways in which the overrepresentation of minority students in special education can be addressed.

- Differentiate two models of second-language acquisition and their implications for special education instruction.

- Describe approaches employed by one teacher in her teaching of language-minority students with special needs.

Questions

R18. Why do the authors raise the issue of school funding in their discussion of the overrepresentation of African American students in special education classes? The authors present two lawsuits regarding test bias, *Larry P. v. Riles* and *Parents in Action on Special Education v. Hannon.* What are the implications of the rulings of the two cases?

R19. How can there be both under- and over-representation of language-minority students in special education? What do the authors see as an incompatibility between a major approach in special education (task analysis and skill-building) and a major approach in bilingual education (the natural language orientation)?

R20. How did Reyes' own experiences as a student influence her approach to teaching? In addition to having students explore and play with language, what other strategies did Reyes employ in teaching language-minority students with learning difficulties?

Why do the authors raise the issue of school funding in their discussion of the overrepresentation of African American students in special education classes? The authors present two lawsuits regarding test bias, *Larry P. v. Riles* and *Parents in Action on Special Education v. Hannon*. What are the implications of the rulings of the two cases?

The Overrepresentation of African American Children in Special Education

The resegregation of educational programming?

Charles J. Russo
Carolyn Talbert-Johnson
University of Dayton

The federal statute that has had the greatest impact on the education of American children in urban settings over the past 30 years is the Individuals with Disabilities Education Act (IDEA; 1996). The IDEA, originally named the Education for All Handicapped Children Act when it was authorized in 1975, is designed "to assure that all children with disabilities have available to them . . . a free *appropriate* [emphasis added] public education which emphasizes special education and related services designed to meet their unique needs" (20 U.S.C. § 1401(c), 1996). Yet, despite almost 30 years of data that have demonstrated that African American children, especially males (Harry & Anderson, 1994), are disproportionately (Artiles & Trent, 1994; Chinn & Hughes, 1987; Dunn, 1968; Maheady, Towne, & Algozzine, 1983; Smith, 1983), and inappropriately (Heller, Holtzman, & Messick, 1982), placed in special education, this unfortunate trend continues.

In addressing the disproportionate placement of African American students in special education, this article applies the definition offered by Chinn and Hughes (1987) as plus or minus 10% of the total percentage of children, based on the overall population of school aged children. Consequently, because African Americans constituted 16% of the public school population in 1992 (U.S. Department of Education, Office of Civil Rights [OCR], 1994), following the standard set by Chinn and Hughes, an acceptable range would be between 14.4% and 17.6% of all children in special education. However, depending on the disability, African American students actually made up as much as 32%, or double their representation, of the population of students in special education (OCR, 1994). Although the authors neither suggest nor support the notion that placements should be based on some form of quota or direct correlation to a minority group's representation in the general population, they do raise questions as to why the percentage of African American students in special education is so disproportionately high.

In light of the equity issues presented by the overrepresentation of children of color in special programming, a trend that may be akin to a form of resegregation, this article is divided into three major sections. The first part reviews the background of special education: its history, salient features of the IDEA, and the key legal issue of test bias—as it is a major factor in the placement of many children with disabilities. The second portion examines the data that reveal that a disproportionately large number of students in these programs are children of color. The article concludes by offering suggestions that may help to lead to the more equitable placement of all children in appropriate educational settings.

Legal Background

History of the Idea

The most significant ruling in American history on the battle for equal educational opportunity is *Brown v. Board of Education of Topeka* (1954) (Russo, Harris, & Sandidge, 1994; Thomas & Russo, 1995). In *Brown*, a case involving racial segregation in public schools, the United States Supreme Court recognized the great importance of providing all children with an appropriate education. In so doing, the Court relied on the Equal Protection Clause of the Fourteenth Amendment when it held that "it is doubtful that any child may reasonably be expected to succeed in life if he is denied the opportunity of an education. Such an opportunity, where the state has undertaken to provide it, is a right which must be made available to all on equal terms" (p. 493).

The Supreme Court's articulation of the need for equal educational opportunity unequivocally establishes *Brown* (1954) as the cornerstone on which all subsequent legal developments protecting the rights of the disenfranchised, including the disabled, are grounded. Therefore it is not surprising that the Supreme Court's reasoning in *Brown* was applied in a number of early special education cases including, perhaps most notably, *Mills v. Board of Education of the District of Columbia* (1972).

Mills (1972) was filed on behalf of seven exceptional African American children who were certified to bring a class action suit representing some 18,000 similarly situated students. The suit charged that the educational needs of the children, many of whom had a variety of disabilities, were not being met by the public schools in the nation's capitol. The federal trial court, in a ruling on the merits of the case, held that the students were improperly excluded from school without due process of the law. The court, in rejecting the school district's argument that it could not afford to pay for all of the educational services that the youngsters required, reasoned that insufficiencies of the system could not be permitted to weigh more heavily on exceptional children.

As such, it held that no child in need of special programming could be totally excluded from public education, whether in a school or an alternative setting. Rather, it mandated that children must be provided with individualized educational services suited to their unique needs, parental notification before any proceeding could take place to consider changing a child's placement, and periodic review to examine the adequacy of the setting. All of these principles enunciated by the court in *Mills* ultimately found their way into the IDEA.

The fact that *Mills* (1972) was litigated in Washington, DC, coupled with related legal developments (Thomas & Russo, 1995) throughout the country, including but not limited to Section 504 of the Rehabilitation Act of 1973 (a law that was originally designed to ensure the rights of workers with disabilities, but which has also played a major part in safeguarding the rights of children with disabilities) provided the impetus for the passage of the IDEA. At its heart, the IDEA mandates that all children with specifically identified disabilities between the ages of 3 (assuming that a state is involved in the early childhood provisions of the Act) and 21 are entitled to a free, appropriate public education (FAPE) in the least restrictive environment. Further, the instruction that is provided to a child with a disability must be individualized to meet his or her unique needs. The IDEA also ensures that a child cannot be deprived of the substantive right to receive a FAPE and accompanying procedural due process safeguards. In special education, procedural due process means that before a child can be tested, classified, or have his or her educational placement changed or modified, the parents must be notified (typically in writing) and must be afforded the right to participate in any meetings to plan the child's placement.

Test Bias

Arguably the most controversial issue surrounding the placement of children in special education is test bias. Yet, despite language in the federal regulations on special education that require that "Testing and evaluation materials and procedures used for the purposes of evaluation and placement of children with disabilities must be selected and administered so as not to be racially or culturally discriminatory" (34 C.F.R. § 300.500(b), 1996), the matter is far from satisfactorily resolved. The first major court case over test bias involving African American students, *Larry P. v. Riles* (1984), emerged from a disagreement in the San Francisco Unified School District (SFUSD) late in 1971. The dispute arose in light of the fact that African Americans made up 28.5% of the student population in the SFUSD, yet represented 66% of children who were placed in classes for the educable mentally retarded (EMR). Moreover, even though only about 10% of California's school-aged population was African American, they accounted for 25% of the state's total in classes for the EMR. After more than a dozen years in court that involved two trial court and two appellate decisions, the Ninth Circuit ruled in favor of the students. The appellate court, in affirming earlier judgments, not only agreed that the SFUSD violated the rights of the students by relying on nonvalidated intelligence (IQ) tests, but also ordered the state to develop plans to eliminate the disproportionate enrollment of African American children in classes for the EMR.

Even as *Larry P.* (1984) made its way through the legal system, a federal trial court in Illinois reached the opposite result. *Parents in Action on Special Education v. Hannon* (1980) was filed on behalf of two African American children who, representing all similarly situated children in the Chicago Public Schools, were placed in classes for the EMH after receiving low scores on standardized IQ tests. In rejecting the students' claims that the tests were biased against African American children, the court examined data that indicated that whereas 62% of the children enrolled in the school system, they accounted for 82% of youngsters in classes for the EMH. At the same time, the court noted that only 3.7% of all African American students in the system were in these classes. Thus the court reached two significant findings. First, it held that even though one item on the IQ test and eight questions on two other measures were either culturally biased or sufficiently suspect such that their use was inappropriate, the disputed items did not significantly affect the scores of the children whose abilities were being evaluated. As such, the court ruled that the use of the questions was not inappropriate. Second, the court reasoned that when the challenged tests were used in conjunction with statutorily mandated criteria for determining a child's appropriate educational placement, they did not discriminate against African American students.

The federal regulation on discrimination free assessment notwithstanding, test bias is an issue that is not likely to go away. However, because the Supreme Court appears to be unlikely to resolve the legal status of test bias, it will continue to be evaluated on a case by case basis. Thus it will be left to educators, psychometricians, and policy makers to ensure that standardized measures employed to evaluate students for placement in special education.

Monitoring by OCR

Even prior to judicial challenges concerning test bias, the Federal Office of Civil Rights (OCR) was created to monitor and enforce compliance with Title VI of the Civil Rights Act of 1964 (1996) by conducting biannual surveys of the schools over student enrollment and placement. In the interim, OCR has also been granted the authority to oversee the enforcement of Section 504 of the Rehabilitation Act. OCR was able to document the overrepresentation of African American children in EMR classes as early as 1974 through 1978 (Smith, 1983), a trend that has continued unabated (Artiles & Trent, 1994; Chinn & Hughes, 1987; Harry & Anderson, 1994). Consequently, in 1979 the OCR created the Panel on Selection and Placement of Students in Programs for the Mentally Retarded. The twofold purpose of this Panel was to assist the OCR to identify potential factors contributing to the overrepresentation of children of color in EMR classes and to help develop procedures to ameliorate this unfortunate resegregative trend. Although no single element has been identified as the cause of the imbalance, there is some evidence that test bias is a substantial factor

(Maheady, Towne, & Algozzine, 1983; Prasse & Reschly, 1986).

Data on African Americans

The statistics concerning African Americans, poverty, and public education are, to put it mildly, less than heartening. The disproportionate numbers of African American children and families, especially in urban areas, living below the poverty level are well documented by the national media. For example, data from the 1990 census indicate that 31.9% of African Americans lived below the poverty level (Jennings, 1994, p. 58). This statistic is further exacerbated relative to special education in light of related data that more than 57% of all African Americans who live below the poverty level reside in urban areas (p. 63).

Turning to education, African Americans currently make up 16% of the public school population, but only 8% of the public school teachers and approximately 4% of teacher educators in institutions of higher learning (Frierson, 1990; King, 1993). The cultural/racial gap between students and instructor is even more pronounced in light of the data that African Americans comprise 28% of all students in special education (National Clearinghouse for Professions in Special Education, 1991). This figure includes 34% of the children in programs for mental retardation, 16% for speech impairments, 22% for seriously emotionally disturbed, and 17% for learning disabilities (Council for Exceptional Children, 1994). Projections are that by the year 2020, children of color will make up 46% of the public school population, yet fewer than 5% of the teachers will be African American (King, 1993). In addition, it is expected that the disproportionate representation of African American students in special education will continue accordingly. The percentage of African American youth in special education programs, especially in the areas of mental retardation and behavior disorders, greatly exceeds their relative percentages in the larger school population (Cartledge, Gardner, & Tillman, 1995).

Demographic studies repeatedly show that minority students, particularly African American males, are disproportionately referred for behavior and learning problems compared to their majority counterparts (Executive Committee of the Council for Children with Behavior Disorders, 1989; Harry & Anderson, 1994). Other related data indicate that, compared to majority populations, culturally different youths with disabilities are more likely to be programmed into punishment facilities such as juvenile court rather than treatment, given more pathological labels than warranted, and less likely to have appropriate family involvement in their treatment plans (Forness, 1988).

The literature supports the notion that African Americans are also disproportionately placed in classes for students with serious emotional and behavioral disorders. However, this rate is not as great as in classes for students with mental retardation (Gollnick & Chinn, 1994). These statistics are alarming for not only African Americans, but for other people of color. Other disturbing statistics include the fact that males are placed in serious emotional and behavioral disorders three and a half times more often than females (OCR, 1994).

According to the American Association of University Women (1992), boys outnumber girls in special education programs by startling percentages. More than two thirds of all students in special education placements are male. In fact, the more subjective the diagnosis, the higher the representation of boys. It is possible that rather than identifying learning problems, school personnel may be mislabeling behavioral problems. Girls who sit quietly are ignored, boys who act out are placed in special education programs that may not meet their needs. Males who are enrolled inappropriately in special education classes face limited educational opportunities and carry a lifelong label.

In light of the nationwide scope of the problem, in the Fall of 1993, the Council of Chief State School Officers, at the behest of the National Association of State Directors of Special Education, analyzed state policies and practices relating to the overrepresentation of minority students in special education (Lara, 1994) in the hope of minimizing or reducing this practice. The results of the study indicated that only 6 of the 32 states that collect annual enrollment data by race and ethnicity have formal follow-up procedures to monitor minority enrollments, to evaluate the adequacy of local policies, and to engage in additional study. Clearly, if the problem of the overrepresentation of African American and other minority students is ever to be ameliorated, states must do a more thorough job of evaluating their actions and planning accordingly.

Recommendations for Change

There are no simple solutions to the problems of disproportionate placement of African Americans and other minorities in special education classes. The authors offer the following seven recommendations to direct the national consciousness to consider ways to help alleviate the problem of overrepresentation of African Americans in special education services.

Restructuring teacher education programs. Insofar as most teacher preparation programs—including those in special education—still function within a framework that is exclusively Eurocentric, few teachers are equipped to deal with different cultures, languages, lifestyles, and values in their classrooms. The result is that many teachers expect all students to conform to the norm. The typical student for whom educators' pedagogy and prescriptions are designed is an endangered species. Highly motivated, achievement-oriented, white, middle-class students from two-parent families are becoming scarce in most school systems, whether rural, suburban, or urban (Irvine, 1992). By the year 2000, these students will be even more atypical. Hodgkinson's (1988) and Coates and Jarratt's (1987) data confirm that divorce; delayed marriage; and the influx of immigrants from Mexico, Asia, and the Caribbean will dramatically change how we will administer schools and instruct students.

One of the challenges facing teacher educators is to prepare future teachers who are capable of maximizing the fit between instruction and students' learning, regardless of racial or ethnic groups, gender, or socioeconomic background. A unique feature of urban schools is the diversity of students who are in attendance. Within these intergroup differences, there are also individual differences in learning rates, attitudes, interests, and motivation levels that schools and teachers must accommodate. Pedagogies should be adapted to reflect the needs of these diverse individuals with curricula changes evident that incorporate multicultural education and a pluralistic approach.

Preparing teachers to become culturally responsive. The increasing numbers of culturally diverse students in the public schools create a corresponding need for well-prepared teachers who can communicate with students within the context of their cultures and/or native languages. Analysis of the 1990–1991 Schools and Staffing Survey (SASS) data showed that 15% of American public schools reported teaching vacancies that could not be filled with fully qualified teachers and that 23% of central city schools had such vacancies. Yet, in contrast, only 13% of urban fringe/large town and rural/small town public schools had similar openings. Across all three types of communities, "the percentage of schools that could not find qualified teachers were greater when minority enrollment was 20% or more than when it was less than 20%. . . . 38% of all schools had teaching vacancies in special education in 1990–91" (Choy, Henke, Alt, Medrich, & Bobbitt, 1993, p. 125).

Schools and institutions of higher learning must design, implement, and evaluate their programs to significantly increase the number of culturally responsive teachers. Several issues must be examined, including the complexity of the problems as well as the need for multifaceted strategies, ranging from intervention in the schooling of at-risk elementary and secondary students to the development of programs that ensure that all students have opportunities to learn in both special and general education settings. New paradigms and reconceptualizations must be related to issues such as the contextualization of instruction and teaching materials, individual needs, reflection and critical inquiry in teaching, redefinition of the teachers' role, cultural immersion experiences, and interpersonal skills training. Because one-shot workshops have not proven to have a lasting impact on preservice students, curricular changes are required. Strategies such as cooperative efforts, working for full inclusion, opportunities to respond, and experiential learning are beneficial in the educational process.

Recruiting teachers of color. Projections are that no more than 5% of public school teachers will be from underrepresented racial/ethnic groups by the end of the decade (American Association of State Colleges and Universities, 1991). This decline may be due to increased career opportunities in other fields, a decrease in higher education enrollment rates by minorities, the growing use of teacher competency testing (where the failure rates for African Americans and other minorities are higher than for Whites), and a dissatisfaction with the teaching profession. Regardless of the reasons, this is a trend that must be reversed.

For special education, the most significant supply/demand issues for the 1990s may center on the deployment of personnel to those locations where recruitment and retention are most difficult; efforts toward more adequate ethnic, racial, and cultural presentation in the personnel force; the skills and knowledge of the educators who are employed; and anticipating changes in the way that local schools will be organized for instruction (Smith-Davis & Billingsley, 1993).

Teachers of color are extremely important to the education of all children, whether in special or regular education, including children of color. King (1993) notes that African Americans serve critical roles as role models and surrogate parents. She asserts that African American teachers are better able to bridge the gap often found between students from low socioeconomic status families and middle-class teachers who tend to have higher expectations than White teachers for students of color. Moreover, according to Irvine (1992), minority faculty should be vigorously recruited and accompanying policies for promotion, tenure, and faculty development should be reexamined for possible bias and disproportionate impact.

A critical concern is the shortage of males in the teaching force. This is a problem of particular significance where disadvantaged children are concerned because they lack positive male role models in their lives. Ancarrow's (1991) analysis showed that two to three times as many general educators were female than male. Teachers from students' racial, cultural, and ethnic background can make an important contribution to the school, enriching both the environment and the curriculum with their diversity. In light of the rapidly increasing diversification of American society, it is in the best interests of schools and society as a whole to recruit and retain a diversity of teachers as it enhances the learning experience of students. And, even where there is a dearth of diversity, all teachers should embrace their task as role models for all students as long as they are understanding, caring, and informed.

Recognizing and valuing individuals first. It is critical to remember that children are first and foremost children. The schools must focus on adapting either the classroom organization or curriculum and instruction to meet the instructional needs of individual students. This is a vital link in school reform. Moreover, cultural and ethnic differences should be embraced and valued in all forms and degrees as reflections of the contributions that different groups of Americans have made to our society. To affirm students means that we validate them for who they are, individuals who are valuable members of the classroom community. Students should be affirmed not only for the qualities that they have in common, but also for their uniquenesses. This can facilitate how they can learn self-respect (Stainback & Stainback, 1992). Educators need to realize that quality education is not just about schools, but about how people want to live their lives as part of a community.

Using assessments as an instrument for guiding instruction. The individualized education programs that guide the progress of children in special education are essentially contracts that govern and monitor a student's progress. As such, it is important to ensure that different forms of assessment are used appropriately, not only to determine the kinds of instruction and services needed by each child, but also to identify individual cognitive and personal strengths. Research must be undertaken to examine the ways in which students are identified for special education and the content of the services they eventually receive. Parental input in the assessment process is essential. In seeking successful collaboration with families, professional educators may have to increase their contacts with and pay more attention to parents. By doing so, educators will help to equalize the balance of power and can help to ensure that parents have the opportunity for sharing their important insights and goals for the children who are in special education (Turnbull, Turnbull, Shank, & Leal, 1995).

Determining best practices for improved student learning. Funding for special education and other federal programs designed to help children from low socioeconomic status families should be blended and made available in urban schools along with state and local resources. This means that a democratic agenda for school reform must include insisting on fair taxation and equal funding for all children. Such a change requires the de-tracking of schools and eliminating the territorial tracking between urban and suburban—not to mention poor and wealthy—districts redistributed in favor of equality. Statements of best practice should include, but are not limited to, age-appropriate placements in local public schools, integrated delivery of services, social integration, transition planning, curricular expectations, home-school partnerships, and systematic program evaluation (Thousand & Villa, 1990). The point here is that the best educational practices should be practiced for all children.

Developing school-home-community partnerships. Due to the rapid changes in contemporary society, schools, families, and communities must learn to share the responsibility of mobilizing resources and expertise (Nettles, 1991). Key issues include providing alternative delivery systems to engage families, community agencies, universities, and the private sector in supporting schools and student success, increasing family involvement in educational activities, and coordinating the linkage with social and health service agencies.

Conclusion

A pressing national concern is to prevent the high proportions of failure among students from diverse racial, ethnic, and socioeconomic backgrounds (Winfield & Manning, 1992). Young males, especially in the African American community, lack role models for the first 6 years of schooling. Further, young males encounter the most conflicts and receive the most punishments in school, and are most often placed in special education and remedial programs (Campbell, 1996). The culture of the school must change to provide learning environments that are responsive to a wide range of students' needs in urban settings. Access to learning for all students, including those from diverse cultures, in equitable environments, enhances the learning experience as well as the development of a positive self-esteem. School reform must address the needs of African American males in urban settings who tend to be the most marginalized group of public school students. Schools should embrace the diversity of the stu-

dent body, respecting and appreciating the rich ethnic and cultural differences in a safe environment conducive to students' learning styles and needs. If schools can accomplish all of these tasks, then perhaps they can escape the conundrum of the overrepresentation, or resegregation, of minority students in special education.

References

American Association of State Colleges and Universities. (1991). Short takes. *AASCU Memo to the president, 32*(22), 1.

American Association of University Women. (1992). *How schools shortchange girls.* New York: Marlowe.

Ancarrow, J. S. (1991). *Characteristics of regular and special education teachers in public schools, 1987–88: E.D. tabs.* Washington, DC: U.S. Department of Education, OSERS, Office of Special Education Programs.

Artiles, A. J., & Trent, S. C. (1994). Overrepresentation of minority students in special education: A continuing debate. *Journal of Special Education, 27,* 410–437.

Brown v. Board of Educ., 347 U.S. 483 (1954).

Campbell, D. E. (1996). *Choosing democracy: A practical guide to multicultural education.* Englewood Cliffs, NJ: Prentice Hall.

Cartledge, G., Gardner, R., & Tillman, L. (1995). African Americans in higher education special education: Issues in recruitment and retention. *Teacher Education and Special Education, 18*(3), 166–178.

Chinn, P. C., & Hughes, S. (1987). Representation of minority students in special education classes. *Remedial and Special Education, 8*(4), 41–46.

Choy, S. P., Henke, R. R., Alt, M. N., Medrich, E. A., & Bobbitt, S. A. (1993). *Schools and staffing in the United States: A statistical profile.* Washington, DC: U.S. Department of Education, National Center for Education Statistics.

Coates, J. F., & Jarratt, J. (1987). *Future search: Forces and factors shaping education.* Washington, DC: National Education Association.

Council for Exceptional Children. (1994). Statistical profile of special education in the United States, 1994.

Supplement to Teaching Exceptional Children, 26(3), 1–4.

Dunn, L. (1968). Special education for the mildly retarded: Is much of it justifiable? *Exceptional Children, 7,* 5–24.

Executive Committee of the Council for Children with Behavior Disorders. (1989). Best assessment practices for students with behavioral disorders: Accommodation to cultural diversity and individual differences. *Behavioral Disorders, 14*(4), 263–278.

Forness, S. R. (1988). Planning for the needs of children with serious emotional disturbance. The national special education and mental coalition. *Behavioral Disorders, 13*(2), 127–139.

Frierson, H. T. (1990). The situation of Black educational researchers: Continuation of a crisis. *Educational Researcher, 19*(2), 12–17.

Gollnick, D. M., & Chinn, P. C. (1994). *Multicultural education in a pluralistic society* (4th ed). New York: Merrill.

Harry, B., & Anderson, M. G. (1994). The disproportionate placement of African-American males in special education programs: A critique of the process. *Journal of Negro Education, 63*(4), 602–619.

Heller, K. A., Holtzman, W. H., & Messick, S. (Eds.). (1982). *Placing children in special education: A strategy for equity.* Washington, DC: National Academy Press.

Hodgkinson, H. (1988). The right schools for the right kids. *Educational Leadership, 45,* 10–14.

Individuals with Disabilities Educ. Act, 20 U.S.C. 1401 *et seq.* (1996).

Irvine, J. J. (1992). Making teacher education culturally responsive. In M. Dilworth (Ed.), *Diversity in teacher education: New expectations* (pp. 79–92). San Francisco: Jossey-Bass.

Jennings, J. (1994). *Understanding the nature of poverty in urban America.* Westport, CT: Praeger.

King, S. H. (1993). The limited presence of African American teachers. *Review of Educational Research, 63*(2), 115–149.

Lara, J. (1994). *State data collection and monitoring procedures regarding overrepresentation of minority students in special education.* Washington, DC: Special Education Program (ED/OSERS). (ERIC Document Reproduction Service No. ED 369 247)

Larry P. v. Riles, 343 F. Supp. 1306 (N.D. Cal. 1972), *aff'd* 502 F.2d 963 (9th Cir. 1974); 495 F. Supp. 926 (N.D. Cal.

1979), *aff'd* 793 F.2d 969 (9th Cir. 1984).

Maheady, L., Towne, R., & Algozzine, B. (1983). Minority overrepresentation: A case for alternative practices prior to referral. *Learning Disability Quarterly, 6*(4), 448–456.

Mills v. Board of Educ., 348 F. Supp. 866 (D.D.C. 1972).

National Clearinghouse for Professions in Special Education. (1991). *The severe shortage of minority personnel.* Washington, DC: U.S. Department of Education, National Center for Education Statistics.

Nettles, S. M. (1991). Community involvement and disadvantaged students: A review. *Review of Educational Research, 61*(3), 379–406.

Parents in Action on Special Educ. v. Hannon, 506 F. Supp. 831 (N.D. Ill. 1980).

Prasse, D. P., & Reschly, D. J. (1986). Larry P: A case of segregation, testing, or program efficiency? *Exceptional Children, 52*(4), 333–346.

Procedural safeguards: Definitions of "consent," "evaluation," and "personally identifiable." 34 C.F.R. § 300.500(b) (1996).

Russo, C. J., Harris III, J. J., & Sandidge, R. F. (1994). Brown v. Board of Education at 40: A legal history of equal educational opportunity in American public education. *Journal of Negro Education, 63*(3), 297–309.

Section 504 of the Rehabilitation Act of 1973, 20 U.S.C. 794(a) (1996).

Smith, G. R. (1983). Desegregation and assignment of children to classes for the mildly retarded and learning disabled. *Integrated Education, 21,* 208–211.

Smith-Davis, J., & Billingsley, B. S. (1993). The supply/demand puzzle. *Teacher Education and Special Education, 16*(3), 205–220.

Stainback, S., & Stainback, W. (1992). *Curriculum considerations in inclusive classrooms: Facilitating learning for all students.* Baltimore: Paul H. Brooks.

Thomas, S. B., & Russo, C. J. (1995). *Special education law: Issues and implications for the '90s.* Topeka, KS: National Organization on Legal Problems of Education.

Thousand, J., & Villa, R. (1990). Strategies for educating learners with severe disabilities within their local schools and communities. *Focus on Exceptional Children, 23*(3), 5.

Title VI of the Civil Rights Act of 1964, 20 U.S.C. 1681 *et seq.* (1996).

Turnbull, A. P., Turnbull, H. R., Shank, M., & Leal, D. (1995). *Exceptional lives: Special education in today's schools.* Englewood Cliffs, NJ: Merrill.

U.S. Department of Education, Office of Civil Rights (OCR). (1994). *1992 elementary and secondary school civil rights survey: National summaries.* Washington, DC: DBS Corporation.

Winfield, L. F., & Manning, J. B. (1992). Changing school culture to accommodate student diversity. In M. Dilworth (Ed.), *Diversity in teacher education: New expectations* (pp. 181–213). San Francisco: Jossey-Bass.

 Article Review Form at end of book.

How can there be both under- and overrepresentation of language-minority students in special education? What do the authors see as an incompatibility between a major approach in special education (task analysis and skill-building) and a major approach in bilingual education (the natural language orientation)?

The Language-Minority Student and Special Education

Issues, trends, and paradoxes

Russell Gersten

Russell Gersten (CEC OR Federation), Researcher, Eugene Research Institute, and Professor, University of Oregon, Eugene.

John Woodward

John Woodward (CEC WA Federation), Associate Professor, University of Puget Sound, Tacoma, WA

The current wave of immigrants to the United States is the largest in history (U.S. Bureau of the Census, 1990). Mexican immigrants over the past 10 years constitute the largest population migration from a single country in U.S. history, doubling in number from 1980 to 1990; currently there are 4.3 million. The total number of Hispanic immigrants (from Mexico and other parts of Latin America) in the United States grew by 2.5 million over the past decade, a 17% increase (De La Rosa & Maw, 1990). In 1982, only 1 in 10 children in U.S. schools was Hispanic, but this ratio will be approximately 1 in 4 by the year 2020 (Pallas, Natriello, & McDill, 1989).

The educational plight of immigrant Hispanic students is a national concern (Suro, 1990). Their rate of grade retention, for example, is extremely high. One in four Hispanic eighth graders, significantly above the national average, has repeated one grade. More importantly, 15.2% of the Hispanic eighth graders sampled by De La Rosa and Maw (1990) had been retained at least twice during their school careers—even though researchers have shown that grade retention is a particularly ineffective means of dealing with learning or motivational problems (Allington & McGill-Franzen, 1989). Hispanics have the highest dropout rate of any ethnic group in the United States. Only 51% of Hispanics age 21 and over possess a high school diploma, compared with 63% for African Americans and 77% for whites (De La Rosa & Maw, 1990).

Some recent immigrants—from Mexico, Central America, and Cambodia and other parts of Southeast Asia—have had very little formal school experience (Foster, 1980; Kleinman & Daniel, 1981; Maingot, 1981; Marx, 1981). In many cases, their parents have also had minimal schooling and students' home exposure to print materials may be quite limited. A substantial proportion of these children will likely perform poorly in school unless school programs are enhanced to meet their needs (Goldenberg & Gallimore, 1991; Reyes, 1992; Teale, 1986).

This combination of educational and demographic factors places tremendous demands on schools in such states as California, New York, Texas, and Florida and large cities like Chicago and Phoenix, which have large numbers of students from language-minority groups. Many smaller communities that have increasing numbers of students from language-minority groups are experiencing similar pressure ("Percentage of Foreigners," 1992). Experts project that these demographic trends will accelerate in the next 10 years (Pallas et al., 1989).

In response to these phenomena, many classroom teachers—particularly in cities and states with large numbers of recent immigrants—have become, often by default, teachers of students for whom English is a second language. Recently, we interviewed educators—special education directors, bilingual education coordinators, principals, and classroom teachers in a large, urban district with a substantial proportion of students from language-minority groups—about perceived problems and policy issues (Gersten, 1991). These educators emphasized the seriousness of the many problems facing classroom teachers, severe personnel shortages, and the uncertain and unclear role of special education in providing solutions. The interviews verified published reports (Baca & Almanza, 1991; Gold, 1992) of severe shortages of adequately trained personnel in both special and general education.

Many teachers, confronted with a struggling student from a language-minority group, are baffled by the student's seemingly unpredictable rate of academic progress (Gersten, Woodward, & Morvant, 1992). Often these teachers turn to special education for assistance because they are unsure of which level of conventional English-language curriculum to use and how to adapt this curriculum to meet the student's needs. They are also uncertain about how to determine whether bilingual students are experiencing problems due to learning disabilities or due to their limited comprehension of the English language.

Yet it is unclear how useful special education can be, because very few special educators are bilingual and have not been trained in second-language instructional techniques.

Rarely is meaningful assistance provided to special education teachers faced with providing second-language instruction (Baca and Cervantes, 1989). Figueroa, Fradd, and Correa (1989) concluded that there is not

a substantive body of empirical data on actual, well-controlled interventions. Bilingual special education does not yet have this body of knowledge [on improving the academic abilities of students with learning disabilities from language-minority groups]. (p. 17)

Often, the services offered are ad hoc, such as providing an untrained tutor who knows the native language but has no teaching experience to solve the problem. As Ruiz (1989) noted: "The wrongs done to . . . language minority students in special education are exceptionally severe: misidentification, misplacement,

misuse of tests, and poor academic performance within special education" (p. 139).

Coexistence of Overrepresentation and Underrepresentation

The related issues of misidentification and misplacement of students from language-minority groups into special education has received the most attention in the research literature. Research documenting recurring severe problems (Chang, 1992; Figueroa, 1989; Mehan, Hertweck, & Meihls, 1986; Mercer, 1973; Moecker, 1992) has led to a focus on the accurate assessment of students from language-minority groups to distinguish those who are truly in need of special education services from students who are not successful in school due primarily to limited English-language capacity (Figueroa et al., 1989; Mercer & Rueda, 1991; Ortiz, 1988).

Currently, a paradoxical condition exists in the field—over-referral *as well as* underreferral.

Overrepresentation of Students From Language-Minority Groups in Special Education

In her seminal research on minorities in special education, Mercer (1973) found that Hispanic students were often erroneously diagnosed as students with learning disabilities or mental retardation and were improperly placed in special education classes. Gearhart and Weishahn (1980) later called this practice a convenient way for administrators to "do something" without truly understanding the students' language needs or dealing with systemic problems.

After conducting an ethnographic study of two elementary schools, Richardson, Casanova, Placier, and Guilfoyle (1989) concluded that classroom teachers often refer students for special education or compensatory education services when they believe that the students are not benefiting from classroom instruction and when the teachers are unsure how to deal with the problem. Richardson et al. concluded that referral often is more a reflection of teacher stress, than a result of carefully diagnosed student learning deficits.

Underrepresentation/Underuse of Support Services for Students from Language-Minority Groups with Academic Needs

One outcome of Mercer's (1973) early research was a series of significant court decisions that resulted in the institution of legal and procedural safeguards to address the inappropriate special education referrals of students from minority groups. Consequently, some districts are reluctant to place students with limited English proficiency in special education because of potential charges of discrimination or misassessment, as well as the fear of lawsuits.

On a national level, there is continuing evidence of overreferral of students with limited English proficiency into special education (Figueroa, 1989; Mercer & Rueda, 1991; Ortiz, 1988). In certain urban districts, however, a fear of legal action, as well as the realization that assessment procedures for these students are of weak validity, has led to a tendency toward *underreferral* of these students for special support services. In at least one large urban district, the problem has been raised by parents and advocacy groups. In this district, the percentage of special education students who are Hispanic is significantly lower than the overall percentage of Hispanic students in the district. This phenomena appears to be increasingly widespread for students with limited English proficiency (Fradd, personal communication, January 1993).

As a result, there is a group of students with learning disabilities or other academic problems, who are limited in their use of English and who are not receiving the kind of assistance they need. Based on our research and interviews with urban administrators, we envision this as a growing problem.

In no way are increased referral rates into pullout special education programs a remedy. However, we are concerned about the large number of students from language-minority groups who are "falling through the cracks." Observational research (Arreaga-Mayer, in press; Campbell et al., 1993; Chang, 1992) is beginning to increasingly document the dire plight of low-achieving students from language-minority groups in general education classrooms when no support is provided.

Differing Theories and Models of Second-Language Instruction

Whether or not low-achieving students from language-minority groups receive special support services, there are serious questions about the present capacity of special education services to offer valid instructional interventions. One reason for this, however, arises from a controversy within bilingual education itself.

Bilingual educators and researchers have long debated the optimal instructional model for providing transitions for students from language-minority groups into the second language of English (Crawford, 1989; Wong-Fillmore & Valdez, 1986). The goal of building competence in English without unduly frustrating students requires a complex balance between the use of the native language and the language to be acquired. Contemporary models differ greatly in the ratio of primary (or native) to English-language instruction provided, particularly during the first 5 years of school. Two issues underlying the controversy are: (a) how quickly students from language-minority groups should be placed in classrooms where English is the sole means of instructional communication; and (b) whether Spanish (or another native language) is merely a bridge to help students learn English as quickly as possible, or whether the goal is for students to become fluent and academically competent in both languages.

In reality, many differing models of bilingual education exist (Ramirez, 1992). For the purposes of this discussion, however, we briefly describe the two major approaches advocated for educating students from language-minority groups and the underlying rationales of these models.

Native Language Emphasis

Wong-Fillmore and Valez (1986) cogently presented the conceptual framework for native-language emphasis:

By reading, we refer here to the act of reconstructing the meaning of a text as intended by the writer, and through this process, gaining access to the information that is encoded. . . . Reading is unquestionably a language-dependent skill. It is not possible to read in a language one does not know, if reading involves the act of making intelligible to oneself written texts of any complexity beyond that of street signs. A prerequisite for true reading, it would appear, is a fairly high level of knowledge of the language in which the text is written. (pp. 660–661)

In other words, until students obtain a reasonably good knowledge of English—particularly in such conceptually complex areas such as reading/language arts and social studies—instruction should be in the native language. Thus, students are not deprived of the experience of learning the core concepts in the normal school curriculum during the years when they are learning English. According to this viewpoint, English-language instruction in complex subjects such as social studies would be nearly incomprehensible, and of little benefit to the student. Premature introduction of students to English-language academic material can be harmful (Krashen, 1982; Moll & Diaz, 1987).

Many contemporary theorists, such as Cummins (1989) or Krashen (1982), believe that once students succeed in complex academic material in their native language, they will transfer this knowledge to the same subjects taught in English. Therefore, it would seem more sensible to teach complex academic content to students in their native language first so that students can understand and discuss challenging material without the added demand of constantly translating or expressing ideas in a second language.

As such, most bilingual approaches typically emphasize academic instruction in the students' primary language and suspend English-language academic instruction, until students demonstrate an adequate grasp of English and exhibit competence in academic areas in their native language (Cummins, 1989; Krashen, 1982).

Advocates of native-language emphasis, such as Cummins (1989) and Moll and Diaz (1987), have noted that another problem with prematurely placing students in academic classes taught in English is that the academic material will be simplified or "watered down" to meet the perceived level of student competence. "A common reaction to the less-than-fluent English of a student is to teach content from a lower grade level and to expect only lower-level cognitive skills, such as simple recall" (Chamot & O'Malley, 1989, p. 114). The predominant use of simplified materials can lead to unnecessary constraints on students' cognitive growth.

Thus there is a widely held belief that native-language instruction in content areas, such as reading, social studies, and language arts, is essential (Goldenberg & Gallimore, 1991; Reyes, 1992). Yet there remains great diversity in opinion and practice regarding how rapidly and in which content areas students should be introduced to English-language instruction, and how long native-language instruction should be maintained (Chamot & O'Malley, 1989; Crawford, 1989; Ramirez, 1992).

Sheltered-English/ Structured Immersion

Another approach to the education of students from language-minority groups is sheltered English (Northcutt & Watson, 1986) or structured immersion (Baker & de Kanter, 1983; Ramirez, 1992). This approach was developed and successfully implemented with English-speaking students in Quebec, Canada. The success of that experiment—documented by significant growth in academic achievement on standardized tests—played a large role in the popularization of sheltered-English/structured immersion approaches in the United States (Genesee, 1984). This approach is currently used most frequently with Southeast Asian students in the elementary grades, and it is increasingly being used with both Hispanic and Southeast Asian students at the secondary level (Chamot & O'Malley, 1989). Researchers have also reported some examples of its use with elementary-age Hispanic students in the United States (Gersten & Woodward, in press; Ramirez et al., 1992).

Sheltered English assumes that an understanding of English can be obtained through well-designed content-area instruction where English is used, *but at a level that is constantly modulated or negotiated* (Chamot & O'Malley, 1989; Long, 1983). Sheltered-English teachers attempt to control their classroom vocabulary, to use concrete objects and gestures to enhance understanding, and to use a wide range of instructional strategies so that students understand the academic material. In some cases, students experience native-language instruction for periods of 30–90 min a day at school. However, English is used for the majority of the teaching day. The goal of sheltered English is for students to learn English while they are developing basic academic abilities and skills and to develop English-language competence while building abilities in the areas of comprehension and problem solving.

In short, during the first few years of elementary school, a student in a sheltered-English program will experience most of his or her day in English, whereas if the student were in a bilingual education program with a strong native-language emphasis, much of his or her day would be in the native language.

Comparing Models of Bilingual Education

To date, research contrasting the effectiveness of structured immersion versus bilingual approaches with more of an emphasis on native-language content-area instruction has produced equivocal findings (Baker & de Kanter, 1983; Cziko, 1992; Danoff, Coles, McLaughlin, & Reynolds, 1977–78; Willig, 1985). Most longitudinal studies have shown little or no difference in achievement between students taught with a native-language-emphasis approach and those taught with a more sheltered-English or structured immersion model.

A possible cause for the consistent lack of significant differences in the various evaluation studies was elucidated by the observational research of Tikunoff (1985). His findings revealed wide variation in *what actually transpires* in bilingual education classrooms, regardless of how the approach is labeled. He observed that, on the average, English was used 60% of the time; and Spanish was used most of the remaining 40%. However, there were large variations from teacher to teacher and school to school. Wong-Fillmore and Valdez (1986) also noted huge variations in practice, and many researchers have found bilingual rooms to be bilingual in name only; in reality, they closely resemble traditional English-language classrooms.

Nine years ago, we noted that "bilingual education . . . [is] relatively easy to write about, yet difficult to implement sensitively on a day-to-day basis" (Gersten & Woodward, 1985, p. 78). As different as the various bilingual models may appear in theory, some of the finer distinctions fade in practice (Tikunoff, 1985). Practical matters, such as high costs and teacher training requirements, are likely to contribute to the considerable variation in practice.

A serious issue common to all approaches is the "double demands" required of students from language-minority groups. Specifically, these students need to acquire a second language, as well as master traditional subject matter in the amount of time most students are asked to learn these subjects in just one language. Overall, it appears that the type of bilingual model selected is less important than the quality of instruction provided (Gersten, 1991; Reyes, 1992; Tikunoff, 1985).

Relevance and Implications for Special Education

For many students from language-minority groups, and for those who teach them, the task of simultaneously learning a new language and mastering the core academic curriculum in this new language is daunting. It is likely that teachers who are unable to cope with many of the demands associated with students from language-minority groups will often look to special education for assistance (Mercer & Rueda, 1991).

The need for special education services also arises from the way teachers provide transitions for students from an almost-all-Spanish to an almost-all-English instructional program. Abrupt transitions almost always have disastrous effects on student achievement and self-concept (Ramirez, 1992). Yet research has shown that this is exactly what schools tend to do with students from language-minority groups (Gersten, 1991; Ramirez, 1992).

Too often, teachers label students caught in these transitions as "at-risk" for special education or school failure. This "policy" is one significant reason for the disproportionate number of inappropriate special education referrals, in the upper elementary grades, of students from language-minority groups.

Another major problem with implications for special education is the variation in models that exists throughout the United States. These variations may exist between neighboring school districts or even within the *same* district. The high mobility of families from language-minority groups increases the likelihood that a child will have been taught with very different approaches at different times in his or her school life. The confusion this can create for a student has been evident in our own observational research (Campbell et al., 1993; Gersten, 1993). The educational history of one of the students (referred to here as Jorge) from the case studies of Campbell et al. (1993) provides a brief illustration.

Jorge was one of 12 "at-risk language minority" students observed by the research team over a 3-year period in a large, racially mixed school district with a sizable low-income population. Jorge spent his first 3 school years in a native-language-emphasis bilingual education program. Virtually all instruction was in Spanish, save for 1 hour of English as a second language. When his family moved to an area served by another school, he entered a sheltered-English program. This meant that Jorge went from a full day in Spanish, where he was learning reading, spelling, and mathematics in his native language, to a classroom where English was the primary language of instruction. Even though the teacher controlled her vocabulary and academic materials, Jorge was well behind his new peers, most of whom were in their third year of English-language instruction. Moreover, his reading was a strange hybrid of the two. He subsequently was referred for special education placement and placed in a room where the teacher spoke only English. Both the special education staff at the school and the school administration were unsure where to begin.

Jorge's case study illustrates an important point. The diversity of viewpoints on second-language programs manifests itself in odd, distressing ways for students from families with high rates of mobility. The stress this diversity of programs puts on students with weak academic abilities is particularly severe.

Whole/Natural Language Versus Skills Emphasis: A False Dichotomy?

In a recent synthesis of findings from research conducted by the Handicapped Minority Research Institutes in the late 1980s, Figueroa et al. (1989) concluded that one of the major flaws in current special education services to students from language-minority groups is the lack of integration between the remedial programs provided by special educators and the students' instructional program in the regular classroom. This problem is hardly unique for this population; Zigmond, Vallecorsa, and Leinhardt (1980) and Allington and McGill-Franzen (1989) have noted similar discrepancies for English-speaking students with learning disabilities. In both instances, the researchers found that remedial, pullout settings tend to emphasize mastery of discrete skills in a nonintegrated fashion.

A major concern among bilingual educators is that the task-analytic, skill-building approach used in many special education programs is both functionally and philosophically incompatible with the natural-language (often called "whole language") approach increasingly used in mainstream classrooms serving students from language-minority groups (Au & Scheu, 1989; Cummins, 1989). Many bilingual special educators (Cummins, 1984; Yates & Ortiz, 1991) believe that the conventional, skill-building approach used in special education is insufficient for meeting the needs of students from language-minority groups because language development will be stifled.

Many second-language programs, therefore, have begun to move toward the increased use of natural language (Cummins, 1989; Saville-Troike, 1982). Both Cummins (1989) and Tharp and Gallimore (1988) have eloquently pled for the conscious integration of natural-language use and genuine dialogue into classroom instruction. These researchers have concluded that conventional emphases—on correct oral reading, proper pronunciation in English, systematic instruction involving vocabulary lists, and English-language grammar and literal comprehension—not only inhibit the language development of students but also hinder their overall cognitive development, by taking most of the meaning and enjoyment out of learning.

This focus on the details of accurate English-language production makes the students appear less competent and able than they really are. When Moll and Diaz followed the same students into a Spanish reading lesson, they observed that these same "low ability" students were able to answer comprehension questions correctly and to develop and expand on ideas in the stories.

Yates and Ortiz (1991) also highlighted the disparity and tensions between conventional special education practice and the emerging model for appropriate instruction of students from language-minority groups and with learning disabilities. They emphasized the importance of *comprehensible* input:

It is difficult for LEP [limited-English-proficient] students to respond appropriately when discussions revolve around leprechauns, blarney stones and the joys of eating corned beef and cabbage if they have no prior experience with these topics. The principle of comprehensible input . . . is violated when teachers use topics, materials and tasks that are linguistically, experientially and culturally unrelated to students' backgrounds. . . . *Teachers should add sufficient context rather than attempting to simplify tasks by breaking them down into what they consider to be smaller, less complex units.* (pp. 15–16, emphasis added)

A more natural, fluid learning environment is necessary for language development. People use language to obtain what they want or to express their thoughts, feelings, and ideas (Fradd 1987). Therefore, it is particularly important that second-language instruction be relevant rather than only a series of drills on grammar and usage.

An Effective Balance

Clearly, we need some reconceptualization of how to teach students from language-minority groups (including those in special education). We need to draw on the developing consensus among bilingual education researchers, while integrating principles of effective instruction and newer cognitive approaches from special education. As recently as 1991, Yates and Ortiz concluded: "The field of bilingual special education is so new that a body of effective practices has yet to be established" (p. 14). Nonetheless, a body of research is emerging from these three areas that suggests practices likely to be effective.

First, research suggests that children must be given interesting reading material that makes sense to them; and the material must explicitly provide links between students' prior knowledge and concepts in the story. Based on extensive work with students from language-minority groups, Barrera (1984) noted how English-language reading can be an excellent medium for the development of English-language competence.

The beginning of second-language reading can be a natural . . . learner-controlled occurrence when children approach reading as a desirable, useful, and meaningful activity. . . . Second-language reading can commence soon after native-language reading begins, or develop virtually alongside it, as long as the learner is making sense of the written language he or she encounters. (Barrera, 1984, p. 170)

Second, an emerging view of effective instruction for students from language-minority groups builds on the concepts of comprehensible input (Krashen, 1982), and "negotiated" interaction (Long, 1983). Ensuring that students understand the concepts that the teacher attempts to convey involves intentional use of redundancy, more frequent use of simple or declarative sentences, frequent checks for student comprehension, and the use of physical gestures and visual cues. Teachers should try to explain ideas of concepts several times using slight variations in terminology and examples.

Fradd (1987) cautions that making material comprehensible should not entail a "watering down" of concepts. It requires the same type of sophisticated modulation of instruction found in the instructional research of such individuals as Graham and Harris (1989) and Palincsar and Klenk (1992).

Third, students from language-minority groups must be pushed to move from learning and producing limited word translations and fragmented concepts, to using longer sentences and expressing more complex ideas and feelings (Barrera, 1984; Gersten, 1993). Special educators often have a relatively easy time breaking complex concepts into small steps, frequently assessing whether students understand the concept taught, and using redundant language and physical gestures as prompts. However, the task of encouraging students to express their ideas in a new language, and in increasingly complex forms, presents a challenge for many special educators.

This emerging sense of effective approaches in bilingual special education suggests that special educators grounded in more task-analytic or behavioral schools of instructional practice can bring their skills to bear in useful ways to meet the needs of students from language-minority groups with academic problems, including those with mild disabilities. However, to fully meet the needs of these students, special education must also increasingly draw on the cognitive tradition, on use of relevant curricular materials, and on the creation of learning environments where students feel comfortable expressing their ideas in a new language.

Conclusion

Rueda (1990) has noted that many issues confronting special education for Hispanic students "are simply manifestations of more fundamental problems that affect the entire field" (p. 126). Among these are the questions from the field of bilingual education of how soon to introduce English-language content instruction and how to handle the complex task of both teaching a second language and developing academic abilities in a relatively short time frame. Similarly, it is essential to have a grasp of the many unresolved issues in the field of special education, such as the advantages and disadvantages of pullout programs, problems in curriculum integration, the proper balance between skills and strategy instruction, and accurate methods of identification and ongoing assessment. An appreciation for the root controversies in both fields is crucial to understanding the dilemmas facing those designing and studying effective programs for students from language-minority groups and students with disabilities or those experiencing difficulty in school.

As we have discussed, emerging research strongly suggests that all students from language-minority groups—including those with disabilities—can profit from some balance of second-language instruction based on contemporary whole-language/process approaches to teaching literacy. This is not to say that such methods provide a complete solution, or that there is no place for some version of systematic instruction with adequate review and practice of targeted skills and strategies. Rather, the issue is one of how to combine these skills and strategies into a viable approach to meet the needs of students with limited English proficiency and with learning disabilities, as well as those not profiting from conventional instruction.

It is easier to critique current practice than to begin building guidelines for special educators to collaborate effectively with classroom teachers on issues related to more effective instruction for these students. The problem is also complicated by a dearth of bilingual special educators. However, with relevant professional development activities, monolingual teachers can also effectively teach these students, an observation supported in recent research on the sheltered-English approach to bilingual education (Allen, 1989; Chamot & O'Malley, 1989; Gersten, 1993).

The task is not easy. Earlier research has detailed problems and argued for more valid, culturally sensitive procedures for assessment and classification. Research has also documented the improper placement of students from language-minority groups into special education, where watered-down curriculums, constricted use of language, and lower teacher expectations have had a detrimental effect on students.

Newer research has shown that, in some areas, the tide is turning; and students with limited English proficiency are referred for special services at a lower rate. However, research has also shown that too many lower performing students from language-minority groups often do not receive adequate instructional assistance from their classroom teachers. Whether students from language-minority groups are underrepresented or overrepresented statistically in special education, it is important that none is underserved and that all receive quality instruction.

References

Allen, V. G. (1989). Literature as a support to language acquisition. In P. Rigg & V. G. Allen (Eds.), *When they don't all speak English.* (pp. 55–64). Urbana, IL: National Council of Teachers of English. (ERIC Document Reproduction Service No. 313 896).

Allington, R., & McGill-Franzen, A. (1989). School response to reading failure: Instruction for Chapter 1 and special education students in grades two, four, and eight. *Elementary School Journal, 89*(5), 529–542.

Arreaga-Mayer, C. (in press). Using ecobehavioral assessment to evaluate effective bilingual special education programs. *Elementary School Journal.*

Au, K. H., & Scheu, J. A. (1989). Guiding students to interpret a novel. *The Reading Teacher, 43*(2), 104–110.

Baca, L. M., & Almanza, E. (1991). *Language minority students with disabilities.* Reston, VA: The Council for Exceptional Children. (ERIC Document Reproduction Service No. 339 171)

Baca, L. M., & Cervantes, H. T. (1989). *The bilingual special education interface* (2nd ed.). Columbus, OH: Merrill.

Baker, K. A., & de Kanter, A. A. (1983). *Bilingual education: A reappraisal of federal policy.* Lexington, MA: Lexington Books.

Barrera, R. (1984). Bilingual reading in the primary grades: Some questions about questionable views and practices. In T. H. Escobar (Ed.), *Early childhood bilingual education* (pp. 164–183). New York: Teachers College Press.

Campbell, J., Gersten, R., & Kolar, C. (1993). *Quality of instruction provided to language minority students with learning disabilities: Five findings from microethnographies.* Technical Report 93-5. Eugene, OR: Eugene Research Institute.

Cazden, C. B. (1992). *Whole language plus: Essays on literacy in the United States and New Zealand.* New York: Teachers College Press.

Chamot, A. U., & O'Malley, J. M. (1989). The cognitive academic language learning approach. In P. Rigg & V. Allen (Eds.), *When they don't all speak English* (pp. 108–125). Urbana, IL: National Council of Teachers of English. (ERIC Document Reproduction Service No. 313 896)

Chang, J. M. (1992, August). *Current programs serving Chinese-American students in learning disabilities resource issues.* Paper presented at the Third National Research Symposium on Limited English Proficient Students, Office of Bilingual Education and Minority Language Affairs, U.S. Department of Education, Arlington, VA.

Crawford, J. (1989). *Bilingual education: History, politics, theory and practice.* Trenton, NJ: Crane.

Cummins, J. (1984). *Bilingualism and special education.* Clevedon, England: Multilingual Matters.

Cummins, J. (1989). A theoretical framework for bilingual special education. *Exceptional Children, 56*(2), 111–119.

Cziko, G. A. (1992). The evaluation of bilingual education. *Educational Researcher, 21*(2), 10–15.

Danoff, M. N., Coles, G. J., McLaughlin, D. H., & Reynolds, D. J. (1977–78). *Evaluation of the impact of ESEA Title VII Spanish/English Bilingual Education Program.* Palo Alto, CA: American Institutes for Research.

De La Rosa, D., & Maw, C. (1990). *Hispanic education: A statistical portrait*. Washington, DC: National Council of La Raza. (ERIC Document Reproduction Service No. 325 562)

Elley, W. B., & Mangubhai, F. (1983). The impact of reading on second language learning. *Reading Research Quarterly, 19*(1), 53–67.

Figueroa, R. A. (1989). Psychological testing of linguistic-minority students: Knowledge gaps and regulations. *Exceptional Children, 56*(2), 111–119.

Figueroa, R. A., Fradd, S. H., & Correa, V. I. (1989). Bilingual special education and this special issue. *Exceptional Children, 56*(2), 174–178.

Foster, C. (1980). Creole in conflict. *Migration Today, 8*, 8–13.

Fradd, S. H. (1987). Accommodating the needs of limited English proficient students in regular classrooms. In S. Fradd & W. Tikunoff (Eds.), *Bilingual education and special education: A guide for administrators* (pp. 133–182). Boston: Little, Brown.

Gearhart, B., & Weishahn, M. (1980). *The handicapped student in the regular classroom* (2nd ed.). St. Louis, MO: Mosby.

Genesee, F. (1984). Historical and theoretical foundations of immersion education. *Studies on immersion education* (pp. 32–57). Sacramento: California State Department of Education.

Gersten, R. (1991, November). *The language minority student in special education*. Paper presented at The Council for Exceptional Children Topical Conference on At-Risk Children and Youth, New Orleans.

Gersten, R. (1993, April). *The language minority student in transition: Exploring the parameters of effective literacy instruction*. Paper presented at the annual conference of the American Educational Research Association, Atlanta, GA.

Gersten, R., & Jiménez, R. (in press). A delicate balance: Enhancing literacy instruction for language minority students. *The Reading Teacher*.

Gersten, R., & Woodward, J. (1985). A case for structured immersion. *Educational Leadership, 43*(1), 75–78.

Gersten, R., & Woodward, J. (1993). *Lost opportunities: Observations of the teaching of language minority students in the intermediate grades*. (Technical Report 93-3.) Eugene, OR: Eugene Research Institute.

Gersten, R., & Woodward, J. (in press). A longitudinal study of transitional and immersion bilingual education programs in one district. *Elementary School Journal*.

Gersten, R., Woodward, J., & Morvant, M. (1992). Refining the working knowledge of experienced teachers. *Educational Leadership, 49*(7), 34–38.

Gold, N. (1992, April). *Solving the shortage of bilingual teachers: Policy implications of California's staffing initiative for limited English proficiency students*. Paper presented at the annual meeting of the American Education Research Association, San Francisco.

Goldenberg, C., & Gallimore, R. (1991). Local knowledge, research knowledge, and educational change: A case study of early Spanish reading improvement. *Educational Researcher, 20*(8), 2–14.

Graham, S., & Harris, K. R. (1989). Components analysis of cognitive strategy instruction: Effects on learning disabled students' compositions and self-efficacy. *Journal of Educational Psychology, 81*, 353–361.

Harris, K. C. (1991). An expanded view on consultation competencies for educators serving culturally and linguistically diverse exceptional students. *Teacher Education and Special Education, 14*(1), 25–29.

Kleinman, H. H., & Danile, J. P. (1981). Indochinese resettlement: Language education and social services. *International Migration Review, 15*, 239–244.

Krashen, S. (1982). *Principles and practice in second language acquisition*. New York: Pergamon Press.

Long, M. H. (1983). Native speaker/non-native speaker conversation in the second language classroom. In M. A. Clarke & J. Handscombe (Eds.), *On TESOL '82: Pacific perspectives on language learning and teaching* (pp. 207–225). Washington, DC: Teachers of English to Speakers of Other Languages.

Maingot, A. (1981). *International migration and refugees: The Caribbean, South Florida and the Northeast*. Miami: Florida International University, Department of Sociology/Anthropology.

Marx, R. (1981). The Iu Mien. *Migration Today, 9*, 21–26.

Mehan, H., Hertweck, A., & Meihls, J. L. (1986). *Handicapping the handicapped: Decision making in students' educational careers*. Stanford, CA: Stanford University Press.

Mercer, J. R. (1973). *Labeling the mentally retarded*. Berkeley: University of California Press.

Mercer, J. R., & Rueda, R. (1991, November). *The impact of changing paradigms of disabilities on assessment for special education*. Paper presented at The Council for Exceptional Children Topical Conference on At-Risk Children and Youth, New Orleans.

Miramontes, O. B. (1991). Organizing for effective paraprofessional services in special education: A multilingual/multiethnic instructional service team model. *Remedial and Special Education, 12*(1), 29–36.

Moecker, D. L. (1992, November). *Special education decision processes for Anglo and Hispanic students*. Paper presented at The Council for Exceptional Children Topical Conference on Culturally and Linguistically Diverse Exceptional Children, Minneapolis.

Moll, L. C., & Diaz, S. (1987). Change as the goal of educational research. *Anthropology and Education Quarterly, 18*, 300–311.

Moll, L. C., Estrada, E., Diaz, E., & Lopes, L. M. (1980). The organization of bilingual lessons: Implications for schooling. *The Quarterly Newsletter of the Laboratory of Comparative Human Cognition, 2*(3), 53–58.

National Assessment of Educational Progress. (1988). Washington, DC: U.S. Department of Education.

Northcutt, L., & Watson, D. (1986). *Sheltered English teaching handbook*. Carlsbad, CA: Northcutt, Watson, Gonzalez.

Ortiz, A. (1988). *Effective practices in assessment and instruction for language minority students: An intervention model*. Arlington, VA: Innovative Approaches Research Project, Office of Bilingual Education and Minority Languages Affairs, U.S. Department of Education.

Ovando, C. J., & Collier, V. P. (1985). *Bilingual and ESL classrooms: Teaching on multicultural contexts*. New York: McGraw-Hill.

Palincsar, A. S., & Klenk, L. (1992). Fostering literacy learning in supportive contexts. *Journal of Learning Disabilities, 25*(4), 211–225, 229.

Pallas, A., Natriello, G., & McDill, E. (1989). The changing nature of the disadvantaged population: Current dimensions and future trends. *Educational Researcher, 18*(5), 16–22.

Percentage of foreigners in U.S. rises sharply. (1992, December 20). *New York Times National*, p. 36.

Poplin, M. S. (1988). Holistic/constructivist principles of the teaching/learning process:

Implications for the field of learning disabilities. *Journal of Learning Disabilities, 21*(7), 401–416.

Ramirez, J. D. (1992). Executive summary. *Bilingual Research Journal, 16*(1 & 2), 1–62.

Reyes, M. de la luz (1992). Challenging venerable assumptions: Literacy instruction for linguistically different students. *Harvard Educational Review, 62*(4), 427–446.

Richardson, V., Casanova, U., Placier, P., & Guilfoyle, K. (1989). *School children at risk.* New York: Falmer Press.

Rueda, R. (1990, July). *Methodological considerations in multicultural research.* Paper presented at Office of Special Education Programs Research Project Directors' Conference, Washington, DC.

Ruiz, N. T. (1989). An optimal learning environment for Rosemary. *Exceptional Children, 56,* 130–144.

Saville-Troike, M. (1982). The development of bilingual and bicultural competence in young children. *Current topics in early childhood education, 4,* 1–16.

Speidel, G. E. (1987). Conversation and language learning in the classroom. In K. E. Nelson & A. van Kleedk (Eds.), *Child Language* (Vol. 6). Hillsdale, NJ: Lawrence Erlbaum.

Suro, R. (1990, November 4). Hispanics in despair. *New York Times,* Section 4A, p. 25.

Teale, W. H. (1986). Home background and young children's literacy development. In W. H. Teale & E. Sulzby (Eds.), *Emergent literacy: Writing and reading* (pp. 173–206). Norwood, NJ: Ablex.

Tharp, R. G. (1982). The effective instruction of comprehension: Results and description of the Kamehameha early education program. *Reading Research Quarterly, 4,* 503–527.

Tharp, R. G., & Gallimore, R. (1988). *Rousing minds to life.* Cambridge, UK: Cambridge University Press.

Tikunoff, W. J. (1985). *Applying significant bilingual instructional features in the classroom.* Rosslyn, VA: National Clearinghouse for Bilingual Education. (ERIC Document Reproduction Service No. 338 106)

U.S. Bureau of the Census. (1990). *How we're changing—Demographic state of the nation: 1990.* Washington, DC: U.S. Department of Commerce, Bureau of the Census.

Wilkinson, C., & Ortiz, A. (1986). *Characteristics of limited English proficient and English proficient learning disabled Hispanic students at initial assessment and at reevaluation.* Austin: University of Texas, Department of Special Education, Handicapped Minority Research Institute. (ERIC Document Reproduction Service No. 283 314)

Willig, A. C. (1985). A meta-analysis of selected studies on the effectiveness of bilingual education. *Review of Educational Research, 55*(3), 269–317.

Wong-Fillmore, L., & Valdez, C. (1986). Teaching bilingual learners. In M. C. Wittrock (Ed.), *Handbook of research on teaching* (pp. 648–685). New York: Macmillan.

Yates, J. R., & Ortiz, A. A. (1991). Professional development needs of teachers who serve exceptional language minorities in today's schools. *Teacher Education and Special Education, 14*(1), 11–18.

Zigmond, N., Vallecorsa, A., & Leinhardt, G. (1980). Reading instruction for students with learning disabilities. *Topics in Language Disorders, 1,* 89–98.

An earlier version of this article was presented at The Council for Exceptional Children's Topical Conference on At Risk Children and Youth in New Orleans in November 1991. This research was supported in part by Grant #H023H00014 of the Division of Innovation and Development of the Office of Special Education Programs of the U.S. Department of Education. The authors wish to express their appreciation for the valuable feedback received from Robert Jiménez and Thomas Keating on earlier versions of the manuscript and thank Damion Jurrens for his assistance in the preparation of the manuscript.

 **Article Review Form at end of book.**

How did Reyes' own experiences as a student influence her approach to teaching? In addition to having students explore and play with language, what other strategies did Reyes employ in teaching language-minority students with learning difficulties?

Conversations with a Latina Teacher about Education for Language-Minority Students with Special Needs

Candace S. Bos
Elba I. Reyes
University of Arizona

Abstract

In this article we describe the beliefs, knowledge, and classroom practices of a successful bilingual special educator. Analysis of in-depth interviews with this teacher indicated that her teaching was shaped by (1) her experiences as a second language learner, (2) her theories of teaching and learning in relation to students with disabilities, (3) her beliefs about how to shape the transition from first language to second language, and (4) the need to involve family and community in students' learning experiences. The teacher emphasized interactive teaching that weaves students' first language and culture into instructional conversations and curriculum, yet at the same time she incorporated direct instruction, practice, and transfer. This blended approach creates learning environments characterized by rich dialogue that promote not only acquisition of English as a second language but also metalinguistic and metacognitive skills and strategies. Teaching strategies for supporting the transition from first to second language and building networks with family and community are discussed.

When language-minority students struggle with academic learning, particularly with language and literacy development, teachers oftentimes use special educators as a resource or refer students for special education services (Gersten & Woodward, 1994; Ortiz & Garcia, 1988). Few special education teachers, however, are prepared to educate language-minority students.

Bos, C. S., & Reyes, E. I., "Conversations with a Latina teacher about education for language-minority students with special needs," *Elementary School Journal, 96* (3), 1996, pp. 343–351. Reprinted by permission of the publisher, the University of Chicago Press, and the authors. © 1996 by The University of Chicago . All rights reserved.

One field that has developed in the last 20 years to address the needs of language-minority students with disabilities, particularly Latino students with learning disabilities, is bilingual special education. Although in the 1970s and 1980s special educators involved with language-minority students focused on establishing the need for bilingual special education services and on issues of valid assessment and placement, in the 1990s increased attention is being given to effective instruction (Baca & Cervantes, 1989).

Despite the growth of bilingual special education and the increasing number of teacher preparation programs in this area, the demand for bilingual special education teachers far exceeds the supply (Baca & Almanza, 1991; Hill, Carjuzaa, Aramburo, & Baca, 1993). Consequently, many educators with limited or no preparation in teaching Latino students with learning disabilities are expected to serve these students.

One way to assist these educators is to describe the beliefs, knowledge, and practices of successful bilingual special educators. In this article we highlight one such teacher (Elba Reyes, the second author). The information presented is based on a series of interviews conducted by the first author with the second author. Over 7 years and in association with other colleagues, we have been developing an interactive model of teaching and learning to promote both literacy and content-area learning in language-minority students with learning disabilities (Bos & Anders, 1992; Bos & Reyes, 1989; Reyes, 1994).

During interview analyses, four major themes emerged that had shaped Elba's teaching as a bilingual special education teacher: her experiences as a second language learner, her theories of teaching and learning in relation to students with disabilities, her beliefs about how to shape the transition from first language to second language, and the need to involve family and community in students' learning experiences.

Experiences as a Second Language Learner

Elba's experiences as a second language learner played an important role in developing her teaching beliefs and practices as a bilingual special educator. She was born in New York City of Puerto Rican parents and lived in a barrio community in which Spanish was used almost exclusively. When she was 5½ she moved to an English-speaking community on Staten Island to live with her aunt and uncle, both of whom spoke English and Spanish well. Elba reported, "My aunt would speak to me in English and then realize that I wasn't understanding her. Then she would speak to me in Spanish. So she was constantly translating." Elba also noted that her aunt was an avid reader. "I remember that almost every day during the summer, we would sit on the beach, both bent over a classic book written in English that my aunt would read and discuss with me."

Six months after she arrived in Staten Island, Elba began to attend a parochial school where instruction was only in English. Since community and school environments were almost exclusively English, Elba reported that she lost most of her ability to speak Spanish and did not learn to read and write in Spanish. Since she was in the early stages of acquir-

ing English, her teachers misinterpreted her limited communication as a cognitive deficit and recommended that she transfer to a public school that had services for "slow learners." Due to her aunt's insistence, this transfer did not occur, and Elba continued in parochial schools through high school. She commented that during those early school years, "There was no one in school to help me learn. The teachers had low expectations for me and didn't take the time to explain concepts and processes that were difficult for me to comprehend as a second language learner. So I had to learn how to learn by myself and with help from my aunt and uncle at home."

Elba took Spanish in high school and reported that she (re)learned it quickly. During high school her aunt encouraged Elba to "play with the two languages." She commented, "I used to write poetry in English and try to figure out how to say and write it in Spanish. So I would apply the Spanish that I was learning to the poetry I was writing." She later attended the University of Puerto Rico where all instruction was in Spanish, and she developed even greater expertise in using Spanish. To deal with exclusive instruction in Spanish during her first semester at the university, she recollected, "I used to take a tape recorder and tape my classes. Then I would listen [to the tapes] when I was doing my work around the house. I also used to read the Spanish texts aloud."

Elba commented that these experiences and the strategies she developed as a second language learner influenced her teaching. This became evident later as she incorporated some of her own learning strategies into her teaching of language-minority students with disabilities. For example, she had students explore and play with language; had students listen to, discuss, and read stories and information multiple times in English through various activities prior to expecting the students to understand and provide verbal and written responses in English; and translated for students to ensure that the information was comprehensible.

Theories of Teaching and Learning

Elba is certified in English as a Second Language (ESL), bilingual education, and special education. She received her training in ESL in the early 1970s as part of the first wave of teachers prepared under the then-new personnel preparation programs authorized by the Bilingual Education Act. She began teaching in a mountain school in Puerto Rico while completing her undergraduate degree. During her first 3 years of teaching in this rural school, Elba developed an interest in students with disabilities. She commented, "I had a class of 52 fourth- and fifth-grade students. I noticed that some of them were different and just didn't fit the mold in that they were not learning easily, nor were they experimenting with their language at the same frequency level or as creatively as the other students. Upon discussing this with other teachers in the school, I learned that I had about 20 students who had qualified for special education. With only one special education classroom for the region, these students were not provided services."

When Elba returned to New York in 1983, she was hired as a bilingual special education teacher because of teacher shortages. In New York, she taught Spanish-speaking 6- and 7-year-old students who were functioning developmentally like 4- and 5-year-olds (i.e., at a preacademic learning stage). She continued her education and obtained a masters degree in special education. After several years, she developed and supervised a Head Start program in which young children with disabilities were integrated.

Most recently, Elba taught in a large, bilingual elementary school (800 students) in a metropolitan district in the Southwest. The school population was about 95% Latino, with approximately 80% of the students also identified as limited English proficient. District guidelines require most students to make the transition from Spanish instruction to English instruction in the fourth grade. As a bilingual special education teacher in this school, Elba taught students who were identified as having learning disabilities, emotional disorders, and mild mental retardation; most were also limited English proficient. The students were in first through fifth grades.

Elba came to view learning as an interactive process and the teacher as a facilitator who uses direct instruction only when needed. Her philosophy of teaching parallels pedagogical theories of second language acquisition as well as the sociocultural theory of teaching (Krashen & Terrell, 1983; Moll, 1990; Vygotsky, 1978).

Elba, however, blended these interactive principles with learning principles associated with spe-cial education. Specifically, within a natural language context, she incorporated direct instruction of strategies and skills, concentrated practice, and systematic transfer. She conveyed how she came to use this blended approach.

At the very beginning when I was teaching special education, I was doing word families, reading comprehension kits, and other activities in which the students learned and practiced skills out of context and without the goal of learning the content they were reading. I used individual student packets, so there was a limited sense of community. It didn't feel like any learning or transfer was occurring, and the students began demonstrating behavior problems.

So I changed back to the way I taught ESL, but I incorporated minilessons for the explicit instruction of skills and strategies. In this context the students could see how the direct instruction tied into their learning both in the resource room and in their general education or bilingual education classrooms. In retrospect, I think that this type of interactive teaching with contextualized, authentic learning yet explicit instruction in skills and strategies is critical for the success of language-minority students with disabilities. However, it is more complex and difficult to orchestrate than using one or the other of the approaches.

Others have also noted that this blended approach to teaching, with its balance of strategy and skill development and the use of meaningful instructional conversations, is difficult for teachers to implement (Anders & Bos, 1992; Gersten, 1996, in this issue; Goldenberg & Gallimore, 1991).

Elba discussed four key strategies for enacting such an approach. First, she believed that students need opportunities to play with and explore language. Initially, this view was based on her experiences as a second language learner and her observations of students experiencing difficulties. Elba thought that students learning a second language needed opportunities to practice and manipulate language. She also observed that students experiencing learning disabilities had particular difficulty using both their first and second languages to mediate learning. Later, her belief was shaped by theories of the natural approach to second language acquisition (Krashen & Terrell, 1983) and by studies of students experiencing academic failure (Bashir & Scavuzzo, 1992; Damico, Oller, & Storey, 1983). In discussing her ESL teaching strategies for these students, Elba commented, "I really encouraged the students to make up lots of nonsense words and to play with the words and see what the sounds did. They were also encouraged to play with real words within the sentence structure. For example, the students would rearrange the word order to see what kind of sentences they could make." Elba commented that students often found the results of playing with sounds and word order funny. She noted, "More importantly, the activities also provided me with information regarding the students' metalinguistic awareness and their level of language development."

Second, Elba built her teaching around the students' background knowledge and sociocultural experiences. In discussing her students with special needs, Elba reported, "It is very important that you know who your students are. Not so much what their problems are, but who they are and what experiences they bring to school. One

way you can do this in the classroom is by letting the students talk about their social lives, their homes and communities, and their language experiences (e.g., what languages they speak and with whom; where, when, and why they developed their English language; how they feel about learning English)."

Elba emphasized the importance of weaving language development and students' sociocultural experiences into instruction. This was demonstrated when she taught reading using social studies. While these students were working on a social studies chapter about communities, class discussion focused on the concept of "services." Elba asked students to give examples of services. Maria responded, "Beds." Because of Elba's knowledge of Maria's parents and their jobs, she encouraged Maria to elaborate on her original response. Maria explained that her mother was a maid and provided a service. Elba noted that students with learning disabilities frequently have the knowledge but fail to activate and use it to assist their comprehension and learning (Torgesen & Licht, 1983). For example, Elba commented, "Often José would not join in the discussion. Because I knew the home environment, I could interject relevant experiences from his life so that he could learn that there is a way to activate and build upon his own experiences." Elba facilitated this form of cognitive scaffolding by promoting students' involvement as active learners.

This same strategy of building on students' knowledge and experiences was evident in Elba's early teaching in Puerto Rico. When speaking of how she used students' first language to support their second language, Elba

noted, "I would introduce the second language using familiar stories. In English I would tell or read stories that the students knew in Spanish, and they listened to the story. At first they didn't necessarily understand it fully, but they knew the gist [of the story] and eventually were able to make the language comparisons."

Third, Elba thought that if she created many opportunities for students to practice their English, they learned English faster. She capitalized on opportunities for students to practice speaking English to each other, learn from each other, and serve in the roles of experts and novices (Vygotsky, 1978). Elba commented, "I always had students at different levels of second language acquisition in the classroom. The less proficient students could hear me and they could hear other students who were in transition and who had mastered some of the language skills, such as [in] manipulating verbs."

Elba talked about how creating this type of interactive classroom requires that the teacher structure the classroom and the activities so that opportunities to practice English occur. For example, when teaching in her special education resource room, Elba usually had students work in groups of two and three. She noted, "Elena and Maria would have the same type of assignments, so they frequently found themselves working together. They would make appointments to work with each other to share their writing and to practice with the books that they were getting ready to read to the kindergarten classes."

Fourth, Elba used direct instruction, concentrated practice, and transfer of learning activities to identify, teach, and generalize specific skills that students needed and had not yet mastered. For example, Elba observed Elena and Maria working together as they practiced their oral reading in English. The girls were working on a story they would be reading to kindergarten classes the following week. Elba noticed that both girls were not using grapho-phonic cues effectively. Although the girls were using the meaning or semantic cues to assist them in decoding unknown words, they were not consistently using basic structural and phonic analysis. Thus, explicit teaching of several basic rules and their application became the focus of skill-oriented minilessons during which the girls practiced word identification. To promote transfer, Elba cued the girls to use the skill when reading their stories, and she watched for transfer.

To incorporate direct instruction and transfer, Elba frequently used minilessons based on students' needs. She commented,

I found ways of incorporating the students' needs into the thematic units because I do believe that students with disabilities need to be explicitly taught skills and strategies. For example, in the classroom the students might be working on using capitalization of proper nouns and commas in a series. I would observe to see if these skills were being used successfully by the students in my classroom. If not, I would develop minilessons for 15 minutes several times a week. A minilesson would include making a transparency and photocopies of one students' writing (with permission) related to the unit on which the students were working. Then we would talk about editing the writing for capitalization of proper nouns and commas in a series. Students would edit their own work and then assist each other. I would

also include these newly learned skills on an editing skill poster that the students could use for reference. Finally, I would watch for those skills to start emerging in their writing and if not to cue them to use the newly learned skills.

Elba's minilessons focused on one or two aspects of language at a time so as not to overwhelm the students.

The Transition from First to Second Language

Elba viewed the transition from Spanish to English as requiring especially careful planning when working with second language learners with learning disabilities. She believed that students educated in the United States, regardless of their disabilities, should have the opportunity to learn to read and write in English. She commented, "We need to teach students to interact in the social and political structure of the United States, which is in English." However, similar to the views of many bilingual educators, Elba thought that, whenever possible, children who enter school not speaking English should develop a strong foundation in and be comfortable with their first language. Then they should use that knowledge to learn English (Cummins, 1984).

Elba used several strategies to assist students such as (a) telling familiar stories in Spanish and English, (b) using techniques of Total Physical Response to build English language vocabulary (e.g., having students "act out" a word or sentence) (Krashen & Terrell, 1983), and (c) teaching English through content-area instruction (Bos & Reyes, 1989; Chamot & O'Malley, 1996, in this issue).

Elba often began English instruction with math. Because of the universality of numeric symbols, teachers in bilingual education classrooms most frequently use math as the first content area for instruction in English. Elba then added social studies. During the transition phase, she initially explained key concepts in both Spanish and English. Elba commented, "In math, I would expose the students to the vocabulary in both languages so that they can see and discuss the similarities, and we would discuss the process or concepts in Spanish and English. In social studies, when some of the students were having difficulty with concepts (e.g., 'services'), we would discuss the concept in Spanish. As soon as the students understood it, we discussed it again in English so that they would get the concept in the English context. Otherwise, the students may continue to think about it in Spanish. I wanted them to [make the] transition cognitively to English."

Regarding second language learners with disabilities, Elba believed that bilingual special education teachers are faced with several dilemmas unique to these learners. First, it may be particularly difficult for students with specific reading disabilities to make the transition from learning to read in Spanish to learning to read in English. Students need to make the cognitive shift between lexicons and language rules. Language-based learning disabilities add difficulties to that transition. Elba noted, "When a student with learning disabilities is finally learning and reading in Spanish and the student is feeling confident as a learner, there is a nice comfort level for the teacher and the student to stay in Spanish. In addition, the IEPs [Individual Education Programs] are often written for instruction to continue in the student's primary language." Yet this transition to English is important for the students' success in general education classrooms.

For students to make the transition, Elba emphasized, they need to discuss how the skills and strategies they used to become good Spanish readers (e.g., making predictions, asking oneself comprehension-monitoring questions, using context combined with basic structural and phonic analysis to decode unknown words) transfer to English. Elba commented, "Building on the student's metacognitive awareness, we would discuss and demonstrate how those same skills and strategies could work for reading and writing in English. I also reminded the students how they had developed good oral language skills in English, had been participating in English instruction in their classrooms in some content-area subjects, and had acquired some sight vocabulary in English." Elba also emphasized the importance of providing opportunities for students to continue reading in Spanish.

Second, Elba needed to solve the dilemma of selecting reading material that built on the students' growing competence with English oral language and at the same time supported their learning in the general education classroom. She commented on the common need of many bilingual special education teachers, "I was always looking for textbooks and easy children's literature that were written in both languages." Elba found that integrating the teaching of reading and writing with content-area instruction, particularly with social studies, pro-

vided a rich milieu for making the transition to reading and writing in English (Bos & Reyes, 1989; Chamot & O'Malley, 1996, in this issue). She noted that as third and fourth graders, students with disabilities often receive content-area instruction in English in their general education classrooms. Many have relatively high oral language conversational proficiency in English but demonstrate much lower academic language skills. For students to develop their reading and writing abilities in English, they also needed to develop higher-level thinking skills in English. Elba elaborated, "What I did was to incorporate the students' higher level of oral language during instruction so that they could develop the critical thinking skills that they needed in English, particularly as they moved into middle school." She engaged students in instructional conversations where they were asked to think about and respond in English to questions such as "Why do you think that?" "How would you prove that?" and "What do you think the process is?" Elba noted, "I engaged the students in these types of higher-level thinking dialogues in Spanish when they were younger, so when they were in fourth grade it was very natural to transition those thinking skills to English."

The Role of Family and Community in School Learning

Elba viewed the family and community as keys to understanding students and as natural motivators for learning within the classroom environment. Home visits were critical in establishing the connection between school and

family. She commented, "Usually I find that if you really want to get to know a parent, you get to know them on their own turf. This is key to developing trust and understanding the parents' perspective. First, get to know the community. Learn where the local grocery store is and what the children do after school. Then schedule the home visit at a time that is convenient for the parents."

Elba particularly stressed home visits with minority parents of children with disabilities. She found that in the home parents were more willing to talk about their fears and aspirations for a child who was struggling in school. Elba commented, "The home environment is not usually as laden with failure. I oftentimes observed the child being successful in the home, for example, riding a bike or helping with dinner."

Meeting with parents in their homes also helped alleviate misunderstanding about the nature of special education programs and prevented miscommunication. Cross-cultural misunderstanding (Harry, 1992) is likely when a child from another culture is placed in a culturally specific classification system such as the categorical disabilities system (e.g., learning disabilities, mental retardation) used in special education. These labels connote varied meanings and hold different implications in different cultures (Harry, 1992). Elba, like other special educators, found that multidisciplinary staffings were often too formal and threatening to serve as a forum for discussing cross-cultural misunderstandings (Marion, 1979; Turnbull & Turnbull, 1986). After making several home visits, Elba noted that parents were more willing to come to school for the parent meetings associated with special education (e.g., multidisciplinary staffings and individual education planning meetings) and more willing to volunteer in school.

Elba also integrated her knowledge about the family and community into classroom learning activities. For example, she learned that one of her students was involved in a home business of making and selling tamales. This topic became the focal point for an integrated unit that involved math as it relates to measurement and money, social studies as it relates to setting up and managing a business, and literacy as students read and wrote about home businesses.

Conclusion

Language-minority students with learning disabilities must not only acquire a second language, they must also overcome language-based disabilities that make language acquisition and literacy development particularly challenging (Carrasquillo & Baecher, 1990). As a result, teachers who work with this population not only must be skilled in special education methods but must blend them with pedagogy of second language acquisition and bilingual education. Only a few teacher education programs, however, provide preparation on how to blend theories from these three fields. Consequently, most teachers continue to be left much as Elba was "to figure it out on her own."

Even the literature provides little information on which to build sound instructional practices. Most research on language-minority students with disabilities has focused on how to identify and assess these students, not on the careful study of effective methods of instruction. Given the status quo, clearly theoretically based instructional research is in order with attention not only to early literacy development but to the transition from first to second language that occurs in upper elementary grades. At the same time, teacher education programs need to incorporate interdisciplinary and transdisciplinary preparation to assure that teachers in training have the opportunity to build their repertoire of knowledge and skills based on various models of teaching and learning.

Finally, this study can be viewed as an initial exploratory study in a line of research that subsequently investigates the beliefs, knowledge, and practices of successful bilingual special education teachers. Such a series of studies could utilize interviews, classroom observations, and student learning to provide evidence for what works—for which students in which subject areas at what stages of second language acquisition and literacy development.

References

Anders, P. L., & Bos, C. S. (1992). Dimensions of professional development: Weaving teacher beliefs and strategic content. In M. Pressley, K. R. Harris, & J. T. Guthrie (Eds.), *Promoting academic competence and literacy in school* (pp. 457–476). San Diego: Academic Press.

Baca, L. M. & Almanza, E. (1991). *Language minority students with disabilities*. Reston, VA: Council for Exceptional Children. (ERIC Document Reproduction Services No. ED 339 171)

Baca, L. M., & Cervantes, H. T. (1989). *The bilingual special education interface*. Columbus, OH: Merrill.

Bashir, A. S., & Scavuzzo, A. (1992). Children with language disorders: Natural history and academic success. *Journal of Learning Disabilities, 25*, 53–65.

Bos, C. S., & Anders, P. L. (1992). A theory-driven interactive instructional model for text comprehension and content learning. In B. Y. L. Wong (Ed.), *Contemporary intervention research in learning disabilities: An international perspective* (pp. 81–95). New York: Springer Verlag.

Bos, C. S., & Reyes, E. I. (1989, December). *Knowledge, use, and control of an interactive cognitive strategy for learning from content area texts.* Paper presented at the annual meeting of the National Reading Conference, Austin, TX.

Carrasquillo, A. L., & Baecher, R. E. (Eds.). (1990). *Teaching the bilingual special education student.* Norwood, NJ: Ablex.

Chamot, A. U., & O'Malley, J. M. (1996). The Cognitive Academic Language Learning Approach (CALLA): A model for linguistically diverse classrooms. *Elementary School Journal, 96*, 259–273.

Cummins, J. (1984). *Bilingualism and special education: Issues in assessment and pedagogy.* San Diego: College-Hill.

Damico, J. S., Oller, J. W. Jr., & Storey, M. E. (1983). The diagnosis of language disorders in bilingual children: Pragmatic and surface-oriented criteria. *Journal of Speech and Hearing Disorders, 48*, 385–394.

Gersten, R. (1996). Literacy instruction for language-minority students: The transition years. *Elementary School Journal, 96*, 227–244.

Gersten, R., & Woodward, J. (1994). The language-minority student and special education: Issues, trends, and paradoxes. *Exceptional Children, 60*, 310–322.

Goldenberg, C., & Gallimore, R. (1991). Local knowledge, research knowledge, and educational change: A case study of early Spanish reading improvement. *Educational Researcher, 29*(8), 2–14.

Harry, B. (1992). *Cultural diversity, families, and the special education system: Communication and empowerment.* New York: Teachers College Press.

Hill, R., Carjuzaa, J., Aramburo, D., & Baca, L. (1993). Culturally and linguistically diverse teachers in special education: Repairing or redesigning the leaky pipeline. *Teacher Education and Special Education, 16*, 258–269.

Krashen, S. D., & Terrell, T. D. (1983). *The natural approach: Language acquisition in the classroom.* Haywood, CA: Alemany Press.

Marion, R. (1979). Minority parent involvement in the IEP process: A systematic model approach. *Focus on Exceptional Children, 10*(8), 1–16.

Moll, L. D. (Ed.). (1990). *Vygotsky and education: Instruction implications and applications of sociohistorical psychology.* Cambridge: Cambridge University Press.

Ortiz, A. A., & Garcia, S. B. (1988). A prereferral process for preventing inappropriate referrals of Hispanic students to special education. In A. A. Ortiz & B. A. Ramirez (Eds.), *Schools and the culturally diverse exceptional student: Promising practices and future directions* (pp. 6–18). Reston, VA: Council for Exceptional Children.

Reyes, E. I. (1994). *Classroom discourse communicative competency of bilingual students with learning disabilities during content learning in three learning environments.* Unpublished doctoral dissertation, University of Arizona, Tucson.

Torgesen, J. K., & Licht, B. G. (1983). The learning disabled child as an inactive learner: Retrospect and prospects. In J. D. McKinney & L. Feagans (Eds.), *Current topics in learning disabilities* (pp. 3–31). Norwood, NJ: Ablex.

Turnbull, A. P., & Turnbull, H. R. (1986). *Families, professionals and exceptionality.* Columbus, OH: Merrill.

Vygotsky, L. S. (1978). *Mind in society: The development of higher level psychological processes.* Cambridge, MA: Harvard University Press.

 Article Review Form at end of book.

WiseGuide Wrap-Up

- Students from minority backgrounds are overrepresented in special education classes. This pattern appears to be a result of bias in the referral, testing, and placement processes, as well as inequities in social conditions.

- The education of language-minority students poses distinct challenges for educators and, in particular, special educators. Teachers need to become well-versed in methods of second-language acquisition and bilingual education.

R.E.A.L. Sites

This list provides a print preview of typical coursewise R.E.A.L. sites. (There are over 100 such sites at the courselinks™ site.) The danger in printing URLs is that web sites can change overnight. As we went to press, these sites were functional using the URLs provided. If you come across one that isn't, please let us know via email to: webmaster@coursewise.com. Use your Passport to access the most current list of R.E.A.L. sites at the courselinks™ site.

Site name: Latino Link: Focusing on Minorities in Special Education

URL: http://www.latino.com/news/1015nspe.htm

Why is it R.E.A.L.? This web page describes a research project focusing on exploring why children from minority backgrounds are overrepresented in special education classes. The site provides a variety of links to related sites pertaining to minority status and special education.

Key topics: minorities

Activity: Select a book from the booklist and try to find it in a local library or bookstore.

Site name: Council for Exceptional Children

URL: http://www.cec.sped.org/

Why is it R.E.A.L.? This is the web page of the Council for Exceptional Children, a professional organization for special educators. Among the divisions of CEC is the Division for Culturally and Linguistically Diverse Exceptional Learners. Professionals in this division of CEC explore the issues of minorities and exceptionality.

Key topics: minorities

Activity: Find out how to join CEC as a student member. What are the benefits of membership?

section 5

WiseGuide Intro Since the 1980s, attention deficit hyperactivity disorder (ADHD) has increasingly become a source of concern for parents and teachers. Students with ADHD generally demonstrate fidgetiness, distractibility, impulsivity, and a short attention span. At present, ADHD is not considered an educational disability; that is, it is not included in the list of disabilities presented in the Individuals with Disabilities Education Act. Rather, it is viewed as a medical condition and it is frequently treated with medication. However, some argue that ADHD should be considered an educational disability and included in future versions of the law. Some students with ADHD receive special education services under the categories of "learning disabled" or "health impaired"; others remain in general education classes while taking medication such as Ritalin.

The two articles in this section present the perspectives of a teacher and a parent on attention deficit hyperactivity disorder. In "Teaching Tommy," second-grade teacher Katharina Fachin describes the many classroom interventions she tried to help Tommy succeed in her second-grade class. Ultimately, his parents, in consultation with her and on the advice of Tommy's pediatrician, elected to try Ritalin. She reports that Tommy's behavior changed considerably and that he was academically more successful.

In "Attention Deficit Hyperactivity Disorder: A Parent's Perspective," Anna M. Thompson describes what ADHD is, how it is diagnosed, and how it is treated. She presents the difficulties involved in finding and adjusting the right dose of medication, particularly as her son became older and developed drug tolerance. Like the first author, Thompson emphasizes the critical nature of parent/teacher communication in working with a student with ADHD.

Learning Objectives

After studying this section, the reader will:

- List behaviors that are used to identify children with attention deficit hyperactivity disorder.

- Grasp the problems associated with testing children for attention deficit hyperactivity disorder.

- Identify a variety of classroom-based approaches to addressing the needs of students with attention deficit hyperactivity disorder.

- Know the types of medications used to treat attention deficit hyperactivity disorder and the side effects of the drugs.

- Differentiate effective and ineffective methods of treating attention deficit hyperactivity disorder.

- Understand the importance of collaboration between school and family in addressing the needs of students with attention deficit hyperactivity disorder.

? Questions ?

R21. Why do you think Katharina Fachin makes the statement, "I do not mean to argue for the use of medication to address the needs of all ADHD students"? What appears to be the greatest lesson that the author learns from her work with Tommy?

R22. Why do you think Anna M. Thompson notes that, when Karl was three, she made the realization that she had to treat ADHD like any other neurological condition? What are the views of the author regarding the role of artificial colorings and preservatives in food as a cause of ADHD? What does she think of psychotherapy as a treatment for ADHD?

Why do you think Katharina Fachin makes the statement, "I do not mean to argue for the use of medication to address the needs of all ADHD students"? What appears to be the greatest lesson that the author learns from her work with Tommy?

Teaching Tommy

A second-grader with attention deficit hyperactivity disorder

Katharina Fachin

Katharina Fachin is a doctoral candidate in the Department of Curriculum and Instruction, University of New Hampshire, Durham. She was previously a second-grade teacher in a New Jersey public school. She wishes to thank Stefne Sears for untiring personal and professional support and Michael Driscoll for his thorough and caring advocacy for children's needs.

Ms. Fachin sees medication as a last resort and believed that Tommy's difficulties could be managed with a comprehensive behavioral and academic program. But, despite her arsenal of classroom interventions, Tommy needed something more.

When Tommy walked into my second-grade classroom on the first day of school, I was happy to see a familiar face. I looked at him with sympathy and hope, wanting to make the year one of learning and of building self-esteem.

Tommy was coming to my class with a difficult year behind him. He had spent first grade in a highly structured classroom, and he had not conformed to its behavioral standards. The behavior modification used with him in that class had included the removal of rewards, and Tommy had experienced little success in keeping the rewards he earned. He was often in trouble, and everyone in the school knew his name. He was three-fourths of a year behind his peers in reading and writing. These experiences led Tommy to believe that he was stupid and bad. I was determined to replace his negative self-image with a positive one based on academic and social success.

Tommy and I already had a history before that first day of school, for I had tutored him once a week from May through July. Originally, Tommy had qualified for home tutoring because of a myringotomy and an adenoidectomy. In preparation for teaching Tommy at home, I talked to his first-grade teacher to find out about his capabilities and to see if she could recommend any materials. I was disappointed when I talked to her because she seemed so negative about him, yet she lacked any precise descriptions of his learning. I met Tommy with the impression that he had had a tough break—a little child facing a teacher who had no hope in him and who lacked the flexibility to meet his needs. Tommy's mother reaffirmed this impression when she described how the teacher wanted him tested and how she was afraid that they just wanted to drug her child so he would be easier to handle.

Tommy snacked on cupcakes and soda as we worked at the kitchen counter. The phone would ring, and siblings would be preparing to go to after-school activities. Tommy wiggled and slid about on the chair, and he would often take bathroom breaks. By remaining firm, I was able to get Tommy to read and write with me. We talked about his interests, and I got to know him. He had a very limited sight vocabulary and could not predict vowel sounds. He could identify most consonants but could not identify the correct vowels, nor was he familiar with how to spell common endings. Although Tommy did

Fachin, K., "Teaching Tommy: A second-grader with attention deficit hyperactivity disorder," *Phi Delta Kappan*, 77(6), 1996, pp. 437–441. Reprinted by permission of the author.

not like to read and write because it was such a struggle, he loved math. Using his fingers, he could calculate all first-grade-level addition and subtraction problems quickly and accurately. Tommy felt very confident of his mathematical abilities.

I became attached to this rough-and-tumble boy with the blue eyes and the big smile. He told me about his daredevil biking stunts and about jumping out of tree houses. Grass stains on his jeans, scrapes on his knees and elbows, and dirty hands were his hard-won war wounds. Tommy struck me as very inquisitive. He spoke of such experiments as creating a pocket of air under water with a bucket. I wondered how I could tap into his creativity in the classroom. Tommy was a very active boy who had trouble maintaining eye contact and concentration, but I attributed these characteristics to his personality, immaturity, diet, and environment. I couldn't understand why a teacher would be so negative about handling him in the classroom.

Over the course of the next school year, I found out why. But I also discovered the joys of teaching Tommy.

Second Grade

Because of my experience tutoring Tommy and my hands-on teaching style, Tommy was placed in my class for second grade. By the third day, I had contacted Dr. Mitchell, our school psychologist. Tommy was singing and making loud noises throughout lessons. He crawled on the floor during transitions and sometimes even during class. As he laughed and shoved

his way through the class to line up, he injured other children. He was playful and destructive at the same time. Instead of picking up the blocks when it was time to clean up, he would scatter them wildly with flailing arms and a big grin. Just when a bucket was filled with blocks, Tommy would dump it.

Throughout that first month I used "time out" with Tommy and had him write about his behavior—to no avail. Positive reinforcement, coupled with ignoring Tommy as a negative consequence, also did not increase Tommy's on-task behavior. Indeed, the research shows that these methods are commonly insufficient for children with Attention Deficit Hyperactivity Disorder (ADHD).[1] I think that ignoring Tommy not only didn't work to improve his behavior but was actually harmful to him. When I made it clear that I was ignoring him, he would feel unloved and bad about himself. On one occasion Tommy curled up in fetal position behind the computer. I had to be careful to let him know that I loved him and believed that he was a good and smart boy. When he needed to be reprimanded, I used a firm monotone voice to correct him succinctly. Still, I felt I had to find a way to help Tommy achieve more success in school.

Token Economy

At the suggestion of Dr. Mitchell, I instituted a token economy system of rewards for Tommy. Tangible rewards coupled with positive verbal reinforcement have been shown to be much more effectual than praise alone.[2] From the very

beginning, though, Dr. Mitchell made it clear that I needed to document Tommy's behavior. In late September I explained the program to Tommy and then later to his mother over the telephone. He could earn play money in $5 bills for raising his hand, keeping his hands to himself, and being a model student. I would not take away any money that he earned. We would count it up at the end of the day and chart it. At the end of the week, Tommy could use the money to purchase time on the computer, time to play with the math manipulatives, or time for drawing in his journal.

As soon as the system was in effect, Dr. Mitchell observed Tommy in the classroom and charted his behavior at one-minute intervals for 30 minutes. Tommy was out of his seat 76.6% of the observed time, he rolled on the rug 16.6% of the time, and he spoke out of turn 63.3% of the time. Moreover, he exhibited aggressive behavior toward property or individuals 26.6% of the time. For example, he crushed some science material on a shelf, and he also tried to throw an object. Only 3.3% of the time were Tommy's eyes on the teacher while he listened and followed directions. For 86.6% of the time Tommy exhibited excessive or incidental movement, and he was off-task 93.3% of the observed time.

Dr. Mitchell called a meeting that included Tommy's father, Dr. Mitchell, the acting principal, and me. I offered specific examples of Tommy's impulsivity, distractibility, and motoric overflow. His father was upset when he heard about Tommy's behavior and acknowledged that he had wanted Tommy tested last year. He even supported the idea of the token economy and said he would have Tommy use his classroom money

> I couldn't understand why a teacher would be so negative about handling Tommy in the classroom. Over the course of the next year, I found out why.

to purchase television time, dessert, and video-game time at home. In the coming months Tommy's father very consistently reinforced the token economy at home and signed the papers for Tommy to be tested.

When we began the token economy in September, Tommy averaged $18 a day for the remainder of that month. During October, he averaged $27 a day, with $10 as the lowest amount and $65 as the highest. For November Tommy averaged $31 a day, with a range from $5 to $110. During December Tommy averaged $51 a day, with a range from $15 to $105. With his parents' support for the system at home and Tommy's own interest in the token economy, I was pleased with the improvement.

Although Tommy was somewhat less disruptive, he would still step on other children as we sat on the rug, make intermittent loud noises, call out to other children, fall out of his chair on purpose, and get up from his desk during lessons. When we used blocks for mathematics, he would play with them and knock them off his desk unless I remained right beside him. If he raised his hand and I didn't call on him immediately, he would get angry and within a minute would be off task. His pencil and notebook could be found anywhere in the room but inside his desk. The situation was most difficult during whole-class times and transitions.

On the other hand, Tommy wanted very much to please me, and he would write me apologies and notes about how he loved me. After the fact, he felt bad about hurting other children and disrupting the class, so I tried to show him affection at every good opportunity.

Despite these difficult times, Tommy also showed his potential to succeed in school. Three days a week for 45 minutes, my instructional support teacher, Mrs. DeVito, worked with Tommy in a small reading group while I worked with two other groups. The fit between Mrs. DeVito's teaching style and Tommy's needs was perfect. Mrs. DeVito enthusiastically and dramatically offered her students positive reinforcement, and Tommy would glow from her praise. She also used a fast-paced, question-and-answer format for lessons that would not allow Tommy to lose focus. He looked forward to his time with Mrs. DeVito and showed great progress in reading. His sight vocabulary and word-attack skills were improving steadily.

ADHD as a Motivational Disorder

This disparity between Tommy's highly distractible and impulsive behavior during whole-class activities and his focused and appropriate behavior in the small reading group was very disconcerting for me. Throughout the year I analyzed and reanalyzed my teaching. I too am a lively and interactive teacher who uses a variety of visual and tactile methods. I made modifications for Tommy so that he could take breaks, vary his tasks more frequently, and stand up while working. I reorganized the classroom so that he was surrounded by calmer children and was seated directly in front of me as I taught. Why couldn't I achieve the same attending behavior as Mrs. DeVito could?

Russell Barkley explains this discrepancy in behavior by charac-

terizing ADHD as a motivational disorder.[3] A child with ADHD can attend well in a highly motivating situation, such as while watching a favorite television program or playing a video game. When the situation is less intrinsically motivating or when there is delayed rather than immediate feedback, the child will display the characteristics of ADHD. This is why the token economy was somewhat successful during whole-class times when Tommy would not be called on as frequently as in a small group.

After seven months, Tommy continued to exhibit frequently every one of the 14 characteristics that the American Psychiatric Association lists as diagnostic criteria for ADHD. (For a list of these characteristics and a brief description of how they can be used in diagnosis, see Anna M. Thompson, "Attention Deficit Hyperactivity Disorder: A Parent's Perspective," page 433, this *Kappan*.)

Interventions

At the classification meeting in December, I found out that Tommy was classified as perceptually impaired because of the discrepancy between his general cognitive ability and his specific achievement in reading and language arts. Although the neurologist had diagnosed Tommy as exhibiting ADHD, this condition was not included in his individualized education program (IEP) in January because the psychologist explained that there was no separate classification in education for ADHD. In January 1995 an IEP was written that allowed Tommy three half-hour sessions in the resource room for language arts and provided an in-class aide each day from 1:30 p.m. to 2:30 p.m.

Resource room. The resource room teacher, Miss Steven, focused on Tommy's spelling. She created an individualized list for him using words from the Dolch list as well as words that exhibited a regular spelling pattern. She scrambled the letters in the words for him to correct, asked him to write his homework sentences in the resource room, and let him write words with colored glue on cards. Using the glue was very motivating for Tommy. When it dried, Miss Steven instructed him to trace over it with his finger. The success of this use of colored glue is consistent with research that suggests that ADHD students "selectively attend to novelty such as color, changes in size, and movement."[4] Tommy went from getting at least 50% wrong on every spelling test to getting all but one word correct. His journal writing also reflected this change.

In-class aide. Tommy was assigned an aide, Mrs. Hellwell, in the last week of February. I gave Mrs. Hellwell a list of appropriate behaviors, inappropriate behaviors, and interventions. She reinforced Tommy's appropriate behavior and provided one-on-one tutoring in the classroom. When he was highly disruptive, she also provided alternative activities. At the end of the day, Mrs. Hellwell monitored Tommy as he counted and charted his earned money. This was a tremendous help to me because it was simply exhausting to manage Tommy and the token economy all day while trying to teach and pay attention to the needs of the rest of the class.

To help with transitions, particularly the transition from lunch recess to afternoon classroom activities, I employed relaxation techniques.[5] I walked the children in from the school yard and asked them to sit at their desks. One row at a time, I called them to lie or sit on the rug. (This usually helped keep Tommy from stepping on anyone.) Then I turned out the lights and talked the children through a breathing exercise; cued them to tense, hold, and relax their muscles; and used guided imagery of peaceful places and activities. Sometimes I encouraged them to think of themselves doing something challenging and achieving success.

At first Tommy wouldn't hold still for these techniques, so I began to sit knee to knee in front of him on the floor as I led the class. After some experience with relaxation, he gradually became able to participate without my sitting with him. As I led the class from a chair, I could see him following my cues for breathing in and out and witnessed his body growing still. Tommy also displayed some enthusiasm for the practices. One day, after I asked the children to try thinking of their own images of succeeding, Tommy told us about how he imagined himself winning a karate match he was nervous about that evening. My long-range goal was to be able to suggest to Tommy that he use the techniques on his own during the day to relax himself. As we walked down the hall, I would say to him, "Tommy, do you notice how you are making loud noises or knocking into the walls? Try breathing like we do after lunch. Can you breathe in a color?" Sometimes he used my suggestions independently, and sometimes I had to take the time to help him use the techniques before we continued walking.

Peer tutoring. At the beginning of the year, the other children in the class thought Tommy was funny and enjoyed his daring and his flouting of classroom rules. Then they became jealous of the extra attention he got from me and tried to imitate his behavior or to win my attention in other ways. Eventually, though, they began to grow angry with him for hurting them or for not waiting his turn or for disrupting class. I felt I had to find a role for the other children in the class.

All through the year I had talked to the whole class about how I was responding to Tommy and had discussed how everyone should act and why. One day, Tommy pulled a chair out from another child, causing her to hit her head hard as she fell. He stared in horror as she cried. A couple of days later, I talked about how we sometimes think of our conscience as a devil on one shoulder and an angel on the other. Tommy called out, "I think my devil killed my angel," and "I'm evil." I asked, "How did you feel when Susan hit her head? A bad person would not feel sad. You have an angel. It just talks to you too late. We need to teach your angel to give you advice before you do something," I had never seen such a look of relief and peace on Tommy's face. I could have cried.

Then I was able to enlist the help of the other students. Each day, a different student, alternating boys and girls, would be a peer tutor and help Tommy's angel "talk." I got an empty desk to put next to Tommy's for his peer tutor. I coached the peer tutor to remind him of proper classroom behavior in a nice way, to set a good example, and to accompany him when he used his money for rewards. Attitudes toward Tommy improved as the other students saw themselves as his helpers and saw Tommy as not a bad kid. Of course, not every match worked, and the boys especially found it difficult not to incite Tommy's off-task behavior and then to goof off with him.

Modifying the behavior modification. After using the token economy for five months, I felt as if Tommy was hitting a plateau. His behavior in whole-class situations was still unacceptable. I decided to buy a digital timer to help him set goals. I would set the timer for five minutes, and he could earn $5 only if he raised his hand before speaking and generally acted appropriately for the full five minutes. I discovered that he tried very hard but could make minutes only about 60% of the time. He never made it to six minutes.

It was February, and Tommy was getting into a lot of trouble on the bus and during recess. He often found himself in the principal's office. His mother was being called every day. I had tried so hard, and yet his year in my class was turning out just like the previous year. The art and physical education teachers came to me out of frustration about his behavior, and we talked about assertive discipline and about ways to manage Tommy. In a letter to Dr. Mitchell, they expressed their concerns about how Tommy was detracting from the learning experiences of the other students in the class.

Changing placement. What else could we try? Dr. Mitchell said that our last resort would be to explore different placement options for Tommy next year. A regular classroom might be inappropriate. Since our district did not have a special education class-

room, that would mean an out-of-district placement. Based on my feelings of loyalty to Tommy and his parents, I asked that I be the one to discuss this with his parents.

I called Tommy's father at the beginning of March and described the situation. I told him that we needed to explore other school placement options if Tommy's behavior did not change. During our telephone conversation I also mentioned that perhaps he and his wife might reconsider taking Tommy to his pediatrician and trying medication. We met two weeks later at parent/teacher conferences to discuss the situation in more depth. I came to the meeting with a prepared presentation detailing Tommy's behavior, the interventions that had been tried, an analysis of his progress, and the options for the future. Tommy's father informed me at that time that they would be taking Tommy to the pediatrician to try medication. They had already reached a decision before our meeting.

Medication. Tommy was on Ritalin for the last month of school. For five days he would take a dose of five milligrams before school, and it would wear off around noon. The first day he was on the medication, he earned the most money he had ever earned in a day, $110. He behaved appropriately for 15-minute intervals. He never lost his sense of humor or energy or bubbliness.

The difference was remarkable. I would see him begin to call out and then stop himself to raise his hand. He would set the timer and look at it to monitor himself.

All his behaviors seemed to indicate that he was more receptive to reinforcers. The entire class responded to Tommy with spontaneous encouragement and praise, though they didn't know he was taking medication. On the first day, one beaming student told me, "This is such a good day!" Tommy was riding so high from the morning that his general sense of feeling good about himself helped him make it through the afternoon. Although he would lose his pencil constantly in the afternoon and rush from one thing to another, he tried successfully to follow classroom rules.

Even on the medication, though, the daily variation in Tommy's behavior remained. Some days he was simply more active than others. For example, on the third morning after he began taking medication, Tommy was still shaking his leg and foot the whole time he was leading the pledge.

Every day I talked to his father after school on the phone to inform him of Tommy's reaction to the medication. His father was so relieved to hear of Tommy's success. He said that he would contact the pediatrician about an afternoon dose.

Tommy continued until the end of the school year with both a morning and an afternoon dose of Ritalin. There were days when I questioned whether or not he was given the dose before he came to school, but I didn't voice these concerns. We also had some difficulty establishing exactly when the second dose should be administered, and I had difficulty remembering to send him to the nurse's office before he exhibited severe off-task behavior.

> More painful than the frustration of trying to deal with the condition of ADHD itself is enduring the criticism that comes from others.

I do not mean to argue for the use of medication to address the needs of all ADHD students. I see medication as a last resort and one that should be used in combination with a comprehensive behavioral and academic program. I offered Tommy an activities-based curriculum to tap into his energy and creativity. I taught abstract ideas concretely and contextually. I consistently used and adapted behavior modification techniques and tried other techniques like relaxation exercises. I let Tommy know that I thought he was a great kid and a talented person, too. I had the class support Tommy as peer tutors and as members of project teams, literature study groups, and cooperative learning groups. The district provided instructional and noninstructional support. But Tommy needed something more to enable him to benefit from these interventions. Tommy's ADHD was severe, and the medication helped him achieve success in the classroom.

From my experience with Tommy and his family. I have come to believe even more strongly that it is vital to gain the trust of parents. Their faith in our efforts and concern for their child must be the basis for communication and teamwork between home and school. I also realize how painful it can be for parents to accept that their child might need extra help and even medication. By fielding my colleagues' complaints about Tommy's behavior, I got a small taste of what parents must feel when they are told by friends, family members, and doctors that they don't know how to discipline their children. More painful than the frustration of trying to deal with the condition of ADHD itself is enduring the criticism and condemnation that come from others. I think that this holds true for the student, the parents, and the teacher.

1. Lee A. Rosen et al., "The Importance of Prudent Negative Consequences for Maintaining the Appropriate Behavior of Hyperactive Students," *Journal of Abnormal Child Psychology*, vol. 12, 1984, pp. 581–604.
2. Linda J. Pfiffner, Lee A. Rosen, and Susan G. O'Leary, "The Efficacy of an All-Positive Approach to Classroom Management," *Journal of Applied Behavior Analysis*, vol. 18, 1985, pp. 257–61.
3. Russell A. Barkley, *Attention Deficit Hyperactivity Disorder: A Handbook for Diagnosis and Treatment* (New York: Guilford Press, 1990).
4. Sydney S. Zentall, "Research on the Educational Implications of Attention Deficit Hyperactivity Disorder," *Exceptional Children*, vol. 60, 1993, p. 143.
5. Sandra F. Rief, *How to Reach and Teach ADD/ADHD Children* (New York: Center for Applied Research in Education, 1993).

Article Review Form at end of book.

Why do you think Anna M. Thompson notes that, when Karl was three, she made the realization that she had to treat ADHD like any other neurological condition? What are the views of the author regarding the role of artificial colorings and preservatives in food as a cause of ADHD? What does she think of psychotherapy as a treatment for ADHD?

Attention Deficit Hyperactivity Disorder

A parent's perspective

Anna M. Thompson

Anna M. Thompson is director of education at Clowes Memorial Hall, Butler University, Indianapolis, and a candidate at Butler for the specialist degree in educational administration.

As a parent and an educator who has spent the last 10 years struggling to assist her own ADHD child, Ms. Thompson gives readers suggestions for managing the challenges that face such children and for enhancing the quality of their lives.

Attention deficit hyperactivity disorder (ADHD) has had many names over the years: organic drivenness, "fidgety Phils," post-encephalitic behavior disorder, minimal brain damage, minimal brain dysfunction, hyperkinesis, hyperactivity, attention deficit disorder (ADD), and attention deficit disorder with or without hyperactivity (ADD/ADHD).[1] A child with ADD without hyperactivity would exhibit all the distractibility of an ADHD child without the physical activity.

Many of the current books available use ADD and ADHD interchangeably. For the purpose of this discussion, I will use ADHD, as that accurately represents my son's diagnosis and my experience as a parent.

What Is ADHD?

ADHD is a neurological syndrome whose classic, defining triad of symptoms includes impulsivity, distractibility, and hyperactivity or excess energy.[2] Studies indicate that approximately 3% to 5% of children in the U.S. can be diagnosed with ADHD. Among children with ADHD who have been referred to clinics, boys outnumber girls by a ratio of approximately 6:1.[3]

ADHD has been defined in a variety of ways over the past 20 years, leading to confusion among education professionals. Most recently ADHD has been described as the display, with developmentally inappropriate frequency, of inattention, impulsivity, and overactivity.[4] To be considered symptoms of ADHD, the behaviors must initially have been exhibited in early childhood (prior to the age of 7) and displayed across a variety of settings (school, home, and play). To meet the diagnostic criteria of the American Psychiatric Association, the child must have been creating disturbances for at least six months, during which time at least eight of the following behaviors must have been exhibited:

1. often fidgets with hands or squirms in seat (though in adolescents this symptom may be limited to subjective feelings or restlessness);

2. has difficulty remaining seated when required to do so;

3. is easily distracted by extraneous stimuli;

4. has difficulty waiting for turns in games or group situations;

5. often blurts out answers to questions before the questions have been completed;

6. has difficulty (not due to oppositional behavior or failure of comprehension) following through on instructions from others;

7. has difficulty sustaining attention in tasks or play activities;

8. often shifts from one uncompleted activity to another;

9. has difficulty playing quietly;

10. often talks excessively;

11. often interrupts or intrudes on others (e.g., butts into other children's games);

12. often does not seem to listen to what is being said to him or her;

13. often loses things necessary for tasks or activities at school or at home (e.g., toys, pencils, books, assignments); or

14. often engages in physically dangerous activities without considering possible consequences (e.g., runs into the street without looking), but not for the purpose of thrill-seeking.

At the age of 3, our son Karl exhibited *all* 14 of these criteria. He was and still is a textbook case of ADHD. At the time he was diagnosed, I would gladly have blamed myself for being a bad parent who did not provide enough discipline rather than admit that anything was wrong with my child. It was only through consultations with Karl's day-care provider, with my family physician, and with a psychiatrist specializing in the diagnosis and treatment of ADHD—as well as

through my own research—that I began to realize that I must treat ADHD like any other neurological condition. If Karl had inherited family genes for epilepsy rather than ADHD, I would have provided him with whatever anti-seizure medication and treatment he needed to help him live a normal life. How could I treat ADHD any differently? This diagnosis gave a name to Karl's problem and encouraged us to learn as much as possible about ADHD.

After consulting with Karl's day-care provider, our family physician was fairly confident that Karl was "hyper." But he did not feel comfortable treating Karl and sought out a local specialist in ADHD to whom we could be referred. He pointed out that a specialist in ADHD could best determine if Karl's problem was ADHD or behavioral in nature. A psychiatrist or neurologist would also be more current on the drugs used to treat ADHD.

Testing

There is no one definitive diagnostic test for ADHD. The most reliable diagnostic tool is the individual's history as elicited from the child, from parents, and, very importantly, from teacher reports. Psychological testing can be helpful in determining an ADHD diagnosis, but it is not definitive.[5] A careful evaluation of ADHD must take into account other conditions that may look like ADHD, some of which must be tested by a physician to be ruled out. Because of a family history of epilepsy, Karl was given an EEG (electroencephalogram) to determine if petit mal might be the cause of his inattentiveness. A negative EEG ruled out this possibility.

For several months after my initial meeting with an ADHD specialist, Karl's teachers and I kept a detailed log of Karl's activity levels. Temper tantrums, aggressive outbursts, and impulsivity were all recorded, as were the conditions prior to each incident. A family history of dyslexia led to testing to determine if learning disabilities were present. I.Q. testing was done at age 4 (Karl scored well above average), behavioral modification techniques were employed, and psychiatric testing was completed. After all of this information was compiled, and after numerous observations of Karl by a specialist, a diagnosis of ADHD was made. Karl's diagnosis was a long, labor-intensive process that was painful at times. Yet the kind of comment I hear most often when I tell a friend, colleague, or educator that Karl has ADHD is "That's an easy excuse/diagnosis for a kid's laziness/lack of discipline/bad behavior." If they only knew what we had been through to reach this diagnosis! A proper diagnosis should include all or most of these components to be sure that the child in question *truly* has ADD or ADHD.

Medication and Treatment

There are two main classes of medication commonly used in the treatment of ADHD: stimulants and antidepressants. The stimulants dextro-amphetamine sulfate (of which Dexedrine is most frequently used) and methylphenidate (trade name: Ritalin) are probably the best-known medications. Dexedrine has been used in the treatment of ADHD since the 1930s; Ritalin, since the early

1960s. A less common stimulant, pemoline (trade name: Cylert) was introduced into the U.S. more recently.[6] George Dupaul and Gary Stoner comment on the use of these medications:

The most widely studied and cost-effective treatment for ADHD is the prescription of psychostimulant medication, such as Ritalin (methylphenidate). These medications can lead to improvements in on-task behavior, impulsivity, social behavior, compliance, and academic productivity in as many as 70%–80% of children with ADHD.[7]

When stimulant drugs are effective, they produce one of the most dramatically positive responses in psychiatry.[8] When Dexedrine was finally prescribed for Karl at the age of 4, we witnessed a miraculous transformation. His patience, attentiveness, fine motor skills, and behavior all improved dramatically. Karl was "like a different child." At the same time, we as parents were concerned about medicating such a young child with such a potent drug, however small the dosage. Ritalin and Dexedrine are both Class II amphetamines and are tightly controlled by the Food and Drug Administration. No refills are permitted, prescriptions cannot be called in by the physician, and the prescription is made out in triplicate so that it can be accounted for. Despite the effectiveness and safety of amphetamines when used properly, these drugs have acquired a bad reputation because of the adults who have abused them. But, as Paul Wender points out,

stimulant drugs have a much different effect on ADHD children than they do in normal adults. Rather than becoming high or excited, ADHD children are in general calmed down by these drugs, and sometimes (rarely) they may even become somewhat sad. Children do not become addicted to these medications: there is absolutely no danger that this will occur.[9]

The same neurological chemistry that makes the ADHD child highly distractible and impulsive prevents a typical reaction to these medications. The medication seems to compensate at a basic level for this difference in chemical makeup, affecting behavior in many diverse areas.

Of the antidepressants used to treat ADHD, desipramine (trade name: Norpramin) is the most commonly used, because most of the research on antidepressants and ADHD has been done on this medication.[10] Desipramine belongs to a class of drugs called tricyclic antidepressants. Although it is a completely different medication, its effect on people with ADHD is similar to that of stimulants. Occasionally, when a stimulant will not work, this antidepressant will work—and vice versa.

Norpramin has several advantages over Ritalin and other stimulants. First, it can be given in a single daily dose; second, it does not produce the jagged peaks and valleys that some people experience on Ritalin; and third, it is not a controlled substance, so there is greater flexibility in prescribing it.

To determine the proper dosage, a child's weight and response to medication are taken into account. The smallest dosage possible is administered until a therapeutic level is reached. This level is determined by the child's behavior, as reported by his or her parents and teachers. Throughout the child's medical treatment, the specialist will rely on the reports of those who have the most frequent contact with the child to decide whether or not to increase the medication. Parents and educators are also in the best positions to observe how long each dose lasts and to help the doctor determine the best spacing of doses. A typical dose of Ritalin can last from three to six hours, depending on the individual's chemistry.

> **Parents of a child with ADHD should receive instruction in behavior management.**

Once a child's dose is fine-tuned, a schedule that works best at school and at home can be determined. If there are problems in both settings, the physician will recommend that the medication be given every day. A drug "holiday" to give the child a break every so often from the medication is also recommended.[11]

Drug Tolerance and Side Effects

As a child who has been on medication for several years becomes older and grows larger, he or she will require an increased dosage. Some children may develop a tolerance to one of the stimulant drugs. In such cases the physician may switch to another drug. If the development of drug tolerance continues to present a problem, the physician may switch to still another of the major categories of medication that are used.

The most frequently reported acute side effects of Ritalin and other stimulants are appetite reduction (particularly at lunch) and insomnia.[12] Other effects reported in the literature include increased irritability, headaches, stomachaches, and, in rare cases, motor and/or vocal tics.[13] At the age of 10, Karl developed a reaction/tolerance to Dexedrine. Despite his medication three times a day, Karl became overactive and irritable, and his grades began to drop. He also developed an annoying and distracting habit of making loud clicking and screeching noises (vocal tics), a practice he was completely unaware of. At this point he had been on Dexedrine for nearly seven years, and our doctor recommended switching him to a comparable dosage of Ritalin. This change quickly eliminated the problems that had been caused by his tolerance for Dexedrine.

The decrease in appetite can result in retarded growth for some children, but studies have shown that the appetite returns in the evening after the drug has worn off. Appetite will also be normal at breakfast, before medication is given. Wender emphasizes that the effects that have been reported are small, and most physicians treating ADHD children feel that the psychological benefits outweigh the possible negative effects on the rate of growth.[14]

The tendency of Ritalin and other stimulants to keep some children awake can also be controlled by the timing of the medication. Eliminating a dose late in the day gives the medication time to wear off so that the child can sleep. If sleeplessness continues to be a problem, it can generally be handled by using pills instead of the long-acting (capsule or suspended release tablet) form of a stimulant.[15] Increased exercise can also help the child to relax and go to sleep more easily.

Some children may also experience other side effects from stimulant medications, such as obsessive-compulsive behavior, a proneness to crying, and anxiety.[16]

By the age of 11, Karl was on the maximum dose of Ritalin for his height and weight (100 milligrams per day). At this level Karl began to wake up in the night crying. He worried about dying and started to develop motor tics and obsessive behaviors. I immediately scheduled an appointment with our specialist to determine what the problem was. She determined that Karl was suffering from side effects because of the level of Ritalin he was taking. She reduced his Ritalin prescription and added a dose of Norpramin to his drug therapy. Within several weeks (it takes a while for Norpramin to reach therapeutic blood level), Karl was back to his "normal" self. Over the past year we have continued to fine-tune this dosage and have arrived at a level that seems to work well for Karl and allows him to function at school and at home.

Other Interventions for ADHD

Medication is not the whole treatment for ADHD. Although inattention and impulsivity can be effectively managed with the appropriate medications, they are not the only problems associated with the disorder: "Children with ADHD . . . may also exhibit difficulties in peer relationships, problems with commands and authority figures, and poor homework completion, study, and organization skills."[17] The scope of the disorder means that multiple strategies and interventions across the school and home environments are necessary to allow the child to be successful. It is important for parents of a child with ADHD to receive supportive instruction in behavior management techniques

that are designed to enhance the child's attention to household tasks and rules.[18] The child's physician, school psychologist, counselor, or special education teacher may steer parents to the appropriate training or literature.

It is crucial that parents receive some guidance regarding their reading about ADHD, as there are many "pop psychology" books, not based on current research, that can create confusion about the treatment and education of the child. One example of such literature would be Ben Feingold's *Why Your Child Is Hyperactive*, which theorizes that ADHD is caused by allergies to artificial colorings and preservatives in food.[19] However, according to Wender,

All the carefully conducted controlled studies—in which the family did not know whether or not the child was on an additive-free diet—have shown that one type of additives (the artificial food colorings) does not produce significant hyperactivity (though it may produce some minor changes in attention in some children).[20]

Wender's own book, *The Hyperactive Child, Adolescent, and Adult*, and his more recent volume, *Attention Deficit Hyperactivity Disorder in Adults*, offer educators and parents objective, accurate, insightful information based on research in the field.[21]

By the time they reach late adolescence, approximately 63% of students with ADHD will have received an average of 16 months of individual psychotherapy.[22] ADHD is not considered to be an emotional disturbance, and parents and educators should not expect counseling alone to alleviate core symptoms. However, counseling can help children deal with the emotional difficulties often associated with ADHD, such as low self-esteem, and thus it can be a valuable component of a comprehensive treatment plan.

Schools and Parents Working Together

Dupaul and Stoner offer the following advice:

When education professionals are involved with children diagnosed with ADHD, their primary professional responsibility must be to promote the child's learning and achievement. In addition, because the diagnosis and treatment of ADHD nearly always involve pediatricians, psychiatrists, and clinical psychologists, collaborative efforts at assessment and treatment will need to be developed and maintained.[23]

Let me add parents to this list of collaborators. From my standpoint as a parent, the most important gift that educators can give my ADHD child is understanding. The most important gift that they can give me is regular, open communication. These two "gifts" allow the parent(s), the ADHD specialist, and the ADHD child to frequently assess educational and emotional progress as well as medical needs. Organized conferences, informal school visits, telephone calls, log books, notes, newsletters, and report cards are all viable means of communicating progress (or lack thereof) to ADHD children and their parents.

School psychologists, teachers, and administrators can all help to promote parent involvement in activities that are likely to foster the ADHD child's learning and achievement. An important key to success for the disorganized ADHD child is for parents to monitor the child assignments and make sure that homework is completed.

For successful treatment of ADHD, it is imperative that the teacher understand what ADHD is and know how to work with ADHD children in the classroom. To assist teachers, Edward Hallowell and John Ratey have put together a list of 50 tips on classroom management of ADHD children.[24] After advising teachers to "Make sure what you are dealing with is really ADHD," they offer specific strategies, such as "Break down large tasks into small tasks," "Try to use daily progress reports," and "Repeat directions, write them down and speak them, repeat directions!" Most of the suggestions have to do with simple skills that are often taken for granted when working with "regular" students but that can be very difficult for the ADHD child. As a parent and educator who has spent the last 10 years struggling to assist an ADHD child and working within the education system, I find this an excellent list for teachers.

Although the challenges facing an ADHD child can seem overwhelming, there is now a sizable body of helpful and sound literature on the disorder. It is my hope that this article has provided readers with a useful perspective and steered them to additional sources of reliable information. If everyone involved in a child's schooling is armed with such information, that child will have far greater opportunities for educational success.

1. Steven W. Garber, Marianne D. Garber, and Robyn F. Spizman, *Is Your Child Hyperactive? Inattentive? Impulsive? Distractible?* (New York: Villard Books, 1995).
2. Edward M. Hallowell and John J. Ratey, *Driven to Distraction: Recognizing and Coping with Attention Deficit Disorder from Childhood to Adulthood* (New York: Simon & Schuster, 1995).
3. Gary J. Dupaul and George Stoner, *ADHD in the Schools: Assessment and Intervention Strategies* (New York: Guilford Press, 1994),p. 3.
4. *Diagnostic and Statistical Manual of Mental Disorders*, 3rd rev. ed. (Washington, D.C.: American Psychiatric Association, 1987).
5. Hallowell and Ratey, p. 42.
6. Paul H. Wender, *The Hyperactive Child, Adolescent, and Adult: Attention Deficit Disorder Through the Lifespan* (New York: Oxford University Press, 1987), p. 59.
7. Dupaul and Stoner, p. 16.
8. Wender, p. 61.
9. Ibid., p. 60.
10. Hallowell and Ratey, p. 240.
11. Wender, p. 65.
12. Dupaul and Stoner, p. 151.
13. Ibid.
14. Wender, p. 68.
15. Ibid., p. 67.
16. Dupaul and Stoner, p. 151.
17. Ibid., p. 171.
18. Ibid., p. 188.
19. Ben Feingold, *Why Your Child is Hyperactive* (New York: Random House, 1975).
20. Wender, p. 77.
21. Paul H. Wender, *Attention Deficit Hyperactivity Disorder in Adults* (New York: Oxford University Press, 1995).
22. Dupaul and Stoner, p. 151.
23. Ibid., p. 203.
24. Hallowell and Ratey, pp. 245–53.

 Article Review Form at end of book.

- Increasing numbers of students are being diagnosed as having attention deficit hyperactivity disorder. Educators are debating whether this disorder should be considered an educational disability and whether it should be included in laws mandating special services for students with disabilities.

- Parents and teachers struggle to meet the needs of students with attention deficits. One of the most difficult decisions parents make is whether to use medication to ameliorate the effects of attention deficits or whether to rely on behavioral methods.

R.E.A.L. Sites

This list provides a print preview of typical **coursewise** R.E.A.L. sites. (There are over 100 such sites at the **courselinks**™ site.) The danger in printing URLs is that web sites can change overnight. As we went to press, these sites were functional using the URLs provided. If you come across one that isn't, please let us know via email to: webmaster@coursewise.com. Use your Passport to access the most current list of R.E.A.L. sites at the **courselinks**™ site.

Site name: Children and Adults with Attention Deficit Disorder
URL: http://www.chadd.org/
Why is it R.E.A.L.? This web site is concerned with providing information about ADD and helping individuals with ADD through support services.
Key topics: attention deficit disorder, parents, law
Activity: Identify the methods recommended for addressing attention deficit disorder in the classroom.

section 6

Learning Objectives

After studying this section, the reader will:

- List a variety of assessment strategies that provide alternatives to norm-referenced testing.

- Describe in detail how teachers can promote learning by using observation, anecdotal records, error analysis, miscue analysis, think-alouds, self-evaluation questionnaires, interviews, journals, learning logs, and portfolio assessment.

- Understand the impact that new technologies can have on the lives of individuals with disabilities.

- Know factors that influence the development of technologies designed to assist individuals with disabilities.

- Identify assistive devices that can help individuals with disabilities in their work and their private lives.

- Know types of technology-based instruction that teachers can employ to help students learn and communicate.

Innovations in Assessment and Instruction

WiseGuide Intro

The education of exceptional learners has changed dramatically in recent years. Two innovations in this period have been the adoption of authentic assessment strategies and the burgeoning of technology-based learning. In this section, we examine these two remarkable innovations.

Until recently, assessment of students with disabilities primarily took two forms. Norm-referenced tests, in which student performance was compared with norms of other children, were used for initial diagnosis of exceptionalities and classification of students in special classes. Teacher-made classroom tests were used to identify students' mastery of specific skills taught in class. Critics of these forms of testing have expressed concern that they do not always meet teachers' needs. In particular, norm-referenced testing has been criticized as not contributing to instructional decision-making.

Advocates of authentic assessment have recommended a variety of assessment methods that have changed the way we evaluate children. These alternative methods have in common an emphasis on assessing children's performance on the actual tasks that they are expected to learn. Rather than giving a student a spelling test at the end of the week, have the student write a letter in which he uses the spelling words. Instead of requiring a student to answer comprehension questions about short passages, have her read a piece of children's literature and have her write about the work in a journal. Many of the newer assessment strategies, such as think-alouds and self-evaluation questionnaires, have a purpose of helping students learn to evaluate themselves. In "Authentic Assessment Strategies," Kathryn Pike and Spencer J. Salend describe a wide variety of approaches that teachers can draw from in obtaining assessment information that can guide instruction.

The next two articles pertain to the contributions being made by technology. Technology is revolutionizing the lives of many people with disabilities. Every year, new technologies are becoming available that are providing individuals with disabilities with new opportunities. In "Technologies That Enable the Disabled," Bruce Felton presents stories of individuals whose lives have been made richer by the technologies that are available to them.

In the classroom, new technologies are helping teachers find ways of promoting student success. Appropriate technologies can be used in some cases to compensate for students' hearing impairment, visual impairment, physical disabilities, and learning disabilities. In "Special Ed Success Stories," Carol S. Holzberg gives five stories describing how technology has been employed to enhance student learning and communication.

Questions

R23. In what way do authentic assessment strategies focus on student abilities, rather than disabilities? Why is student participation in assessment so important?

R24. What factors account for the increased success of firms specializing in technology for persons with disabilities? What are the benefits of technology for persons with disabilities?

R25. What are the features of technology that can help students with disabilities? A common criticism is that computer instruction relies too heavily on drill and practice. What counter-examples of this are presented in this article?

In what way do authentic assessment strategies focus on student abilities, rather than disabilities? Why is student participation in assessment so important?

Authentic Assessment Strategies

Alternatives to norm-referenced testing

Are you up on your authentic assessment lingo? Quick now, in 100 words or less, what are the following: anecdotal records, error analysis, miscue analysis, think-alouds, observation, self-evaluation questionnaires/interviews, journals/learning logs, portfolios.

And how do you use these assessments in your classes? Is this too much to ask of a teacher, when standardized tests are available and easy to administer? This article explains how to incorporate authentic assessments into everyday practice—and how to learn from the process.

You can use these strategies with students across a range of abilities and ages; as with any generic instructions, you should tailor the use of these strategies to the unique needs of your students and classrooms.

Kathryn Pike
Spencer J. Salend

Kathryn Pike, Elementary Coordinator, Windham-Ashland-Jewett Central School, Windham, New York. **Spencer J. Salend** *(CEC Chapter #615), Professor of Educational Studies, State University of New York at New Paltz.*

Observation

Observation should be an integral part of your assessment process. If you regularly observe your students, you can obtain valuable information about their academic and behavioral performance. Since learning occurs all day, observations can take place throughout the school day both in and outside the classroom.

Goodman (1978) suggested that teachers engage in "kid-watching," which involves watching students and *documenting* these observations. For example, an observation regarding spelling performance might provide insights into the extent to which a student uses the dictionary and thesaurus for assistance in writing, or the discrepancy between a student's word choices in verbal and written communication.

You can structure your observations through the use of observational recording systems such as event, duration, or interval recording (Koorland, Monda, & Vail, 1988; Salend, 1994). You may also structure observations by setting aside a portion of the day for observing designated students.

However, observations need not always be structured. You can informally observe students during various content area activities and jot down observations of significant behaviors, such as "Yolanda read her piece aloud to a friend and asked for advice" or "When encountering a word he does not know, Jason frequently seeks the assistance of the teacher or a peer rather than attempting to figure out the word."

Figure 1. Checklist to examine students' understanding of narrative text.

Figure 2. Sample anecdotal record.

| Student: _____ |
| Teacher: _____ |
| Date(s): _____ |

Directions: Use the following system to record student behavior:

  N = Student does not engage in the behavior.

  B = Student is beginning to engage in the behavior.

  D = Student is developing the behavior.

  P = Student has proficiency in the behavior.

Support your notations with comments.

Narratives	Behavior	Date(s)	Comments
Names characters			
Describes the setting			
Identifies time/place			
Identifies problems			
Identifies solutions			
Predicts story outcomes			
Identifies mood			
Describes author's view			
States theme of story			

Setting: Student in fourth-grade class during Writers' Workshop activities.

3/6—Monica spent the initial 10 minutes of workshop time staring out the window, sharpening pencils, and doodling. Once she started writing, she produced a draft on building model airplanes.

3/9—Monica had difficulty getting started during the first 15 minutes of the session. She read her draft to peers in the Writer' Circle and then started working on revisions.

3/11—Monica spent the first part of the session looking for papers and getting organized. She had difficulty proofreading her own copy and then started to draw illustrations for her story.

Many teachers use commercially produced or teacher-made checklists to guide the observation. Whereas checklists are useful in focusing attention on small segments of learning, they often fail to provide information on the learning process. Therefore, you may want to supplement your checklists by including narrative statements to support or document the statements that have been checked or by using an anecdotal record. Figure 1 shows a sample checklist to guide an observation.

Anecdotal Records

An anecdotal record is a narrative description of the significant behaviors that occurred during an observation. Anecdotal records can focus on student products or the processes students use to complete these products (Rhodes & Nathenson-Mejia, 1992).

You can analyze a narrative record of observations over a period of time to determine a student's developmental patterns, as well as his or her strengths and weaknesses, progress, and responses to specific instructional strategies. For example, the anecdotal record in Figure 2 reveals

that Monica has difficulty beginning a task. Aside from assisting Monica with proofreading, Monica's teacher could assist her by providing her with additional time during the prewriting stage of the writing process and devising strategies to help her begin her writing. Alberto and Troutman (1990) offer guidelines for analyzing information reported in an anecdotal record.

You can devise various strategies to help you collect and organize anecdotal reports. Some teachers store data concerning each student in a three-ring binder that is sectioned off alphabetically by students' last names, while others maintain a separate notebook for each content area. Others prefer to use a card file system, whereby they record relevant data and observation dates on index cards that are filed and reviewed periodically. Some teachers initially record their observations on Post-its or gummed labels and later date and glue or staple these observations to the student's card or file folder (Pike, Compain, & Mumper, 1994).

Error Analysis

Another means of observing students and noting the learning strategies they use is error analysis. Error analysis allows you to examine students' responses to identify areas of difficulty and patterns in the ways students approach a task. You can then review student performance by identifying the mastery of skills and patterns in the methods a student uses to approach a task. You can use error analysis to enhance the value of assessment data obtained through other assessment procedures (Gickling & Thompson, 1985) and to adjust instruction to facilitate student performance (Grimes, 1981).

Though teachers often use error analysis when assessing mathematics skills (Enright, 1983), it also can be used across content areas. You can involve students in the error analysis process by (a) providing students with a set of items that require students to produce a permanent product; (b) examining the permanent product to identify error patterns; (c) querying the student concerning the strategies he or she employed in working on the items; (d) developing and teaching the student an instructional strategy to remediate the error pattern; and (e) assessing the effectiveness of the instructional strategy on the student's performance (Salend, 1994).

Miscue Analysis

In reading, error analysis is often referred to as miscue analysis. Miscues are viewed as being a natural and expected part of the reading process. In miscue analysis, teachers are concerned with the quality of the miscue and how the miscue helps or hinders the readers' efforts to comprehend the material.

Miscue analysis involves listening to students read orally, recording oral reading errors, and then analyzing the miscues to see whether the miscues are semantically or syntactically acceptable and look or sound like the actual word. When conducting a miscue analysis, you are also examining the metacognitive behaviors of students, such as the self-correction strategies the students employ when encountering unknown words or difficult text. As such, miscue analysis provides you with insights into the reading process and allows you to examine the reading strategies of your students. By knowing what strategies students use, you can help them develop more effective strategies and increase their repertoire of strategies.

Think-Alouds

"Think-aloud" is the name of an assessment strategy whereby students verbalize their thoughts as they are performing an activity. In a sense, like a radio sports announcer, the student gives "play by play" accounts of his or her thoughts when performing the task. You can use think-alouds to gather data about how a student approaches a task. Think-alouds help students to become aware of their thought processes while learning and provide you with information that is useful for planning instruction (see box on think-alouds). You can implement think-alouds by asking the students to state the processes used while they are performing a task (Meyers & Lytle, 1986).

Think-Alouds in Practice

Andrews and Mason (1991) used think-aloud procedures to assess the reading strategies employed by deaf and hearing readers. Deaf students, using manual communication, and hearing students, using their voices, were asked to read a sentence, identify the missing word or phrase in a sentence, and communicate the strategies they used to arrive at their answer. When students failed to think aloud, the teachers prompted them by using probing questions such as, "What are you doing now?" or "What are you thinking?" or "How are you finding the answer?" (Andrews & Mason, p. 538). Similarly, Meyers and Lytle (1986) used think-aloud procedures to assess students' understanding of what they read. Students read sentences and stated their thoughts while reading. Their think-aloud responses were then categorized in terms of their ability to understand the material presented, analyze text features, and expand on and judge the text. Instructional strategies were then developed to help students become more competent readers.

Think-alouds help students gain insights and control over their own learning and thereby enable teachers to help students become self-reflective, self-directed learners. However, students do not spontaneously "think aloud" and therefore must be taught to use this technique. You can encourage students to use think-aloud procedures by modeling the process and talking as you work through a problem. In addition, you can use probing questions to help students learn to think aloud and to increase the quality of their responses (Afflerback & Johnston, 1984).

Self-Evaluation Questionnaires and Interviews

An important aspect of authentic assessment is having students

Figure 3. Checklist on writing.

Question	Yes	No
Did I pick an interesting topic?		
Did I think about my topic before I began to write?		
Did I stick with my topic?		
Have I left anything out?		
Did I read my writing aloud?		
Did I make changes from the suggestions of others?		
Did I find and correct misspelled words?		
Did I capitalize correctly?		
Did I check my punctuation marks?		

Reminder: The Importance of Assessment

Many important decisions regarding student's educational program—particularly students with exceptional needs—are based on data collected through the assessment process. These educational decisions include the following:

- Establishing a student's need for special education services.
- Determining the related services that students will need to benefit from special education services.
- Specifying the objectives that will comprise a student's educational program.
- Grouping students for instruction within a particular classroom or subject area.
- Identifying potential instructional strategies to be used with a student.
- Providing data to assist educators who are teaching with disabilities in general education settings.
- Evaluating the effectiveness of the student's educational program.

evaluate their own learning. Since self-evaluation may be new to many students, you should offer instruction and provide students with numerous opportunities to engage in self-evaluation. You can obtain self-evaluation data by interviewing students or having students complete questionnaires or checklists. By tailoring questions to students' ages and levels of development, you can use these instruments to collect data from students concerning their perceptions of their educational needs, progress in mastering class content, and strategies for completing a task. For example, Figure 3 shows a simple checklist on writing that students might use.

Similarly, a self-evaluation conference with a student concerning his or her reading performance might focus on the following questions:

- What are some things you do well when you read?
- What are some areas in reading that cause you difficulty?
- How is your reading improving?
- What areas of your reading would you like to improve? (Pike et al., 1994).

Since students with special needs may have reading or writing problems, you may need to administer survey or checklists items in an interview format for these students and record their responses.

Journals and Learning Logs

Students also can engage in self-evaluation through journals or learning logs. At the end of a class session, students can write comments in their logs regarding (a) what they learned, (b) how they learned it, (c) what they do not understand, (d) why they are confused, and (e) what help they would like to receive. You and the students can then review the journals and develop instructional goals and strategies to address areas in need of remediation (see box [on learning logs]).

For example, Davison and Pearce (1992) used student journals to assess and increase the math performance of students from culturally and linguistically diverse backgrounds. Students' journals contained entries regarding reactions to math lessons and problems they were experiencing with these lessons. One student wrote:

Today I learned a new word. It's called *perimeter*. Perimeter means a distance around the pattern, and we used a square for 1 unit to measure the pattern, and it was fun and easy. (Davison & Pearce, 1992, p. 151).

Periodically, you can ask students to respond in their journals to specific information that has been covered in class (see box [on learning logs]). For example, after instruction in decimals, you could ask students to respond to these questions:

- What are decimals?
- Why do we use decimals?

Using Learning Logs in Any Subject

- If you wanted to teach decimals to someone else, how would you teach them?

- How do you feel about learning decimals?

- What part of learning about decimals do you find easy? hard?

- Write a story to go with this problem: 9.7 + 4.3 = 14.

Students who have difficulty writing can maintain an audio log by recording their responses on an audiocassette.

Portfolio Assessment

Portfolio assessment is a collaborative assessment process in which students and teachers compile information about the student across multiple contexts throughout the school year.

Portfolios examine the learning *process,* as well as the *products* of learning (Pike et al., 1994). Because portfolio assessment focuses on products that result from real classroom activities, it establishes a clear link between assessment and instruction.

Although many teachers have kept samples of student work in folders for years, work folders and portfolios differ in intent and philosophy. Unlike work folders, which students add to on a daily basis, portfolios are archival in nature. They contain samples gathered over time that are reviewed periodically by students, teachers, and parents to document progress, process, and development.

While portfolio assessment can be used with all students, it is particularly meaningful for students from culturally and linguistically diverse backgrounds whose progress may not be accurately measured by traditional testing strategies. For example, a series of audio recordings of language samples over time can be included in the portfolio for second-language learners to examine and document their increasing proficiency in learning English. By collecting language samples on a regular basis, these students' growing command of English can be documented by examining the amount of description provided, the use of more complex sentence structures, and the growth of vocabulary.

Both you and your students should select the types of items in portfolios and should relate them to the goals specified in students' instructional programs. In selecting products to include in portfolios, you and your students should consider what the selected piece demonstrates about each student's learning and how the piece provides insights into the instruction needed for each student (see box on what goes in a portfolio).

Salinger (1991) proposes that teachers periodically hold a "Portfolio Selection Day," in which students and teachers examine work that could be included in portfolios. On this day, students can be given time to review products saved in their work folders for possible inclusion in their portfolios. Teachers can structure the selection process for students by providing a framework for selecting products.

It is helpful to place a caption on each selected piece to provide reviewers of the portfolio with sufficient information to understand what the documents were intended to demonstrate. Captions should be short statements that include (a) an identification of the document, (b) a

What Goes in a Portfolio?

Ask students to choose the following items from their work folders (several subjects are represented here):

- A sample from your learning log where you wrote about a math lesson.
- A piece of writing where you identified words you did not know how to spell.
- A record of books you have read.
- Your best piece of writing.
- A piece of work of which you are really proud.

Samples that may be placed in portfolios include checklists, written responses in journals, selected daily work samples, unit projects, teacher observations, audio and video recordings, and parent and student interviews and surveys. Portfolios also can contain assessment data collected through self-evaluation questionnaires, think-alouds, and error analysis.

After an item has been included in a portfolio, both the item and an analysis of the relevant information depicted in the item should be included in the contents of the portfolio (Valencia, 1990). The portfolio should also contain captions for the various items and a summary sheet.

A Comparison of Traditional and "Authentic" Assessments

Traditional Assessment

Traditionally, educational decisions are based on assessment data collected through the use of teacher administered norm referenced, standardized tests (Salend, 1994). Norm-referenced testing offers educators information that allows comparisons of the student's performance to norms that are based on the scores of others. While norm-referenced testing is often employed to determine eligibility for special education services, it fails to provide specific information for planning, implementing, and evaluating a student's educational program. Norm-referenced test scores tend to be static and reflect only one score on a particular day under certain conditions. They do not reveal a student's attempts toward determining correct answers, nor do they acknowledge the student's efforts.

Authentic Assessment

Authentic assessment refers to a variety of informal and formal student-centered strategies for collecting and recording information about students. Authentic assessment practices seek to facilitate student learning by linking assessment and instruction. Authentic assessment procedures emphasize both the process and products of learning, and place value on input from teachers and students (Anthony, Johnson, Mickelson, & Preece, 1991). Teachers who effectively use authentic assessment practices continuously observe and interact with their students to discover not only what students know, but also how students learn. For authentic assessment to be meaningful for students and teachers, it should encompass the following principles:

- Assessment should be linked to what students are actually learning and what they might be learning.
- Assessment should be viewed as a continuous and cumulative process.
- Assessment should be conducted throughout the school day and across the curriculum.
- Assessment results should be based on data from a variety of assessment strategies.
- Assessment should occur during real learning experiences.
- Assessment should be a collaborative process on the part of students and teachers.
- Assessment findings should be easily communicated to students, parents, professionals, administrators, and other decision makers (Department of Education, Wellington, 1989; Pike, Compain, & Mumper, 1994).

Effective authentic assessment strategies involve students in the assessment process and make them the focus of all evaluation activities. Research indicates that student academic achievement levels and study behaviors are enhanced when students are involved in establishing the standards for performance (Brownell, Colleti, Ersner-Hershfeld, Hershfeld, & Wilson, 1977). Salend (1983) found that students' performance levels as measured via self-assessment procedures were superior to the performance levels determined by a multidisciplinary planning team using standardized assessment instruments.

Figure 4. A sample summary sheet.

Student: _____

Teacher: _____

Date: _____

Contents: *Included in this portfolio are: miscue analysis of oral readings, retelling of stories, survey interview sheets, writing samples.*

Analysis: *Through data collected via think-alouds and interviews and analysis of oral readings, it appears that Dexter initially perceived reading as "word calling" and did not attend to meaning. He felt he was not a reader and that he was incapable in school. Over the year, his reading performance data reveal that he began to pay more attention to the author's message as opposed to merely focusing on pronouncing the words. His miscues began to make sense, and he started to make self-corrections as needed. At the end of the school year, he could retell what he read and was reading with more enthusiasm.*

description of the context in which the document was produced, and (c) an explanation of why the piece was chosen. You should encourage students to assist in writing captions.

In addition to the captions, a summary sheet (see Figure 4) should accompany the portfolio. The summary sheet synthesizes the information that is presented in the portfolio and allows you to organize the contents of the portfolio to facilitate the instructional decision-making process (Wolf, 1989).

Portfolios should be reviewed periodically by teachers, students, parents, and administrators. Portfolios can be shared with others during conferences, which allow participants to examine each student's portfolio in comparison to the goals of that student's instructional program. In addition, at the end of the school year, portfolios can be forwarded to new teachers (Gropper, n.d.).

If the amount of data contained in portfolios becomes unwieldy, teachers and students can collaboratively determine which items should be shared with the students' new teachers and which items should go home to be shared with parents. In any case, the summary sheets and analyses will provide new teachers with the needed insights into the students' learning behaviors.

Summary

The exclusive use of norm-referenced standardized tests in

making instructional decisions has limitations. As a result, alternatives to norm-referenced testing have been proposed. Effective authentic assessment strategies can help educators and students make sound educational decisions. These assessment strategies reflect a changing philosophy toward learning and learners—an outlook that focuses on student abilities, not disabilities, and that expands to involve students in the assessment process. Authentic assessment procedures make assessment a more positive and valuable experience for students, teachers, and parents.

References

Afflerback, P., & Johnston, P. (1984). Research methodology on the use of verbal reports in reading research. *Journal of Reading Behavior, 16,* 307–322.

Alberto, P. A., & Troutman, A. C. (1990). *Applied behavior analysis for teachers* (3rd ed.). Columbus, OH: Merrill.

Andrews, J. F., & Mason, J. M. (1991). Strategy usage among deaf and hearing readers. *Exceptional Children, 57,* 536–545.

Anthony, R. J., Johnson, T. D., Mickelson, N. I., & Preece, A. (1991). *Evaluating literacy: A perspective for change.* Portsmouth, NH: Heinemann.

Brownell, K. D., Colletti, G., Ersner-Hershfeld, R., Hershfeld, S. M., & Wilson, G. T. (1977). Self-control in school children: Stringency and leniency in self-determined and externally imposed performance standards. *Behavior Therapy, 8,* 442–455.

Davison, D. M., & Pearce, D. L. (1992). The influence of writing activities on the mathematics learning of Native American students. *The Journal of Educational Issues of Language Minority Students, 10,* 147–157.

Department of Education, Wellington. (1989). *Keeping school records.* Wellington, New Zealand: Author.

Enright, B. E. (1983). *Enright Diagnostic Inventory of Basic Arithmetic Skills.* North Billerica, MA: Curriculum Associates.

Gickling, E. E., & Thompson, V. P. (1985). A personal view of curriculum-based assessment. *Exceptional Children, 52,* 205–218.

Goodman, Y. (1978). Kid watching: An alternative to testing. *National Elementary School Principal, 57,* 41–45.

Grimes, L. (1981). Error analysis and error correction procedures. *TEACHING Exceptional Children, 14,* 17–21.

Gropper, N. (n.d.). *Steps in conducting portfolio assessments.* New Paltz, NY: Department of Elementary Education, State University of New York at New Paltz.

Koorland, M. A., Monda, L. E., & Vail, C. O. (1988). Recording behavior with ease. *TEACHING Exceptional Children, 21,* 59–61.

Meyers, J., & Lytle, S. (1986). Assessment of the learning process. *Exceptional Children, 53,* 138–144.

Pike, K., Compain, R., & Mumper, J. (1994). *New connections: An integrated approach to literacy.* New York: Harper Collins.

Rhodes, L. K., & Nathenson-Mejia, S. (1992). Anecdotal records: A powerful tool for ongoing literacy assessment. *The Reading Teacher, 45*(7), 502–509.

Salend, S. J. (1983). Self-assessment: A model for involving students in the formulation of their IEPs. *Journal of School Psychology, 21,* 65–70.

Salend, S. J. (1994). *Effective mainstreaming: Creating inclusive classrooms* (2nd ed.). New York: Macmillan.

Salinger, T. (1991, November). *Getting started with alternative assessment methods.* Workshop presented at the New York State Reading Association Conference, Lake Kiamesha, New York.

Valencia, S. (1990). A portfolio approach to classroom reading assessment: The whys, whats, and hows. *The Reading Teacher, 43,* 338–340.

Wolf, D. P. (1989). Portfolio assessment: Sampling student work. *Educational Leadership, 46*(7), 35–39.

 Article Review Form at end of book.

What factors account for the increased success of firms specializing in technology for persons with disabilities? What are the benefits of technology for persons with disabilities?

Technologies That Enable the Disabled

High-tech or low, devices enrich work

Bruce Felton

With meetings, paperwork, phone conferences and a travel schedule that eats up three weeks a month, Urban Miyares doesn't get much reading done during the workday. So Mr. Miyares, a San Diego businessman who runs the Disabled Businesspersons Association, rises at 6 most mornings and spends an hour or so catching up on E-mail, reports and business magazines before leaving for the office. In the evening, he picks up where he left off, typically reading into the small hours.

Although Mr. Miyares is blind, Braille is of little use to him because the diabetes that destroyed his vision also deadened the nerve endings in his fingertips. Instead, he reads with a remarkable device called a Kurzwell Reading Edge optical scanner, which takes about five seconds to absorb a page of print and begin converting it to spoken text.

Mr. Miyares exemplifies the degree to which so-called adaptive or assistive devices have allowed people to sidestep their disabilities and perform at peak levels. Some devices, like his Kurzwell scanner, rely on highly sophisticated technologies; others are as low-tech as amplified telephones and motorized wheelchairs.

"If I had been born 50 years earlier, I'd be sweeping floors instead of running a business," said Christopher D. Sullivan, a former Wall Street technical analyst who is deaf and heads Merrill Lynch's Services for Deaf and Hard of Hearing Investors in Plainsboro, N.J. "Technology is what makes the difference."

In recent years, an entire technology sub-sector has burgeoned with the express purpose of capitalizing on the growing market for assistive devices. A spokesman for Henter Joyce Inc., a company based in St. Petersburg, Fla., that specializes in computer screen reading devices for the blind, would not disclose earnings figures, but said its work force had tripled to 24 in the last year. LC Technologies, a small company in Fairfax, Va., that makes eye-activated computers, said orders had increased sharply in the last six months. And, according to Voice Information Associates, a market research firm in Lexington, Mass., the market for speech-to-text products, projected at $410 million in 1997, should top $4.3 billion by 2001.

Top-tier technology companies like Xerox, which makes the Kurzwell scanner, likewise joined the parade.

But this isn't to suggest that all mainstream technology companies have kneed and elbowed one another in the race to make their existing products accessible.

"It's only been two years since Microsoft finally agreed to make its Windows software accessible to the disabled," said Lawrence Scadden, who is blind and serves as a senior program officer for the National Science Foundation in Washington. "I'm positive they made the decision only when the states of Massachusetts and Missouri and the Social Security Administration said they wouldn't buy Windows because it wasn't usable by blind persons."

Luanne LaLonde, the accessibility product manager for Microsoft, said, "It's no secret that these actions brought pressure on us to place even greater emphasis on an effort that had already been in place." She added that the company had made accessibility a priority for six years and that Windows 98, the next version of its signature operating system, "will be inherently even more usable by vision-impaired users," with automatic adjustments of screen size and contrast, among other features.

Not surprisingly, technology has made its greatest difference in the seven years since the passage of the Americans With Disabilities Act. Along with banning employment discrimination against disabled persons, the act requires businesses with 15 or more employees to provide "reasonable accommodation," a catch-all phrase that ranges from gadgets that allow disabled workers to do their jobs to ramps and widened doorways that let them get to their jobs in the first place.

Large companies appear to have moved most quickly toward making those accommodations. "The problem is that 80 percent of all jobs are with smaller businesses, where there is more misinformation and discrimination," said Doris Fleischer, co-author, with Frieda Zames, of "From Charity to Confrontation: The Modern Disability Rights Movement," soon to be published

by Temple University Press. "Big companies doing business with the Federal Government have been required to provide accommodations since 1973. Smaller companies, which typically don't depend on Federal contracts, are still struggling to accept the idea."

One common fear is that accommodating disabled workers is expensive. "Building a one-step ramp to make a store wheelchair-accessible costs less than $400," said Dr. Fleischer, who teaches humanities at the New Jersey Institute of Technology. "Mounting a table on blocks so that a mobility-impaired employee can use it costs virtually nothing. These are minimal investments, but they open a large and invaluable talent pool to employers."

Just how large is open to debate. The National Organization on Disability, based in Washington, says 49 million Americans are disabled, with 29 million of prime working age, from 21 to 64, of whom half are employed. But some say those figures are low. "Start counting people with dyslexia, diabetes and other hidden disabilities, and you're over 100 million," Mr. Miyares said.

Whatever number is used, the disabled account for a sizable part of the work force. As the general population ages, adaptive technologies continue to evolve and employers become more welcoming, that segment seems sure to grow. Some disabled workers will rise to the top of their professions, others will coast and the vast middle will perform adequately—the same as their able-bodied colleagues.

Then there will be those like Mr. Miyares, Mr. Sullivan and others who rely on technology to help them push the limits of cre-

ativity and grit and force a careful reconsideration of what it means to be disabled. Some of their stories follow.

Composing Music

Trading a Guitar for a Computer

Endowed with large hands, dazzling virtuosity and a brilliant future, musician-composer Jason Becker learned that he might be suffering from amyotrophic lateral sclerosis a week after he was hired as lead guitarist for David Lee Roth, the rock star. The year was 1989 and Mr. Becker was 19.

Amyotrophic lateral sclerosis—better known as Lou Gehrig's disease after the New York Yankees superstar who died in 1941—is a degenerative neuron impairment that gradually shuts down the muscles, bringing atrophy and paralysis. It is incurable and often fatal, but Mr. Becker's grim diagnosis "sort of went in one ear and out the other," he wrote recently in A.L.S. Digest, a magazine published on the World Wide Web. "All I knew was that I'd just joined Dave's band and I was going to be the guitarist."

He performed with the band even as his symptoms advanced. When his hands weakened, he switched to lighter-gauge strings and then a guitar with an easier action. He started taking more than 100 vitamins a day and bought a $200 pair of Nike Air Jordans in an effort to steady his shaky balance. Finally, he quit the band and, after a brief stay in Los Angeles, moved back into his parents' house in the San Francisco Bay area.

In 1991, unable to play the guitar without pain and shaking, Mr. Becker began composing on a Macintosh Classic computer linked to an electronic keyboard and a digital synthesizer. Later, as his condition worsened, he tapped out musical lines on the keys of an on-screen keyboard with a device held in his mouth. He also wore a wireless "Head Mouse," which allowed him to control a cursor and compose on screen solely by moving his head. A result of those efforts is "Perspective," a haunting compact disk recording of his music that departs radically from his hard-rock roots. It was released this year by Apallon International.

"Not playing guitar has been the hardest thing about having A.L.S.," Mr. Becker said in a recent E-mail message. "It has also made composing more difficult. But the music from 'Perspective' just flowed out of me, almost as if it came from somewhere else."

Since the release of "Perspective," Mr. Becker's muscle control has continued to erode. At 27, he can no longer speak or walk, and has limited movement in only three fingers.

He lives next door to his parents in Richmond, Calif., communicating with them and his fiancée, who take turns caring for him, largely by means of an alphabet board designed by his father. If he's in distress, or simply needs to have a fly brushed away from his face, he rings an electric bell that sits in his lap.

In Mr. Becker's current condition, the devices he used even a few months ago to compose music are largely useless to him.

"Jason is in a kind of artistic holding pattern, waiting for a technology that will let him resume composing," said his friend and computer guru, Mike Bemesderfer.

That may come in the form of the Eyegaze computer from LC Technologies. At the heart of the $20,000 system is a retooled casino surveillance camera that tracks the user's gaze with an infrared beam. While looking at a grid of characters displayed on the screen, the user is able to type by allowing his or her gaze to settle on the desired key for a fraction of a second. Mr. Becker took the system for a spin recently at his home. As he shifted the gaze of his left pupil from key to key, letters, and then words and sentences, appeared.

But Eyegaze does not lend itself to composing and orchestrating—not at the moment, anyway. That is because it lacks an eye-activated mouse, which Mr. Becker needs to operate his music software. A spokeswoman for LC Technologies said that such a device was under development and could be available next year.

The composer is eager to try it. "There's music that's been in my head for years," he said. "I can't wait to make it a reality."

Serving Investors

Brokers Converse with Deaf Clients

Deaf since infancy, Chris Sullivan attended a special school at which pupils who used hand signals were smacked with a ruler. "The idea was to read lips and to speak like hearing people," he said. "Signing was considered a sign of weakness."

Mr. Sullivan learned his lesson well: as a successful Wall Street investor and entrepreneur, he lived exclusively in the world of the hearing, with no deaf friends, no interest in deaf organizations and, almost as a matter of pride, no knowledge of American Sign Language. Even his first wife had normal hearing.

All that is changed now. Mr. Sullivan, 50, is married to a deaf woman, signs fluently and subscribes to Deaf Life and Silent News along with Forbes and Institutional Investor. And at Merrill Lynch's offices in Plainsboro, N.J., he runs a first-of-its-kind service focused solely on the needs of deaf and hard-of-hearing investors.

The needs of such investors were not foremost on Mr. Sullivan's mind when he joined Merrill as a technical analyst in October 1987. At another firm, where he had tracked the commodities markets, he had proved himself a canny reader of tea leaves. But he was caught off guard, along with much of the rest of the world, when the stock market cratered two weeks after he started at Merrill. Over the next four months, he worked 90 to 100 hours a week feeding market data and forecasts to jittery clients and helping Merrill rebuild from the wreckage.

Around the same time, Mr. Sullivan's new wife, Vicki Joy, was doggedly trying to raise his consciousness about being deaf. "She introduced me to other deaf people, got on my case to learn signing, exposed me to deaf culture," Mr. Sullivan said.

Notwithstanding his successes, he learned that deaf people often found Wall Street distinctly user-unfriendly. "If you wanted investment advice or a product brochure, you'd have to have a hearing friend make the call for you," he said. "A lot of people decided it wasn't worth the trouble."

In 1990, he gave up tracking the market to set up the unit serving the deaf and hard of hearing. Technology has figured large in the success of the unit, which began with $21 million in assets and today has more than $628 million.

Mr. Sullivan recalled that a few years ago, a cadre of 85 financial consultants served the unit's clientele. "It was easy to find new business," he said, "because the market was totally untapped and clients tended to be clustered in clubs and community groups, ripe for the taking."

But the consultants quickly reached a point where they could not handle more clients. Small wonder: "Even a simple phone conversation with a deaf client using a TTY took way too long," Mr. Sullivan said. A TTY—or telephone teletypewriter—has a small display screen and keyboard and attaches easily to virtually any standard phone. The system, which is subsidized by small fees paid each month by all phone users, allows users to converse by typing.

"With our sales force turning down leads for lack of time, I had visions of the business imploding." Mr. Sullivan said. "I was very nervous."

Deliverance came with the Americans With Disabilities Act. The law laid the foundation for Relay, a telecommunications service, which went into operation in 1993 and lets the deaf communicate easily with those who hear.

A specially trained operator acts as go-between, conveying the hearing person's spoken words to the deaf person on a TTY, and reading aloud the TTY messages to the hearing person. The process takes longer than a conventional phone call, but it is measurably faster than TTY—and frees the hearing person from having to install special equipment.

"With Relay, we suddenly had all 13,000 Merrill financial consultants in a position to take on as much new business as we could give them," Mr. Sullivan said. "Business surged."

Building Businesses

A Devoted Reader Can Be a Listener

For entrepreneurs with disabilities, Urban Miyares likes to point out, one of technology's most compelling benefits is the way it screens them from their customers.

"Reading an E-mail I've sent, or talking to me on the phone, there's no way you can tell what I look like," said Mr. Miyares, who founded the Disabled Businesspersons Association in 1985, a year after losing his sight. "Technology gives me the time to win your trust and build my business—without having to overcome your reluctance to deal with a blind person."

The diabetes that eventually left Mr. Miyares blind had first surfaced in 1968, when he was an infantry leader in Vietnam. Besides deadening the nerve endings in his hands and feet, the disease would leave him with wobbly balance; the impact of bomb explosions and mortar fire also damaged his hearing.

Medically discharged from the Army, Mr. Miyares moved to New Jersey and started a construction company—the first of nearly a score of enterprises he began over the next 15 years, including a hardware store, a public relations firm and a German restaurant. He made enough money to start the Disabled Businesspersons Association and finance it out of his own pocket

for the first 11 years. It is now supported by private donations.

The association, which operates out of a one-room office at San Diego State University, enlists volunteers to help people with disabilities to get back to work.

"For many disabled people, self-employment is often the best road back to the workplace, even if their ultimate goal is a salaried job," Mr. Miyares said. "It's a way of rebuilding your confidence and gaining work experience on your own terms."

Because so much of Mr. Miyare's work involves reading, the Kurzweil scanner he uses, which costs about $5,000, has proven an essential part of his success.

"The clarity is excellent, but it's always going to be slower than normal sight-reading," he said. "You can save time and get more reading in by turning up the speed," Mr. Miyares typically revs up the device to two and a half to three times the speed of normal speech.

But it is important then to take one more step. Regularly switching between male and female synthesized voices, Mr. Miyares said, breaks the monotony and "keeps me from starting to talk like a robot, too."

Writing Columns

A Torrent of Words and Stylistic Risks

On a recent Tuesday morning, Brian Dickinson awoke with a mild fever and a gnawing realization that he had picked a bad time to get sick. Tuesdays are when the 59-year-old newspaperman normally files the second of two weekly columns for The

Providence Journal-Bulletin in Rhode Island.

Another writer might have welcomed a guilt-free day in bed to surf the channels and catch up on reading. But Mr. Dickinson, a fixture of New England journalism since 1964, misses deadlines rarely—and never in good humor. Besides, enforced idleness isn't his idea of a good time. Mr. Dickinson normally writes from eight to nine hours a day, seven days a week.

Like Mr. Becker, the young musician, Mr. Dickinson has amyotrophic lateral sclerosis, which has stripped him of the power to speak, swallow, move his legs or arms, wiggle his fingers or turn his head. But because he deals with words rather than musical notes, Mr. Dickinson is producing some of the best work of his life, thanks to the Eyegaze computer.

Seated in a wheelchair, his arms resting limply before him on a pillow, Mr. Dickinson pumps out a steady stream of columns and book reviews, composes letters and E-mail, and shoots the breeze with his wife, Barbara, and their three grown sons.

In short bursts, he can hit 40 words a minute, but the going is usually slower and bumpier. No problem there: by budgeting three days to write each 800-word column, he builds in ample time for "planning, reflection and reorganizing," he told a visitor, conversing via the keyboard. "Having A.L.S. has freed me to take risks with style—plus I have an indulgent editor," he said. "Over the years, I've learned the importance of turning in letter-perfect copy, but it's especially important now, because revising is so time-consuming."

Before his illness, Mr. Dickinson was best known as a political commentator. He traveled often and widely, filtering his views of world and national events through a liberal lens. These days, his writing is more droll and contemplative, and less tied to breaking news. "The Labor Day holiday always seems to lack a clear identity," he wrote recently. "If the purpose is to recognize us all for toiling all summer, the term 'Labor Day' is a howler. No one works any harder in summer than he absolutely must."

Mr. Dickinson discusses his illness in print a few times a year; otherwise, his prose doesn't yield a whisker of evidence that there is anything wrong with his body. His first symptom—a tingling in his right leg—appeared in 1992. When he grew too weak to type, he composed his columns orally with a Dragon Dictate voice-recognition device, which converts speech into type. Eventually, he recalled, his speech failed, "so that the machine couldn't understand me."

Later, he pecked out his columns on a specially configured computer with the one finger he could still move. Ultimately, that ability vanished as well. He began using the Eyegaze system in 1995.

For all its world-of-tomorrow remarkableness, the Eyegaze system isn't without its nits. "It can be hard on the eyes, and after a few hours of gazing, I take a break for eyedrops," he said. Also, a cough or a random glint of light from Mr. Dickinson's eyeglasses can send the cursor skittering out of view, stopping him in his tracks while he takes the time to recalibrate the camera beam.

Occasionally, that requires help. "There are times he's sat there stuck for 45 minutes before someone has walked into the room and fixed the problem," his wife said.

In all fairness, sometimes the villain isn't a computer glitch, but old-fashioned creative block. "If I get stuck, or need a break, I flip to a game screen and play solitaire." Mr. Dickinson said. "It's no different from when I worked in a newspaper office. If I hit a wall, I'd go out for coffee or schmooze with my colleagues about the Red Sox."

 **Article Review Form at end of book.**

What are the features of technology that can help students with disabilities? A common criticism is that computer instruction relies too heavily on drill and practice. What counter-examples of this are presented in this article?

Special Ed Success Stories

Educators all over the country find that technology-based instruction helps kids achieve learning success. Here are some examples of the dramatic impact technology can have on students with special needs.

Carol S. Holzberg, Ph.D.

Carol S. Holzberg, Ph.D., is an anthropologist and computer journalist. She writes for several publications, works as a computer consultant, and serves as computer resource person at the Shutesbury and Swift River Elementary Schools in Massachusetts.

For Libby Blondin, speech and language clinician at the Minors Lane Elementary School in Louisville, Kentucky, one of the most powerful features of technology is that it allows her students to show their teachers, family members, and peers how much they know. "A lot of times people see a child with special needs and think that child is stupid or can't do anything," she says. "It's up to us to figure out how to get the best out of them so that they can showcase what they've got."

For a number of the students in the school's two special education classrooms, computers serve

as a key communications device. Using a Hawk input board, a small programmable device that evolved from Texas Instruments' older Touch and Say machine, students who are severely physically challenged can participate in regular classroom activities. "We can set it up so that it says out loud the vocabulary words kids need to know to participate in a lesson," Blondin explains. "For example, we might program it with the days of the week so that when they go into a class for calendar time, they can press a button and the Hawk will say, 'It's Monday.' They don't have the voice to say it themselves, but they can say it using the machine."

Even for children who have the physical ability to talk, technology is often the tool that motivates them to express themselves. "We have a few students who use the computer better than their 'regular education' peers," Blondin says. "Two children I am

thinking of don't talk a whole lot when questions come up, but we can get them to do it on the computer. It enables us to see how much they really do know."

Whether technology is being used to mainstream higher-functioning students or to help students with more severe developmental disabilities understand basic cause and effect, Blondin is impressed by how it motivates young people. "Whenever we do something at the computer, everybody wants a turn," she says. "When the computer goes on, kids who usually have trouble paying attention suddenly start pulling their chairs over and calling, 'Me first!'"

The Minors Lane teachers are also enthusiastic about the benefits of technology with the students who are mainstreamed into their classes. "They see the kids in there using the computers successfully and independently," Blondin notes. "And it's not just

Carol S. Holzberg, "Special ed success stories," *Technology & Learning,* October 1996, vol. 17, no. 2, pp. 35–41. Reprinted by permission.

when I'm in there helping them. They use them the whole day. It allows them to be independent and it's a lot more fun than pencil and paper."

Walking—and Signing—with Rosie

"When you can't hear, it's hard to know what's going on," says Gerald Pollard, CD-ROM project director at Austin's Texas School for the Deaf. That's why deaf children often lose interest in conventional electronic storybooks, even though these multimedia-rich learning tools are wildly popular in the hearing world. CD-ROM storybooks build literacy skills by providing a wealth of visual stimulation, audio reinforcement, and reading encouragement for hearing children. However, the animated lip movements of the characters lack sufficient detail for lip reading. Other storybook options, like clicking on a word to hear it pronounced, also have little to offer the hearing impaired.

There's more to deafness than just the absence of sound, explains Pollard. The disability also slows down language development, resulting in reading difficulties for many children with hearing problems. So Pollard and colleague Denise Hazelwood decided to reinvent the interactive storybook. By adding a sign language component to the printed text and humorous animations, they hoped to make popular stories accessible to deaf children.

Pollard and Hazelwood approached the Macmillan Publishing Company, which gave them the green light to transform Pat Hutchins's entertaining children's title *Rosie's Walk* into a sign language CD. The Austin-based teachers applied for and received a three-year grant from the U.S. Department of Education, and began work on transforming a 30-year-old children's classic into an online treasure that both hearing and deaf children could enjoy.

The CD of *Rosie's Walk* is now on the market. This multimedia storybook recounts the barnyard adventures of a hen named Rosie and the mishaps of a hungry fox who would love to eat her for lunch. The humorous story has enough music, sound effects, and voiced narration to hold the attention of hearing kids. It also includes over 120 QuickTime sign language movies in both Signed English and American Sign Language, plus five entertaining games to build vocabulary and reading skills. A Secret Words option enables viewers to click on screen objects to see related words, signs, and animations.

While *Rosie's Walk* is the first signed children's CD of its kind, Pollard hopes it won't be the last. Plans are in the works for the release of four signed Aesop's fables and two signed O. Henry short stories. He says deaf students are attracted to the technology and eager to learn from it. They see the results of what they do on screen and really appreciate a story told in their first language. At the same time, hearing children enjoy the storybook because each page combines voice, sound effects, and animation with sign language demonstrations for familiar words and phrases.

Computers That Teach the "Write" Stuff

Textbooks are not the primary instructional medium for sixth-graders at John Rolfe Middle School in Richmond, Virginia. Instead, teachers and students rely on technology, according to Jane Middleton, a special education teacher at the school. Middleton team-teaches the sixth grade in a "collaborative classroom" with two regular education teachers. Together they accommodate 30 students, 20 of whom have special needs.

Most of the students Middleton works directly with are mildly learning disabled; many have difficulty with writing or reading. Some struggle with more severe limitations. Middleton believes (and achievement on school-administered literacy tests affirms) that student performance improves with technology. Computers, tape recorders, video laserdisc players, LCD projection panels, and CD-ROM drives enable youngsters "to work around their disabilities," she says, " so they can participate in content appropriate to their age level."

Many of Middleton's students find computer-based laserdiscs and CD-ROMs easier to work with than conventional print materials. "If they have difficulty with reading and organizational skills, they really can't manage without a tremendous amount of support," she explains. "But with CD-ROM programs like *Microsoft Encarta*, *Grolier's Multimedia Encyclopedia*, and StarPress Multimedia's *Material World*, they can work more independently."

The multimedia software is not only informative and easy to use, Middleton suggests, it also serves as an economical alternative to expensive textbooks. To keep learning materials up-to-date, the school has opted to purchase more CD-ROM and laser videodisc technology than new science texts.

Technology turns Middleton's students into more active learners because it gives them all a chance to participate. With computer assistance, for example, she was able to enlarge the type size on the assignment sheets of a student whose work was at the level of tracing and copying, making it easier for that student to complete assignments. Parent volunteers have recorded textbooks on tape for students who prefer listening to reading. And some children overcome writing limitations by dictating their work into a tape recorder.

Technology is also a time saver. When Middleton prepares tests, she prints individualized exam pages for each student. "All tests do not look alike," she explains, "because most students need less text on a page." With computer help, she can modify an exam to meet each student's needs. It doesn't take her much time to make those changes because she has to type in questions only once.

According to Middleton, research shows that the more you separate special needs students from regular education students, the less they absorb. They begin to exhibit a phenomenon called "learned helplessness," losing confidence in their ability to do anything themselves and gradually trying less and less. With computers, she can present her students with both a challenge and a solution. As a result, they begin to believe in themselves again. "We really worked to find a way that they can participate with other students" she says. "Thanks to computers, many youngsters in the class do not know who is in special education and who is not."

My Right Foot

Kate Moore works as a speech language pathologist at Cotting School, a publicly funded, independent school in Lexington, Massachusetts, for children with moderate to severe learning, physical, and communication disabilities. Students range in age from three to 22. Many have very identifiable neurological problems, requiring that they receive their education in smaller chunks and at a slower pace than regular education students.

Motor and sensory impairments prevent these youngsters from achieving age-appropriate developmental milestones, or from succeeding in a regular mainstream classroom. Some students may have movement limitations. Others have processing difficulties which affect their language comprehension or visual perception. "By virtue of their physical and in some cases sensory limitations (whether auditory, visual, or tactile)," says Moore, these students "are more dependent on others to help them through normal activities, such as turning a page. The technology assists them in coping with large quantities of information more independently."

At the computer, a child who can use the mouse can easily page forward or backward through a reading assignment in the same way as a student who uses a regular textbook. With technology, children can work alone on the machine "even if they only have the use of one finger or a head pointer," says Moore. "They can still turn pages themselves and move from text to questions or from a teacher's worksheet to the

text. Extremely skilled kids can even move from copying that text to pasting it into a word processor."

While all learning is heavily collaborative at certain stages, Moore believes it's very important for her students to acquire skills that allow them to work independently. "They must be able to make their own needs known and do more for themselves," she says. "Technology helps them learn. It also gives them a way to demonstrate comprehension and expressive output without that intense teacher-student collaboration or facilitation."

As an example, Moore points to the case of an 11-year-old boy with severe cerebral palsy. He has limited hand use, low vision, and no functional speech. However, thanks to a Ke:NX interface (from Don Johnston), he can run a computer with a single switch, accessing it with a simple head movement. With this setup, he can use a word processor, word prediction software that allows for faster writing, and a variety of other programs for recreation and learning. Moore is enthusiastic about the sense of accomplishment the technology provides. "This is a child who came to us with only 'yes' and 'no,'" she says. "He currently has an expressive vocabulary of over 100 words, and he feels extremely proud to be able to demonstrate his own learning and acquisition of skills."

Another wheelchair-bound student with severe cerebral palsy operates a Ke:NX-equipped computer with his right foot and a single switch. The interface allows this 16-year-old to run any educational software, but he really enjoys using the computer to access

America Online and the Internet. He's also learning *PageMaker*. While he's dependent on someone to get paper out of the printer for him, he can run communication software to make those requests.

"Technology motivates kids who have a hard time meeting normal curriculum demands," Moore says. "It's colorful and bright, with few distractions. It allows these students to bring interesting things back to share with their families and their community, and it gives them the autonomy to decide what they want to do with their own motor systems."

All Together Now

"Inclusion" classrooms at Dupont Elementary School in Commerce City, Colorado, combine both special education and regular education kids with special services delivered to the child in the classroom. About one-third of the students in Michael Cummings's fifth-grade inclusion class have special needs, because of emotional, physical, and learning disabilities.

A simple word processor is an extremely powerful tool for helping Cummings's students experience success. He describes a former student who had extremely limited finger control: "For him to write his name with a pencil took about 20 minutes. Usually the activity ended up being so frustrating that he would tip a desk over, wad up the paper, and throw it away, or break his pencil. When I put him on a computer, he was able to punch in the letters and type his name as well as any other student. It was the first time he had enjoyed that kind of success. He didn't have to

be different any more." This student's triumph spilled over into other areas. He began to sit still for longer periods of time. He was more willing to heed advice. He accepted constructive criticism. Eventually he became a much better student and went on to write a five-page report.

According to Cummings, one of the greatest strengths of the computer is that it "doesn't have a preconceived bias about what kids can or cannot do. It has tremendous patience. It won't call them stupid or look at them like they can't learn. It just keeps coming back with helpful suggestions." A spelling checker, for example, has helped many of his students develop their language skills in a non-threatening way. "I've seen them experiment," Cummings says. "They go for the bigger and better words or choose words that they've heard before. All of the sudden they've increased their vocabulary as well as their spelling skills."

Cummings believes that technology works because it puts kids in charge of their own learning and enhances what they do well. "The more we can get them to take controlled risks," he explains, "the more they learn. The more they are successful, the more risks they take. Success breeds success."

Signs of the Times

T & L profiled Susan Abdulezer several years ago, when as a graphic arts teacher at JHS 47 School for the Deaf in New York City, she developed a student-run desktop publishing business called Fingerprints Press. While Abdulezer has moved on to other

projects, deaf students at the school continue to work at Fingerprints Press, designing and selling a variety of sign language products, greeting cards, t-shirts, and buttons. The money they earn from sales helps the school buy high-end Macintosh computers and other equipment.

Today, Abdulezer wears two hats. She's still on staff at JHS 47, but she's also multimedia coordinator for special education in the New York City public schools. Heading up a technology-rich multimedia center located on the premises of the School for the Deaf, she runs year-long multimedia seminars for teachers in New York's special education district.

Under her direction, teachers sign up for eight full-day sessions to learn how to develop customized software and adapt computers for special needs populations. By the time they complete the course, they've had hands-on experience with every kind of digital input, including scanners, cameras, frame grabbers, and screen capture software. They learn their way around *HyperStudio's* authoring environment, *Adobe Photoshop's* image editor, and *Adobe Premier's* digital video editor. Abdulezer also teaches teachers how to gather information and do research over the Internet and how to use this online information in multimedia projects.

To complete the course, participants must turn in an original multimedia project. Abdulezer takes these projects, records them on CD-ROM, and gives each participant a copy. Teachers then return to their classrooms with examples of 20 or so multimedia projects they can replicate with their students.

Abdulezer recently won a Smithsonian Innovation in Technology award for Education and Academia. She received this coveted prize for her outstanding work in the world of information technology. The particular project that attracted such favorable review was her CD-ROM-based instruction toolkit called *StreetSigns: A City Kid's Guide to American Sign Language.*

Designed in collaboration with deaf children and faculty, *StreetSigns* features 650 signed concepts, grouped into 24 language categories. Students sketched illustrations for the categories, drawing inspiration from various aspects of their urban experience. For example, they represented the "Numbers and Calculation" category with an illustration of Wall Street. A picture of Central Park symbolizes "Nature," while a drawing of youngsters hanging out on a street corner is the visual metaphor for "Social Interaction."

Abdulezer taped students as they used American Sign Language to communicate the various signs for each category. After consulting with deaf staff members to ensure the accuracy of sign language content, she converted the signs into QuickTime movies for output on classroom computers. According to Abdulezer, *StreetSigns* is both a stand-alone application with core sign language vocabulary, and a video source for students and teachers who may wish to embed signs in their own multimedia projects. It does for multimedia project development what "canned" clip art did for desktop publishing.

 Article Review Form at end of book.

WiseGuide Wrap-Up

- Authentic assessment refocuses assessment so that it involves actual tasks that students are expected to perform, rather than invented tasks used solely for the purpose of testing. Portfolios, observation, and journals are some of the methods used in authentic assessment. The purpose of authentic assessment is to obtain information that can effectively guide instruction.

- Technology has provided a vast array of new opportunities to individuals with disabilities. By enhancing their opportunities to learn, communicate, and be productive at their jobs, new technologies have made significant contributions to the quality and meaningfulness of the lives of individuals with disabilities.

R.E.A.L. Sites

This list provides a print preview of typical **coursewise** R.E.A.L. sites. (There are over 100 such sites at the **courselinks**™ site.) The danger in printing URLs is that web sites can change overnight. As we went to press, these sites were functional using the URLs provided. If you come across one that isn't, please let us know via email to: webmaster@coursewise.com. Use your Passport to access the most current list of R.E.A.L. sites at the **courselinks**™ site.

Site name: Catalyst: A Resource for Technology in Special Education
URL: http://home.earthlink.net/~thecatalyst/
Why is it R.E.A.L.? At this site, the Western Center for Microcomputers in Special Education produces a quarterly newsletter about technology in special education.
Key topics: technology, microcomputers
Activity: Find the Center's most recent newsletter and summarize in a paragraph the newsletter's major story.

Site name: Assistive Technology Project
URL: http://www.cc.ndsu.nodak.edu/at/
Why is it R.E.A.L.? This site is supported by North Dakota State University and is dedicated to helping students with disabilities through assistive technology. It covers both legal and procedural issues.
Key topics: technology, accommodations
Activity: Find the procedures that college students with disabilities should follow to obtain accommodations in teaching and testing.

Site name: National Center to Improve Practice in Special Education through Technology, Media, and Materials
URL: http://www.edc.org/FSC/NCIP/
Why is it R.E.A.L.? This site directs you to workshops on technology in special education. It also links you to a library of resources.
Key topics: technology, resources
Activity: Identify how voice recognition technology is helping students who have difficulty with writing.

section

7

Inclusion
The Issue of the 21st Century

 Since the passage of Public Law 94-142, the Education for All Handicapped Children Act, in 1975, educators have struggled with the issue of when and how students with disabilities should participate in classes with their nondisabled peers. At the heart of the issue is the interpretation of the clause indicating that students with disabilities should be educated in the "least restrictive environment." The "mainstreaming" movement of the late 1970s and 1980s led to placement of some students with disabilities in regular classes, but only if they were academically prepared. For example, some students with learning disabilities who were placed in special classes might spend part of their school day in the regular class if they were judged able to perform at grade level.

In the 1990s, the "inclusion movement" began. This movement was based on the belief that students with disabilities should have the opportunity to be educated with their nondisabled peers regardless of their academic level. Further, they should be full members of a class, not visitors. However, advocates of inclusion stress that participation by students with disabilities in regular classes depends on the provision of appropriate supports provided in the regular classroom setting to help students succeed. This might mean that a student with mental retardation has a paraprofessional in the regular class who is present to explain concepts that the teacher is presenting to the class. Or, a special education teacher might co-teach with a regular education teacher who has three students with learning disabilities in the class.

Inclusion, which is occurring in various forms in more and more schools, is the subject of fierce debate among special educators. Some believe that inclusion is the next stage in the evolution of educational opportunity for students with disabilities; others fear that inclusion will lead to a loss of the rights and services for which advocates for special education struggled. The debate continues and efforts to understand inclusion will continue into the twenty-first century.

The articles in this section present a variety of positions on the inclusion issue. Mara Sapon-Shevin, in "Full Inclusion as Disclosing Tablet," contends that the inclusion issue reveals the weaknesses of our educational system. She examines a variety of myths about inclusion and concludes that inclusion both can and should be implemented.

Diane Bricker, in "The Challenge of Inclusion," explores inclusion of very young children with disabilities. She calls on the field to examine the complexities of successful inclusion, rather than looking at inclusion as a purely moral or legal issue.

Dianne L. Ferguson, in "The Real Challenge of Inclusion," argues that inclusion should be part of a larger reform of schools. She contends that regular education and special education together need to reinvent schools to make them more responsive to all forms of diversity. Arguments against full inclusion are voiced by James M. Kauffman, John Wills Lloyd, John Baker, and Teresa M. Riedel in "Inclusion of All Students with Emotional or Behavioral Disorders? Let's Think Again." These authors believe that teachers in regular education settings are not likely to be able to implement the educational strategies that are known to work with these populations. Finally, Michael Mahony, in "Small Victories in an Inclusive Classroom," describes his experience as a ninth-grade English teacher with three included students. He identifies the instructional adaptations and teaching methods that he employed to make his classroom an effective learning environment for all of his students.

Questions

R26. How do you respond to Sapon-Shevin's question, regarding educational research, whether the burden of proof should rest on those who wish to segregate students with disabilities? She contends that students with disabilities can learn "functional life skills" in regular classes. How persuasive is her argument?

R27. What is Bricker's purpose in presenting the *Narratives from the Sandbox?* What is her greatest concern regarding the role of special education in educational reform?

R28. How does Ferguson's definition of inclusion differ from more traditional definitions? What does she mean when she describes included students as being "*in*, but not *of*, the class"?

R29. What are the major concerns of Kauffman et al. regarding the inclusion of students with emotional and behavioral disorders in regular classes? What kind of definition for inclusion do they propose?

R30. In what way did Mahony's flexibility extend to his grading? What are some of the teaching practices described in this article that contributed to the included students' success?

How do you respond to Sapon-Shevin's question, regarding educational research, whether the burden of proof should rest on those who wish to segregate students with disabilities? She contends that students with disabilities can learn "functional life skills" in regular classes. How persuasive is her argument?

Full Inclusion as Disclosing Tablet

Revealing the flaws in our present system

Mara Sapon-Shevin

Mara Sapon-Shevin is professor of education at Syracuse University.

If we include a student like Travis, we'll have to change our curriculum . . . .

If we include students like Larissa, we'll have to change our teaching methods too—lecture just doesn't work with those kids . . . .

If we include a student like Justin, the other kids will destroy him. . . . The kids in my class have no tolerance for kids who are different in any way . . . .

And if we have to plan for a student like Marianna, our teachers will need time to meet and plan together . . . .

The above statements are representative of the hue and cry that has been raised by the prospect of full inclusion in many school districts. Full inclusion, the movement to include students with disabilities as full-time members of general education class-

rooms, has come under sharp criticism of late, and has been blamed for a host of problems— overworked teachers, falling academic standards, lack of discipline, and poor teacher morale (Willis, 1994). Although some of these criticisms are consistent with the often inadequate and half-hearted ways in which inclusion has been implemented, negative responses to planning and implementing full inclusion tell us as much (or more) about the quality and responsiveness of the schools as it does about the challenges presented by the students themselves.

When children are being taught proper dental hygiene, the dentist sometimes gives them a little red pill to chew after they have brushed. The red dye sticks to any areas that have been inadequately brushed, thus making it obvious where problems remain. These pills are called "disclosing tablets" because they disclose the areas that require further attention.

It is possible to look at full inclusion as a disclosing tablet. Attempting to integrate students with significant educational and behavioral challenges tells us a lot about the ways in which our schools are unimaginative, underresourced, unresponsive, and simply inadequate. Full inclusion did not create these problems, but it shows us where the problems are. Children who stretch the limits of the system make it painfully clear how constricting and narrow those limits are. Full inclusion reveals the manner in which our educational system must grow and improve in order to meet the needs of all children.

Consider again the original set of complaints cited at the beginning of the article. What do these statements tell us about our schools?

We'll have to change the curriculum . . . .

Yes, we will need to change the curriculum if we want to include students with disabilities. But don't we believe that the cur-

Sapon-Shevin, M., "Full inclusion as disclosing tablet: revealing the flaws in our present system," *Theory into Practice,* 35(1), 1996, pp. 35–41. Copyright 1996 College of Education. The Ohio State University. This article was part of a theme issue on "Inclusive Schools: The Continuing Debate." Reprinted by permission.

riculum already needs changing, is changing, and will be improved for all children by being reconceptualized more broadly and divergently?

We'll have to change the way we teach . . . .

Yes, we will need to look at teaching structures and practices. Teachers whose teaching repertoires are limited to frontal, lecture style instruction will need to explore more interactive, engaging ways of teaching. Isn't that what the research tells us needs to happen anyway?

We'll have to pay close attention to the social dynamics . . . .

Yes, including a child with a significant difference will mean that we need to pay closer attention to the social climate of the school. But, clearly, if children who are "different" in any way are routinely mocked, scorned, or excluded, this is not a productive learning environment. Why do we assume that a classroom in which a child with Down's Syndrome would be teased is a comfortable classroom for children who are African-American, overweight, from single parent families, or non-English speaking? Wouldn't improvements in classroom climate have a salutary effect on all students?

We'll have to support teachers in their efforts at change . . . .

It is true that including a student with a disability will require that teachers have time for collaborative planning and preparation. The kinds of creative, multi-level instruction and assessment necessitated by full inclusion make it imperative that teachers be given adequate time to think and plan together. But doesn't all good teaching require planning and preparation? And don't all teachers rise to higher expectations when they are treated as profes-

sionals who need thinking and planning time?

There is bad news and good news about full inclusion—and it is the same news. The "news" is that to do inclusion well will require changes in curriculum, pedagogy, staff development, school climate, and structures. This can be characterized as "bad news" because it means that mere tinkering on the edges of existing structures will not work; simply dumping children with disabilities into classrooms without adequate preparation, commitment, and support will certainly not work. But this same news—the need for wide-ranging change—is good news because there is considerable evidence that the kinds of changes necessitated by inclusion are consistent with and often can be a catalyst for broader, far-reaching school restructuring and reform efforts (Stainback & Stainback, 1992; Villa, Thousand, Stainback, & Stainback, 1992).

Like all reform efforts, the range of policies and practices implemented in the name of full inclusion has varied tremendously in quality and depth. Some school systems have simply eliminated costly special education services and teachers in the name of inclusion, dumping those students into inadequately prepared and supported classrooms. But in other schools, full inclusion has served as a spark, an organizing principle for wide-ranging change. In these schools, the inclusion of students with disabilities has been part of school reform and school restructuring that reaches far beyond the handful of labeled students identified as the purview of "special education" (Villa et al., 1992). Like all reform movements that are clouded by misinformation, debated by experts, and shrouded by emotion, it can be difficult to

discern what full inclusion really means.

This article explores the vision and possibilities of full inclusion by addressing and responding to myths about full inclusion that block thoughtful and comprehensive implementation. Responding to these myths can help us to better understand the promise and the practice of full inclusion.

Myth: Inclusion is being imposed on schools by outside ideologues and unrealistic parents who do not accept their child's disability.

Inclusion did not spring, fully-formed, from any particular group. The evolution of the movement can be traced through changes in language and terminology. Twenty years ago, our efforts were directed toward "mainstreaming"—putting selected students with disabilities into general classrooms when a good "match" could be made. When those efforts proved inadequate to the task of changing classrooms so that students would fit in, we focused our efforts on "integration"—trying to mesh the systems of general and special education. Those efforts taught us about the need for unified services and collaboration and the importance of good communication and problem solving.

We have now articulated our task as inclusion—changing existing classrooms and structures so that all students can be served well within a unified system. Rather than merging two systems, we are trying to create a new, improved, more inclusive system for all students.

While parents have certainly played an important role in the inclusion movement, they have not acted alone. Teachers and administrators have shown great leadership in designing creative solutions to the problems inherent within pullout programs and remedial education. In the best case scenarios, parents and teachers have worked together to create programs that are effective and realistic. Inclusion is a product of many people's rethinking of the nature and quality of special education, as well as a by-product of new ways of thinking about teaching and curriculum.

Myth: Inclusionists only care about students with significant disabilities.

This is a complaint often raised by those whose primary concern is for students with mild disabilities, particularly learning disabilities. They fear that the educational needs of their students will get lost in the shuffle of full inclusion, while students with extensive challenges (of which there are fewer) will become the organizing focus of inclusion. These are valid concerns, and no inclusion advocate I know is callous to the very real learning needs of students with mild disabilities who are often abandoned without support in general education classrooms under the name of inclusion.

But, by definition, inclusion involves changing the nature and quality of the general education classroom. And there is no reason that the instructional strategies and modifications provided for students with learning disabilities in segregated settings cannot be provided in more typical classrooms if we are willing to reconceptualize those classrooms.

Justin Maloney (1994/1995) of the Learning Disabilities Association of America argues against full inclusion and for a continuum of services; yet, she herself acknowledges that

Students with learning disabilities would have a better chance of success in the general education setting if more of the strategies developed by special education, such as collaborative learning, cooperative teaching, peer tutoring and some of the innovative scheduling and planning developed in education reform models, became commonplace, rather than showpieces. (p. 25)

Myth: Inclusionists are driven only by values and philosophy—there is no research and no data.

The research in the field of inclusion is relatively recent, because it is difficult to collect data on programs and options until they exist. Advocates of full inclusion provide data indicating that students with disabilities educated in general education classrooms do better academically and socially than comparable students in non-inclusive settings (Baker, Wang, & Walberg, 1994/1995). Those who do not support inclusion cite studies indicating that special education programs are superior to general education classrooms for some types of children (Fuchs & Fuchs, 1994/1995).

The controversy about the research and what it tells us is indicative of more fundamental disagreements about (a) what counts as research and (b) what research is of value and what it is of value for. Should inclusion programs have to prove they are better than segregated programs, or should the burden of proof be on those

who would maintain students in more restrictive environments? What data are collected? Are reading scores the best indications of student success? Is growth in social and communicative skills considered of primary or secondary importance? And what about benefits to "typical" students? How should these be measured and valued? The lack of agreement on the quality and value of the research data gathered to this point is indicative of more basic conflicts about the value and purposes of inclusion.

Myth: Segregation is not inherently a problem— it is only *bad* segregation that is a problem.

Many anti-inclusionists have been angry about parallels drawn between racial segregation (Brown v. Board of Education's "segregation is inherently unequal") and the segregation of students with disabilities. Kauffman (quoted in O'Neil, 1994/1995) asserts:

Certainly racial segregation is a great evil, and segregation that is forced and universal and unrelated to legitimate educational purposes certainly is wrong. But when separate programs are freely chosen and placement decisions are made on a case-by-case basis—not forced, not universal—I think it's inappropriate to call that segregation. (p. 9)

But most of the segregation that has been part of special education has been forced, has *not* been freely chosen, and has *not* been made on a case-by-case basis. Often parents have been forced to accept segregated special education services or nothing and have not been presented with a range of options. More importantly, it is not clear that segregating students with disabilities is directly related to a legitimate educational purpose! When all school districts offer parents and their children the choice of a well-developed, fully inclusive classroom, then we may be able to talk differently about the advisability and appropriateness of more segregated settings; until then, we cannot call segregation a legitimate choice.

Myth: The system isn't broken—why are we messing with it?

The eagerness with which educators embrace school reform in general and inclusion in particular is definitely related to the extent to which they believe that the existing system needs changing. Inclusion advocates do not believe the system (two systems, actually) is working. The disproportionate number of students of color in special education, the lack of mobility out of special education settings, the limited community connections for students with disabilities, and the human and financial costs of supporting two separate systems of teacher education, classroom programs, and curricular materials and resources have led many educators to welcome changes in the ways in which special education services are conceptualized and delivered.

Even those who recognize the need for change, however, do not necessarily agree on the nature or extent of that change. Some supporters of maintaining a continuum of services believe that we only need to do special education "better" to make it work. Inclusion advocates tend to look for more systemic, structural change; they do not see the problems as being linked to the quality

or commitment of those who provide services but as more basic, requiring changes in more than just personnel.

Myth: Inclusionists think we need change because special educators are bad or incompetent.

This myth is closely related to the previous one. Those who promote inclusion in no way impugn the hard work, motives, or competence of special educators. Rather, they seek to find new ways to use those talents and skills so that all students can benefit from highly specialized teaching strategies and adaptations.

Myth: Inclusion advocates believe special educators are extinct (or should become that way).

Again, closely linked to the above two, inclusion will require that special educators reconceptualize their roles, acting more often as coteachers or resources than as primary sources of instruction or services. Conceiving of special education as a set of services rather than as a place allows us to conceive of special educators as educators with special skills, rather than as educators who work with "special" children.

Myth: It takes a special person to work with "those kids."

Idealizing the special educator as someone with unique personality characteristics (often patience) and a set of instructional tricks foreign to general education class-

room teachers has served to deskill general education teachers, removing the motivation and the need to develop a wider repertoire of skills. "Those kids" need good teaching, as do all students. Our goal should be to have skilled (special education) teachers share what they know with others, rather than to isolate them in ways that minimize their breadth and long-term effectiveness.

Myth: Inclusion is beyond the reach of the already overburdened general education teacher.

There is no question that many general education teachers are overburdened and under-supported. Adding students with disabilities without committing the necessary resources and support is unethical as well as ineffective. We must make huge improvements in the kinds and quality of support we provide for teachers. Although many general education classroom teachers initially say, "If I take that kid, I'll need a full-time aide," more experienced inclusion teachers identify many kinds of support as important (sometimes eliminating the need for a full-time aide), including: planning and collaboration time with other teachers, modified curriculum and resources, administrative support, and ongoing emotional support.

Myth: We're talking about the same "regular classrooms" you and I grew up with.

This myth is a difficult one. It is true that many special education programs were developed because the "regular" classroom was inadequate for the learning needs of children with disabilities. So talk of "returning" such students seems illogical—if those classrooms were not good before, why should they be appropriate now? The answer is that inclusive classrooms are not and cannot be the same rigidly structured, everyone-on-the-same page, frontal teaching, individually staffed classrooms we all remember. Successful inclusion involves radical changes in the nature of the general education classroom.

Myth: The curriculum of the general education classroom will get watered down and distorted.

There is a fear that inclusion will force teachers to "dumb down" the curriculum, thus limiting the options for "typical students" and especially for "gifted and talented" students. The reality is that the curriculum in inclusive classrooms must be structured as multi-level, participatory and flexible.

For example, all the students might be working on the Civil War, but the range of books and projects undertaken and the ways in which learning is pursued can vary tremendously. Some students might be working on computer simulations, while others might write and perform skits or role plays. A wide range of books on the Civil War could allow students who read at a range of levels to find and share information. Inclusion invites, not a watered-down curriculum, but an en-

hanced one, full of options and creative possibilities (Thousand, Villa, & Nevin, 1994).

Myth: Special services must take place in special places.

Those who are fearful or antagonistic about full inclusion believe that we must maintain a *continuum of placements* in order to serve all children well. Inclusion advocates support the need for a *continuum of services* (e.g., occupational therapy, speech therapy, physical therapy) but propose that those services be provided in the most integrated way possible, sometimes in the general education classroom and sometimes with other nonhandicapped students participating.

Inclusion does not mean abandoning the special help and support that students with disabilities truly need. Rather, it means providing those services within more normalized settings and without the isolation and stigma often associated with special education services.

Myth: Without special education classes, children with disabilities will not learn functional life skills—the things they really need to know.

In many special education classes, students are still learning money skills by working with pretend coins and bills, doing workbook problems. In more inclusive settings, a student with a disability

may be working at the school store, making change, and interacting with real customers using real money. Creative teachers (with adequate support) can find numerous ways to incorporate functional life skills into more typically "academic" settings, often benefiting all the students in the class.

Myth: The only way to keep "special children" safe is to keep them away from other children. If you include them you are setting them up to be victims; you are setting them up for failure. They can only feel good about themselves if they're with their "own kind."

No parent wants their child to be a victim of cruelty or violence, friendless and alone, abandoned and outcast in school. But when we think of the bigger picture—the future beyond school—it becomes evident that we cannot keep students with disabilities safe by sheltering them. They must learn repertoires of accommodation and adaptation (how to deal with teasing and rejection) and, more importantly, we must take active steps to shape the understanding, commitment, and active friendship of students without disabilities who will be the lifelong peers of people with disabilities.

When students grow up together, sharing school experiences and activities, they learn to see beyond superficial differences and disabilities and to connect as human beings. This applies to differences in race, religion, economic status, and skill and ability, as well as physical, emotional, and learning differences. It is vital that all students feel safe and welcome in the world, and inclusion provides us with an excellent way to model and insist on a set of beliefs about how people treat one another with respect and dignity.

Myth: Inclusion values "social goals" above "educational goals."

The accusation that inclusion advocates only care about "social" integration and that valuing social growth means that academic progress is not considered relevant or important has persisted for many years. In fact, all learning is social and all learning occurs in a social environment. Learning to talk, make friends, ask questions and respond, and work with others are all educational goals, important ones, and foundational ones for other learning.

There is little doubt that certain specific, concrete drill and practice skills can be better taught within intensified, one-on-one instructional settings; what is less clear is that those are the skills that matter or whether such learning will generalize to more "normal" environments. There is also little evidence that most special education settings are particularly effective at teaching academic skills. Some of the original motivation for mainstreaming, then integration, and then inclusion, was the recognition of the low expectations and distorted goals that were

set for students with disabilities within more segregated settings.

Myth: Inclusion is a favor we are doing for children with disabilities at the cost of other children's education.

There is no evidence that the education of other students suffers in any way from the inclusion process. Al Shanker, president of the American Federation of Teachers (AFT) and a leading anti-inclusion force, commented on the students pictured in the Academy Award-winning film, *Educating Peter* (Wurtzberg & Goodwin, 1992), which detailed the classroom experience of Peter, a boy with Down's syndrome, during his third grade year:

I wonder whether the youngsters in that class had spent a whole year in adjusting to how to live with Peter and whether they did any reading, whether they did any writing, whether they did any mathematics, whether they did any history, whether they did any geography.

And it seems to me that it's a terrible shame that we don't ask that question. Is the only function of the schools to get kids to learn to live with each other? Would we be satisfied if that's what we did and if all the youngsters came out not knowing any of the things they're supposed to learn academically?

Will any of them, disabled or non-disabled, be able to function as adults? (Shanker, 1994, p. 1)

The answer, Mr. Shanker, is that their teacher, Martha Stallings (1993, 1994) reports that the students in her class all had a wonderful year, learned their math and their history and their geography, did a great deal of writing

and reading, and learned to be decent caring human beings as well. That seems like an incredibly successful year to me!

Will any of them be able to function as adults? Yes, they will function as adults who, in addition to knowing long division and the states and their capitals, also know how to actively support a classmate who is struggling and know not to jump to early conclusions about whether or not someone can be a friend.

Myth: It takes years of planning and preparation before you can start to do inclusion.

Planning and preparation certainly help inclusion to work well. And there is no denying that adequate lead time and thoughtful groundwork improve the quality of what can happen when students with disabilities are included. But it is also true that no teacher, school, and district ever feel truly ready to begin inclusion, and what is most necessary is ongoing support and commitment. Even schools that are well known for their inclusion programs acknowledge that there are always new issues and concerns. Although some aspects of the inclusion process become easier, they still require time and planning because every child and every situation is different.

The AFT has requested an inclusion moratorium, citing the many problems that schools experience when they attempt to implement inclusion. Shanker (1994/1995) cites lack of adequate preparation for teachers and lack of ongoing support as the two major barriers to successful inclusion. I would agree with his analysis completely. His conclusion, however, is quite different from mine. His solution to the lack of preparation and support is to call for a moratorium on inclusion. My solution is to commit the resources we know are required to do inclusion well.

Myth: If we just ignore inclusion long enough and hard enough, it will go away.

I cannot imagine that parents who fought so hard for the right to have their children included in general education classrooms will be willing to go back to segregated programming. And teachers who have experienced successful inclusive teaching are not likely to want to return to a segregated system. But is society willing to commit the funds and the human resources necessary to do inclusion well? That is a larger question that brings us to the very heart of our values and our priorities about children and their educational futures.

Conclusion

Examining these myths and the responses to them allows us to see how much is affected by our decision to include students with disabilities and how much change will be required for it to be successful. At stake is not just our special education programs, or even our educational system. What is at stake is our commitment as a democracy to educate all children to the best of their abilities and to teach them all to be responsible, caring citizens, cognizant of their interrelationships and their mutual needs. A stirring song by Bernice Reagan, performed by the group "Sweet Honey in the Rock," says, "We who believe in freedom cannot rest until it comes." An appropriate paraphrase for *this* struggle might be: We who believe in inclusion cannot rest until it's done (well)!

References

Baker, E.T., Wang, M.C., & Walberg, H.J. (1994/1995). The effects of inclusion on learning. *Educational Leadership, 52*(4), 33–35.

Fuchs, D., & Fuchs, L.S. (1994/1995). Sometimes separate is better. *Educational Leadership, 52*(4), 22–26.

Maloney, J. (1994/1995). A call for placement options. *Educational Leadership, 52*(4), 25.

O'Neil, J. (1994). Can inclusion work? A conversation with Jim Kauffman and Mara Sapon-Shevin. *Educational Leadership, 52*(4), 7–11.

Shanker, A. (1994, Fall). A full circle? Inclusion: A 1994 view. In *The Circle.* Atlanta: Georgia Governor's Council on Developmental Disabilities.

Shanker, A. (1994/1995). Full inclusion is neither free nor appropriate. *Educational Leadership, 52*(4), 18–21.

Stainback, S., & Stainback, W. (1992). *Curriculum considerations in inclusive classrooms: Facilitating learning for all students.* Baltimore: Paul H. Brookes.

Stallings, M.A. (1993, May). When Peter came to Mrs. Stallings' class, *NEA Today,* p. 22.

Stallings, M.A. (1994, December). *Educating Peter.* Presentation at the Association for Persons with Severe Handicaps Conference, Alliance for Action, Atlanta.

Thousand, J.S., Villa, R.A., & Nevin, A.I. (1994). *Creativity and collaborative learning: A practical guide for empowering students and teachers.* Baltimore: Paul H. Brookes.

Villa, R.A., Thousand, J.S., Stainback, W., & Stainback, S. (1992). *Restructuring for caring and effective education.* Baltimore: Paul H. Brookes.

Willis, S. (1994, October). Making schools more inclusive. *ASCD curriculum update,* pp. 1–8.

Wurtzberg, G., & Goodwin, T. (1992). *Educating Peter.* Home Box Office Video.

 Article Review Form at end of book.

What is Bricker's purpose in presenting the *Narratives from the Sandbox*? What is her greatest concern regarding the role of special education in educational reform?

The Challenge of Inclusion

Diane Bricker

University of Oregon

Introduction

Intervention programs for young children with disabilities were initiated in the United States in the early 1970s. From an inauspicious beginning, few programs, little information, and no trained personnel, the field of early intervention/early childhood special education has grown into a fully legitimate enterprise in North American and many other industrialized nations. In these countries, there exist legal and legislative foundations for offering services to children birth to 5 years, a solid knowledge base to direct assessment, intervention and evaluation efforts, and a growing cadre of professional personnel. These professionals are specifically trained to offer services, conduct research, and formulate policy focused on young children with disabilities (Bricker, 1989). The progress has been substantial. As we move toward the 21st century, however, early intervention and early childhood special education personnel have many issues to address and problems to solve if improvement in

what we do and how we do it is to continue.

Perhaps one of the more troubling and dramatic issues facing us is the integration or inclusion of young children with disabilities into community-based programs. This issue is troubling because of its complexity and dramatic because of the emotional responses it engenders. The complexity of inclusion centers on what the concept means as well as how to involve young children with disabilities in community-based programs so that all parties, with and without disabilities, benefit. Likewise, the issue triggers in many individuals strong emotional reactions because of its human rights interpretation; that is, individuals with disabilities are entitled to equal participation in school, recreation, and other publicly supported community activity.

I am worried that the call to arms emanating from full-inclusion camps is too dogmatic, simplistic, and value laden. (This sentence should not be interpreted in any way as support for segregated programs.) During the last 10 years, the rhetoric for full inclusion has grown increasingly strident, and full inclusion is often

presented as a moral imperative. The right thinking, politically correct "good" guys support and work for full inclusion whereas those who are opposed to it or who suggest cautious implementation are placed together on the wrong side of the fence. This dichotomous assignment leaves me lined up with those on the wrong side. Given my history and long-term involvement in developing integrated programs for young children with disabilities, this assignment is at best puzzling and at the very least disconcerting. So, after all these years of demonstration programs, research, and writing, how did I end up on the wrong side of the fence?

At the outset, I need to make clear that my disagreement is not conceptual. I believe that the goal of full inclusion as articulated by The Division For Early Childhood of the Council for Exceptional Children (1993) is correct:

Inclusion, as a value, supports the right of all children, regardless of their diverse abilities, to participate actively in natural settings within their communities. A natural setting is one in which the child would spend time had he or she not had a disability. Such settings include but are not limited to home and family,

Bricker, D., "The challenge of inclusion," *Journal of Early Intervention, 19*(3), 1995, pp. 179–194. Reprinted by permission.

play groups, child care, nursery schools, Head Start Programs, kindergartens, and neighborhood school classrooms.

Rather, my difficulty comes in the simplistic and naive declarations about how to achieve this goal. The content of many written documents and verbal presentations suggest that we, like the Nike commercial, "Just do it." On the contrary, I believe considerable thought and planning are required to ensure that integration efforts are successful for children, parents, teachers, and the larger community. Therefore, the approach taken in this paper is to address the challenge of inclusion through an analysis of the complexity and emotionality surrounding it.

Definitions

The terms *mainstreaming, integration,* and *inclusion* are used frequently by those of us associated with intervention programs for infants, toddlers, and preschoolers with disabilities. Historically, there appears to have been a progression in the use of these terms, beginning with *mainstreaming,* moving to *integration,* and currently *inclusion.* Mainstreaming initially referred to the reentry of children with mild disabilities into regular education programs. Although the use of the term mainstreaming has broadened over time, it has never fit particularly well when discussing young children with disabilities for two reasons. First, the applicability of the term to infants and toddlers is questionable. For example, what would be a mainstream placement or activity for a 6- or 18-month-old? (I was once involved in a discussion where a professional stated that home-based programs should not be sup-

ported because "mainstreaming" was difficult to implement in most homes!) What indeed could they be reentered into? A second and more substantive problem is the limited number of public school programs for nondisabled children, particularly 3- and 4-year-olds, which seriously reduced the "mainstream" options available to preschool-age children with disabilities. In effect, public school mainstreaming approaches are not applicable to prekindergarten programs.

Early efforts to combine young children who were disabled and nondisabled into a single program began in the 1970s (Bricker, 1978). The preferred term to describe this combination was integration or developmental integration (Guralnick, 1978). The general usage of the term was to describe the systematic and careful combining of toddlers and preschool-age children who had disabilities and those who did not into the same classroom setting, as opposed to the educational practice of segregating children with disabilities into separate programs. The term *integration* has endured in the field of early intervention/early childhood special education; however, since the 1990s, the term *inclusion* has gained in popularity and frequency of use.

In a recent paper, Dianne Ferguson (in press) makes an interesting distinction between the terms integration and inclusion. She argues that the essential message of integration was to remediate "social discrimination by ending stigmatizing and discriminatory educational exclusion and segregation" (p. 5). "Inclusion, unlike integration, did not depend on being segregated in the first place. Rather than ever separating students on the basis of

disability . . . students should simply be included, by right, in the opportunities and responsibilities of public schooling" (p. 6). This distinction is important for it moves the concept of the inclusion of children with disabilities into public schools and community-based programs from preferred best practice to a legal and moral mandate.

Issues

As with any controversial concept or approach, inclusion has its strong advocates and detractors (Fuchs & Fuchs, 1994). An issue of concern is that the emotional debate engulfing inclusion appears to have encouraged many advocates to make inclusion a cause. As such, advocates have directed the debate at the program level rather than the child level, or perhaps, said differently, at the conceptual rather than the practical level. That is, concern or attention to the individual needs of children and families is superseded by commitment to the cause of inclusion. This is troubling because the value or validity of the conceptual position seems to be determined, in large measure, without concern for its applied worth. MacMillan, Semmel, and Gerber (1994) frame the issue in the following way:

Certainly, advocacy on behalf of children is desirable; however, the brand of advocacy we have seen has increasingly been "program advocacy" rather than "child advocacy." Advocacy . . . has been characterized by the uncritical advancement of a point of view in the absence of, or a disregard for, the evidence on the effects of that "program" on children. (p. 447)

Primacy of program advocacy over child advocacy is troubling for at least two reasons.

First, the focus of attention is often on placement, which deals with relatively superficial aspects of the process of inclusion—a point few challenge. Analyses of individual child and family goals and outcomes are, at best, secondary to the highly visible dimension of placement. Yet with some reflection most of us might agree that the more important dimension of genuine inclusion is the meaningful participation of the child in the range of offered program activities and events, not merely the placement of the child into an integrated program.

Placement of a child with disabilities and his or her special aide in a program designed for nondisabled children does not meet the criteria of inclusion if the intervention activities are conducted largely apart from the other children. Neither does a program in which children with disabilities are present but do not participate in most program activities. Meaningful inclusion involves much more than placement. Genuine inclusion means that during large circle time, the child with disabilities sits next to the other children, sings the songs, and participates in other planned activities to the fullest extent possible. Children with disabilities may not perform at the same level as the other children but they are respected and included for their contributions. So, too, in small group and play activities, the child with disabilities is a participating member. If the children go for a walk, the child in a wheelchair goes also. At story time, the child with the augmentative communication system contributes using his or her nonvocal mode of communication. Appropriate materials are provided so the child with limited visual acuity can engage meaningfully in program activities.

A second troubling issue surrounding program or placement advocacy appears to be the advocates' unwillingness to accept anything less than the placement of children with disabilities into programs designed for nondisabled children, regardless of their quality (Fuchs & Fuchs, 1994). Parents may feel forced to place their children in settings they might not otherwise select. For example, many child care programs are staffed by poorly trained personnel who receive minimum wage. Parents may genuinely fear for the safety of their child in such settings but may feel enormous pressure from professionals to acquiesce to an integrated placement. Parents can have legitimate concerns about the treatment of their child by other children. They may be wary of the subtle or not so subtle messages delivered to their child by adults and other children if program staff are not prepared to counter negative or destructive perceptions.

Some parents may believe that placement in a segregated program is best for their child for a variety of legitimate reasons (Stoneman, 1993). For example, parents may feel that placement in an early intervention program with qualified staff who can design and deliver effective intervention services may maximize child progress so that their child has an increased probability of placement in a regular kindergarten or first grade program. For these parents, decisions may have to be weighed as long-term versus short-term outcomes. Current placement in a noninclusive program may seem a better choice if the child's chance for future placement into regular education is enhanced.

We should be examining first the child's needs, then the family's values, the desired outcomes, and the short-term versus the long-term effects of specific approaches and placements. Placements should be congruent with at least these four areas.

Narratives from the Sandbox

In 1992, Eileen Hughes, then a doctoral student at the University of Oregon, conducted a qualitative investigation she called *Narratives From the Sandbox* (Hughes, 1992). The study was designed to assist in understanding how young children with disabilities use augmentative communication systems to interact with their nondisabled peers. Dr. Hughes spent 120 hours observing three preschool-age children with disabilities during which she filled 850 pages of field notes. These notes provide a rich source for examining the reactions and interactions among teachers, allied health professionals, and the children involved in three community-based early education programs. From her range of observations I have selected some examples that are not meant to be representative nor random. They illustrate, however, what I believe happens all too often when young children with disabilities are added on to programs designed for nondisabled children.

Becky was a 5-year-old child diagnosed with oral apraxia and a developmental delay. She was enrolled in a summer preschool program that had a history of including young children with disabilities, but Becky was the only child with a disability enrolled in her class at the time of Dr. Hughes' observations. The program was designed around a Montessori educational model. Becky was included in the program by mutual choice of program personnel and her parents.

In the first week of school, Becky fell out of the small chairs in the class. . . . Because Becky lost her balance on the small chairs in the classroom, she used a slightly larger chair positioned against the wall at the table. While this was the solution to the tipping chairs, it created a place away from the children and hence a special place for Becky. . . . The children came to learn that this was her place and never used it themselves. If she was bothering them, they directed her back to this place. (When Becky comes back, Ashley is standing in front of her chair as she paints. Becky goes to move Ashley's chair; Ashley tells her, "This is mine. Yours is the one over there," pointing to Becky's table and chair against the wall. The teacher tells Becky, "Here is one [manipulative from the shelf]. Now go to your table.") There were a few occasions by the end of the summer school session in which Becky initiated finding a chair at another table (and did not fall out). However, by this time, the children had learned that Becky's place was against the wall. (p. 151–52)

Becky was the oldest and tallest child in the class, which prompted this observation by a 5-year-old peer: "She is a baby. She wears diapers. She is not trained to go to the bathroom. Do you know what? She is old" (p. 158). Other observations by Dr. Hughes suggested that the nondisabled peers perceived Becky as different and responded accordingly.

The children in Becky's summer school program were quick to tell Becky "no!" or to tell her what to do. When Becky played in the sink, Ashley noticed and told her, "No, Becky." When Becky went to grab a puzzle piece in the center of a group activity, Ellie tells her, "No, Becky." Raoul told Becky not to sit next to him in circle. Becky is led down the hall by a peer and told, "Come on, Becky." (p. 188)

Given that no adult intervention occurred, these interactions are troubling for two important reasons. First, it is hard to believe that such interactions will lead nondelayed children to have or to develop a positive, constructive attitude about Becky specifically or children with disabilities in general. Second, it is equally hard to imagine that these interactions are helping Becky develop a positive self-image.

A second participant, Eric, was 4 years old and was diagnosed with a neuromotor impairment that interfered significantly with his speech production and general motor control. Like Becky, Eric was enrolled in a community-based preschool program with a history of including children with disabilities. Program staff were proud of "their history as one of the first preschools in town to 'integrate children with special needs' " (Hughes, 1992, p. 62). The program did not offer the children formal educational activities but rather followed a developmentally appropriate practice model.

Eric was swinging in the blue swing that was purchased especially for him by his family. It is made so he can sit with support. A girl with disabilities from another class was pushing him, and Joan, an instructional assistant, was standing next to him. Two women stood next to her (they were professionals here to evaluate Eric). Eric was smiling and appeared to be enjoying the ride. The woman with the pad was leaning in front of the swing as she talked to Eric. "Isn't that nice she is pushing you?" Her tone reflected talk to a younger child. "Oh, Tonya gave you a *big* push (she emphasizes the word "big"), and you like that." Eric smiles and laughs. She continues and starts playing almost a peek-a-boo game by moving her face away then moving back when the swing came forward. Eric laughed hard as she continued. At one point the woman asked Eric if she could swing, and he shook his head, no.

A little blond girl sucking her thumb was standing not far from me and looking over at the swing. I turned to the girl and asked, "Can you use that swing?" She looked at me, turning her head and wrinkling her face. She replied, "No, 'cause I am a *big* girl" (she emphasizes the word "big"). I said, "Who is the swing for?" She answered. "Eric." She said it matter-of-factly and without thinking, like, "Of course. Why are you asking?" (2/27/92)

Dr. Hughes asks Krissa, one of Eric's schoolmates, how Eric talks to her. While painting at an easel Krissa says,

"Well, he kinda talks like sign language. Different than me. He wants to say he wants to be on the rug with earphones." (Eric is often positioned on the rug and today he is seated with the other children listening to a story using earphones.) "I don't know if he is American or not. I am American. He is different than Jade, Martin, and me. He is kind of different." (She stops painting and stares at her picture.) "No one ever asked me that question before." (6/9/92)

A final example is instructive. Marsha, Tammy, and Eric are painting. Marsha and Tammy begin blowing on their paint brushes. Eric moves the brush to his mouth to imitate the girls and participate in the activity. The teacher observes Eric's action:

Teacher: "Uh, Uh, not in your mouth." (She goes to move the brush down.)

Eric: "Aauh." (Vocalizes sounding like a laugh.)

Teacher: "Is that funny?"

Eric: "Yeah."

Teacher: "It is?"

(Marsha and Tammy are looking at Eric. He goes to blow on the paintbrush again.)

Teacher: "No, no, no, no." (She goes to wipe the dot that he has put on his face; she takes the smock with her hand and wipes his face.) "It is soap, ecck." (Eric turns away and Marsha and Tammy are watching.)

Tammy: "I hate soap." (Marsha smiles. Eric was going to put the brush up to his mouth again, like the other two girls.)

Teacher: "Uh, uh." (She moves Eric's brush down to the paper.)

Then to further quote Dr. Hughes: "The interactive exchange continued, with the two girls leaving Eric to focus on his paper. This was an example of how a teacher unknowingly intervened with a child in a manner that may have blocked further integration with peers" (p. 218).

These examples seem particularly significant when one recalls that Eric and Becky were placed in receptive programs. That is, these programs welcomed children with disabilities and had a history of providing services to children with special needs. Although it is likely that none of the examples presented above were traumatic to Becky or Eric as individual occurrences, we should, I believe, be concerned with the potential cumulative ef-

fects of such interactions on children both with and without disabilities. What kinds of messages do we send children when we make it clear they require special chairs, activities, and attention from adults? What perceptions are formed when professional staff speak to and treat children with disabilities different from nondisabled children? Dr. Hughes often noted a young nondisabled child closely watching the interactions and communicative exchanges between Becky and Eric and an adult. What were these young children learning from these observations and what attitudes were they forming? Our empirical base for knowing is nonexistent.

The successful inclusion of young children with disabilities into community-based programs is multidimensional and complex. Undoubtedly, we can find examples of successful inclusion of children with disabilities into community-based programs in which little thought, consideration, or training occurred prior to the child's inclusion; however, I think that these instances are rare. Consistently successful inclusion requires attention to far more than placement; it must also address attitudes, resources, and curricula.

Successful Inclusion: The Long Run

Some leaders in education argue that the genuine actualizing of inclusion will require major school reform (Ferguson, in press; Snell & Drake, 1994). For example, Strain and Smith (1993) contend that for inclusion to be broadly and meaningfully accomplished general education reform and restructuring are needed. The na-

ture of that reform requires that "All students are perceived as members of the school community, possessing a social place and roles that result in every student experiencing a 'natural fit' with the life of the school" (Ferguson, in press, p. 16).

Although many may agree that such reform is necessary, there is considerable controversy over the nature and extent of the reform as it relates to inclusion (Fuchs & Fuchs, 1994). Particularly germane to our topic is the role and place of special education in more general school reform if we are to incorporate all children into a single, cohesive program. What role is special education to maintain? Do we support a parallel structure between regular and special education as currently exists or do we blend them into a unified system? Gallagher (1994) points out the significance of this issue:

We should be clear in our understanding that the issues here involve more than just educational efficiency. . . . They are, instead, issues of power and influence. If special education becomes merely a minor part of the general education system, then special education loses its voice in the power circles of the educational system and loses much of its ability to influence policy in that system. (p. 527)

If all children are placed in regular education programs, then will special education, or for young children, early intervention, lose its ability to control resources, to advocate for children, and to fight for resources for children with disabilities? Without maintaining a presence at the decision-makers' table, do we run the risk of seeing hard-won resources dwindle away or being reallocated to nondisabled children? Conversely, if special education functions separately from the general education system, what are the chances that regular education will take on the responsibility of meeting all children's needs?

The relationship between regular education and special education including early intervention will likely undergo change as we move toward the 21st century. The nature of that change will have much to say about how, when, and where children with disabilities are involved in public education. Until then, the inclusion of children with disabilities into educational and child care, community-based programs, and public school programs is likely to proceed child by child. It may proceed more efficiently and effectively if the integration of each child is considered and carefully done.

Successful Inclusion: The Short Run

As noted above, I believe successful inclusion of young children with disabilities is influenced by three general factors: attitude, resources, and curricula. Each of these factors is probably necessary but in and of itself not sufficient. That is, the teaching staff could have a positive and supportive attitude but without the necessary resources the staff may be unable to include the child with disabilities in the majority of program activities except in the most superficial manner. Furthermore, these factors are probably interactive, leading to the conclusion that successful inclusion is a multidimensional and complex process worthy of considerably more study than it has received.

Attitude

In an insightful review chapter, Stoneman (1993) makes a strong case for the importance of attitude in successful integration of young children with disabilities. Using a model developed by Triandis (1971), Stoneman describes attitude as three-dimensional, having a cognitive, affective, and behavioral component.

The cognitive component is the idea or knowledge that the person holding an attitude has about its referent. . . . The affective component . . . is the emotional reaction elicited by the referent. . . . The third component of an attitude, behavioral intent, is a predisposition to act in a certain manner, to either speak or avoid contact. (pp. 224–225)

This definition suggests the pervasiveness of attitudes in shaping our perceptions and actions.

For inclusion to be successful, positive and constructive attitudes about disability and young children who have disabilities need to be fostered. Adults, including parents, caregivers, teachers, and allied health professionals need to have cognitive, affective, and behavioral reactions that support integration efforts. In addition, these same supportive attitudes need to be conveyed to both nondisabled children and children with disabilities if inclusion efforts are to be successful. The complexity of successful inclusion plus the large number of personnel often associated with the integration of young children into community-based programs requires, I believe, that specific strategies be used to reach the goal of fostering positive and constructive attitudes in adults and young children. Those strategies include selection, training/awareness, and maintenance/vigilance.

Selection

Until information becomes available on how to include children into a wide range of classrooms and programs successfully, it seems wise to select carefully, when possible, a child's placement. Early intervention personnel and parents should look for programs that have teachers, other staff, and parents of nondisabled children who are enthusiastic about including a child with disabilities in the program. Avoiding placement where staff and other parents have reservations and are reluctant to accommodate the special needs of the child with disabilities seems the wise course of action at present.

Training/Awareness

Even in programs where staff and parents appear to hold constructive attitudes about inclusion, additional training will likely be needed to assist adults in managing challenging questions and situations. Most professionals and paraprofessionals prepared to work with nondisabled children know little about disabilities, about how impairments may affect children, or what strategies to use in addressing questions and problems in ways that expand and enhance positive attitudes in young children. Parents of nondisabled children also may require information and the opportunity to ask questions to assist them in understanding and appreciating a particular child's disability. Teaching staff and caregivers need to understand that it is normal for young children to ask questions about children who have impairments and that such questions and ensuing discussions should be encouraged and explored to the children's satisfaction, while being respectful of the child with disabilities.

An important outcome for training should be increased awareness by adults of the potential impact their words and actions may have on the attitudes of young children. Children, in large measure, acquire their attitudes about people and events from their primary caregivers (Stoneman, 1993). In addition to assigning Becky to a special table and chair, little effort was made to support children's overtures to Becky. For example, when the children asked to play with Becky's augmentative communication device, the teacher was quick to tell them *no*. Opportunities to address children's questions or to encourage positive interactions between Becky and her nondisabled peers were not exploited. Becky's classmates' exclusionary attitude reflected, at least in part, the teacher's attitude and interactions with Becky. This teacher would likely be shocked to know that she may have been engendering in Becky's peers a negative attitude toward Becky and perhaps toward all children with disabilities. Training that promotes awareness of the impact of adult's attitudes and actions on children might do much to reduce the type of negative incidents observed by Dr. Hughes (1992).

Maintenance/Vigilance

Even with the provision of training, program staff and caregivers need strategies to assure the maintenance of positive and constructive attitudes. It is easy to miss or misuse opportunities to promote healthy attitudes. Adults can unknowingly send the wrong kind of message even when engaged in therapeutic activities. The staff member who initiated infantile language games with Eric while pushing him on his swing was sending a message to Eric and another child who was watching close by. That message may have been that Eric is a baby. My hunch is that this was neither the goal nor intent of this staff member; however, this may have been the message that Eric and the other child received.

For inclusion to be more than episodically successful, program staff and caregivers need to be vigilant in maintaining positive attitudes. Parents and staff members should observe and monitor their interactions and conversations with children and also note those of other adults. When the wrong message is being sent, corrective action is in order.

Resources

A second set of factors critical to successful inclusion can be subsumed under the heading of resources (Peck, Furman, & Helmstetter, 1993). Resources can include (a) access to specialists, (b) collaborative planning and decision making, and (c) appropriate environment and equipment. Depending upon the child and program other resources may be required as well.

Access to Specialists

Head Start and early intervention/ early childhood special education programs are specifically designed to provide services to children who are at risk and disabled. These programs may have avail-able a cadre of specialists who provide consistent support and comprehensive services to children and families, whereas most community-based child care programs are designed for children who are typically developing and, therefore, rarely have staff members with the necessary experience or training to work effectively with children who have special needs (Wolery et al., 1994). Access to specialists is important for two reasons. First, children with disabilities may need specialized assessment and management procedures that require, at least initially, observation or handling by one or more specialists. Second, the program staff will probably require training on how to assist the child who has special needs. They may also require regular consultation to aid them in addressing problems as they arise.

When asked about the inclusion of young children with disabilities into programs designed for typically developing children, the concern parents of both disabled and nondisabled children most often raise is whether the child with disabilities will receive adequate attention and instruction (Stoneman, 1993). This same concern is felt by many professionals who watch inclusive placements for young children with disabilities fail because program staff do not have consistent access to specialists. In these situations, staff, children, and parents struggle to meet the child's needs with a likely unsatisfactory outcome for everyone. These failed or unsatisfactory attempts may not only do damage to the child and family but also impede subsequent efforts at integration. Careful consideration should be given to the availability of specialists before placing children with disabilities into community-based programs (Wolery et al., 1994).

Collaborative Planning and Decision Making

A recent study conducted by Peck and his colleagues (Peck et al., 1993) reported that integrated programs that survived over time were those in which collaborative planning and decision making occurred. It is not surprising that mainstream programs in which administrative and direct service personnel work together are more likely to endure over time. Program staff with the best intentions can face a difficult situation if the administration is unsympathetic to and unsupportive of inclusion. The addition of children with disabilities generally requires minor to major program modifications. An administration that will not support required modification, such as release time for staff training, clearly jeopardizes the success of inclusion efforts. Similarly, an administration that makes an important decision, to admit a child with disabilities, without including the direct-service personnel in the decision making will probably be unsuccessful.

Appropriate Environment and Equipment

Some community-based educational and child care settings are not appropriate for children with specific disabilities without extensive modifications. Without assurance that the necessary modifications will occur, these placements should be avoided. For example, it may not be wise to

place children who require wheelchairs in programs located in buildings with stairs and small doorways.

Besides requiring accessible and safe environments, many children with disabilities require specialized equipment if they are to be maximally independent. Children with motor impairments may require special chairs or standing tables, children with sensory impairments may require special curricular material, and nonvocal children may require augmentative communication devices. Appropriate use of this equipment often requires extensive training of program staff by specialists. Hughes (1992) observed that Eric rarely used his augmentative communication device and Becky used her device primarily when her mother was present. Program staff generally resisted using this technology because they had reservations about its appropriateness in a curriculum for young children. They felt the technology often interfered with meaningful "communication" between the child and others (Hughes, 1992).

As with Becky and Eric, program staff may not use specialized equipment, despite recommendations from specialists, if they do not believe the equipment is appropriate for their setting. Thought should be given to the needs of each child prior to placement, and children should be placed in programs where these important environmental and equipment needs can be met. As Peck (1993) points out, successful integration of children with disabilities requires facing and solving multiple problems and dilemmas simultaneously.

Addressing the resource needs of children with disabilities prior to placement in a community-based program is fundamental to successful inclusion.

Curricula

The final set of factors that effect successful inclusion are associated with program content or curriculum. Curriculum refers to the substance of the interventions and treatments offered to children who participate in a program. It appears that some curricular approaches foster and encourage interaction between children with and without disabilities whereas other approaches do not. Curricular approaches that build on the consistent use of daily activities, events, and interactions appear to support inclusion goals, whereas approaches that rely on formal structure, artificial activities, and adult-directed interactions may actually interfere with the genuine integration of children with disabilities into program events and activities.

Program staff members interested in the meaningful inclusion of young children with disabilities should design their curriculum to include (a) naturalistic approaches that encourage participation in meaningful activities of interest and relevance to children and (b) activities that promote interactions between children.

Activity-Based Curricula

As indicated above, successful inclusion efforts employ the use of meaningful activities that occur regularly (e.g., outdoor play time, washing up for snack), are child initiated (e.g., children ask for a specific book to be read, child initiates playing peek-a-boo), and are planned by staff but are *authentic* for children (e.g., taking a walk, washing baby dolls). Activity-based approaches easily promote children's genuine participation in program activities because teachers and interventionists using these approaches appropriately are able to vary the content of activities for all participating children (Bricker & Cripe, 1992). For example, when engaged in a pretend food preparation activity, children can initiate a variety of actions appropriate to their cognitive, linguistic, and motoric developmental level. The developmentally youngest children can stir, pour, and use simple one-word labels for their actions. More developmentally advanced children can cook in pots, set the table, and use sentences to discuss their activities. Staff members will probably see many opportunities to encourage the development of new skills and to encourage verbal and behavioral interactions among all participating children. Largely teacher-directed approaches, using carefully structured activities and massed-trial formats, do not lend themselves to the easy and successful inclusion of children functioning at a variety of skill levels.

Naturalistic approaches, such as activity-based intervention, used by early interventionists and early childhood special educators also are compatible with developmentally appropriate practice often used in community-based programs for young children. The compatibility and similarity of these two approaches (Novick, 1993) suggests that teaching staffs in community-based programs will be better able to manage children with disabilities using an activity-based approach than if they are required to provide isolated, direct instruction for the child.

Promoting Interaction

Within the program with an activity-based format, personnel need to encourage activities that promote interaction between children with disabilities and nondisabled children. A number of studies have reported that nondisabled children tend not to choose their disabled peers for play or interactions unless adults encourage the inclusion of the child with disabilities (Odom & Brown, 1993). When interactions are promoted through the introduction of appropriate activities or when spontaneous interactions occur and are supported, children with disabilities can become active participants with their nondisabled peers. Again Dr. Hughes' (1992) observations of Becky and Eric provide relevant examples.

Meona is not doing a puzzle at another table and isn't able to fit all the pieces together. She says, "Maybe Becky would help?" Paula (the teacher) answers, "Maybe she will." Meona goes over to Becky who is standing by the shelf, and says, "Do you want to help me?" (p. 187)

Becky does not respond and Meona walks away saying, "I think she wants to help me." Unfortunately the teacher lets this wonderful opportunity to encourage an interaction between Becky and Meona slip away. With subtle adult support Becky may have been able to assist Meona, resulting in an interaction that was positive for both children and certainly supportive of an inclusion goal.

Eric and Thomas, a nondisabled child, are looking through a small plastic ring and are giggling at each other. The teacher approaches, comments on the fun the boys are having, and then expands the interactive exchange to include other children.

Lory (the teacher): "Look at Teresa. See if she laughs like that."

Lory: "Try Masha. See what she does."

Lory: "It makes everybody laugh."

Thomas: "How can we stop laughing?"

Lory: "Look at Eric. See if he laughs." (p. 175)

The activity continues on for some time to the children's delight. The teacher in this instance not only supported the interaction between Eric and Thomas but also was able to expand the activity to include several other children. She was careful to assure that Eric maintained his participation.

Programs that promote these natural and satisfying interactions among children are probably doing much to ensure the child with disabilities feels a part of the larger group. These interactions also probably enhance nondisabled children's attitudes and willingness to include children with disabilities in their activities.

Summary

Whether called integration, mainstreaming, or inclusion, the placement of children with disabilities into settings designed for their nondisabled peers is an important goal. The challenge is not to "just do it," but to do it in ways that maximize children's growth in critical areas of development and foster communication, understanding, and acceptance between children with and without disabilities.

A major theme of this paper has been the tendency of many professionals to see inclusion as a moral and legal issue that can be addressed exclusively at the conceptual level. The complexity of successful implementation of inclusion is overlooked or given little attention. As Rick Brinker noted (personal communication, February 26, 1993),

The issue of integration in early childhood programs is very important. Like many things in education we tend to bulldoze ahead based on 'principle' with little thought given to how to make that principle truly supportive of the development of all children. Of particular concern is the fact that little empirical effort is invested in describing what is happening in the integrated environment, and how to support efforts so better things happen.

The debate over inclusion will not diminish but will continue into the 21st century, capturing important and finite resources. At the heart of this debate is the acceptance and treatment of individuals with disabilities. The debate can continue as it has—one largely devoted to conceptual arguments—or it can shift to careful and considered examination of all facets of the inclusion process. The latter strategy is far more likely to yield outcomes that will make better things happen for children and for families.

References

Bricker, D. (1978). A rationale for the integration of handicapped and non-handicapped preschool children. In M. Guralnick (Ed.), *Early intervention and the integration of handicapped and non-handicapped children* (pp. 3–26). Baltimore: University Park Press.

Bricker, D. (1989). *Early intervention for at-risk and handicapped infants, toddlers, and preschool children.* Palo Alto: VORT Corporation.

Bricker, D., & Cripe, J. (1992). *An activity-based approach to early intervention.* Baltimore: Paul Brookes.

Edgar, E., & Polloway, E. (1994). Education for adolescents with disabilities: Curriculum and placement issues. *Journal of Special Education, 27,* 438–452.

The Council for Exceptional Children. (1993, April). *Statement on inclusive schools and communities.* Reston, VA: Author.

Ferguson, D. (in press). Is it inclusion yet? Bursting bubbles. In M. Berres, D. Ferguson. D. Knobloch, & C. Woods (Eds.), *Restructuring schools for all children.* New York: Teachers College Press.

Fuchs, D., & Fuchs, L. (1994). Inclusive school movement and the radicalization of special education reform. *Exceptional Children, 60,* 294–309.

Gallagher, J. (1994). The pull of societal forces on special education. *Journal of Special Education, 27,* 521–530.

Guralnick, M. (1978). *Early intervention and the integration of handicapped and nonhandicapped children.* Baltimore: University Park Press.

Hughes, E. (1992). *Narratives from the sandbox: A qualitative study of communicative interactions of young children with augmentative and alternative communications systems and their peers.* Unpublished doctoral dissertation, University of Oregon, Eugene.

Lamorey, S., & Bricker, D. (1993). Integrated programs: Effects on young children and their parents. In C. Peck, S. Odom, & D. Bricker (Eds.), *Integrating young children with disabilities into community programs: Ecological perspectives on research and implementation* (pp. 249–270). Baltimore: Paul Brookes.

MacMillan, D., Semmel, M., & Gerber, M. (1994). The social context of Dunn: Then and now, *Journal of Special Education, 27,* 466–480.

Novick, R. (1993). Activity-based intervention and developmentally appropriate practice: Points of convergence. *Topics in Early Childhood Special Education, 13,* 403–417.

Odom, S., & Brown, W. (1993). Social interaction skills interventions for young children with disabilities in integrated settings. In C. Peck, S. Odom, & D. Bricker (Eds.), *Integrating young children with disabilities into community programs: Ecological perspectives on research and implementation* (pp. 39–64). Baltimore: Paul Brookes.

Peck, C. (1993). Ecological perspectives on the implementation of integrated early childhood programs. In C. Peck, S. Odom, and D. Bricker (Eds.), *Integrating young children with disabilities into community programs: Ecological perspectives on research and implementation* (pp. 3–16). Baltimore: Paul Brookes.

Peck, C., Furman, G., & Helmstetter, E. (1993). Integrated early childhood programs: Research on the implementation of change in organizational contexts. In C. Peck, S. Odom, and D. Bricker (Eds.), *Integrating young children with disabilities into community programs: Ecological perspectives on research and implementation* (pp. 187–206). Baltimore: Paul Brookes.

Peck, C., Odom, S., & Bricker, D. (1993). *Integrating young children with disabilities into community programs: Ecological perspectives on research and implementation.* Baltimore: Paul Brookes.

Snell, M., & Drake, G. (1994). Replacing cascades with supported education. *Journal of Special Education, 27,* 393–409.

Stoneman, Z. (1993). The effects of attitude on preschool integration. In C. Peck, S. Odom, and D. Bricker (Eds.), *Integrating young children with disabilities into community programs: Ecological perspectives on research and implementation* (pp. 223–248). Baltimore: Paul Brookes.

Strain, P., & Smith, B. (1993). Comprehensive educational, social and policy forces that affect preschool integration. In C. Peck, S.

Odom, and D. Bricker (Eds.), *Integrating young children with disabilities into community programs: Ecological perspectives on research and implementation* (pp. 209–222), Baltimore: Paul Brookes.

Triandis, H. (1971). *Attitude and attitude change.* New York: John Wiley & Sons.

Wolery, M., Holcombe-Ligon, A., Brookfield, J., Huffman, K., Schroeder, C., Martin, C., Venn, M., Werts, M., & Fleming, L. (1993). The extent and nature of preschool mainstreaming: A survey of general early educators. *Journal of Special Education, 27,* 222–234.

Wolery, M., Venn, M., Holcombe, A., Brookfield, J., Martin, C., Huffman, K., Schroeder, C., & Fleming, L. (1994). Employment of related service personnel in preschool programs: A survey of general early educators. *Exceptional Children, 61,* 25–39.

Paper prepared for the Australian Early Intervention Association Annual Conference, University of Melbourne, Melbourne, Australia, August 18–20.

Support for the preparation of this paper came in part from Grant Nos. H024B1006 and H024D10011 from the U.S. Department of Education, Office of Special Education Programs, to the Center on Human Development, College of Education. University of Oregon.

Address correspondence to **Diane Bricker**, Early Intervention Program, 5253 University of Oregon, Eugene, Oregon 97403-5253.

 Article Review Form at end of book.

How does Ferguson's definition of inclusion differ from more traditional definitions? What does she mean when she describes included students as being "*in*, but not *of*, the class"?

The Real Challenge of Inclusion

Confessions of a 'rabid inclusionist'

The new challenge of inclusion is to create schools in which our day-to-day efforts no longer assume that a particular text, activity, or teaching mode will "work" to support any particular student's learning, Ms. Ferguson avers.

Dianne L. Ferguson

Dianne L. Ferguson is an associate professor in the College of Education, University of Oregon, Eugene.

About a year ago, a colleague told me that my work was constrained by the fact that "everyone" thought I was a "rabid inclusionist." I was not exactly sure what he meant by "rabid inclusionist" or how he and others had arrived at the conclusion that I was one. I also found it somewhat ironic to be so labeled since I had been feeling uncomfortable with the arguments and rhetoric of both the anti-inclusionists and, increasingly, many of the inclusionists. My own efforts to figure out how

to achieve "inclusion"—at least as I understood it—were causing me to question many of the assumptions and arguments of both groups.

In this article, I wish to trace the journey that led me to a different understanding of inclusion. I'll also describe the challenges I now face—and that I think we all face—in trying to improve our schools.

The Limits of Our Reforms

Despite our best efforts, it was clear to my husband and me that even the possibility of "mainstreaming" was not open to our son Ian. Although mainstreaming

had been a goal of the effort to change the delivery of special education services since the late 1960s, the debates never extended to a consideration of students with severe disabilities. Indeed, it was only the "zero reject" provisions of the Education for All Handicapped Children Act (P.L. 94-142) in 1974 that afforded our son the opportunity to attend school at all—albeit a separate special education school some 20 miles and two towns away from our home. What that landmark legislation did not change, however, were underlying assumptions about schooling for students designated as "disabled."

Since special education emerged as a separate part of public education in the decades spanning the turn of the century, the fundamental assumptions about students and learning shared by both "general" and "special" educators have not changed much. Despite periodic challenges, these assumptions have become so embedded in the culture and processes of schools that they are treated more as self-evident "truths" than as assumptions. School personnel, the

Ferguson, D. L., "The real challenge of inclusion: Confessions of a 'rabid inclusionist'," *Phi Delta Kappan, 77*(4), 1995, pp. 281–287. Reprinted by permission of the author.

families of schoolchildren, and even students themselves unquestionably believe:

- that students are responsible for their own learning;

- that, when students don't learn, there is something wrong with them; and

- that the job of the schools is to determine what's wrong with as much precision as possible, so that students can be directed to the tracks, curricula, teachers, and classrooms that match their learning-ability profiles.

Even our efforts to "integrate" and later to "include" students with severe disabilities in general education failed to challenge these fundamental assumptions. Indeed, these special education reform initiatives have served more to reinforce them.

Unlike mainstreaming, which was grounded in debate about where best to provide the alternative curricular and instructional offerings that students with disabilities need, the reform initiatives of integration and later of inclusion drew much more heavily on social and political discourse. From a democratic perspective, every child has a right to a public education. For those moderately and severely disabled students who had previously been excluded from schooling on the ground that they were too disabled to benefit, the application of a civil rights framework gave them the same status as any minority group that was widely disenfranchised and discriminated against.[1] The essential message of integration was to remediate social discrimination (not so much learning deficits) by ending stigmatizing and discriminatory exclusion.

We sought this more "normalized" schooling experience for Ian, advocating actively for placement in a typical public school rather than in a separate school. Unfortunately, the efforts of professional educators to balance the right of students to be educated with the still unchallenged and highly individualized deficit/remediation model of disability most often resulted in the delivery of educational services along some continuum of locations, each matched to the constellation of services believed to "fit" the identified type and amount of student deficit and disability.

For someone like our son, with multiple and severe disabilities, the result was self-contained classrooms that afforded only the briefest contact with nondisabled students. The integrationists' promise that the mainstream would tolerate and perhaps even incorporate more differences in abilities remained largely unfulfilled. Even when some students found themselves integrated into general education classrooms, they often did not reap the promised rewards of full membership.

Yet we could see the promise of something else. Ian's first experience in a *public* school was when he was about 10. He was assigned to a new self-contained classroom for "severely and profoundly handicapped" students. This new classroom was located in the "physically handicapped school," where all students with physical disabilities were assigned because the building had long ago been made accessible, unlike most other school buildings in town.

Because we hoped he would have some involvement with nondisabled peers, we lobbied the school administration for a policy that permitted two kinds of "mainstreaming": one kind for students who could learn alongside their peers with some extra teaching help and another kind for students like Ian, who could not learn the same things but might benefit by learning other things. It took months of discussion, but finally the grade 5 class down the hall from Ian's self-contained room invited him to join it for the "free" times during the day when students got to pick their own games and activities. The teacher was skeptical but willing and sent students to collect him for some part of nearly every day.

One day a small group of students invited Ian to join them in a Parcheesi game. Of course, he had no experience with the game and probably didn't grasp much of it. It could be argued, I suppose, that his lessons (at the separate school and class) on picking things up and putting them into cans offered him some ability to participate, but he would not be just another player like the other fifth-graders. The students, with no adult intervention, solved this participation problem by making him the official emptier of the cup of dice for all the players—something he could not only do, but relished. His role was critical to the game, and he got lots of opportunities to participate, since he was needed to begin every player's turn.

Ian's experience in Parcheesi expanded over the year to include some integration in music, lunch, and recess with these same students. More important were the lessons his participation began to teach us about the possibilities of integration that we and others had not yet fully explored, especially regarding the ways that learning, participation, and membership can mean different things for very different children in the same situation.

However it was being implemented, integration also contained a critical flaw in logic: in order to be "integrated" one must first be segregated. This simple point led to the first calls for inclusion. According to this new initiative, all students should simply be included, by right, in the opportunities and responsibilities of public schooling. Like integration, however, these early notions of inclusion focused primarily on students with moderate to severe disabilities who most often were placed along the continuum of service environments furthest from general education classrooms.

Unfortunately, neither integration nor inclusion offered much practical guidance to teachers who were engaged in the daily dynamics of teaching and learning in classrooms with these diverse students. The focus on the right to access did not provide clear direction for achieving learning outcomes in general education settings. Essentially, both of these reform efforts challenged the logic of attaching services to places—in effect challenged the idea of a continuum of services. However, the absence of clear directions for how services would be delivered instead and the lack of information about what impact such a change might have on general education led some proponents to emphasize the importance of social rather than learning outcomes, especially for students with severe disabilities.[2] This emphasis on social outcomes certainly did nothing to end the debates.

Inclusion as 'Pretty Good' Integration

The inclusion initiative has generated a wide range of outcomes—some exciting and productive, others problematic and unsatisfying. As our son finished his official schooling and began his challenging journey to adult life, he enjoyed some quite successful experiences, one as a real member of a high school drama class, though he was still officially assigned to a self-contained classroom.[3] Not only did he learn to "fly," trusting others to lift him up and toss him in the air (not an easy thing for someone who has little control over his body), but he also memorized lines and delivered them during exams, learned to interact more comfortably and spontaneously with classmates and teachers, and began using more and different vocal inflections than had ever before characterized his admittedly limited verbal communications. Classmates, puzzled and perhaps put off by him at the beginning of the year, creatively incorporated him into enough of their improvisations and activities to be able to nominate him at the end of the year not only as one of the students who had shown progress, but also as one who showed promise as an actor. He didn't garner enough votes to win the title, but that he was nominated at all showed the drama teacher "how much [the other students] came to see him as a *member* of the class."

Ian's experiences in drama class helped me begin to understand more fully that *learning* membership was the most important dimension of inclusion and

that it was an extraordinarily complex phenomenon, especially within classrooms.[4] It also prompted me to question other bits of the conventional wisdom about inclusion: Is inclusion all about place? Must it be full time? Is it okay for learning to take second priority to socialization and friendship? Does one always have to be traded for the other? Will students learn things that they can use and that will make a difference in their lives? Who will teach, and what will happen to special educators? And so on.

A three-year research effort followed, during which I learned a good deal about what inclusion is and isn't. Perhaps the most troubling realization was that—even when students were assigned to general education classrooms and spent most (or even all) of their time there with various kinds of special education supports—their participation often fell short of the kind of social and learning membership that most proponents of inclusion envision and that Ian achieved in that one drama class. Even to casual observers, some students seemed set apart—immediately recognizable as different—not so much because of any particular impairment or disability but because of what they were doing, with whom, and how.

During the years of our research, my colleagues and I saw students walking through hallways with clipboard-bearing adults "attached" to them or sitting apart in classrooms with an adult hovering over them showing them how to use books and papers unlike any others in the class. Often these "Velcroed" adults were easily identifiable as "special education" teachers because the students called them by their first names while using the more formal Ms. or Mr. to refer to the general education teacher. The included students seemed *in*, but not *of*, the class. Indeed, we observed teachers who referred to particular students as "my inclusion student." It seemed to us that these students were caught inside a bubble that teachers didn't seem to notice but that nonetheless succeeded in keeping other students and teachers at a distance.

In trying to change everything, inclusion all too often seems to be leaving everything the same. But in a new place.

We also saw other students "fitting in," following the routines, and looking more or less like other students. But their participation seemed hollow. They *looked* like they were doing social studies or math, but it seemed more a "going through the motions" than a real learning engagement. Maybe they were learning in the sense of remembering things, but, we wondered, did they know what they were learning? Or why? Or whether they would use this learning in their lives outside of school?

Even the protection of an individualized education program (IEP)—a key component of P.L. 94-142 and now of the updated Individuals with Disabilities Education Act (IDEA)—seemed yet one more barrier to real membership. Special education teachers became "teachers without classrooms," plying their skills in many places, following carefully designed and complicated schedules that deployed support personnel in the form of classroom assistants to teach, manage, and assist the "inclusion students" so that they could meet the goals and objectives of their IEPs. Classroom

teachers struggled to understand how to "bond" with their new students.

Even more challenging was how to negotiate teaching. The peripatetic special educator usually remained primarily responsible for writing IEPs that only distantly related to the classroom teacher's curriculum and teaching plans. At the same time the general educator would strive to assume "ownership" of the shared student's teaching, often by following the instructions of the special educator. Special educators who were successful at moving out of their separate classrooms struggled with the sheer logistics of teaching their students in so many different places. They also struggled with whether they were teachers of students or teachers of other teachers. And some wondered what would happen to them if the general educators ever "learned how" to include students without help.

Bursting Bubbles

Gradually I came to see these examples and the experiences that have been detailed elsewhere as problematic for everyone precisely because they failed to challenge underlying assumptions about student learning differences.[5] Too much inclusion as implemented by special education seems to succeed primarily in relocating "special" education to the general education classroom along with all the special materials, specially trained adults, and special curriculum and teaching techniques. The overriding assumptions remain unchanged and clearly communicated.

- These "inclusion" students are "irregular," even though they are in "regular" classrooms.

- They need "special" stuff that the "regular" teacher is neither competent nor approved to provide.

- The "special" educator is the officially designated provider of these "special" things.

In trying to change everything, inclusion all too often seems to be leaving everything the same. But in a new place.

My colleagues and I also saw lots of examples of things that did not remain the same, examples like my son's experience in drama class. The challenge was to try to understand what made these experiences different.

Gradually I began to realize that, if inclusion is ever to mean more than pretty good integration, we special educators will have to change our tactics. To resolve the debates about roles, ownership, accountability, student learning achievements, the meaningfulness of IEPs, and the achievement of genuine student membership in the regular classroom, we must begin with the *majority* perspective and build the tools and strategies for achieving inclusion from the center out rather than from the most exceptional student in. Devising and defining inclusion to be about students with severe disabilities—indeed, any disabilities—seems increasingly wrongheaded to me and quite possibly doomed to fail. It can only continue to focus everyone's attention on a small number of students and a small number of student differences, rather than on the whole group of students with their various abilities and needs.

Inclusion isn't about eliminating the continuum of placements[6] or even just about eliminating some locations on the continuum,[7] though that will be one result. Nor is it about discontinuing the services that used to be attached to the various points on that continuum.[8] Instead, a more *systemic* inclusion—one that merges the reform and restructuring efforts of general education with special education inclusion—will disassociate the delivery of supports from *places* and make the full continuum of supports available to the full range of students. A more systemic inclusion will replace old practices (which presumed a relationship between ability, service, and place of delivery) with new kinds of practice (in which groups of teachers work together to provide learning supports for all students).

Inclusion isn't about time either. Another continuing debate involves whether "all" students should spend "all" of their time in general education classrooms.[9] One form of this discussion relies largely on extreme examples of "inappropriate" students: "Do you really mean that the student in a coma should be in a general education classroom? What about the student who holds a teacher hostage at knife point?" Other forms of this argument seek to emphasize the inappropriateness of the general education classroom for some students: "Without one-to-one specialized instruction the student will not learn and his or her future will be sacrificed." Another version of the same argument points out that the resources of the general education classroom are already limited, and the addition of resource-hungry students will only further reduce

what is available for regular education students.

Of course these arguments fail to note that labeled students are not always the most resource-hungry students. Indeed, when some students join general education classrooms, their need for resources diminishes. In other instances, the labeled student can bring additional resources that can be shared to other classmates' benefit. These arguments also fail to note that the teaching in self-contained settings, as well as the resource management, can sometimes be uninspired, ordinary, and ineffective. Consider how many students with IEPs end up with exactly the same goals and objectives from year to year.

Like the debates about place, debates about time miss the point and overlook the opportunity of a shift from special education inclusion to more systemic inclusion. *Every* child should have the opportunity to learn in lots of different places—in small groups and large, in classrooms, in hallways, in libraries, and in a wide variety of community locations. For some parts of their schooling, some students might spend more time than others in some settings. Still, the greater the number and variety of students learning in various locations with more varied approaches and innovations, the less likely that any student will be disadvantaged by not "qualifying" for some kind of attention, support, or assistance. If all students work in a variety of school and community places, the likelihood that any particular students will be stigmatized because of their learning needs, interests, and preferences will be eliminated. All students will benefit from such variety in teaching approaches, locations, and supports.

The Real Challenge of Inclusion

Coming to understand the limits of inclusion as articulated by special educators was only part of my journey. I also had to spend time in general education classrooms, listening to teachers and trying to understand their struggles and efforts to change, to help me see the limits of general education as well. The general education environment, organized as it still is according to the bell curve logic of labeling and grouping by ability, may never be accommodating enough to achieve the goals of inclusion, even if special educators and their special ideas, materials, and techniques become less "special" and separate.

It seems to me that the lesson to be learned from special education's inclusion initiative is that the real challenge is a lot harder and more complicated than we thought. Neither special nor general education alone has either the capacity or the vision to challenge and change the deep-rooted assumptions that separate and track children and youths according to presumptions about ability, achievement, and eventual social contribution. Meaningful change will require nothing less than a joint effort to reinvent schools to be more accommodating to all dimensions of human diversity. It will also require that the purposes and processes of these reinvented schools be organized not so much to make sure that students learn and develop on the basis of their own abilities and talents, but rather to make sure that all children are prepared to participate in the benefits of their communities so that others in that community care enough about what happens to them to value them as members.[10]

My own journey toward challenging these assumptions was greatly assisted by the faculty of one of the elementary schools in our research study on inclusion. Most of our research had really centered on the perspectives of special educators. While we talked with many other people in the schools, our access had always been through the special educator who was trying to move out into the school. Finally, however, we began to shift our attention to the *whole* school through the eyes of *all* its members. For me, it was a shift from *special education research* to *educational research* that also happened to "include" special education teachers and students. I began to learn the language of schooling, became able to "talk education" rather than just talk special education, and sought that same bilingualism for my students and colleagues through a series of reframed research and demonstration projects.

Learning about various reform agendas within education that support and facilitate systemic inclusion enormously reassured and encouraged me, and I have begun to refocus my efforts toward nurturing them. For example, in response to the changing demands of work and community life in the 21st century, some initiatives within general education reform and restructuring are focusing on students' understanding and use of their own learning rather than on whether or not they can recall information during tests. Employers and community leaders want citizens who are active learners and

No longer must the opportunity to participate in life wait until some standard of "normalcy" is reached.

collaborators as well as individuals who possess the personal confidence and ability to contribute to a changing society.[11]

In response to these broader social demands, teachers at all levels of schooling are trying to rethink curriculum. They are looking for ways to help students develop habits of learning that will serve them long after formal schooling ends. In pursuit of this goal, they are moving from seeking to cover a large number of "facts" to exploring in more depth a smaller number of topics of interest and relevance to students.[12] An important aspect of this curriculum shift is that not all students will learn exactly the same things, even within the same lesson or activity.

These changes in general education are being pursued because of increasing social complexity and student diversity. Educators are less and less confident that learning one standard, "official" curriculum will help students achieve the kind of competence they need to lead satisfactory lives. Greater numbers of educators are concerned not so much that some bit of content knowledge is learned, but rather the students use their learning in ways that make a difference in their lives outside of school. The difficulty in making this happen in classrooms is that students bring with them all manner of differences that teachers must take into consideration. These include different abilities, of course, but also different interests, different family lifestyles, and different preferences about schools and learning. Students' linguistic backgrounds, socioeconomic sta-

tus, and cultural heritage must also be considered when making curriculum and teaching decisions. Finally, some students have different ways of thinking and knowing—sometimes emphasizing language, sometimes motor learning, sometimes artistic intelligence, and so on.[13]

To general education teachers who are experimenting with these kinds of curricular and teaching reforms, students with official disabilities become different in degree rather than in type. Tailoring the learning event for them might require adjustments or supports not needed by some other students. But the essential process remains the same for all. Fear of "watering down" the official curriculum remains only for those classrooms that have not responded to the need for more systemic reform of curriculum and teaching. Classrooms and teachers seriously engaged in preparing students for the future have already expanded and enriched the curriculum to respond both to the demands for broader student outcomes and to the different interests, purposes, and abilities of each student.

A New Inclusion Initiative

These are just a few of the ongoing discussions within general education. There are many more. Some, like the pressure to articulate new national standards and benchmarks, are less clearly supportive of student diversity. Reform initiatives are emerging from all parts of the system—from the efforts of small groups of teachers to those of state and federal policy makers. Often these various pressures for change contradict one another, but in the end all will have to be accommodated, understood, and transformed into a single whole.

Changing schools at all, never mind actually *improving* them, is an extraordinarily complex and arduous task. Public education is like a web: each strand touches many others, depending upon as well as providing support for the entire structure. Any change, even a small one, ripples through the web, sometimes strengthening, sometimes weakening the whole. When many things change at once, it is a time of both great risk and great energy.

Public education is in just such an exciting period of change. Perhaps for the first time, changes in all parts of the system can begin to converge. My own journey to understand inclusion has led me to propose my own definition of inclusion:

Inclusion is a process of meshing general and special education reform initiatives and strategies in order to achieve a unified system of public education that incorporates all children and youths as active, fully participating members of the school community; that views diversity as the norm; and that ensures a high-quality education for each student by providing meaningful curriculum, effective teaching, and necessary supports for each student.

Perhaps there are "rabid inclusionists," foaming at the mouth over some specific change and having but little awareness of the challenge their agenda represents to fundamental assumptions. I suppose that there are also "rabid separatists," just as fanatically insisting on preserving the present system and similarly unaware of the fundamental assumptions that influence their positions.

My own journey led me to a different destination. It led me to take the risk of admitting that I have changed my mind about many things. (Perhaps it would be more accurate to say that I have not so much "changed" my mind as "clarified" and expanded my thinking.) I am still an advocate for inclusion, but now I understand it to mean much more than I believed it meant when I first began to study and experience it through my son. As I and others who share this broader understanding work to create genuinely inclusive schools, we will be encouraging people in schools, on every strand of the complex web, to change in three directions.

The first shift involves moving away from schools that are structured and organized according to ability and toward schools that are structured around student diversity and that accommodate many different ways of organizing students for learning. This shift will also require teachers with different abilities and talents to work together to create a wide array of learning opportunities.[14]

The second shift involves moving away from teaching approaches that emphasize the teacher as disseminator of content that students must retain and toward approaches that emphasize the role of the learner in creating knowledge, competence, and the ability to pursue further learning. There is a good deal of literature that seeks to blend various theories of teaching and learning into flexible and creative approaches that will accomplish these ends. The strength of these approaches is that they begin with an appreciation of student differences that can be stretched comfortably to incorporate the differences of disability and the effective teaching

technology created by special educators.[15]

The third shift involves changing our view of the schools' role from one of providing educational *services* to one of providing educational *supports* for learning. This shift will occur naturally as a consequence of the changes in teaching demanded by diversity. Valuing diversity and difference, rather than trying to change or diminish it so that everyone fits some ideal of similarity, leads to the realization that we can *support* students in their efforts to become active members of their communities. No longer must the opportunity to participate in life wait until some standard of "normalcy" or similarity is reached. A focus on the support of learning also encourages a shift from viewing difference or disability in terms of individual limitations to a focus on environmental constraints. Perhaps the most important feature of support as a concept for schooling is that it is grounded in the perspective of the person receiving it, not the person providing it.[16]

The new challenge of inclusion is to create schools in which our day-to-day efforts no longer assume that a particular text, activity, or teaching mode will "work" to support any particular student's learning. Typical classrooms will include students with more and more kinds of differences. The learning enterprise of reinvented *inclusive* schools will be a constant conversation involving students, teachers, other school personnel, families, and community members, all working to construct learning, to document accomplishments, and to adjust supports. About this kind of inclusion I can be very rabid indeed.

1. John Gliedman and William Roth, *The Unexpected Minority: Handicapped Children in America* (New York: Harcourt Brace Jovanovich, 1980).

2. Jeff Strully and Cindy Strully, "Friendship as an Educational Goal," in Susan Stainback, William Stainback, and Marsha Forest, eds., *Educating All Students in the Mainstream of Regular Education* (Baltimore: Paul H. Brookes, 1989), pp. 59–68.

3. Dianne L. Ferguson et al., "Figuring Out What to Do with Grownups: How Teachers Make Inclusion 'Work' for Students with Disabilities." *Journal of the Association for Persons with Severe Handicaps,* vol. 17, 1993, pp. 218–26.

4. Dianne L. Ferguson, "Is Communication Really the Point? Some Thoughts on Interventions and Membership," *Mental Retardation,* vol. 32, no. 1, 1994, pp. 7–18.

5. Dianne L. Ferguson, Christopher Willis, and Gwen Meyer, "Widening the Stream: Ways to Think About Including Exceptions in Schools," in Donna H. Lear and Fredda Brown, eds., *People with Disabilities Who Challenge the System* (Baltimore: Paul H. Brookes, forthcoming): and Dianne L. Ferguson and Gwen Meyer, "Creating Together the Tools to Reinvent Schools," in Michael Berres, Peter Knoblock, Dianne L. Ferguson, and Connie Woods, eds., *Restructuring Schools for All Children* (New York: Teachers College Press, forthcoming).

6. Michael Giangreco et al., " 'I've Counted on Jon': Transformational Experiences of Teachers Educating Students with Disabilities," *Exceptional Children,* vol. 59, 1993, pp. 359–72; and Marlene Pugach and Stephen Lilly, "Reconceptualizing Support Services for Classroom Teachers: Implications for Teacher Education," *Journal of Teacher Education,* vol. 35, no. 5, 1984, pp. 48–55.

7. Russell Gersten and John Woodward, "Rethinking the Regular Education Initiative: Focus on the Classroom Teacher," *Remedial and Special Education,* vol. 11, no. 3, 1990, pp. 7–16.

8. Douglas Fuchs and Lynn S. Fuchs, "Inclusive Schools Movement and the Radicalization of Special Education Reform," *Exceptional Children,* vol. 60, 1994, pp. 294–309.

9. Lou Brown et al., "How Much Time Should Students with Severe Intellectual Disabilities Spend in Regular Education Classrooms and Elsewhere?," *Journal of the Association of Persons with Severe Handicaps,* vol. 16, 1991, pp. 39–47; and William Stainback, Susan Stainback, and Jeanette S. Moravec, "Using Curriculum to Build Inclusive Classrooms," in Susan Stainback and William Stainback, eds., *Curriculum Considerations in Inclusive Classrooms: Facilitating Learning for All Students* (Baltimore: Paul H. Brookes, 1992), pp. 65–84.

10. Dianne L. Ferguson, "Bursting Bubbles: Marrying General and Special Education Reforms," in Berres, Knoblock, Ferguson, and Woods, op. cit.: and Terry Astuto et al., *Roots of Reform: Challenging the Assumptions That Control Change in Education* (Bloomington, Ind.: Phi Delta Kappa Educational Foundation, 1994).

11. See, for example, Anthony D. Carnevale, Leila J. Gainer, and Ann S. Meltzer, *The Essential Skills Employers Want* (San Francisco: Jossey-Bass, 1990).

12. David T. Conley, *Roadmap to Restructuring: Policies, Practices, and the Emerging Visions of Schooling* (Eugene: ERIC Clearinghouse on Educational Management, University of Oregon, 1993); Robin Fogarty, "Ten Ways to Integrate Curriculum," *Educational Leadership,* October 1991, pp. 61–65; Jacqueline G. Brooks and Martin Brooks, *In Search of Understanding: The Case for Constructivist Classrooms* (Alexandria, Va.: Association for Supervision and Curriculum Development, 1993); Nel Noddings, "Excellence as a Guide to Educational Conversations," *Teachers College Record,* vol. 94, 1993, pp. 730–43; Theodore Sizer, *Horace's School: Redesigning the American School* (Boston: Houghton Mifflin, 1992); and Grant Wiggins, "The Futility of Trying to Teach Everything of Importance," *Educational Leadership,* November 1989, pp. 44–59.

13. Thomas Armstrong, *Multiple Intelligences in the Classroom* (Alexandria, Va.: Association for Supervision and Curriculum Development, 1994); Howard Gardner, *Multiple Intelligences: The Theory in Practice* (New York: Basic Books, 1993); and Gaea Leinhardt, "What Research on Learning Tells Us About Teaching," *Educational Leadership,* April 1992, pp. 20–25.

14. Linda Darling-Hammond, "Reframing the School Reform Agenda: Developing Capacity for School Transformation," *Phi Delta Kappan,* June 1993, pp. 753–61; Jeannie Oakes and Martin Lipton, "Detracking Schools: Early Lessons from the Field," *Phi Delta Kappan,* February 1992, pp. 448–54; and Thomas M. Skrtic, *Behind Special Education: A Critical Analysis of Professional Culture and School Organization* (Denver: Love Publishing, 1991).

15. Conley, op. cit.; Robin Fogarty, *The Mindful School: How to Integrate the Curricula* (Palatine, Ill.: IRI/Skylight Publishing, 1991); Brooks and Brooks, op. cit.; Nel Noddings, *The Challenge to Care in Schools* (New York: Teachers College Press, 1992); Sizer, op. cit.; and Wiggins, op. cit.

16. Philip M. Ferguson et al., "Supported Community Life: Disability Policy and the Renewal of Mediating Structures," *Journal of Disability Policy,* vol. 1, no. 1, 1990, pp. 9–35; and Michael W. Smull and G. Thomas Bellamy, "Community Services for Adults with Disabilities: Policy Challenges in the Emerging Support Paradigm," in Luanna Meyer, Charles A. Peck, and Lou Brown, eds., *Critical Issues in the Lives of People with Severe Disabilities* (Baltimore: Paul H. Brookes, 1991), pp. 527–36.

 Article Review Form at end of book.

What are the major concerns of Kauffman et al. regarding the inclusion of students with emotional and behavioral disorders in regular classes? What kind of definition for inclusion do they propose?

Inclusion of All Students with Emotional or Behavioral Disorders? Let's Think Again

James M. Kauffman, John Wills Lloyd, John Baker, and Teresa M. Riedel

James M. Kauffman is a professor of education at the University of Virginia, Charlottesville, where John Wills Lloyd is an associate professor. John Baker, formerly a middle school teacher in the Greene County (Va.) Public Schools, lives in Paradise, Utah. Teresa M. Riedel, an aquatics instructor in Greenbelt, Md., taught elementary school in the Albemarle County (Va.) Public Schools.

While we attempt to make regular schools and classrooms inclusive in the best sense for as many students as possible, we should not be guided by overgeneralizations or become detached from the realities of classroom teaching, the authors warn.

Nearly all teachers have at least one student who fits the current federal definition of being "seriously emotionally disturbed"—or, in today's preferred terminology, having an "emotional or behavioral disorder."[1] Such students may be severely antisocial, aggressive, and disruptive; they may be socially rejected, isolated, withdrawn, and nonresponsive; they may show signs of severe anxiety or depression or exhibit psychotic behavior; they may vacillate between extremes of withdrawal and aggression; and they nearly always have serious academic problems in addition to their social and emotional difficulties. These students' problems are severe, pervasive, and chronic—not minor, situational, or transitory.

In many appeals for the restructuring or reform of special education, the call is for inclusion of all students with disabilities, and no attempt is made to disaggregate the population.[2] Consequently, we must consider the nature and extent of the problems we will face if inclusion of all students with emotional or behavioral disorders in regular schools and classes becomes a reality.

Current national statistics show that less than 1% of public school students are identified as having emotional or behavioral disorders, and the majority of these students are now served in separate classes or facilities.[3] Clearly, then, regular classroom teachers will need to be prepared to teach and manage not only those students with emotional or behavioral problems whom they are already teaching, but also additional students who present even more difficult challenges to pedagogy and behavior manage-

Kauffman, J. M., Lloyd, J. W., Baker, J., & Riedel, T. M., "Inclusion of all students with emotional or behavioral disorders? Let's think again," *Phi Delta Kappan, 76*(7), 1995, pp. 542–546. Reprinted by permission of the author.

ment. Although we hope that general education will become more accommodating to students with disabilities, we doubt that regular schools and classrooms will ever be able to provide an appropriate education for all students with emotional or behavioral disorders.

Nature and Extent of the Problem

Study after study over the past three decades has indicated that some 6% to 10% of children and youths have emotional or behavioral problems that seriously impede their development and require treatment if these students are to function adequately in school and in the larger society.[4] Federal data suggest that 70% to 80% of children needing mental health services do not receive appropriate care.[5] Other reports indicate that many children do not receive any mental health services until their problems become so extreme as to require residential treatment.[6]

Many students with serious emotional or behavioral disorders remain in regular classes and receive little or no special help of any kind. They are unlikely to be identified for special education unless their problems are severe, complex, and global—so severe that they require comprehensive and intensive intervention.[7] Thus only those with the worst emotional or behavioral disorders have been removed from regular classes, and their return would undoubtedly tax the most competent of classroom teachers. The following brief descriptions of two children, provided to us by teachers of our acquaintance, illustrate the severity of problems faced by many regular classroom

teachers before children are even identified for special education.

Tom, a third-grade boy with serious academic deficits, has exhibited severe behavior problems with every teacher he has had. In first grade, he frequently urinated in the classroom and other inappropriate places and picked fights with other children. Now, not only is he highly aggressive, but also he frequently steals from the teacher and his classmates and is labeled a thief by his peers. His mother does not see his stealing as a serious problem; his father is in jail. Neither Tom nor his mother is receiving any counseling or mental health services. The school's pre-referral team has found no strategy to control his aggressive behavior. In the middle of his third-grade year, Tom was placed with an exceptionally strong male teacher, who finds it impossible to control Tom's behavior and to teach the rest of his class at the same time. This teacher wants Tom to be evaluated for special education.

Pat, a fifth-grade girl, is at or above grade level in all academic areas but has been highly oppositional and defiant of all teachers since kindergarten. Large for her age and strong, she pushes, hits, and threatens her peers, who are fearful of her and will not initiate any interaction with her. She sometimes bangs her head on her desk or the floor, shouting, "I'm no good" or "I want to die." Pat was evaluated for special education only after terrorizing her classmates and a substitute teacher by tying the cord of a classroom window blind around her neck and jumping from a table, bringing the blinds crashing down with her in an apparent suicide attempt.

In anticipation of the demands of dealing with an influx

of more challenging students, we might ask two questions. First, what are the strategies that research and experience have shown to be most effective in working with these students? Second, what is the likelihood that these strategies can be employed consistently and effectively in regular schools and classrooms?

Strategies That Work

Programs for students with emotional or behavioral disorders have been accused of overemphasizing external control of behavior.[8] However, programs that do not establish control of disruptive behavior give teachers no opportunity to teach academic and social skills. Effective programs for students with emotional or behavioral disorders provide the necessary control of aggressive and disruptive behavior, but they also offer a rich curriculum that helps students learn self-control, attain academic competence, and acquire employment-related attitudes and skills that will improve their chances of living happily and successfully in their communities.

Special education and mental health services for students with emotional and behavioral disorders have a substantial history, and a variety of programs have produced significant benefits.[9] Regardless of their differences in philosophy or conceptual orientation, the most effective programs share the following characteristics.

- *Systematic, data-based interventions.* Intervention strategies are chosen on the

Many students with serious emotional or behavioral disorders remain in regular classes and receive little or no special help of any kind.

basis of the best available data regarding their effectiveness with the specific problems exhibited by individual students, and these strategies are implemented with a high degree of fidelity.

- *Continuous assessment and monitoring of progress.* Each student's progress is monitored frequently, usually daily. Decisions about changes in intervention strategies are based on the measurement of progress, and the student often monitors his or her own progress in addition to having it monitored by program staff.

- *Treatment matched carefully and specifically to the nature and severity of students' problems.* One program is not assumed to be appropriate for all who are categorized as having emotional or behavioral disorders. Rather, each student's specific problems are assessed, and the intervention plan is based on the emotional or behavioral characteristics he or she exhibits. Program personnel understand that many kinds of interventions are required to address the diversity of students' problems.

- *Multi-component treatment.* The program includes a combination of services to address all aspects of the problem, including academic and social skills, social and family services, counseling or psychological therapy, and pharmacological treatment as necessary. Services are not provided piecemeal or in isolation. Rather, services are coordinated and mutually supportive.

- *Provision for frequent guided practice of academic and social skills.* It is not assumed that emotional, behavioral, or academic skills are to be learned merely by talking about them. Rather, teachers give students frequent practice and coach them in actually using the skills. Teaching and practice may begin in "safe" settings in which success is virtually guaranteed, and then problems or lessons of graduated difficulty are provided to ensure continued success. Teachers design instruction carefully, so as to avoid those situations in which failure to use the skills has serious negative consequences.

- *Programming for transfer and maintenance.* Intervention across environments or settings is programmed as necessary to produce generalized improvement and maintain gains. Improvement is not assumed to be permanent or self-sustaining, and improvement in one situation is not assumed to produce automatic improvement in another. Program personnel give extraordinary attention to the specific conditions under which the student who has acquired social and academic skills will be expected to use them.

- *Commitment to sustained intervention.* "One-shot" interventions assumed to be "cures" are avoided. Program personnel understand that most severe emotional or behavioral disorders are developmental disabilities, not transient problems, and that most students with these disorders may require prolonged, if not lifelong, support services.[10]

Regular School and Classroom Implementation

Few if any of the strategies that are successful with students who have emotional or behavioral disorders are unique; many of the same techniques are appropriate in some form for other students. It is not so much particular features that set successful programs apart, but the precision, duration, and intensity of those features. As we have noted, many students with emotional or behavioral disorders are not now identified for special education; they (along with some of those who *have* been identified) are maintained in regular classrooms, albeit marginally and with poor results. Some of these students would probably benefit from regular classrooms in which some of the program features we have discussed were implemented, and in all likelihood some of the students now served in special classes or schools could be appropriately served in regular classes, were adequate strategies employed.

Nevertheless, observational studies suggest that most regular classrooms are not characterized by the strategies known to be effective with these students.[11] Very significant changes in what teachers know and do will be required before a majority of regular classroom teachers are prepared to create the minimum conditions necessary for the success of students with behavioral and emotional disorders while also providing an appropriate program for the nondisabled students.[12]

Knowing what is needed to help students is not the same as

being able to provide it. Many teachers, administrators, and mental health workers are frustrated because they do not have the resources to do what they know needs to be done. The resources that are lacking are most often human resources—enough properly trained personnel to allow the time and concentration necessary to address students' problems effectively. There is also a lack of appropriate settings in which intensive, sustained, and often highly personal services can be provided.

In our current research on placement, we have interviewed teachers, administrators, and mental health personnel who provide special programs for students with emotional and behavioral disorders. They have described to us the conditions necessary for helping these students: 1) a critical mass of trained, experienced, and mutually supportive personnel located in close physical proximity to one another and 2) a very low pupil/staff ratio (approximately 5:1 for students in day or residential treatment and 1:1 for the most severely disabled students). Not only are these conditions seldom met, but we suspect that very few school systems, let alone regular classroom teachers, will ever be prepared or willing to accept some students with emotional or behavioral disorders. Consider the difficulty of teaching a regular class while simultaneously addressing the needs of the students described in the following vignettes, which are drawn from our own classroom experience.

Johnny, a child with emotional and behavioral disorders, is included in a regular second-grade class. He begins the school day by kicking apart the puzzle a girl is assembling on the floor. He then takes another boy's paper and runs around the room tearing it up and laughing, ignoring the teacher's instructions to stop. Told to go to the time-out area, he drops to the floor, kicking, pounding the floor with his fists, and crying loudly. When he refuses to stop this behavior the teacher instructs her other 22 students to follow "Plan A"—stop their activities and return immediately to their desks to read or write independently. The teacher then asks a neighboring teacher to supervise her class while she escorts Johnny to the office. Johnny refuses to leave the classroom, so the teacher summons the principal. Johnny ignores the principal's instruction to follow him to the office, so the teacher and principal physically remove him, screaming, kicking, and crying.

Matt, a seventh-grader, attends a modified self-contained classroom for students with "serious emotional disturbance" but is included in a regular homeroom and goes to lunch with his regular classroom peers. When in his regular homeroom, Matt is prone to jump onto a desk and, when asked to get down, to leap from desk to desk proclaiming loudly, "You can't catch me!" until flinging himself upon a student below. On one occasion he rigged the wiring of his homeroom's overhead projector so that someone touching the metal casing would receive an electrical shock (his prank was reported to the teacher by another student before anyone was hurt). Matt has torn down the entire ceiling of the rest room, destroying fixtures, and started fires in the rest room, although he is escorted there and back by a female aide. His inability to handle unstructured time in his homeroom and unsupervised activities elsewhere in the school is a contrast

to his successes in the highly structured special class.

Given what we know about effective programming for students with emotional or behavioral disorders, the outlook for public schools' resources in the foreseeable future, and the movement to include all students with disabilities in regular schools and classes, we need to assess the probability that inclusion will produce the results we want. Studies of the inclusion of students with emotional and behavioral disorders indicate that it is indeed an arduous task and that a careful case-by-case approach is the only responsible course of action.[13]

At the outset, if we are seriously to consider the placement in regular schools and classes of all students with emotional or behavioral disorders, we must have answers to at least the following questions.

1. How will nondisabled students be affected by the modifications of the regular classroom that are necessary to manage and teach students with emotional and behavioral disorders? Especially, how will the educational and social development of students who need far less classroom control and structure be affected?

2. How will schools justify to parents the placement in regular classrooms of students known to be highly volatile, disruptive, and perhaps violent? Will the physical and psychological safety of other students and the benefits of an orderly learning environment be jeopardized?

What are the legal liabilities of school personnel involved in the inclusion of these students?

3. As special schools and classes are eliminated as placement options, what alternatives are most likely to be used for these students? If school personnel are forced to choose between keeping students with emotional and behavioral disorders in regular schools and classes or simply not identifying them for special education so that they can be suspended and expelled, how will these students be guaranteed an appropriate education?

4. What will be the benefits to students with emotional or behavioral disorders of being included in regular classrooms? If they have not previously imitated appropriate peer models or benefited from the instructional program in the regular classroom, what assurances can be given that they will now imitate positive models and benefit from instruction?

5. What training would be sufficient to allow regular classroom teachers to deal with these students? What training will regular classroom teachers be given, when, and by whom?

6. Which teachers will be asked to include more students with emotional and behavioral disorders in their classrooms? Will the most capable teachers be asked to assume a disproportionate share of the responsibility for these students?

7. What additional support services will be provided to regular classroom teachers? Will the necessary number of trained personnel be available before these students are included?

8. How will the success of inclusionary programs be assessed? What criteria will be used to ascertain that inclusion is having positive effects on both nondisabled students and those with emotional and behavioral disorders? What will be done if such criteria are not met?

An Alternative Definition of Inclusion

A narrow, highly restrictive definition of inclusion requires that all individuals occupy a common space, regardless of whether that space has the features appropriate for their needs; it assumes that every place can be structured to serve every individual's needs. A more adaptive and humane definition of an inclusive school system is one that allows for a variety of placements that offer the conditions under which every individual feels safe, accepted, and valued and is helped to develop his or her affective and intellectual capacities. Such a definition recognizes that in some cases there will have to be different placements for different individuals.

This is not a new idea but is merely a reiteration of the mandate of the Individuals with Disabilities Education Act of 1990—a law with features that some seem to have ignored.[14] Research, the history of human services to people with emotional and behavioral disorders, and personal experience suggest that regular schools and regular classrooms are not now and are extremely unlikely ever to be places in which all students with disabilities experience the conditions described above. The demands on regular classroom teachers' time, the lack of concentrated support personnel, and the severity of children's problems preclude the effective education of some students in regular schools and classrooms.[15] On the other hand, we know that special schools and classes can be made safe, accepting, valuing, and productive environments for these students.

A century ago, overenthusiasm for the institution as the sole placement option for people with disabilities resulted in great injustices and the needless exclusion of many individuals from regular schools and communities. Perhaps overenthusiasm for the regular school and the regular classroom as the sole placement options for students with disabilities has the potential for creating an equal tyranny. While we attempt to make regular schools and classrooms inclusive in the best sense for as many students as possible, we should not be guided by overgeneralizations or become detached from the realities of classroom teaching.

> Many teachers, administrators, and mental health workers are frustrated because they do not have the resources to do what they know needs to be done.

1. The terminology "emotional or behavioral disorder" is preferred by the National Mental Health and Special Education Coalition: for discussion, see Steven R. Forness and Jane Knitzer, "A New Proposed Definition and Terminology to Replace 'Serious Emotional Disturbance' in Individuals with Disabilities Education Act," *School Psychology Review,* vol. 21, 1992, pp. 12–20.

2. See, for example, Alan Gartner and Dorothy K. Lipsky, *The Yoke of Special Education: How to Break It* (Rochester, N.Y.: National Center on Education and the Economy, 1989); *Winners All: A Call for Inclusive Schools* (Alexandria, Va.: National Association of State Boards of Education, October 1992); and William Stainback and Susan Stainback, "A Rationale for Integration and Restructuring: A Synopsis," in John W. Lloyd, Nirbhay N. Singh, and Alan C. Repp, eds., *The Regular Education Initiative: Alternative Perspectives on Concepts, Issues, and Models* (Sycamore, Ill.: Sycamore Press, 1991), pp. 226–39.

3. U.S. Department of Education, *To Assure the Free Appropriate Public Education of All Children with Disabilities: Sixteenth Annual Report to Congress on the Implementation of the Individuals with Disabilities Education Act* (Washington, D.C.: U.S. Government Printing Office, 1994).

4. Nancy A. Brandenberg, Robert M. Friedman, and Starr E. Silver, "The Epidemiology of Childhood Psychiatric Disorders: Prevalence Findings from Recent Studies," *Journal of the American Academy of Child and Adolescent Psychiatry,* vol. 29, 1990, pp. 76–83; and Institute of Medicine, *Research on Children and Adolescents with Mental, Behavioral and Developmental Disorders: Mobilizing a National Initiative* (Washington, D.C.: National Academy Press, 1989). For a review and discussion of prevalence studies, see James M. Kauffman, *Characteristics of Emotional and Behavioral Disorders of Children and Youth,* 5th ed. (Columbus, Ohio: Merrill/Macmillan, 1993).

5. *Children's Mental Health Problems and Services—A Background Paper* (Washington, D.C.: U.S. Office of Technology Assessment, OTA-BP-H-33, 1986).

6. Jane Knitzer, *Unclaimed Children: The Failure of Public Responsibility to Children and Adolescents in Need of Mental Health Services* (Washington, D.C.: Children's Defense Fund, 1982); and *Invisible Children Project: Final Report and Recommendations of the Invisible Children Project* (Alexandria, Va.: National Mental Health Association, 1989).

7. See *Invisible Children Project;* and Richard E. Mattison and Alan D. Gamble, "Severity of Socially and Emotionally Disturbed Boys' Dysfunction at School and Home: Comparison with Psychiatric and General Population Boys," *Behavioral Disorders,* vol. 17, 1992, pp. 219–24.

8. Jane Knitzer, Zina Steinberg, and Brahm Fleisch, *At the Schoolhouse Door: An Examination of Programs and Policies for Children with Behavioral and Emotional Problems* (New York: Bank Street College of Education, 1990).

9. See, for example, Peacock Hill Working Group, "Problems and Promises in Special Education and Related Services for Children and Youth with Emotional or Behavioral Disorders," *Behavioral Disorders,* vol. 16, 1991, pp. 299–313; Michael H. Epstein et al., "Improving Services for Students with Serious Emotional Disturbances," *NASSP Bulletin,* January 1993, pp. 46–51; and Frank A. Fecser, "A Model Re-ED Classroom for Troubled Students," *Journal of Emotional and Behavioral Problems,* Winter 1993, pp. 15–20.

10. Peacock Hill Working Group, op. cit.

11. Richard E. Shores et al., "Classroom Interactions of Children with Behavior Disorders," *Journal of Emotional and Behavior Disorders,* vol. 1, 1993, pp. 27–39; and Philip S. Strain et al., "Naturalistic Assessment of Children's Compliance to Teachers' Requests and Consequences for Compliance," *Journal of Applied Behavior Analysis,* vol. 16, 1983, pp. 243–49.

12. John W. Lloyd and James M. Kauffman, "What Less Restrictive Placements Require of Teachers," in James M. Kauffman et al., eds., *Issues in the Educational Placement of Pupils with Emotional or Behavioral Disorders* (Hillsdale, N.J.: Erlbaum, 1995), pp. 317–34.

13. Douglas Fuchs et al., "Toward a Responsible Reintegration of Behaviorally Disordered Students," *Behavioral Disorders,* vol. 16, 1991, pp. 133–47.

14. See Barbara D. Bateman and David J. Chard, "Legal Demands and Constraints on Placement Decisions," in Kauffman et al., pp. 285–316.

15. Pete Idstein, "Swimming Against the Mainstream," *Phi Delta Kappan,* December 1993, pp. 336-40.

Article Review Form at end of book.

In what way did Mahony's flexibility extend to his grading? What are some of the teaching practices described in this article that contributed to the included students' success?

Small Victories in an Inclusive Classroom

Take a high school English class and add several students who've always been in small, special education classes. For best results, discard plans based solely on what a typical 9th grader should do.

Michael Mahony

Michael Mahony is the Chair of the English Department for grades 6–12 and teaches English at Hastings High School, Mount Hope Blvd., Hastings-on-Hudson, NY 10706 (e-mail: mahony@1-2000.com).

Here is an English teacher's dilemma: How does one teach special education students and a handful of other students who find English difficult while also teaching students for whom reading and writing come easily? That is the quandary I first faced in the 1993–94 school year when I began teaching the most mixed group of 9th graders I had ever encountered. Of the 20 students in my English class, some could read sensitively and write cogently; others had difficulty reading complex sentences; a few could not produce complete sentences or coherent paragraphs.

Educators might call this class an inclusion class because it included three students who never took classes in a general education curriculum. They had spent their first nine years of public education in classes of fewer than five students, taught by professionals specially trained to understand their learning problems. I preferred not to label this class an *inclusion* class because the term implies that, for some, the curriculum will be less rigorous than a general 9th grade English class. Indeed, initially this was a real concern among a few parents. But my reading list and writing as-signments were similar to those I used for my other classes, with fundamental changes only in classroom activities.

The most exciting moments came when students working together were able to make sense of literature and talk about it in their own terms.

Further, here at Hastings High School, we do not include everyone, as the term implies, only those students who we believe might benefit from such a class. Our general policy is very fluid. Some special education students remain in their small, self-contained classes for only one or two subjects, or they may return to these classes if they don't do well in a larger general class. We also rotate teachers and ask for volunteers. For example, last year, another English teacher took over my mixed class, and I'll rejoin the same group of students this coming year when they'll be 11th graders.

Open Questions

How did this mixed class come about? Much had to do with wondering. Educators in our small school district in the Hudson River Valley wondered whether more special education students would benefit from being in a general education class. They encouraged teachers in all subjects to open their classrooms to special education students. For that reason—and because of the federal mandate to place these students in the least restrictive environment—we have fewer self-contained classes than we have had in the past.

There is, of course, fiery argument over whether such mixed classes are educationally sound. A study by Chira (1993, p. A17), for example, shows that when special education students are placed in general education classes, they fail 61 percent of the time, as compared to 14 percent in special education classes. But this raw statistic does not distinguish among the different kinds of classes that special education students are thrown into. Some programs provide little or no support for the general curriculum teacher or the special education student. The statistic remains disturbing, but it should not preclude a long-term examination of classes where these students appear to be prospering.

I entered the fire relatively ignorant of the details of the debate, but wondering whether the presence of a special education teacher in my class—one who was alert to learning problems—would make me a better teacher. An aging literature buff, my shtick was reading, writing, and literature. Although I had taught special education students, they were deemed able to work in a large class as long as they received special assistance, usually tutoring by a special education teacher at some point in the school day.

Further, I had never taught as part of a team. My teaching partner, Andy Lubitz, was also in the dark. Although he was an experienced special education teacher and learning specialist, he had never taught English to a group of students, nor did he have extensive training in literature.

A Honeymoon and Hurdles

The first two weeks of classes were like any other year. Students exuded enthusiasm, studiousness, and optimism. When Andy led the class through an activity, I mingled and helped students when necessary. Several weeks passed before either of us sensed the need to interrupt or amend activities when students needed further explanations or more time to understand concepts or finish reading. But classes rarely proceeded as planned.

My special students' first hurdle was learning how to act in a large group. Adam, the seemingly most limited of the three, was accustomed to more informal gatherings and kept shouting out answers. Because I call on students to answer other students' questions, the special students were occasionally disconcerted. They expected more of an authority in the class and wanted immediate answers to questions. Sheila, our one student with emotional problems (I'm using pseudonyms throughout), refused to engage in discussion and declined virtually every time she was called upon. Group discussion, in which the students had to listen patiently to their peers, was strange and occasionally tedious for the three students.

For the special education students, being part of a large class meant making new friends and encountering more challenges than they ever would in a group of five.

Adam: An Important Contributor

Andy and I spent most of our time struggling with how to teach Adam. Adam expressed enthusiasm in disruptive ways, such as by being excessively talkative. Some of his manic activity was out of his own control. Yet Adam knew himself to be intelligent; he saw this class as an opportunity to show his friends that he was. The one thing we had going for us was that he wanted to be in the class despite its challenges.

On occasion we spoke to Adam after school about his behavior, giving him the typical explanation: We were responsible for 20 students; everyone was entitled to speak. We praised his verve but insisted that he follow some basic rules. He understood our reasoning, but still felt frustrated when he couldn't speak up when he knew an answer. Still, he usually cooperated with gentle reminders to raise his hand, open his book, or take notes. Only on those days when he broke his glasses while playing with them or lost his notebook or keys did his anxiety demand attention.

Adam also had great difficulty reading aloud in class, and often misread words. (We required every student to read at least one sentence aloud, but they could then call on someone else to continue.) From the beginning, Andy or I would read Adam words and sentences he could not decipher so that he would gain confidence. He soon was eager to read aloud.

Whenever possible, we gave Adam dramatic roles that he could improvise rather than read. His best moment was when he played the role of Puck in Shakespeare's *A Midsummer Night's Dream*. His classmates explained to him that Puck was tormenting the lovers in the woods. Adam deftly interacted with the students who were reading their parts, usually a sure way to antagonize. Tickling students' noses when they were engaged in heated argument was not in Shakespeare's script, but it did express Puck's impishness and enlivened his character for the other students.

Adam's writing was his severest shortcoming. At first his many perceptual and motor disabilities made it torturous for him to write. In addition, Adam's spelling was so erratic, and his handwriting so poor, that he could not decipher words he had written the previous day. After much experimentation and failure, we came up with two partial solutions. The best one was having Adam dictate to one of us.

While the class worked on an essay in the computer lab, I typed Adam's words verbatim, including expletives and wandering thoughts. I would then give him a printed copy to review for errors. He would make corrections (sometimes by himself, sometimes with my or Andy's help). After revising his essay, he would print it out for a grade. In an effort to get him to write more independently, I began to dictate the main ideas and have Adam fill in the blanks. This approach could be simplified with a dictating computer program, but I have yet to find one that is adaptable for student use.

To help Adam remember what he learned, I insisted that he record key words from the class in a notebook. To help him—and others who had difficulty taking exact notes—we designated a different student every few days as the class secretary. This student would type notes on a laptop computer. I would proofread the notes and perhaps do them over if necessary, then distribute them to any students who wanted them. I also gave the special education students the opportunity to serve as the secretary.

By April, Adam's notes were legible and coherent. By the end of the year, he wrote an article for a newspaper that his group was preparing. He advised 8th graders about what to expect in 9th grade. It was funny and included serious as well as light-hearted advice. Despite these accomplishments, Adam continued to have

difficulty writing extended, logical arguments. He was able to dictate compositions that reflected organized thought and developed ideas. In addition, some of his comments and questions precipitated our most important class discussions of the year. Adam's classmates considered him an important contributor to the class.

Sheila: A Changed Person

Sheila was not sociable with other students and had a reputation of wanting to be left alone. She often would sit in front of a computer screen all day, unable to hold conversations with other people or look anyone in the eye. She was terrified of reading or speaking in front of a group, especially peers. To give her more confidence, Andy began discreetly previewing her questions and responses. We called on her when we knew she was prepared and her remarks were sound. If they weren't, we asked her to listen to other students' answers and ask them how they arrived at their conclusions.

Sheila's major obstacle was that she would not complete any of the daily homework assignments. As far as we could tell, she was able to follow the class and comprehend whatever reading we assigned. She frankly admitted that she preferred TV and electronic games to homework. Andy and I told her she had to complete all assigned work to stay in the class. We encouraged her to see us after school.

Gradually, as I talked to her in the hallways, asking her about her work and after-school activities, she became much more at ease with me. She began coming

to my classroom after school to ask questions about the reading. She became eager to get good grades.

Upon finding encouragement in the classroom, Sheila began handing in her compositions and essays. They were always late, but nonetheless thoughtful and articulate. Her creative writing reflected a vividly macabre imagination. She told us proudly that she was inspired by Stephen King. We never penalized her for late papers.

Perhaps as a way of getting attention, Sheila engaged in minor but aggravating pranks outside of class, such as hiding a classmate's glasses. She was regularly called to the assistant principal's office. This antagonistic behavior notwithstanding, she was beginning to be sociable with adults and peers. Several teachers remarked that she was a changed person. Her former science teacher said her newfound confidence was striking. She definitely succeeded in a general curriculum class, ultimately performing better than many of the regular students. We finally gave her an 80 average overall.

Able: A Late Bloomer

Able was our most disappointing special education student. I'll call him Able because he had seemed the most likely to succeed. He was articulate, perceptive, and intelligent. He did not appear to have any anxiety about the classroom. But it was not until the fourth quarter that he began to complete his writing and reading assignments and answer test questions.

Able's previous special education teachers told us his reluc-

> Each special student presents a unique combination of challenges that require individual attention and planning.

tance or inability to work was a longstanding problem that nobody could convincingly explain. Nevertheless, we did stumble on a way to engage him. Each day we distributed a form to the entire class that we actually had designed primarily for students who took notes poorly or not at all. We asked students to list four things that they had learned. We also asked them to summarize the most important point of the lesson and to think of an important question to ask for the next class meeting. This gave students a simple goal: If they completed the form, they would get credit for keeping accurate notes.

Able bought into the plan, conscientiously completing the sheet every day. One day in the last quarter, he came to class early and told us he had read Neil Simon's *Brighton Beach Memoirs* (1984) and thought it funny and realistic. He had read the play—in which Simon chronicles his turbulent youth—in its entirety, even though we had assigned only a few pages for that evening. He went on to complete the writing assignments and even wrote an article for the class newspaper. He liked the frankness and honesty of the characters in talking about their life together. The play had struck a chord.

In retrospect, Able may have taken a significant step toward realizing his abilities, even though he learned only a small part of the year's curriculum. He was scheduled to return to a smaller special education class where he could get more attention. Instead, he surprised us by taking a regular English class in summer school, earning a *B*. So the plans changed—he remained in the general class after all.

Rigor and an Open-Ended Approach

I must admit that by the end of the honeymoon period, I realized the class was exhausting. I found out what is probably obvious to any experienced special education teacher: Each special student presents a unique combination of challenges that require individual attention and planning. I could not plan based on a general idea of what a 9th grader should do; I had to think of what each student was doing, then figure out what each should do next. I realized why small special education classes are a good idea: They are practical. I consoled myself, however, by recognizing that my three special kids were learning about literature and, as adolescents do, thriving on being with friends and peers.

Our success was due in part to our class structure. Andy and I spent most of our time questioning and exploring. I usually began by determining what students already knew about the topic and then built on their knowledge or insights. This approach allowed students to talk to one another and gave special education students a chance to show off what they knew.

For example, we introduced the short story "Antaeus" by asking whether anyone had ever heard of the character. When no one had, I broadened the questioning by noting that Antaeus was a famous mythical character. I then asked whether anyone knew any mythological stories. Students responded by summarizing myths they were familiar with. Next, I asked whether students knew the way myths from the past influence modern stories.

After students shared their ideas, I told them the story of the mythical Antaeus. We then read the first few paragraphs of the short story and considered the possible connections between the story and the myth. Because students were free to speculate, they could answer without fear of being wrong.

We then focused on careful reading of the story. By this time, most students had enough information to argue for one interpretation over another. After this lesson, I went on to define literary allusion. The students were able to explain the importance of allusion for Antaeus.

One of the visible improvements in the class as a whole was an ease with the improvisational mood. Some students enjoyed clarifying ideas for others, and Andy and I repeatedly insisted on having students solve problems of understanding by asking others in the class to explain things to them.

This is not to say that students did not also study words and grammar and correct their writing and misreading. But the most exciting moments came when students were able to make sense of literature and talk about it in their own terms—with some help from two interested teachers.

Grading: How Do You Define Success?

In addition to figuring out how to teach such a diverse class, the other nagging quandary was how to evaluate work. In the past I had assessed my students primarily by evaluating their writing— whether it was clear and cogent and reflected thoughtful analysis of literature. I had an imaginary model of what I could expect from 9th graders: They should be able to organize ideas into coherent paragraphs, present a thesis and prove it, and so forth.

But what of a student who could write no more than a sentence? Could you expect the same final product? I began by thinking you could—stubbornly insisting on it. If I had stuck to that standard, however, I would have perpetrated a gross injustice on Adam. Adam came to my class unable and unwilling to write compositions or even paragraphs.

In looking through his portfolio of writing, I saw enormous strides. He ended up with 80s, but he had learned more than many students who received 80s at the beginning of the year. His 80 percent did not mean the same thing as another student's 80 percent. As McCrory Cole (1992, p. 13) argues, "In heterogeneous classrooms, success for one student may not be defined in the same way as for another." Rather, success "will fall on a continuum, and what is most important is that students are progressing on the continuum."

Certainly not everyone shares this assumption about

Statistics should not preclude a long-term examination of classes where special education students appear to be prospering.

grades. If it is to be applied—and something like it should be if special education students are to be included in general curriculum classes—we need to adopt alternative forms of grading and assessment. Adam's report card would have been more meaningful if it had included a narrative evaluation of his work as well as a numeric one. This would have helped teachers and parents understand the skills he had mastered so that they could set realistic learning goals. For special education students in general classes, traditional grading can become punitive rather than evaluative.

Two Are Better Than One

Did Andy's presence make me a better teacher, as I set out to discover? It did. Further, having two teachers gave us flexibility: we could solve many problems by giving some students individual attention when they needed it.

From the beginning, I wanted the special education teacher to be involved with the entire class. I thought all students would benefit by having an additional teacher to instruct them whenever necessary. When working with groups or individuals, Andy and I gravitated to the special students, but several of the more reticent students clearly enjoyed the presence of an additional teacher. The rest of the class could continue to work uninterrupted.

In the end, all but one student could boast of success, and the only repeated complaint was that too much was required to get a high grade. My year ended with a fuller understanding of myself as a teacher and a fuller understanding of all my students, but especially three special kids.

References

Chira, S. (May 19, 1993). "When Disabled Students Enter Regular Classrooms." *The New York Times*. pp. A1, A17.

Cole, C.M. (1992). *Collaboration: Research and Practice: CASE Information Dissemination Packet*. Bloomington. Ind.: Council of Administrators of Special Education, Inc., Indiana University Deptartment of School Administration.

Simon, N. (1984). *Brighton Beach Memoirs*. New York: Random House.

 Article Review Form at end of book.

WiseGuide Wrap-Up

- Inclusive education is the education of all children in their age-appropriate classrooms, regardless of their disabilities. In inclusive education, all students have full membership in the class. Inclusive education is intended to give children at all levels opportunities to learn together academically and be together socially. Inherent in inclusive education is the requirement that students with disabilities receive supportive services in their classrooms.

- Inclusive education has been the subject of intense debate. Supporters of inclusion cite the social benefit for students with disabilities as well as for their non-disabled peers. They also note that inclusion is an issue of social justice; they argue that participation in the regular education class is an individual's right. Opponents of inclusion claim that it is difficult if not impossible to educate students with disabilties among their same-age peers, given their various needs and characteristics. Some contend that both populations of students will be short-changed.

R.E.A.L. Sites

This list provides a print preview of typical **coursewise** R.E.A.L. sites. (There are over 100 such sites at the **courselinks**™ site.) The danger in printing URLs is that web sites can change overnight. As we went to press, these sites were functional using the URLs provided. If you come across one that isn't, please let us know via email to: webmaster@coursewise.com. Use your Passport to access the most current list of R.E.A.L. sites at the **courselinks**™ site.

Site name: Special Education Inclusion (Educational Issues Series)

URL: http://www.weac.org/resource/june96/speced.htm

Why is it R.E.A.L.? This site provides information on practices, definitions, legal background, and research pertaining to inclusion.

Key topics: inclusion, law, research

Activity: Find a description of the most recent court case pertaining to inclusion. What was the resolution of the case?

....

Site name: The Renaissance Group

URL: http://www.uni.edu/coe/inclusion/index.html

Why is it R.E.A.L.? The Renaissance Group is a consortium of universities with teacher education programs focusing on inclusion. It discusses the "Whats" and "How-To's" of inclusion. The site includes information regarding philosophy, requirements for teacher preparation, legal background, descriptions of inclusive classrooms, resources, and organizations.

Key topics: inclusion, resources, law, teacher education

Activity: Find four strategies for working with students with disabilities in the regular education classroom.

....

Site name: Consortium on Inclusive Schooling Practices

URL: http://www.asri.edu/cfsp/brochure/abtcons.htm

Why is it R.E.A.L.? This site provides a catalog of products related to inclusion that have been produced by funded projects. It also includes a variety of papers on critical issues relating to inclusion, Internet links, and information on assistive technology.

Key topics: inclusion, technology

Activity: One of the links to this site is a paper on the impact of standards-based reforms of education on students with disabilities. Find the paper and identify the three major implications of the standards movement on the education of students with disabilities.

....

Index

Notes:
Entries in boldface type are authors of Readings.

Complexity, as characteristic of innovation, 86
Comprehensible input, as basis for bilingual instruction, 114
Computers
    adapting for disabled people, 157
    advances in, 82
    special education applications, 154–58
    use by disabled people, 149, 150, 151, 153
Conlin, Michelle, 58
Consortium on Inclusive Schooling Practices, R.E.A.L. site, 199
Contrast pairs, for describing people, 33 n.4
Control, for disabled people, 16–17, 19
Cooperative learning, in transition services, 41, 94
Council for Exceptional Children
    full inclusion goals of, 169–70
    R.E.A.L. site, 126
    support for special education placement, 41
Counseling, use with ADHD, 137–38
"The Country of the Blind", short story by H. G. Wells, 22
Court decisions, regarding assisted suicide, disabled people's resistance to, 18–19
Cultural diversity
    and authentic assessment, 146
    teachers-sensitivity to, 104
Culture
    constructions of disability, 24–25, 27–29
    defining, 22–23
    as disability, 26, 28–33
    function of, 23
    limitations of, 23
Cummings, Michael, 157
Cumulative data review, in vocational education assessment, 73
Curriculum, and inclusion, 84–85, 166, 176–77, 185
Curriculum-based measurement, 44–46

D

Deafness
    cultural responses to, 24–25
    financial services for, 151–52
    multimedia storybooks for, 155
Decentralization of services, trend toward, 88–89
Delayed, versus retarded, effects of terminology, 9
Deno, Stanley, 43
Department of Education
    growth of special education authority, 51
    top 10 priorities of, 83
    and vocational education for disabled people, 69
Deprivation approach, of culture to disability, 27, 29–30, 31
Detracking
    arguments against, 41
    arguments for, 39, 40

See also Inclusion
Development
    effect of disabilities on, 11
    and school failure, 27
Developmental delays, and Down syndrome, 8
Dexedrine, for treatment of ADHD, 135–36, 137
Dickinson, Brian, 152–53
Difference approach, of culture to disability, 27–28, 29–30, 31
Disability
    cultural constructions of, 24–25, 27–29
    culture as, 26, 28–33
    effect on development, 11
    employing people with, 13–14, 91, 150
    and equal access, 81–82
    ethnographic study of, 22–33
    language of, 9–10, 26, 33 n.4 (see also Labeling)
    learning disabilities (see Learning disabilities)
    as minority group status, 14
    number of Americans with, 14, 88, 150
    and self-advocacy, 15–17, 79, 93
    severe, 72, 164
    and special education (see Special education)
    technology solutions for, 149–53
    and victimization, preventing, 166–67
    and vocational education, 68–80, 81–86, 87–91
    and withholding of medical care, 18–21
The disAbility Information and Resources site, R.E.A.L. site, 36
Disabled Businesspersons Association, 149, 152
Disabled persons
    college transition services for, 92–95
    legislation for, 88–89
    school-to-college transition programs for, 92–96
    unemployment rate among, 91
    victimization of, 166–67
    vocational education for, 68–80, 81–86, 87–91
Discipline, and special education, 50
Discrimination, special education as remedy, 42
Diversity
    among educators, 104–5
    and inclusion, 186
    in schools, 88
    teachers-sensitivity to, 104
    teaching, 85
Division for Innovation and Development, 43
Do Not Resuscitate order, 19
Dowdy, Carol A., 68
Down, J. Langdon, 8
Down syndrome
    and Bloomington Baby case, 20–21
    incidence of, 6–8
    killing of infants with, 20–21
Drop-out rates, among minorities, 91

Drug tolerance, with ADHD medications, 136–37

E

Educable mentally retarded, overrepresentation of African Americans as, 102
Education
    establishment's approach to disability, 25–27, 27–28
    failure in, 33
    improving environment for, 84
    of special educators, 42
    vocational (see Vocational education)
    See also Special education
Education Department. See Department of Education
Education for All Handicapped Children Act
    and inclusion, 160
    zero reject provisions of, 180
    See also Individuals with Disabilities Education Act (IDEA)
Edwards-syndrome, 7
Efficacy studies, criticism of, 43
Ehman, Joe, 19
The Eighteenth Annual Report to Congress, R.E.A.L. site, 64
E-mail, 82
Emotional disorders, inclusion and, 188–93
Employment
    future trends in, 82–83
    of people with disabilities, 13–14, 150
English as second language. See Bilingual education; Language-minority students
Entrance examinations, 94
Environment, effect on disability, 30
Equipment, for inclusive school programs, 176
Eric, in Hughes observational study of inclusion, 172–73
Error analysis, in authentic assessment, 143–44
Ethnic diversity, teachers-sensitivity to, 104
Ethnicity
    and access to vocational education, 71
    and employment trends, 82
Ethnic minorities. See Minorities
Ethnography, and disability, 22–33
Eusthenopteron, 7
Euthanasia, 18–19
Evers, Rebecca B., 68
Exceptionality, defining, 1
Exit criteria, for special education, 56
Exterminators, literacy program for, 31–33
Eyegaze computer, 151, 153

F

Fachin, Katharina, 128
Failure
    in educational culture, 32–33
    in standardized testing, 33

leaving special education, 40–41
professional development of, 90
recruiting for special education, 175
recruiting minorities as, 104–5
Teaching strategies
for bilingual special education, 113–14,
120–24
for full inclusion, 163
for special education, 43, 45
Technology
applications in special education, 154–58
importance in workplace, 88
solutions for disability, 149–53
Telephone teletypewriter, 152
Test bias, against ethnic minorities, 102–3
Testing
for ADHD, 135
for aptitudes, 73
authentic assessment, advantages of, 140
bias against minorities in, 102–3
with curriculum-based measurement,
44–45
norm-referenced, for disability
screening, 140, 147
standardized, 31, 32–33
trends in, 89
See also Assessment
Think-alouds, 144–45
Thompson, Anna M., 134
Time-series research, on special
education, 44
Token economy rewards system, 129–30

Tommy, attention deficit hyperactivity
disorder case study, 128–33
Torticollis, 6
Tracheoscopy, 7
Transfer and maintenance, in special
education programming, 190
Transition services
for disabled people, 68–80, 96
model for, 92–95
Translocation, as variation of Down
syndrome, 8
Transportation, as part of vocational
rehabilitation, 78
Treatment, withholding, 20–21
Triability, as characteristic of innovation, 86
Trisomies, types of, 7
Trisomy 21. *See* Down syndrome

U

U.S. Education Department. *See*
Department of Education
U.S. Office of Special and Rehabilitation
Services, R.E.A.L. site, 64
Unemployment, among disabled people,
14, 91

V

Validation, of special education
practices, 45

Varenne, Hervé, 22
Vertebral anomalies, in newborn with
Down syndrome, 6
Victimization, and disability, 166–67
Vineland Adaptive Behavior Scales, 74
Vocational education, for disabled people,
68–80, 81–86
Vocational rehabilitation, for disabled
people, 68–80
Vocational services, of International Center
for the Disabled, 13–14

W

Wartenberg, Jeremy, 58, 60
Wellman, Mark, 39
Wells, H. G., 22 , 33 n.5
Wender, Paul H., 137
Whitestone, Heather, 39
Whole-language approach
effect on special education growth, 56
impact on learning disabled, 62
special education and, 113, 115
Wide Range Interest Opinion Test, 74
Windows software, features for disabled
people, 149–50
Wircenski, Jerry L., 81
Wircenski, Michelle D., 81
Women, employment trends among, 82
Woodward, John, 108

Putting it in *Perspectives*
-Review Form-

Your name:_____   Date: _____

Reading title: _____

Summarize: provide a one sentence summary of this reading: _____

_____

_____

_____

Follow the Thinking: how does the author back the main premise of the reading? Are the facts/opinions appropriately supported by research or available data? Is the author's thinking logical?

_____

_____

_____

_____

_____

Develop a Context: answer one or both questions: how does this reading contrast or compliment your professor's lecture treatment of the subject matter? How does this reading compare to your textbook's coverage?

_____

_____

_____

_____

_____

_____

Question Authority: explain why you agree/disagree with the author's main premise?

_____

_____

_____

_____

_____

_____

COPY ME! Copy this form as needed. This form is also available at http://www.coursewise.com Click on: *Perspectives*.